THE FARM FIASCO

THE FARM FIASCO

JAMES BOVARD

ICS Press

Institute for Contemporary Studies
San Francisco, California

Inquiries, book orders, and catalogue requests should be addressed to ICS Press, Institute for Contemporary Studies, 243 Kearny Street, San Francisco, California, 94108. (415) 981-5353. FAX: (415) 986-4878.

Portions of this book were previously published in the *Wall Street Journal*, the *New York Times*, and *Reader's Digest*.

The analyses, conclusions, and opinions expressed in ICS Press publications are those of the author and not necessarily those of the Institute for Contemporary Studies, the Institute's officers and directors, or others associated with, or funding, its work.

Distributed to the trade by Kampmann & Company, Inc., New York, New York.

Library of Congress Cataloging-in-Publication Data:

Bovard, James.
   The farm fiasco / James Bovard.
   p.   cm.
   Bibliography   : p.
   ISBN 1-55815-001-3 : $18.95
   1. Agriculture and state—United States. 2. Agricultural subsidies—United States. 3. Agriculture—Economic Aspects—United States. 4. Farms—United States. I. Title.
HD1761.B663 1989
338. 1'873—dc20   89-7482
                                    CIP

Contents

Foreword

Farm subsidies are an anamoly. Their greatest expansion came under the Reagan administration, which was elected in 1980 with the explicit promise to reduce government interference in the economy. Last year the government paid out $26 billion in agricultural subsidies, an amount approaching one-fifth of the federal budget deficit. Few believe it was money well spent. But much worse than the waste is that farm subsidies are harming American agriculture itself, historically one of the nation's most productive enterprises.

Reforming farm policy has proved terribly difficult. This is partly due to the system of political payoffs now operating in Washington, as well as to the wide currency that certain myths about farming have achieved. This book, written by the nation's best-known critic of federal farm policy, attacks the problem head-on. We hope that Mr. Bovard's study will spark a long-needed debate over the farm fiasco.

—Robert B. Hawkins, Jr.
President, Institute for
Contemporary Studies

San Francisco
April 1989

Chapter 1

Introduction

Federal farm policy is trampling individual rights, sacrificing the poor to the rich, and giving congressmen and bureaucrats vast arbitrary power over American citizens. For sixty years, the U.S. government has devotedly repeated the same agricultural policy mistakes. Unfortunately, the federal safety net is slowly strangling American agriculture. Farm policy is the perfect example of politicians' inability rationally to plan and control economic development.

Farm subsidies—roughly $25 billion a year in federal handouts and $10 billion more in higher food prices—are the equivalent of giving every full-time subsidized farmer two new Mercedes Benz automobiles each year. Annual subsidies for each dairy cow in the United States exceed the per capita income for half the population of the world. With the $260 billion that government and consumers have spent on farm subsidies since 1980, Uncle Sam could have bought every farm, barn, and tractor in thirty-three states. The average American head of household worked almost one week a year in 1986 and 1987 simply to pay for welfare for fewer than a million farmers.

In 1930, the *New York Times*, surveying the wreckage of agricultural markets after the federal government tried to drive up wheat prices, concluded, "It is perhaps fortunate for the country that its fingers were so badly burned at the very first trial of the scheme."[1] Despite an unbroken string of failures, the federal government has continued disrupting agriculture ever since. The trouble with farm programs is not that they are malfunctioning in the late 1980s, but that they have never worked well and Congress has never fixed them. Almost all the mistakes of the past are still being repeated: only the names of the secretaries of agriculture and of the farm-state congressmen have changed.

"Prosperity through organized scarcity" is the goal of many U.S. Department of Agriculture (USDA) farm programs. The USDA rewarded farmers for not planting on 78 million acres of farmland in 1988—equivalent to the entire states of Indiana and Ohio and much of Illinois. Government shut down some of the best American farmland in an effort to drive up world wheat and corn prices. Supply controls—paying farmers to plant less—are introduced only after politicians and bureaucrats have mismanaged price controls. The federal government pays farmers not to grow seven of the four hundred crops produced in America largely because Congress insists on paying farmers more than those seven crops are worth. Government first artificially raises the price of the crop and then attempts to artificially reduce crop production.

Each year, the USDA's marketing orders force farmers to abandon or squander roughly 500 million lemons, 1 billion oranges, 100 million pounds of raisins, 70 million pounds of almonds, and millions of plums and nectarines. The USDA endows major fruit and nut cooperatives with the power to effectively outlaw competition and to force farmers to let much of their crop rot or be fed to animals. To preserve federal control of the lemon business, the USDA effectively bans new technology that would boost fruit sales and benefit both growers and consumers. The USDA assumes that farmers gain more from higher prices than they lose from being forced to abandon much of their harvest.

"Handouts in lieu of exports" is the core of farm policy. For sixty years politicians have driven American farmers out of world markets and onto the government dole. The federal government decided in the 1930s that American farmers could not compete with foreign farmers and proceeded to close the borders to imports, undermine exports, and drive up domestic farm prices. The leading export sector of the U.S. economy was effectively confined to a government hospital because politicians said it could not survive on its own. But each time

Congress has driven American crop prices above world prices, Congress drove American farmers out of the world market. Taxpayers have paid out more than $400 billion since 1930 in part to compensate farmers for politicians wrecking farm export markets.

Federal farm programs are the biggest source of unfair competition in rural America. The USDA has bankrupted cattlemen in order to enrich dairymen, bushwhacked dry bean growers in order to reward wheat growers, and clobbered soybean growers in order to benefit corn growers. USDA bureaucrats have forced Arizona farmers to abandon three-quarters of their lemon crop in order to enrich California lemon growers, and the USDA sanctions the crushing of independent dairymen in order to make huge dairy cooperatives all-powerful. Congressmen talk of the sanctity of the family farmer, and then routinely sacrifice weak farm groups to other farm groups with more political clout.

Farm programs are government out of control: Programs perennially have no concept either of waste or of failure. The USDA is paying eleven-year-old children $50,000 a year not to plant corn. The Farmers Home Administration made almost a billion dollars in loans to farmers who were already technically bankrupt in 1985 just to keep them on their tractors one more year. Since 1980, the federal sugar policy has cost the equivalent of over $2 million for each sugar grower, and the USDA has spent over $1 million for each full-time rice grower since 1985. Yet no matter how much money government wastes, politicians ask only one question: "Is government being generous enough to farmers?"

Thanks to political mismanagement, one of America's leading industries is becoming a ball-and-chain on the American economy. Every year between 1983 and 1987, the total cost to consumers and taxpayers of welfare for farmers equaled or exceeded total farm income—even though many farmers and most farm products received no subsidy. Federal subsidies for wool, cotton, rice, and honey are so lavish that they routinely exceed the value of the entire subsidized crop. In 1987 the entire corn harvest was worth only $12.1 billion, yet the USDA spent $12.0 billion on corn subsidies—the same amount government spent on food stamps for 20 million Americans. Though American farmers may potentially be the world's most efficient wheat producers, annual subsidies for wheat production are double or triple the amount of the 1980 Chrysler bailout.

Farm policy is a classic example of the debilitating effects of providing welfare for businessmen. The more welfare American farmers have received, the less competitive they have become. Every farm handout program has reduced efficiency, raised costs of production, or increased federal control over farmers. Many farmers have gone bankrupt because they received too many subsidized government loans. Farm policies have helped caused boom-and-bust cycles in farmland values, shattering many farmers' livelihoods in the process. Handouts have encouraged farmers to spend their time "farming Washington" rather than maximizing their own productivity. According to Larry Johnson of the National Corn Growers Association, farmers now spend more time standing in line at local USDA offices than it would take them to plant crops on all the acres the USDA pays them to keep idle.[2]

Farm policy discussions have focused largely on the beneficiaries of federal intervention, with little consideration of the victims. The USDA estimated that the 1987 farm program, by paying farmers to leave more than 70 million acres unplanted, destroyed more than a quarter million jobs for farmworkers and others in related industries. By driving American dairy prices to triple world price levels, the USDA contributes to calcium deficiencies among the poor and osteoporosis in the elderly. The squandering of capital and labor resources in agriculture decreases American manufacturing and service exports by $10 billion a year, according to a study by a former USDA chief economist.[3]

Federal agricultural policy is based on the superiority of government central planning over private decision-making. There are many similarities in how Congress and the USDA manage American agriculture and how Eastern European governments manage their industries. In Poland and in California, government policy is designed almost solely for the benefit of the producer, with open contempt for consumers. In Hungary and in Mississippi, prosperity often depends more on political connections than on economic achievement. In Bulgaria and in Montana, government programs reward producers for neglecting quality and maximizing the quantity of their output. In Czechoslovakia and in Illinois, the government pays not according to whether a product is sold, but whether it is produced. In Eastern Europe there are stockpiles of unused, often worthless manufactured goods; in the United States, we have our mountains of surplus cheese, butter, and increasingly infested wheat and corn. In East Berlin and in Washington, planners routinely set prices for domestic products with an open contempt for the rest of the world. In Rumania and on Capitol Hill, economic planners scorn the future and attempt to prohibit innovations that would disrupt government control.

Eastern European economies have their five-year plans and Congress has its five-year farm bills. Both Eastern European and American government agricultural plans are usually out of date by the time the plans are finally printed up—but politicians stick to the plans and ignore reality. Federal agricultural planners in the 1980s may not be socialists, but they share with Eastern European planners a faith that government coercion is superior to voluntary agreement—that the plan is more important than individual rights—and that the more power government has, the better off society will be. Rexford Tugwell, USDA assistant secretary, declared in 1934, "Russia has shown that planning is practical. . . . The success and enthusiasm of Sovietism almost guarantees an unlimited rise in Soviet standards of living."[4] Though farm policy-makers have abandoned the 1930s rhetoric, they have retained the 1930s programs.

Farm Programs and the Nature of the Modern State

Farm policy is the best American example of industrial policy in action. Agriculture is our most controlled, regulated, and subsidized industry. Agricultural policy is perhaps most valuable for what it reveals about how politicians manage the economy. The same rationales for intervention, the same caliber of analyses, and the same failures that characterize farm policy-making are repeated in federal intervention in many other sectors of the economy.

Farm policy is a study of a political system unable to correct its economic mistakes. Political and bureaucratic inertia are the dominant forces in American agricultural policy. While congressmen ceremoniously label every second or third farm bill an "agriculture adjustment act," politicians and bureaucrats themselves refuse to adjust to the new realities of world agriculture. The federal government paid farmers not to work in 1988 primarily because it paid farmers not to work in the 1930s; the government is effectively destroying much of the orange and lemon crop this year mainly because the USDA also condemned citrus harvests in the 1940s. The most important test of farm policy has become not whether it succeeds or fails, but whether the same thing was done last year.

The history of federal agricultural policy is largely the history of a Sisyphean struggle against the gradual, inevitable decline of crop prices. Wheat, corn, oat, and cotton prices have been gradually declining in real terms for more than 150 years, and have nose-dived in comparison to units of labor required to purchase them. Prices have declined because the cost of production has declined, thanks to the invention of tractors, new seed varieties, better fertilizers, and other innovations. Politicians have perennially misunderstood this economic trend and cited the decline in crop prices as proof of market failure and proof of the need for political intervention. They proclaim that because wheat prices are lower now than they were ten, twenty, or thirty years ago, society is treating farmers unfairly and farmers deserve recompense. Farm policy is a case history of politicians attempting to control what they could not understand.

When the federal government took control of agriculture in the 1930s, many people believed that agriculture should be managed by politicians for the public good rather than by private individuals for their own selfish gain. But buying votes is the only farm policy most congressmen understand. For politicians, votes and campaign contributions have always been more important than supply and demand. The federal farm-welfare system has always been more concerned with re-electing politicians than with benefiting farmers.

Farm programs have survived only because the farm lobby and many congressmen have successfully perpetrated an image of farmers as hardship cases. Yet the average farm family income has exceeded the median American family income every year since 1964. The average full-time farmer earned more than $152,000 in 1987. The net worth of the average full-time farmer is more than ten times higher than that of the average American family. The average full-time farmer is a millionaire, yet farmers as a class pay no income taxes. The essence of agricultural policy is hollering about poor farmers and giving money to rich farmers.

The Choice America Faces

Federal farm programs have become far more expensive and more self-defeating in the 1980s. President Reagan preached about the "miracle of the marketplace," and then bragged that his administration had given more money to farmers than had any administration in history. The federal government took over de facto daily control of major crop prices, and the USDA devastated self-reliant farmers with covert schemes to drive crop prices up or down. The U.S. government now holds or guarantees half of all farm debt. Though the 1985 farm bill has been saluted as a "historic turning point in agricultural policy," farm policy is still based on maximum political manipulation—on allowing politicians vast arbitrary power over farmers in order to attempt to boost "farm income."

We have a choice, in agriculture and elsewhere in American society, between more control and more freedom. There is a farm revolution occurring around the world. Crop yields are soaring on every continent, costs of production are falling rapidly, and comparative advantages among nations are shifting. From China to Tanzania to Argentina, politicians are admitting their failures and reducing government controls over farmers. Yet Congress and the USDA remain devoted to trying to perpetuate the agricultural production patterns of the 1930s and the agricultural prices of 1910.

The main effect of farm programs is to force farmers to do inefficiently what they would have done efficiently without subsidies, to force Americans to pay more for food, to drive up the price of farmland (thereby decimating American farmers' competitiveness), and to squander pointlessly tens of billions of dollars a year. Every subsidized crop will still be grown in America even if the USDA never hands out another bushel of greenbacks. The issue is not whether the United States will have ample food in the future, but whether politicians will continue controlling American agriculture.

Farm programs raise moral questions that go to the heart of the welfare state. Do politicians and bureaucrats have a right to coerce

people in an attempt to benefit them? Is the government entitled to
sacrifice one individual's rights to boost another individual's profits?
Are politicians morally justified in using taxpayers' dollars for
programs that are guaranteed to make society poorer?

Agricultural policy epitomizes the mindless paternalism of
modern times. The USDA is a bureaucratic Leviathan that, because it
was created to benefit farmers, continues grinding away regardless of
how many farmers it harms. After almost sixty years of Keystone
Kops economic planning, politicians continue their stranglehold on
American farming—like a feeble monarch that refuses to relinquish
power regardless of how badly he mismanages his domain. The
government's "enlightened despotism" over farmers is increasingly
absurd, increasingly wasteful, and increasingly costly both to farmers
and to the American economy.

♦ *Chapter 2* ♦

The USDA's Sixty-Year War Against the Market

The history of agricultural policy is a history of endless political fina-gling—of bureaucracies always lagging behind the pace of events, of policy-makers' appalling misperceptions that repeatedly destroyed farmers' independence, of politicians refusing to admit their limita-tions, and of farmers refusing to admit their responsibility. Recent American agricultural history consists of a hundred schemes designed to harvest votes and scorn markets, of politicians forever discovering new wrenches to throw into the agricultural economy's engine—and of a perennial contempt for the rights and livelihood of individual farmers.

We cannot understand the current farm policy quagmire without examining how politicians brought us here. Despite a vast increase in farm productivity, a massive restructuring of agriculture, and an 80 percent decrease in America's farm population, we have essentially

The author wishes to thank the staff of the U.S. Department of Agriculture's History Office and USDA chief historian Douglas Bower for assistance in gathering information for this chapter. Readers should not presume that the USDA's historians necessarily agree with the views expressed in this chapter.

the same farm programs in the late 1980s that we had in the early 1930s. Government farm programs have been impervious both to failure and to change.

The Early Days

Agriculture had a special place for the Founding Fathers. Thomas Jefferson celebrated the farmer as the foundation of American democracy. Farmers rallied at the bridge at Concord, formed the core of the infantry in the Revolutionary War, and led the way in securing America's new frontiers. Most Americans were farmers, and the prosperity of farmers was equated with national prosperity.

Since politicians lauded farmers' virtues, it was not surprising that politicians sometimes offered cash rewards for such virtue. One of the first farm subsidies in the United States involved a protection for Southern sugar growers. In 1816, Congress legislated a 3-cent–per-pound tariff on imported sugar. This pegged American sugar prices at about double the world price. In 1832, Henry Lee, writing for the Free Trade Convention assembled in Philadelphia, denounced the sugar tariff as a scam on the American working class to benefit fewer than 500 plantation owners:

> Admit the principle, that a particular class of men or a particular state has a right to government aid, for the prosecution of a business, which could not be prosecuted without it, and there is no limit to the rightful claims of individuals and states.[1]

The legislature of Louisiana petitioned Congress, observing that "the General Government, if it did not compel [sugar growers to produce sugar], invited them to attempt it."[2] Thus, Louisiana politicians argued, the government was obligated to continue protecting sugar growers. In the same way that farm aid supporters warn today of the collapse of rural America if subsidies are curtailed, sugar tariff supporters warned of the devastation of the South if the sugar tariff were abolished. As one Southern statesman noted, "The ruin of the sugar planters would depreciate slave property in the United States by $100,000,000."

In the middle of the nineteenth century, American agriculture was prospering, providing more than 80 percent of the country's exports and helping to pay for the Industrial Revolution. Farmers were a relatively prosperous class. In 1862 Congress passed the Homestead Act, which promised 160 acres of free land to anyone who would stay on his claim for five years. The act was intended to reward Union war veterans and entice foreign immigrants to help develop the American West. Between 1850 and 1900, land in farms increased from 300 million to 840 million acres. By the 1880s, farming was, thanks partly to government land giveaways that encouraged overproduction, in a major depression. Farmers, urged by activists to raise "less corn and more hell," targeted their criticism on middlemen, the railroads, the Liverpool Wheat Pool, and the Chicago Board of Trade. Some farm groups advocated the nationalization of the railroads; others advocated "free silver"—a huge increase in the coinage of silver in order to spur inflation and make it easier for farmers to pay their debts.

While government policies caused surpluses and depressed farm income in the 1880s, many politicians prospered by preaching to farmers about their need for, and entitlement to, government relief. Congress also attempted to prohibit or discourage innovations that might affect farm income. The invention of margarine, for example, was seen as a dire threat to the dairy industry. Senator Henry W. Blair proposed a federal law to require margarine to be colored red or blue to discourage consumers from buying it. Congress eventually enacted a heavy tax on oleomargarine, which the Supreme Court later struck down as unconstitutionally discriminatory.

The years before World War I were the most prosperous for American farmers up to that time. The prewar years became the standard by which all subsequent comparisons of farm and nonfarm incomes would be judged. After the start of World War I, grain prices rose, as much of Europe's best cropland was covered by armies instead of seeds and fertilizer. For the 1915–16 crop year, wheat averaged 98 cents a bushel, which was then considered a good price.

When the United States entered the war, the government imposed a price floor, guaranteeing farmers at least $2 a bushel for their wheat to encourage increased production. President Wilson declared, "Food will win the war"—and farmers planted another 40 million acres. Liberal export credits to Allied nations drove wheat prices far above the government-guaranteed level. Yet many farmers suspected that the government was manipulating markets in order to hold down prices. Though wheat soared to more than $3 a bushel, many farm groups were confident that it would rise to $4 when the government got out of the market.

By the end of the war, America's farmers were more prosperous than city residents. Many farmers were exempted from the draft and profited greatly from the high wartime prices. Farm income exceeded nonfarm income by 50 percent in both 1918 and 1919. By 1920, almost 60 percent of the farmers in Minnesota, Montana, Kansas, Missouri, Illinois, and Iowa had automobiles and almost 70 percent had telephones. At the same time, nationwide, less than half of all American families owned cars.[3]

How Government Wrecked the Farm Economy in 1920

It was widely believed in the 1920s and 1930s that agriculture was permanently depressed after World War I, and that a federal takeover was necessary because agriculture was so severely imbalanced that farmers could not survive without government help. Chester C. Davis, administrator of the federal Agriculture Adjustment Administration, reflected farmers' opinions in 1934 when he declared, "The situation in the last fourteen years has cried out for [government] agricultural planning, production adjustment, and farm income insurance."[4] The events from World War I onward are crucial to an understanding of the road to the federal takeover of agriculture.

A few months after the Armistice in November 1918, prices for hogs, corn, and other farm products naturally began to edge downward with the expectation of a fall in demand. Corn prices fell sharply in January 1919, after the War Trade Board removed restrictions on the import of Argentinian corn. The United States, Argentina, and Australia all had huge wheat surpluses available to send to Europe after the end of hostilities. While the U.S. government continued to guarantee American farmers $2.25 a bushel for their wheat, the Australian government was guaranteeing its farmers 98 cents a bushel and Argentina was selling its wheat to the Dutch for $1.26 a bushel. Treasury Secretary Carter Glass favored ending export credits, but

Herbert Hoover and the U.S. Food Administration considered the huge surplus a grave threat to the stability of domestic farm prices that had to be exported at any cost. Officials in the Wilson administration believed that farmers were morally entitled to high prices for their harvest. Julius Barnes, the head of the U.S. Food Administration, which was sitting on a mountain of surplus wheat, declared, "Shall the United States, with its surplus wheat, enter a worldwide competition for its sale and thereby break down its own price, or shall it assume that what wheat it has for sale shall be at our price—pronounced fair to our producers?"[5]

Congress anxiously deliberated the wheat situation in early 1919. As Congressman James Young of Texas observed, "The farmer has a guaranteed price on his wheat and has no right to kick because the wheat farmer is the most prosperous farmer in the United States."[6] High food prices in the cities were spurring social unrest, with housewives marching in the streets of New York and a handful of Bolshevik agitators terrifying the Justice Department.

In March 1919 Congress pegged the price of wheat through mid-1920 at $2.26 a bushel—more than double the prewar price—and expanded the War Finance Corporation to subsidize more exports to Europe. Wheat acreage expanded by 20 percent in 1919 (and was more than 50 percent above the 1917 acreage) as thousands of corn, oat, and barley farmers became wheat farmers. Even though many city residents were denouncing "wheat profiteers," Congress perpetuated the war economy for wheat for two years after the war and persuaded farmers to greatly increase their wheat supplies. The appropriations of the War Finance Corporation for export subsidies were justified to help get rid of the wheat surplus—even though Congress simultaneously provided farmers with incentives to continue overproducing wheat.

In May 1920, the War Finance Corporation stopped making export loans "on the ground that our agricultural export business was holding up well enough."[7] At the same time, the U.S. Grain Corporation stopped buying wheat—and many farmers rejoiced, because they believed that government intervention was the only thing keeping wheat prices from going to $4 a bushel.[8]

In June 1920, the Democratic presidential nominee, James W. Cox, urged in his acceptance speech that "we increase to our utmost the area of tillable land." Henry Cabot Lodge, in his keynote speech at the Republican convention, urged, "To keep up on increased production, particularly should every effort be made to increase the productivity of the farms."[9] Herbert Hoover, the chief of the Food Relief Administration and a dominant influence on farm policy, warned, "Our agricultural production is decreasing, and unless we can stem this tide of decrease we shall soon be dependent on overseas supplies."[10] Politicians were certain that American agricultural exports had been permanently increased.

Both politicians and farmers were surprised when wheat prices rapidly plummeted more than 50 percent. Granaries in Europe were already bulging with American grain. The high price obtained through mid-1920 was due largely to subsidized export credit and the government price guarantee. Thanks to government signals, farmers continued overproducing wheat long after the wheat market was glutted.

Farmers were damaged far more by the government-caused speculative bubble after World War I than by their expansion of production in 1917 and 1918. Farmers plowed up an extra 20 million acres after the end of World War I; huge surpluses accumulated and depressed prices throughout the early 1920s. As historian James Shideler notes, "Speculative frenzy in land prices was one of the most notable features of the postwar years in agriculture, and a source of great future trouble for farmers."[11] In 1949 economist Warren Hickman observed, "These emergency measures of Herbert Hoover and Bernard Baruch were extremely short-sighted, and the ultimate collapse of American farm prices in 1921 was more spectacular than the collapse would have been in 1919."[12] Theodore Saloutos and J. D. Hicks observed, "Probably the factor which contributed more than any other to the deepness of [the agricultural depression of the 1920s and early 1930s] was the land boom that had accompanied the war prices."[13]

The U.S. economy suffered a sharp depression in 1920–21, and then quickly recovered. Agriculture was slower to recover than was the rest of the economy, though this should have been no surprise. During the Napoleonic Wars, European agricultural production had increased sharply in response to threats of blockade. After 1815, production continued to be higher than its prewar levels, and farmers suffered heavily until the late 1820s, when supply and demand again began to balance out.[14]

The farm crisis of 1920 provoked a flock of conspiracy theories and xenophobic outbursts. Henry Adams Bellows, editor of *Northwestern Miller*, wrote in 1924, "The farmer from 1920 to 1924 . . . regarded the economic abstractions of supply and demand as mere dust thrown to blind his eyes. Political leaders, capitalizing on his rebelliousness, told him that he was being systematically robbed, and that all he needed was adequate legislation against the robbers."[15] If the farm crisis of 1920 had been properly diagnosed, Herbert Hoover might have been kept out of the presidency and the nation conceivably might have avoided the Great Depression. Hoover later became the only American politician to twice wreck the American agricultural economy.

The Path to Federal Takeover of Agriculture

Congress responded to the agricultural collapse of 1920 with the Emergency Tariff Act of 1921 to help farmers by taxing food imports and keeping out foreign competition. As H. L. Mencken observed, "Potatoes carried a duty of 50 cents a hundredweight—and the potato growers of Maine, eager to mop up, raised such an enormous crop that the market was glutted and they went bankrupt, and began bawling for government aid."[16]

Even though World War I had turned the United States into the largest creditor in the world, the Harding administration pushed one tariff bill after another through Congress. Even though farmers relied heavily on exports for prosperity, few groups were more supportive of protectionism than farmers. As *The New Republic* observed in 1925:

> Protectionist arguments are now advanced fervently by a great part of the farm press; they appear in the resolutions of the most powerful farm organizations. . . . The new farm protectionists' . . . ideal is the complete disappearance of export surpluses, so the tariff may operate effectively upon the whole range of agricultural production.[17]

The tariff did not protect agriculture in general, but it was a gold mine for a few strong lobbies—just as agriculture programs are today. In 1926, U.S. wool prices were almost triple world prices, butter prices were 50 percent above world market prices, and sugar prices were double world market prices.

The takeover of agriculture by the federal government in the 1930s was based on the belief that agriculture had been permanently depressed after World War I. Yet the agricultural depression of the 1920s was largely an illusion—"a statistical artifact rather than an economic fact," as economist H. Thomas Johnson observed in 1961.[18] One organization did more than any other to promote the idea that agriculture was permanently in need of federal aid: the U.S. Department of Agriculture (USDA). This was one of the greatest bureaucratic coups in history—defining the problem in such a way that the only solution was a massive expansion of government power.

There were many farm bankruptcies in the 1920s, but these were largely due to the government-induced speculative land binge of 1919–20 that left many farmers with large mortgages. At their peak in 1927, the rate of bankruptcies among farmers was 1.8 per 100—a rate lower than the rate for all American businesses. According to a 1935 USDA report, while farm income had averaged $4.6 billion a year during the golden era of 1909–14, it averaged $7 billion a year from 1923 to 1929.[19] Average farmland values stayed above pre–World War I levels throughout the 1920s, and crop prices were generally higher than they had been before the war. In 1933, economist G. M. Peterson concluded that "the economic position of the farmer compared very favorably with the average for over 95 percent of the entire population . . . during [the 1920s] when the agriculture industry is supposed to have been in a state of continued depression while other classes enjoyed prosperity."[20] Joseph S. Davis, an economist at Stanford University, observed in 1938: "In retrospect, in the light of revised data and a truer perspective, [the mid- to late 1920s] should properly be regarded as moderately prosperous and relatively normal for agriculture."[21]

So why were people convinced that farmers were miserable? Largely due to the invention of "parity." The USDA's Bureau of Agricultural Economics concocted a formula for comparing farm and nonfarm family income—and farm lobbies seized it as a way to prove that the economy was inherently unfair to farmers because crop prices, when compared with industrial prices, appeared to be lower after World War I than they had been before the war. As H. Thomas

Johnson noted, "Most of the statistical measures of the agricultural 'depression' . . . were generated at the USDA."[22] "The conclusion that the agriculture sector was thrust into a position of economic inequality after 1920 was based largely on the failure of the parity ratio to return to the prewar level."[23] As historian William D. Rowley noted:

> The Bureau of Agricultural Economics research focused on the relation of agriculture to the distribution of national wealth. In relation to other segments of the economy, did agriculture reap its fair share on the open market? Agricultural economists invariably gave a negative answer.[24]

Herbert Hoover, who himself favored extensive government intervention, denounced the Bureau of Agricultural Economics as the "father" of congressional legislation designed to impose federal controls on crop prices and dump drop surpluses on world markets. Hoover concluded in 1924, "Being naturally Socialistic in my mind they turn to Socialism as a solution."[25]

The parity formula was designed to significantly understate farm income. Even though more than 25 percent of farmers had jobs off their farms, parity did not count their off-farm income. In fact, the more money farmers earned off the farm, the poorer they would appear to be. If off-farm income had been included, then farmers likely would have achieved parity. And the formula exaggerated farmers business costs—by counting half the cost of passenger automobiles as a farm expense, for example.

The concept of parity presumed that there had been no change in the cost of production for major crops; yet farming underwent a mechanical revolution in the 1920s. Farmers bought almost a million tractors in the 1920s, resulting in a revolution in productivity and a sharp decrease in production costs. In Kansas, mechanization in the 1920s reduced by 50 percent the number of man-hours required to raise an acre of wheat.[26] Wheeler McMillen observed in 1929, "The tractor farmer can plow four to eight times as many acres a day as a man with a two-horse team."[27] As historian Vernon Carstensen observed in 1960:

> It almost seems that many [agricultural economists] were reluctant to acknowledge [in the 1920s] that the tractor had been invented and there seems to have been a tendency among some to regard it merely as a different kind of horse—one that used kerosene instead of oats.[28]

H. C. Taylor, chief of the USDA's Bureau of Agriculture Economics, urged farmers not to purchase expensive new machinery like tractors, convinced that the additional expense would not be justified by higher productivity.

USDA economists slanted other numbers in order to produce an appearance of agricultural depression. For instance, in July 1927, the USDA's monthly report, *Crops and Markets*, showed gross returns and income for farmers for each year of the 1920s, with the years 1919–20 as the base. By using a base of the two most prosperous years in the history of American farming, the report easily made it look as though farmers were suffering badly in the 1920s.[29] Yet, even with the USDA's slanted parity measure, the gap between farm income and nonfarm income was not that great, as Table 2-1 shows. USDA economists and farm-lobby leaders were calling for a federal takeover of agriculture even though the official measures showed a difference of less than 15 percent between farm and nonfarm income.[30]

In its 1923 yearbook, the USDA announced that American wheat farmers were no longer competitive and that "our wheat production should be placed gradually on a domestic basis and then should keep pace with our growth in population and domestic demand." The USDA averaged the costs of producing wheat on the plains of Kansas

Table 2-1

Comparison between Farm and Nonfarm Income, 1921–29

Year	Farm Income as Percent of Nonfarm Income
1921	80%
1922	87
1923	89
1924	89
1925	95
1926	91
1927	88
1928	91
1929	92

SOURCE: H. Thomas Johnson, *Agricultural Depression in the 1920s* (New York: Garland), 1985.

and the mountainsides of West Virginia and concluded that the United States as a whole could not compete. The USDA observed, "Looking ahead beyond this season, prospects are not good for marketing a surplus of wheat at satisfactory prices." The USDA then predicted that wheat prices would stay depressed for many years and recommended creating a government corporation to dump American wheat on world markets: "The prime duty of such an export corporation would be to restore . . . the prewar relation between [the price of] wheat . . . and other commodities."[31]

The USDA's analysis presumed that farmers could not voluntarily adjust to changed market conditions. But between 1919 and 1925, farmers reduced their wheat acreage in response to market prices from 74 million acres to 52 million acres. In 1924, less than eight months after the USDA's announcement that wheat exports were doomed, the market price of wheat began to rise without any government help; by 1925, wheat was $1.50 a bushel, far above prewar prices, and farmers in the most productive parts of the United States were expanding their wheat acreage. Farmland in western Kansas, the best wheatland in the country, increased in value until 1932, because Kansas wheat producers' costs of production were so low that growing wheat was profitable even at prices that drove North Dakota farmers out of business.

In the 1920s, as in the 1980s, there was fierce debate among farmers about whether foreign markets were a blessing or a curse. Even though the United States exported 40 percent of its wheat, 55 percent of its cotton, and 33 percent of its tobacco in 1929, many farmers and politicians scorned foreign sales as an impediment to domestic farm prosperity. Farm lobbies and politicians were confident that farm prices could easily be inflated if America would only close its borders to the rest of the world. As Frank C. Platt, a farmer, exclaimed in 1925, "Everyone must realize that the U.S. cannot compete with other countries in the production of agricultural products. The wages we pay . . . are so much higher that, if we are to compete with other countries, we must sell below cost."[32] But at the time, America's main agricultural competition came not from starving peasants in undeveloped countries, but from prosperous farmers in New Zealand and Canada.

The USDA's recommendation that the United States abandon world markets stemmed largely from its belief that farm prices were unfairly low. It was not a question of whether American farmers could compete, but whether world market prices were as high as the USDA thought American farmers deserved. Most of the apparent unfairness of farm prices was due to the USDA's deceptive parity measure and an inability to understand the mechanical revolution in farming. The USDA was apparently not interested in objectivity: H. C. Taylor declared in 1929 that it was farm economists' duty to see that farmers got higher prices and a larger share of the national income.[33]

The more mechanized farming became, the larger the gap became between innovative and traditional farmers. The 1920s saw a rapid drop in costs of production for the most efficient producers, leading them to expand production and drive down prices; meanwhile, less innovative farmers with much higher costs of production suffered. Many analysts concluded that, since the marginal American farmer could not compete with foreign farmers, the United States should surrender its export sales altogether.

Even in the 1920s, federal agricultural policy was a tangle of contradictions. While farmers were complaining of low crop prices, the federal government launched twenty-five reclamation projects to create new cropland in the desert—at huge expense to taxpayers. Twenty-four of the projects were failures. In early 1929, Millard Peck, a senior USDA economist, estimated that potatoes produced on federal irrigation projects drove down potato prices 4 cents a bushel, or a total of $15,664,220; extra cotton production drove prices down two-fifths of a cent a pound, or $40,000,000; and federal projects cost wheat farmers $5 million. Peck concluded, "If production is increased [crop] prices are depressed; if production is not increased, the nation receives no compensation for the expense involved in reclaiming the arid lands."[34] Economist G. S. Wehrwein observed, "In agriculture, public policy creates more farms to compete with farms already established, adding to, if not creating an abundance which means low prices to those already engaged in farming."[35]

The Federal Farm Board Solves the Farm Problem

Herbert Hoover, in his speech accepting the presidential nomination in 1928, promised to create a Farm Board to "establish for our farmers an income equal to those of other occupations." On July 15, 1929, Hoover told the new Farm Board, "I invest you with responsibilities and resources such as have never before been conferred by our government in assistance to any industry."[36] The Farm Board's $500 million budget was larger than any ever authorized for a nondefense expenditure. In short order the Farm Board wrecked the export markets for America's two most important crops.

Immediately after its creation, the Farm Board decided to boost the income of American farmers by cornering the world grain market and driving up prices. In August 1929, the Farm Board pressured the federal credit banks to liberalize their loans to agricultural coopera- tives to help them make more generous loans to farmers so that farmers could hold their crops off the market. In November 1929, the chairman of the Farm Board declared: "Anyone selling wheat or cot- ton at the present market price is foolish."[37] By December 1929, Farm Board officials were preaching to farmers to reduce production and abandon exports so that the government could drive their prices up for them.

In order to support its crop-withholding advice, the Farm Board set up a Grain Stabilization Corporation that began desperately buying up wheat. The board managed to boost U.S. prices to 18 cents a bushel above the Canadian prices. Bernard Ostrolenk, in *The Surplus Farmer*, noted, "The Farm Board's position was that of a continual purchaser of wheat normally exported, at prices from 18 to 20 cents above world prices."[38] Exports of wheat nose-dived. Ostrolenk con- cluded, "Because of the crop-withholding advice of the Farm Board, exports during 1929 and 1930 were between 40,000,000 and 50,000,000 bushels less than the preceding year."[39] The Farm Board was certain that a world shortage of wheat was imminent and that importing nations would soon come begging to America. Instead, Canadian and Argentinian farmers reaped larger profits because of the Farm Board's action.

The Farm Board's massive cache of wheat further depressed world prices, since every grain dealer in the world knew that the United States would eventually dump its surplus on the market:

> It was this large carry-over then which created the wheat emergency. . . . The Farm Board had advised the farmer to gamble with his crop instead of urging him to market it, and these repeated statements of the Board had led farmers to believe that by withholding their wheat and cotton they could get higher prices. . . . During 1930 it was the known surplus of agricultural commodities in the U.S. which forced farmers to face the most drastic price cuts in a decade. . . . [40]

The Farm Board also wrecked the cotton market, America's largest cash export. Harvey Parnell, governor of Arkansas, complained in 1932 that the Farm Board had "done more to destroy the cotton market" than any other factor except high tariffs.[41] In 1930, as in 1960, 1970, and 1988, the federal government's agricultural policy made a mockery of the policy-makers' rhetoric. The Farm Board intervened to drive farm prices up and then begged farmers to plant smaller crops. But farmers paid more attention to prices than they did to bureaucrats, so harvests grew instead of shrinking. In August 1931, the Farm Board urged Southern farmers to destroy every third row of cotton; Southern politicians suggested that farmers instead destroy every third member of the Farm Board. J. W. Garrow of the American Cotton Shippers Association told the Senate Agriculture Committee in 1931, "By spreading overconfidence among growers that government would maintain cotton prices at a high level, the Farm Board has made a major contribution to the present large surplus."[42] Thanks to the Farm Board, 1931 was the first year since the Civil War that "consumption of foreign-grown cotton throughout the world exceeded that of American cotton."[43]

In a hare-brained effort to enrich farmers, the Farm Board destabilized the grain trade, razed U.S. exports, and created a massive price-depressing surplus, greatly weakening American agriculture. Lionel Robbins, a British economist, observed in 1934, "The grandiose buying organizations by which Hoover tried to maintain agricultural prices had the effect of demoralizing markets altogether, by the accumulation of stocks and the creation of uncertainty."[44] Argentinian, Canadian, and Australian farmers weathered the Great Depression far better than American farmers did largely because their governments did not abandon export markets. Canadian and Australian exports actually increased in the 1930s. The prices of American wheat and cotton declined far more than those of other domestic crops between 1929 and 1932.

Geta Feketekuty, an economist at the U.S. trade representative's office in the White House, observed, "The world protectionist binge of the 1930s started as a result of efforts to protect American farmers from low world market prices."[45] After the federal government had driven U.S. crop prices far above world prices, politicians had no choice but to close U.S. borders or abandon their price-boosting scheme. The Farm Board debacle convinced many farmers that foreign trade was the only thing standing between them and far higher prices. The farm bloc put its weight behind an extreme protectionist measure, the Smoot-Hawley Tariff Act, that boosted tariffs on agricultural products far more than it boosted tariffs on industrial products.

The Smoot-Hawley Act turned a bad recession into a worldwide depression. In the year after Smoot-Hawley was enacted, U.S. foreign trade decreased more than 50 percent. Jude Wanniski noted, "Smoot-Hawley had a major impact on spurring the stock market crash and led to a worldwide trade war that devastated both America and Europe."[46] Once the United States stopped purchasing European goods, Germany and other European powers were forced to default on their debts to the United States. This helped cause a wave of bank failures and panic across the country.

Farmers suffered during the Great Depression because of other federal policies as well. The Federal Reserve Bank reduced the money supply by one-third between 1929 and 1932, thereby causing a huge drop in price levels.[47] Farmers with mortgages were hurt badly by the deflation, since the price of their crops fell sharply while their mortgage payments became much higher in real dollars. The deflation-caused mortgage crunch was a major cause of desperation in the farm belt.

The single most devastating expense for farmers in the early 1930s was higher taxes. In 1933 an article in the *Journal of Farm Economics* noted that "the taxes paid by farmers as an entire group have, within the past few years, exceeded the interest paid on farm mortgages. The farmer of today performs . . . two days [of work] per week for the state for a privilege of working the land."[48] Farmers were taxed heavily because most local and state governments relied on property taxes for most of their income, and because "farm land was still listed on the tax rolls at figures approaching the extravagant prices of the immediate post-war years."[49] As crop prices declined, taxes as a percentage of income skyrocketed. An estimated 25 percent of the farms that went bankrupt between 1931 and 1933 were sold for failure to pay taxes.[50] E. C. Young, an economist at Purdue University, declared in 1935 that "the depression would not likely have developed into an agricultural crisis had it not been for the tax and mortgage load."[51]

Though much of the farm crisis of the early 1930s was the result of high taxes and government mismanagement of the currency, many agricultural economists and politicians insisted that the problem was in the inherent nature of the business and could only be solved by a government takeover of agriculture.

A Temporary Farm Dictator

In 1933, Franklin Roosevelt took office amid promises to revolutionize agriculture. The *New York Times* reported on March 12, 1933, shortly after Roosevelt's inauguration, that Agriculture Secretary Henry Wallace and farm leaders were appealing to Roosevelt for the appointment of a "farm dictator" to solve the farm crisis. Wallace and others were certain that only by vesting vast arbitrary powers in a farm dictator could American agriculture be saved.

The New Deal looked upon agriculture as though the "production problem" had already been solved, and the only thing missing was proper control of farmers and consumers. Wallace denigrated the use of labor-saving devices. Assistant Secretary of Agriculture Rexford Tugwell declared in 1934, "Today our primary need is not to stimulate enterprise, but to order and plan it in the public interest."[52] M. L. Wilson, USDA undersecretary in 1934, declared, "Technological efficiency alone is seldom or never all-important."[53] Farm programs were launched with a contempt for efficiency and a neglect of productivity—attitudes that have not changed in fifty-six years.

The original agricultural planners had unlimited faith in their capacity as benevolent despots. Roosevelt's Agricultural Adjustment

Act (AAA) was launched in 1933 at the same time as the National Industrial Recovery Act that restricted working hours, restrained industrial output, and allowed businesses to form committees to dictate restraints on competition. (One industrial code limited the number of stripteases that could be performed in a burlesque show.) Both acts assumed that prosperity could be secured by restricting production and boosting prices—prosperity through "universal monopoly and universal scarcity." This panacea was soon abandoned for business, but it is retained to the present day for agriculture.

The 1933 Agriculture Adjustment Act opened with a "Declaration of Emergency" and noted that the act should "cease to be in effect whenever the President finds and proclaims that the national emergency in relation to agriculture has ended." Wallace proclaimed that the emergency justified temporary programs to pay farmers to kill 6 million baby pigs and plow up 10 million acres of cotton. The administrator of the AAA, George Peek, celebrated the cotton plowup as "an epoch in American Agriculture. . . . History has been made during these days."[54] The USDA was ridiculed for "solving the paradox of want amidst the plenty by doing away with the plenty."[55] The USDA's promise of higher cotton prices persuaded many cotton farmers to plant as much as they could, making the 1933 cotton harvest as large as that of 1932.

Roosevelt's brain trust was convinced that raising farm income was the key to reviving prosperity. At a time when one-quarter of the American work force was unemployed, the federal government imposed a heavy tax on food items in order to raise revenue for farm aid. Thanks to the heavy taxes, food consumption declined in 1935 even below the levels of previous depression years.[56]

Farmers' attitude toward government assistance depended largely on whether or not they were successfully standing on their own two feet. The *New York Times* reported in May 1933 that "it is the unmortgaged farmers who shies away from an elaborate machinery of federal supervision; the mortgaged farmer does not care how many federal agents camp in his barnyard to count his planted acres and his pigs."[57] Unmortgaged farmers voted heavily against all phases of federal control in a 1933 Midwest poll. After one year's experience with the Agricultural Adjustment Administration, Kansas farmers—

the nation's most efficient wheat producers—again voted heavily
against continued federal controls.[58]

The AAA set American crop prices far above world market prices.
As a result, agricultural exports plummeted. While U.S. exports of
automobiles between 1932 and 1934 rose by 110 percent and iron and
steel manufactures exports by 125 percent, exports of major farm commodities collapsed. Cotton exports fell from 14 million bales in 1929 to
3.5 million in 1938. In 1931, the United States exported 131 million
bushels of wheat; in 1934, after the government paid farmers to slash
production, the United States was a net *importer* of wheat. Agricultural
economist O. B. Jesness summed up the government's attitude toward
crop exports: "It has been common among representatives of the AAA
to express the view that foreign markets are gone and that all we can
do is mourn their loss."[59] Agricultural economist B. H. Hibbard
reported in *The Nation* in 1934 that the AAA "put a thousand times as
much effort into reduction of output at home as they put into the
effort to restore foreign trade during their first year in control."[60]
Economist Theodore W. Schultz denounced New Deal farm programs
for "putting a 'Chinese Wall' around our export farmers."[61]

Politicians first wrecked the agricultural export markets, and then
used the loss of exports to justify taking over American farmers' businesses. USDA Assistant Secretary M. L. Wilson declared, "Concerted
cooperated crop control for American agriculture just now is necessary to compensate for the virtual loss of the foreign market."[62]
Another AAA administrator, Chester Davis, declared that "unless and
until the U.S. recovers the lost export markets, the adjustments in
[crop] production will have to be made."[63]

The destruction of export markets is the key to understanding the
New Deal farm policy—and all subsequent farm policy. Federal
policies have decreased farmers' efficiency, greatly increased their
costs of production, and routinely priced American farmers' harvests
out of the world market. Politicians then cite the lack of exports as
proof of the need for political control over farming. This is how the
New Deal justified production controls, and why the USDA rewarded
American farmers for idling 78 million acres of farmland in 1988.

American farmers were badly hurt by the loss of export markets
in the 1930s. As agricultural economist Ashner Hobson observed in
1935, "The cause [of surpluses] is not so much that we are producing

more, but rather that we are selling less abroad. . . . While declining agricultural exports may not have caused the depression, certainly their loss contributed substantially to its severity."[64] But the AAA had complete faith in its ability to enrich farmers by manipulating farm markets. And it was extremely difficult to manipulate markets as long as the United States was still tied to world prices. President Roosevelt in 1935 even bragged about his administration's destruction of farm exports: "Now, with export surpluses no longer pressing down on the farmers' welfare, with fairer prices, farmers really have a chance for the first time in this generation to benefit from improved methods."[65]

Since the 1930s, politicians have viewed farm prices as tickets for votes rather than as signals to producers and consumers, and have believed that they can drive up prices without disrupting agriculture. The Roosevelt administration manipulated prices with carefree abandon. As Treasury Secretary Henry Morgenthau noted in his diary:

> On the night of October 16th [1933], as I was spending a quiet evening at home, the telephone rang. It was the President. "We have got to do something about the price of wheat," he said, strain and weariness apparent in his tone. "I can't take it any longer. . . . Can't you buy 25,000,000 bushels for Harry Hopkins and see if you can't put the price up?" I started in on the buying game first thing in the morning. Wheat was perched precariously at 64 and 7/8 when I placed the first order for one million bushels. By the end of the day we had worked it up 10 cents. "Squeeze the life out of the shorts," FDR said to me, with the old fight in his voice, "and put the price up just as far as you can."[66]

Jesse Jones, the chairman of the Reconstruction Finance Corporation, had a similar tale about cotton prices:

> One afternoon in 1933, President Roosevelt called me to the White House and, as soon as I entered his office, said: "Jess, I want you to lend 10 cents a pound on cotton. Cotton was then selling around 9 cents. The law which created the RFC stated clearly that we should lend only on "full and adequate security." Therefore, to lend 10 cents a pound on cotton when it was selling at 9 and less, was not easy. I did not tell the President we could not do it. I took it to be my job to find a way to do it because I thought cotton was worth more than 10 cents and that to lend that amount of it would be very helpful and entail no loss to the government.[67]

By promising farmers far more than the market value of their crops, the New Deal encouraged farmers to produce far more than could be sold at government-controlled prices. Politicians encouraged farmers to overproduce, and then cited crop surpluses as proof of the need for political management of agriculture. Politicians soon realized that to benefit farmers, they must control them. In 1934 the government imposed heavy taxes on all cotton and tobacco farmers who refused to limit their production as the government demanded. The Roosevelt administration proposed vastly expanding federal controls over other crops in 1934, but Congress rebuffed the idea.

Many of the architects of federal agricultural policy in the 1930s thought the Soviet economic system was superior to that of the United States. Rexford Tugwell, the assistant secretary of agriculture, praised the Soviet Union for its "operation of industry in the public interest rather than for profits . . . ."[68] (Tugwell was accused of learning all he knew about agriculture from a visit to Moscow.) The AAA was a hotbed of radicals and, according to historian Arthur Schlesinger, there was a communist clique in the legal and policy-making branch, where Alger Hiss worked. Schlesinger is careful to point out that "nothing of importance took place in AAA as a result of [the communists'] presence in AAA which liberals would not have done anyway."[69] It is unclear whether Schlesinger's remark was intended as a compliment to the liberals or to the communists.

The federal government in the 1930s and early 1940s attempted many experiments with local socialism. In 1935 Tugwell declared, "Redistribution of our essential wealth, the land, is the clearest mandate our society has received from economic necessities of the present depression."[70] George Mitchell, who was the assistant administrator of the USDA Resettlement Administration, declared in 1941 that the "ownership of [private] property is the greatest detriment to our national prosperity."[71] The Farm Security Administration (FSA) bought more than a million acres of land and then locked many poor farmers into ninety-nine-year leases with close supervision. The FSA intended to supervise the farming of the farmer, his son, and his grandson, and was denounced for trying to introduce serfdom into America. The FSA also stirred controversy by paying the poll tax for white farmers in Southern states; many alleged that the FSA would be pressuring its clients on how to vote. Many of the FSA's local socialized farm projects became renowned for their phenomenally low productivity.

FDR's farm programs were a tangle of contradictions. At the same time the Roosevelt administration was paying farmers to plant less, the Tennessee Valley Authority, the Grand Coulee Dam, and other dams were justified partly as creating millions of new acres of farmland. In 1933, officials of the Roosevelt administration spoke of a massive plan to resettle 6 million unemployed city and town residents on the land to work as "subsistence farmers." The economist Otis Durant Duncan observed, "The addition of more insolvent families to the farm population will undoubtedly lower the average per capita wealth of all farm people."[72] Will Rogers commented,

> Well, we had thought that that foolishness had pretty well died out, but no, this year it springs up again. The government decided that the West should be settled again. The first settling on unoccupied land didn't take, so they would, as they say in the movies, try a "retake." So now they have issued an ultimatum that every ranchman shall take down all his "Drift" fences, all his pastures that are government land, and give the old ad reader in the papers another chance to starve to death. Principally they offer it to ex-soldiers. War wasn't tough enough, they are going to dare 'em to live on a government claim.[73]

Joseph S. Davis, who had been the chief economist of the Federal Farm Board, declared in 1935 that AAA programs "have put the brakes on business recovery" by shutting down much of the cotton and corn support industries.[74] In 1930 roughly 40 percent of all American farmers were tenants or sharecroppers. Yet the New Deal farm programs were designed almost solely for the benefit of landowners. As former USDA chief economist Don Paarlberg observed, "the agricultural elite, generally the large landowners, managed to retain most of the program benefits for themselves rather than share them with tenants or employees."[75] In 1934 the USDA paid cotton producers to slash cotton production, giving the landlord four cents a pound and the sharecropper only one-half cent per pound for production foregone. William B. Anderson reported in *The Nation* in early 1935:

> In the richer Delta country there was relatively little unemployment until the winter of 1933–34, when the reduction program began to

exert its influence. We believe it is fair to say that over the whole cotton belt about one-third of the present rural unemployment can be directly referred to the [cotton] reduction program.[76]

David Eugene Conrad, historian, noted that sharecroppers,

prevented from receiving their "rightful share" of parity payments and forced from the land by the cotton-acreage reduction program, . . . found their protests ignored by both their landlords and the conservative element among the Washington administrators of the act. Bureaucrats sympathetic to tenant interest were forced to resign their jobs in the Agricultural Adjustment Administration.[77]

New Deal agricultural programs were a dismal failure at returning prosperity to the farm. Ezra Taft Benson, secretary of agriculture under President Eisenhower, noted that "cash farm income, less government payments, did not reach the 1929 level until 1941, a war year."[78] Farmland values continued to decline throughout the 1930s and only began rising after World War II became imminent. The continuing decline of farmland value was the clearest vote of no confidence in government agricultural controls by farmers. The parity ratio (for what it is worth) was lower every year of the 1930s than it had been in any year of the 1920s.

The explicit goal of the farm programs created in the 1930s and perpetuated to the present day was to keep as many people in farming as possible. Farm programs have failed miserably: Since 1933 the farm population has fallen from 30 million to less than 5 million today. It is not surprising that the government effort failed to prevent the great migration off the land, but if the USDA and twenty-five sessions of Congress had somehow succeeded, American farmers would likely have become a permanently poverty-stricken class.

In judging the New Deal farm programs, it is important to keep in mind that the United States recovered far more slowly from the Great Depression than did most other industrialized countries. Willford I. King, writing in the *Journal of Farm Economics* in 1935, noted that by 1934, Great Britain, Chile, and Japan had all recovered to near their 1929 industrial output levels.[79] The United States sought to achieve prosperity by raising taxes, restricting production, and causing artificial scarcities to boost prices; other countries did not pursue such radical measures and fared far better. Though the economy was slightly stronger after Roosevelt's inauguration than it had been in 1932, in 1937–38 the economy nose-dived and unemployment was again at 25 percent. The apparently permanent collapse of the American economy helped make the United States a weak presence during the rise of Hitler and the approach of World War II.

The Abuse of Statistics, the Expansion of Government

The increase in federal aid to, and control over, farmers in the 1930s was based on a perception that farmers as a class were much poorer than were other Americans. But the statistical justification for this expansion of federal power was shaky at best and deceptive at worst. The USDA intentionally juggled numbers to make farmers appear needier than they actually were. This set a precedent that has continued to the 1980s and still dominates farm policy debates.

Roosevelt's speeches on agriculture frequently referred to "6 million" struggling farmers. In reality, there were probably fewer than 3 million full-time farmers. Anyone with three acres of land was defined as a farmer. A change in the Census Bureau's method of counting farms in 1930 and in 1935 led to a "fictitious increase of small [farms] and a declining per-capita income."[80] Half of all farms generated farm products with a gross value of less than $1,000 and accounted for only 11 percent of all commercial agricultural production. A million and a half "farm operators" produced less than 4 percent of commercial output. A study for the National Industrial Conference Board concluded in 1936, "These establishments have relatively heavy interest, taxes, and other expenses, and very little offsetting gross income from agricultural production. Their inclusion thus grossly inflates the expenses to be charged against commercial and total agricultural production in arriving at estimates of the net farm income of farm operators."[81] USDA measurements of farm income did not count off-farm income. Yet according to the 1935 Census, "Just over 30 percent of all farm operators . . . reported working off their farms for pay for an average of 100 days during the preceding year."[82] H. Thomas Johnson notes, "Nonagricultural earnings were equal in amount to about one-half of the net income of farmers from farming in the late 1930s when the USDA began to estimate these figures."[83]

The USDA's and the Census Bureau's estimates of gross farm income were extremely inaccurate, being based on limited samples and sometimes excluding entire crops. The Social Science Research Council, in a study by J. D. Black, a well-known agricultural economist, concluded, "Easily as much as ten percent of the income from some major farm products may be missed in some states and much more than this of some minor products."[84] A major component in the comparison of farm and nonfarm standards of living was food grown by farmers and consumed by farm families. Even though the Social Science Research Council and others urged the USDA to value this food at retail prices in order to provide a fair comparison of the actual living standards and diets of farmers and nonfarmers, the USDA calculated the cost of food at wholesale prices—and this figure alone could have accounted for half of the reputed difference between farm and nonfarm living standards. The USDA also significantly undercounted the amount of food consumed on the farm.

The USDA calculated the depreciation of farm buildings and farm equipment at a rate far faster than that used by the Treasury Department for income tax purposes. In its comparison of prices that farmers received and prices that farmers paid, the USDA omitted all mail-order purchases made by farm families. Instead, its cost calculations were based on an extremely limited survey of rural store prices, which were, not surprisingly, much higher than the mail-order prices.[85]

The parity measure was the usual "proof" that farmers deserved more. AAA Administrator Chester C. Davis declared in 1934, "Parity is justice now."[86] Parity presumed that there was no significant change in the value of items that farmers purchased. But in the "Index Numbers of Prices Paid by Farmers for Commodities Bought," published in 1935, the USDA admitted that "the quality and utility of many of the farm machinery items, as well as other items the farmers buy, change over a period of years. Engineers have estimated that the wearing quality and capacity of 25 items of farm machinery in 1932 averaged about 170 percent of prewar machinery. This means that the prices in recent years represent machines of greater producing capacity than in the prewar years."[87] Yet even though the USDA admitted that the parity measure was thus grossly misleading as to the value of farmers' purchases, it continued relying on parity and cited parity measures to prove that the federal government needed to maintain control over farmers.

The USDA manipulated numbers to make it appear that farmers were worse off than they actually were. In its 1934 announcement on the financial condition of farmers, the USDA declared that farmers suffered a 3.1 percent negative return on their investments. The baseline for this calculation was the value of farms, farm equipment, and farm inputs in 1929. The price level of all goods in the United States had fallen sharply between 1929 and 1933. If, as it had done previously, the USDA had based its 1934 estimates of farmers' return-on-investment on current (1934) farmland and farm equipment values, farmers would have been shown to have a 4.4 percent positive return.[88] But that figure would have not helped the USDA to justify expanding farm programs.

In 1936, the National Industrial Conference Board concluded, "In 1935, the fully employed salaried employee and wage-earner incomes for the country as a whole were between $100 and $200 above those of farm operators, as was the case in 1933. If the unemployed in manufacturing and retail trade are taken into consideration, farm operators' incomes were about the same as the average for salaries and wages in these industries."[89]

Farm income statistics were also misleading because roughly half of all farmers lived in the South, and in general Southerners had far lower incomes than people living in other parts of the country. (As mentioned earlier, tenants and sharecroppers in the South were hurt by the federal government's efforts to shut down the cotton plantations in order to drive up cotton prices.) If Southern sharecroppers, often still living as semi-chattels even after the abolition of slavery, are excluded from comparisons of farm and nonfarm income, farmers would likely have had comparatively higher incomes.

After the Depression

Even after the start of World War II, the USDA failed to release controls on production. The huge USDA bureaucracy had spent its career throttling production; once the war began, it was difficult to teach an old dog a new trick. The USDA was so worried about the possibility that a huge crop surplus would result after the war's end that it continued controls on production until 1944. As political scientist Charles Hardin observed, the USDA was "skeptical about the predictions of European postwar food needs" and reluctant to provide storage facilities to store surplus U.S. grain.[90] The Twentieth Century Fund reported in 1953 that, thanks in part to U.S. food production cutbacks during the war years, much of Western Europe "came desperately near to mass starvation in 1946 and 1947."[91] Only good weather and bumper harvests in the immediate postwar years prevented disaster.

During the war the USDA created an extremely generous system of price supports for potatoes. Potato production soared; in 1948, the government spent $206 million buying a third of the potato crop. The government was soon buried in potatoes and ended up dashing them with kerosene and leaving them to rot in such places as alongside New Jersey highways. The nation was outraged, and in 1951 Congress abolished potato price supports. The USDA learned its lesson: Never again would it allow a surplus crop to rot near the highways of New Jersey.[92]

In 1953, Dwight Eisenhower took office and appointed Ezra Taft Benson as agriculture secretary. Benson wanted to return farming to the free market, but Congress refused, instead setting price supports at roughly double world prices and imposing mandatory production controls on wheat and corn farmers. In 1955–56, the USDA arrested or sued more than 1,500 farmers for growing more wheat than was permitted. Stanley Yankus, a farmer in Michigan who grew wheat illegally to feed his chickens, told the House Agriculture Committee in 1959, "I am not fighting for the right to grow wheat. I am fighting for the right to own property. If I am forbidden the use of my land, then I do not own it. How can you congressmen justify the laws which have destroyed my means of making a living?"[93] But since Congress was still in the business of taking care of farmers, farmers had to be prohibited from using their own property as they wished.

By the mid-1950s, it was obvious that farm policies had not saved the small farmer and were providing windfalls for large farmers. Eisenhower, in his 1954 farm message, declared:

> The chief beneficiaries of our price support policies have been the 2 million larger, highly mechanized farming units which produce about 85 percent of our agricultural output. The individual produc-

tion of the remaining farms, numbering about 3.5 million, is so small that the farmer derives little benefit from price supports.[94]

Economist D. Gale Johnson compared farm and nonfarm income in 1954, at a time when the average annual income of nonfarm families was about $5,100:

> If we consider the incomes of the 1.23 million farm families that operate farms which sold 73 percent of all farm products in 1949, we find that their net income was $6,350, or perhaps about $6,750 in dollars of nonfarm purchasing power. That is, the recipients of almost all of the gains from increased prices due to price supports would have been farm families with an average income above that of nonfarm families.[95]

Yet even though farm payments were effectively targeted to wealthy farmers, farm-state politicians and farm lobbies continued to use the struggling family farmer as the justification for all agricultural subsidies and restrictions.

By 1960, the United States was spending over a billion dollars a year just to store surplus commodities. In 1961, when the Kennedy administration took office, Agriculture Secretary Orville Freeman decided that surplus production was the problem and quickly launched a program to bring independent corn growers to their knees. Freeman told a congressional committee in 1965 that the USDA "purposely [dumped government-held surplus corn on the markets] in order to move our prices down far enough so that they would be way below the support level, the loan level, so that we would thereby get compliance. That was the whole intent and purpose and thrust of the program."[96] Getting "compliance" simply meant forcing farmers to follow government orders. Freeman and his advisers decided that the United States needed less corn and, in order to force all corn farmers to accept government restrictions on corn acreage, the USDA wrecked the corn market.

In 1963, wheat farmers voted in a national referendum on whether to continue mandatory federal controls over wheat production. At the time, farm programs were being fiercely criticized. Freeman promulgated a "loyalty oath," requiring all farmers elected to USDA local committees to swear "to support all government farm programs." A USDA committee in South Dakota used tax dollars to set up a miniature railroad exhibit at the state fair, showing a sidetrack with a rail-road wreck and two signs that read: "Do not let Farm Program opponents sidetrack you onto a dead end," and "Free Enterprise Wrecked This Train." USDA employees told farmers that the election issue was simple: "Two-dollar wheat versus one-dollar wheat." The USDA blanketed farmers with more than 5 million copies of seven different pamphlets urging them to vote in favor of it. In an article in the *Reader's Digest*, John Strohm noted that "federal workers high-pressured banks into buying newspaper ads plugging for a yes vote."[97] Despite the government's high-handed pressure, wheat farmers rejected continued mandatory government controls and the end of the New Deal era appeared to be on the horizon.

Farm programs in the 1960s were a costly, ineffective failure. As the *Wall Street Journal* noted in a June 27, 1967, editorial on farm income during the 1960s, "producers of livestock, poultry and such uncontrolled crops as potatoes and soybeans enjoyed rising incomes while producers of crops—wheat, feed grains and so on—under governmental control programs saw their incomes decline." *Barron's* noted on June 17, 1968, "Virtually half of the farmer's net income today comes from cultivating Washington. . . . Since the number of farms has declined in the past seven years by over 20 percent . . . government cash payments per farm have soared from $175 to $978." Kermit Gordon, former budget director, estimated in 1965 that "80 percent of U.S. agriculture assistance goes to the million farmers whose average income exceeds $9,500 [more than $30,000 in 1988 dollars] while the other 20 percent of assistance is spread thinly among the remaining 80 percent of farmers."[98] Charles Schultze, in a study for the Brookings Institution, concluded that the "total cost [of agricultural subsidies] in 1969 measured as the sum of direct outlays in federal funds and the amount [extra] paid by consumers of agricultural products, roughly equaled the cost in the same year of all federal, state, and local welfare programs, including Medicaid."[99]

In 1972 the USDA paid American farmers to idle 60 million acres—the biggest acreage reduction since the Great Depression. At the same time, the USDA paid its largest export subsidies in history ($700 million) to the Soviets to help them buy a quarter of the American wheat crop. As the General Accounting Office noted, the USDA kept subsidizing exports even after the Soviets had effectively cornered the U.S. market. Congressman Pete du Pont declared, "It appears that more thought goes into selling a can of soup off a grocery shelf than went into the 1.1 billion bushels of wheat sale."

Despite a worldwide wheat shortage, the USDA continued rewarding farmers for not planting more crops. A *New York Times* editorial on April 3, 1973, slammed the Nixon administration for its "inexcusable failure" to end all acreage-reduction programs. The USDA did not formally announce the end of restrictions on wheat planting until mid-August 1973—after wheat had topped $5 a bushel (more than $13 in 1988 dollars). USDA was supposed to have a reporting system for foreign crop purchases, but the system failed to monitor the massive Soviet purchases, which helped quadruple wheat prices and signaled the onset of a decade of world inflation. If the United States had not idled 60 million acres of cropland, it is likely that wheat prices would have risen far less.

After 1973, Agriculture Secretary Earl Butz urged American farmers to plant fencerow-to-fencerow. Once exports began increasing, politicians assumed that they would increase forever, and that American farmers should be encouraged to produce as much food as possible at any cost. During the export boom of the 1970s, U.S. support and target prices were usually lower than were world crop prices. But between 1975 and 1982, Congress and three presidents raised the support price, in real dollars, for wheat by 43 percent, corn by 38 percent, cotton by 31 percent, and rice by 44 percent. Target prices were raised by an equal or greater amount. Yet at the same time that American price supports were soaring, the real cost of production of major crops was falling around the world. Once again politicians were on the verge of pricing American farmers out of world markets.

In January 1980, President Carter embargoed grain sales to the Soviet Union in retaliation for the Soviets' invasion of Afghanistan. Though Carter's desire to punish the Soviets was commendable, the grain embargo was a senseless, ineffective method. Wheat is a fungible commodity: if the U.S. doesn't sell to the Soviets, the Argentinians and Australians will. It would have made far more sense to impose an embargo on all U.S. bank lending to the Soviet bloc. The grain embargo was a typical example of the nationalism and myopia of agricultural policy, and of how poorly American politicians understand international markets.

The Carter administration estimated that the boycott would reduce Soviet meat consumption by up to 10 percent. Within days after the boycott was announced, the Soviets were easily buying up wheat on the world market—and U.S. grain prices dropped sharply. In farm-lobby lore, the 1980 embargo created a permanent obligation of society to the American farmer. But a comprehensive study published by the USDA in 1986 concluded that the government "actually overcompensated farmers" for the Soviet grain embargo—that is, that farmers received more in new handouts than they lost in foreign sales.[100] The government gave farmers new and more generous payments for storing their wheat—assuring them that they could "store their way to prosperity." But the federal program effectively "locked up" the grain. In 1982 and 1983, U.S. grain exports fell partly because farmers were not allowed to sell grain because of federal regulations.

In the 1980s, farm program costs exploded. Saving the farmer became a popular cause. Country music singers organized concerts to raise money for struggling farmers—but a nationally televised concert with more than a dozen well-known singers raised less money than the USDA paid to persuade a single California farm to slaughter its dairy cows. Though few people contributed their own money to farmers, many concert-goers did make the effort to send in form letters to congressmen demanding mandatory controls to boost crop prices.

Historical Price Trends vs. Federal Agricultural Policy

The history of American agricultural policy is largely the history of a political struggle against changes in relative prices. Much of farm policy since 1933 can be explained by a misunderstanding of long-term price trends. The real price of major farm commodities has been slowly declining over the past several centuries. The real price (in constant dollar terms) of chickens has declined by 80 percent since 1930; the real price of eggs has declined by over 70 percent since 1930; the real world market price of sugar has declined by over 50 percent since 1930. Figure 2-1 puts sugar prices in historical perspective.

The price of wheat, measured in units of the average manufacturing wage, has fallen by 90 percent in the last two centuries. Prices have

FIGURE 2 - 1
Historical Trends in Sugar Prices, 1801–1984

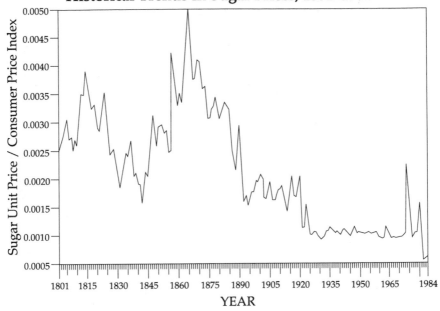

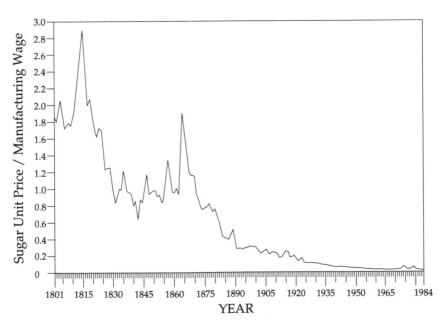

SOURCE: Julian Simon, University of Maryland.

FIGURE 2 - 2
Historical Trends in Wheat Prices, 1801–1984

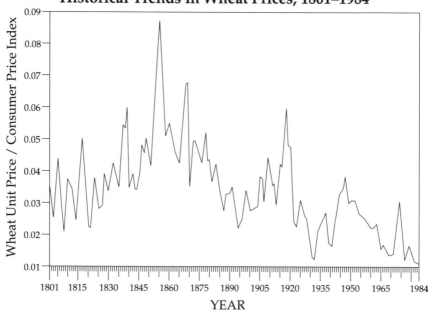

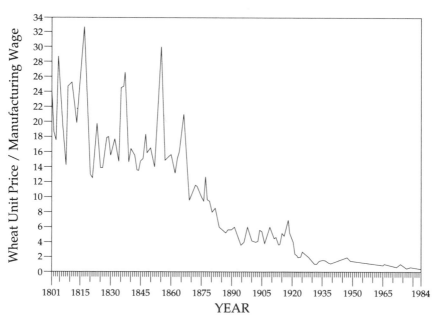

SOURCE: Julian Simon, University of Maryland.

risen sharply during wars and during the 1970s world inflationary boom. But the long-term trend has been unmistakably downward. The productivity of labor used for wheat production tripled between 1800 and 1900. In the 1980s, with new seed varieties available throughout the world, wheat yields have soared and the price of wheat has fallen sharply around the globe. Figure 2-2 shows the fluctuations of wheat prices.

Crop prices have fallen primarily because the costs of production have continued to fall. Mechanical inventions, the development of new seeds and fertilizer, the development of sound management techniques on the farm, and the success of private and government-funded research have all helped drive down the cost of wheat production. But in the same way that most USDA measures understate farm income (by exaggerating the number of farmers), most official measures also overstate the cost of wheat production. As a result, politicians and policy-makers often have the mistaken idea that farmers are being pauperized—even as farmers have become a financial elite.

Politicians have long tended to view falling food prices as an economic problem rather than as a natural and inevitable result of technological progress and an opportunity for the citizens to have a better diet. The farm problem is largely that farm prices are not as high as politicians think they should be. Each decade, as prices trend downwards, politicians and farm lobbyists have warned that wheat production is no longer profitable and that society will soon have a severe wheat shortage unless immediate action is taken to raise wheat prices. Yet in every decade farmers have produced more wheat than they produced in the previous decade. As prices have fallen, production has steadily risen. Politicians argue that falling prices force farmers to produce more, so as to make up in volume what they lose in profit margins. Though some farmers might temporarily react this way for a very short period, this is a poor explanation for long-term historical trends. Julian Simon, a University of Maryland economist and a pioneer in the analysis of long-term commodity price trends, observed that "politicians have refused to admit the obvious—and thereby have justified endless unsuccessful schemes that disrupted the American agricultural system. Crop cost-of-production and crop prices will continue to decline, regardless of how many politicians rant and rave on the floors of Congress."[101]

Chapter 3

Seven Myths of Farm Policy

Our farmers round, well pleased with constant gain,
Like other farmers, flourish and complain.

—George Crabbe
The Parish Registry, 1807

Agricultural policy-making is dominated by mythology. The 1985 farm bill was based on the same creeds that dominated the 1933 Agricultural Adjustment Act. As former USDA chief economist Don Paarlberg noted, "In developing the Food Security Act of 1985, the Congress paid little attention to economic analyses."[1] Agricultural debates have largely consisted of conjuring and waving intellectual relics—with policy-makers showing an unwavering loyalty to the beliefs of their ancestors.

It is impossible to understand farm policy without knowing how many farmers there are, their comparative wealth, the broad differences in their business ability, and the effect of agriculture on the national economy. USDA statistics have almost always understated farmers' income and overstated farmers' costs of production, thus perennially misleading the public about the true wealth of American farmers. Misleading statistics—or statistics that are abused by politicians—are the source of much of the "farm crisis" of the last half century.

A handful of key ideas have dominated government agricultural policy-making since the 1920s. Each of these ideas is an illusion, and each has helped disrupt the American economy. From the number of farmers to farm income, from farmers' costs of production to widespread misconceptions on the nature of farmers and of bankruptcy, farm policy has been based on meaningless definitions and meaningless numbers.

There Are 2.2 Million Farms in America

If we defined corporations as Uncle Sam defines farms, every eight-year old with a lemonade stand would have to file a corporate tax return. If a person sells only $1,000 a year in farm commodities, he is classified as a farmer. If a person sells a single horse for more than $1,000, the USDA labels the person a farmer. The federal government says there are 2.2 million farms. Yet in the 1982 Census of Agriculture, one million of these so-called farmers denied that they were farmers, claiming some other occupation. Two-thirds of these so-called farmers lose money from farming most years; they are primarily gentlemen farmers, hobby farmers, or tax farmers. *The American Journal of Agricultural Economics* reported that between 1980 and 1982, off-farm income accounted for 99 percent of family income for 72 percent of all U.S. farms. In 1986, 55 percent of so-called farmers' income came from off the farm. Most farmers receive most of their income from nonfarm jobs, and reliance on actual farm income is now lower than ever before. Yet in public discussions of the farm crisis, most commentators look only at so-called farmers' on-the-farm income. Since most so-called farmers lose money farming most of the time, there is always ample ground to proclaim a farm crisis.

The USDA classifies farmers according to their total sales. The 1,612,000 farms with a gross sales volume of between $1,000 and $40,000 lost an average of $223 each in 1979, $948 in 1980, $1,370 in 1981, $721 in 1982, $1,195 in 1983, $1,320 in 1984, and $531 in 1985. In 1986, the 1.6 million smallest farmers each had an average profit of $139—less than the cost of applying fertilizer and pesticides to four acres of corn cropland.[2] Obviously, these folks are not in farming for the money. As Marvin Duncan, vice president of the Kansas City

Federal Reserve Bank notes, "One could almost disregard about 1.7 million farmers. They are economically irrelevant. They have almost no impact on the food supply."[3]

For the 286,000 farms with sales between $40,000 and $100,000, the average annual farm income during the 1980s was $8,099—including an annual average government handout of $6,006. These farms had an average off-farm income of $11,191. These farmers are considered full-time by some and part-time by others. But since this class earns most of its income from off-farm sources, it is not dependent either on farming or on farm programs for economic survival. Emanuel Melichar, former chief agricultural economist for the Federal Reserve system, observed in 1984 that "on many of these farms, the operators either are underemployed during much of the year or have a relatively inefficient operation." H. O. Carter of the Agricultural Issues Center at the University of California at Davis observed, "As a group, these smaller farmers are declining in numbers because they are not large enough to compete with their larger, more efficient neighbors."[4]

Commercial farmers are those who sell over $100,000 in farm products a year. In 1987 there were 301,000 farmers in this class, and their income from farming averaged $136,255. The average off-farm income for this group was $15,916, making their average total income more than $152,171. In 1987 the USDA gave, in direct payments to the 29,000 largest farms, an average of $46,073—an amount that exceeded the net worth (including the value of house and cars) of over half the families in America. The USDA estimated that the average total federal outlay for the largest subsidized 16,240 farms in 1985 was $105,000 each.[5]

Many congressmen and farm lobbyists insist that farmers in the $40,000–$99,999 sales class are full-time farmers. Counting these farmers as full-time farmers essentially doubles the number of farmers, and the more farmers there appear to be, the more easily farm subsidies can be justified. To better understand the issue, consider the number of hours of work required to produce enough corn to garner $40,000 in gross income. According to the USDA, the average corn yield is 119 bushels an acre, and it takes 3.1 hours of labor to plant and harvest each acre of corn. The target price for corn in 1987 was $3.03 a bushel. This means that the average farmer would have collected, per acre, $360.57 in revenue, including federal subsidies. To sell $40,000-worth of corn, a farmer would have to harvest 111 acres, which require

Table 3-1

Subsidies for Farmers, by Gross Annual Sales, 1985

Gross Annual Sales	Percentage of Total Farmers	Number of Farmers Receiving Subsidies
$500,000+	56%	16,240
$250,000–$500,000	62	40,920
$100,000–$249,999	66	138,600
$40,000–$99,999	57	167,580
Total Subsidized Farmers:		**363,340**

SOURCE: U.S. Department of Agriculture, *Farmline*, December 1986/January 1987, p. 5.

only 344 hours of work during the course of the year. This is clearly not a full-time job (defined as 2,000 hours a year) even though during planting and harvesting seasons, farmers routinely work more than 60, 70, or 80 hours a week. The average farm income of farmers in the $40,000–$99,999 sales class during the 1980s was $8,099—slightly more than the annual salary of someone employed as a minimum-wage dishwasher.

The important question for farm policy is not how many farmers there are, but how many farmers receive federal aid. Table 3-1 shows the estimates made by the USDA's Economic Research Service in 1986 of the percentage of farmers in each sales class that received federal subsidies.

Subsidized farmers in the $40,000–$99,999 class, rather than being the backbone of American democracy, are actually relatively ineffi-cient government contractors. As with other government contractors, it is often government regulations and restrictions that make them inefficient. Direct federal payments per farm in this class far exceeded average net farm income in 1983 and 1984.[6] And the cost to taxpayers is actually much higher than the cost of direct federal handouts; the Senate Budget Committee examined agricultural subsidies for the year 1982, and concluded that "comparison of total direct and indirect benefits reveals that indirect benefits exceeded direct benefits by more than 400 percent."[7] Almost half the farmers in this sales class receive no direct government benefits; in 1985, the average farmer in the $40,000–$99,999 class had a net farm income of $10,642; the average federal outlays per subsidized farm were $15,000.[8]

If we presume, for the sake of argument, that half of the farmers with annual sales of between $40,000 and $99,999 are full-time farmers, about 300,000 full-time farmers receive government subsidies (see Table 3-1). This is roughly equal to the population of Albany, New York; Birmingham, Alabama; or Charlotte, North Carolina. This is the size of the group we are speaking of when debating the necessity of federal farm subsidies.

While farm programs have striven for over half a century to save the small farmer, farm operations and farm income have become more concentrated. As the Congressional Budget Office noted in 1984,

> Today, about 12 percent of all farms produce most of the nation's food and fiber. These farms, with annual gross sales over $100,000, accounted for 68 percent of the total cash receipts from the sale of farm products in calendar year 1982. These approximately 300,000 farmers had an average income from all sources of nearly $90,000. And in recent years they received about 90 percent of total net farm income . . . and have an average net worth of about $1.2 million.[9]

Lloyd Teigen of the USDA's Economic Research Service observed that "more than 80 percent of the farm output is produced by fewer than 20 percent of the farms which reap virtually all of the industry net farm profits."[10] One percent of the farms routinely earns 50 or 60 percent of net farm income. Two million, one hundred thousand farms account for only 5 percent of farm profits.[11] Sixty-five percent of the USDA's payments to farmers now goes to about 135,000 feed-grain, cotton, and rice farms.[12] Yet public policy is still premised on the notion that there are millions of farmers, almost all of whom need continued federal aid and protection.

Farm lobbies and farm-state congressmen proclaim that farmers are the backbone of American democracy. But even if we count the $40,000–$99,999 farmers as full-time farmers, the total number of farmers is roughly 573,000—less than the number of postal workers, beauty and barbershop employees, or textile sewing-machine operators in the country. If we look only at subsidized farmers, we find fewer federally dependent farmers than there are bartenders, taxi and bus drivers, or social workers.[13]

Federal aid to states and counties is based partly on the number of farms in each locale. Any change in the definition of *farm* would alter the allocation of federal aid. Naturally, congressmen from areas with large numbers of hobby and tax farmers fiercely oppose a definition of *farm* that has any relevance to the late twentieth century. And by exaggerating the number of farmers, politicians can more easily justify increasing farm aid. By refusing to make an intelligent classification of what is and is not a farm, the federal government guarantees the misspending of billions of dollars on farm and rural programs. By using statistics that greatly exaggerate the number of farms, congressmen and the farm lobbies can more easily frighten the public with the specter of mass dislocation in rural America. Only one in twelve families in rural America today is a farmer—even with the government's "sell a horse, be a farmer" definition.[14]

Farmers Are Poorer than City Folks

For over forty years, federal farm policy has been dominated by myths about farmers' poverty. For over a century, politicians have been basing their rhetoric on the poor family farmer. Even though farmers are now far richer than nonfarmers, pleading farm poverty is still a good way to shake down taxpayers. A 1987 USDA publication, *Agricultural Parity: Historical Review and Alternative Calculations* by Lloyd D. Teigen, concluded that the total farm and off-farm income of farm families had exceeded the median American family's income every year since 1964 (see Table 3-2).[15]

And even this comparison understates farmers' advantage over nonfarmers. Congress has created a welter of tax write-offs for farmers that allow them to shelter far more of their income than other Americans. In 1983, when net farm income was $12.7 billion, farmers and farm investors claimed a net loss of $9.3 billion for tax purposes.[16] The *Washington Post* reported that "Nebraska farmers can get 'conservation' tax credits for leveling hilly sand dunes to plant crops, even though erosion is usually increased."[17] This creates an even greater disparity between real farm and nonfarm income. In addition, the cost of living for farmers is significantly lower; thus, the farmer's dollar goes further than does the nonfarmer's dollar. Agricultural economist

Table 3-2

Average Farm Family Income
as Percent of All Family Income,
1960–87

Year	Median Income of All Families	Average Income of Farm Families	Average Farm Family Income as Percent of All Family Income
1960	$5,620	$4,946	88.0%
1961	5,735	5,434	94.0
1962	5,956	5,782	97.1
1963	6,249	6,204	99.3
1964	6,569	6,638	101.1
1965	6,957	7,325	105.3
1966	7,532	8,575	113.8
1967	7,933	8,279	104.4
1968	8,632	9,008	104.4
1969	9,433	10,268	108.9
1970	9,867	10,848	109.9
1971	10,285	11,287	109.7
1972	10,116	13,955	125.5
1973	12,051	19,746	163.9
1974	12,902	20,413	158.2
1975	13,719	18,266	133.1
1976	14,958	19,365	129.5
1977	16,009	18,267	114.1
1978	17,640	23,207	131.6
1979	19,587	25,709	131.3
1980	21,023	26,503	126.1
1981	22,388	25,849	115.5
1982	23,433	26,794	114.3
1983	24,580	29,048	126.8
1984	23,620	30,215	127.9
1985	27,376	32,908	120.2
1986	29,458	37,125	126.0
1987	30,853	42,754	138.6

Method of calculation was revised to compensate for previous understatement of farm income.
SOURCES: Lloyd D. Teigen, *Agricultural Parity: Historical Review and Alternative Calculations*, report prepared for U.S. Department of Agriculture, 1987; "Economic Indicators of the Farm Sector—Farm Sector Review, 1986," U.S. Department of Agriculture, January 1988, p. 51; *Money Income of Households, Families, and Persons in the U.S.*, U.S. Census Bureau, Series P60, #156.

Dale Hathaway estimated in 1963 that farmers can achieve a standard of living comparable with that of nonfarmers on only 86 percent of the income.[18]

Farmers not only have higher incomes than do nonfarmers, but also most farmers are far wealthier than other Americans. The Census Bureau concluded in 1986 that the median net worth of American households was $32,677 (meaning that an equal number of households were worth less than, and more than, $32,677), and that the mean, or average, net worth of American households was $78,734.[19] According to the USDA, as of December 31, 1987, the average net worth of full-time farmers with sales of more than $100,000 a year was $1,003,000.[20] If we assume that half the $40,000–$99,999 farmers are full-time farmers, this would provide an average net worth for full-time farmers of $822,118—still significantly above the asset eligibility cutoff for food stamps and Aid to Families with Dependent Children. The average full-time farmer is worth more than ten times as much as the average American household, and more than twenty times as much as half the households in America.[21] If the average full-time farmer sold his farm and put the $822,118 into an annuity yielding 9 percent a year and never worked another day in his life, he would still have an annual income of $73,990—more than double that of the average American family.

Farmers have been wealthier than nonfarmers for decades. Even in the depths of the Great Depression, the average farm net worth exceeded nonfarm net worth. Wheeler McMillen, the editor of *Country Home*, noted in 1936 that the average farm family had a net worth of $9,668, while the average nonfarm family had a net worth of $8,709.[22] By 1962, the average farm net worth was four times greater than nonfarm net worth.[23] But because there is political profit in portraying farmers as indigent, this fact has been little recognized in public debate.

Federal aid to farmers has helped boost farmland values and widen the gap between farmer and nonfarmer net worth. As a result of higher land values, it is now extremely difficult for an individual to get started in farming without family connections. Former USDA chief economist Don Paarlberg notes, "We are drifting toward a structure of agriculture which approaches . . . a wealthy hereditary land-owning class, with new entrants almost ruled out unless they are well-to-do."[24] One percent of the U.S. population now owns almost one-third of the nation's ranch and farmland.[25] The National Agricultural Forum reported in 1984 that "eight percent of the households in America own the vast majority of the land . . . 63 percent of U.S. households own no land."[26] The longer we continue to believe farmers are poor and give them more money, the higher the entry barriers for new farmers will be, and the greater the inequality between farmers and nonfarmers.

Any comparisons of farm and off-farm income also must consider the comparative work week. The image of the farmer toiling year-round from before dawn to after sundown is long since outdated. *Washington Post* reporter Julius Daschau observed in 1964, "The crop rotation among prosperous farmers in the Midwest is corn, soybeans, and Miami Beach in the winter."[27] In the *Atlantic Monthly*, Gregg Easterbrook observed that well-equipped crop farmers "face three months of heavy work during planting and two more at harvest," and often have little work to do the rest of the year.[28] There is a new "Robotic Driver" electronic guidance system that automatically steers a tractor in the field. The farmer can smoke a pipe, play the banjo, or read *Playboy* while the robot does the job more accurately and faster (the farmer still needs to be on board to turn the tractor around at the end of each row).[29] According to the USDA, cotton and tobacco farmers average only 34 hours of work for 45 weeks a year. Dairy farmers, on the other hand, work an average of 68 hours a week for 51 weeks a year—much more than the average American.[30]

Farmers Are Entitled to the Same Income that Nonfarmers Receive

Parity is the doctrine that farmers are morally entitled to an income equal to that of nonfarmers, and has been the rallying cry of farm groups since the 1920s. Farm groups have always implied or proclaimed that society is to blame if the typical farmer earns less than the typical nonfarmer—and that the government has a duty to intervene to make recompense. Parity is a doctrine of "fair exchange value," which means that if farmers receive less than so-called parity values, society has treated them unfairly. Parity declares that society treats farmers immorally if crop prices fall relative to other prices.

The official parity calculation is based on the ratio of farm prices to nonfarm prices between 1910 and 1914. The USDA picked out the most prosperous years, excluding wartime, for farmers in American history, and then proceeded to gouge the taxpayers for most of the next seventy-five years because farm prices were not as high. No one would try to drive across the country with a 1912 road map—but that is how the government makes agricultural policy. Parity is still the legal foundation for the dairy, honey, wool, orange, and lemon programs. If current farm legislation expires in 1990 without being replaced, farm programs will automatically revert to so-called permanent legislation and parity will set the standard for all commodity programs.

Parity is based on the idea that the comparative cost of production for agricultural and industrial goods has not changed for almost eighty years and that farmers have not become more efficient. Lloyd Teigen of the USDA observes that "the average corn farm produces more than 21 times the corn produced per farm in 1910–14, and cotton farmers produce 44 times the 1910–14 average."[31] Corn yields per acre have increased 450 percent, wheat yields are up 400 percent, and milk per dairy cow has tripled.

How would the public react if American television manufacturers stormed Capitol Hill to protest the fact that the price of television sets had fallen sharply in real terms over the past few decades? Yet this is what farmers do almost every year. Most of the complaints about unfairly low crop prices in this century have stemmed largely from a refusal to admit that the cost of producing these crops has fallen steadily, thereby leading naturally to lower prices. This is a trend that has been proceeding continuously for at least 200 years, and has been fought tooth-and-nail by politicians for at least a century. Parity is a Luddite concept that implies that the American economy should be frozen to provide farmers with the same comparative advantage that their great-grandfathers enjoyed. Parity is also a protectionist concept, based on the idea that government should isolate the American economy in order to boost farm prices.

In a free society, no individual or group has a moral right to the same income as any other individual or group. A group's income is the result of millions of voluntary decisions of that group and other groups throughout the economy. If people are unsatisfied with their incomes, they are free to change professions. But farm lobbies have always thought that the answer was not for some people to leave farming, but for the American economy to be shackled to benefit farmers. Yet there is no reason to equalize farmers' and city folks' income that would not justify forcibly equalizing the incomes of all professions. Parity has always been "socialism for one class."

Parity is implicitly based on the idea that all farmers are alike, and that with a few deft adjustments, government can assure an economic balance between farmers and nonfarmers. But the differences among the incomes of different farmers is as wide as the difference between farmers and nonfarmers. Parity makes no sense when setting prices for individual crops because some farmers have ten acres and some ten thousand. In taking a per-bushel or per-hundredweight measure of parity, Congress and the USDA can set prices without regard to the windfalls that large farmers can receive.

Politicians and some farm-group leaders have often used the parity doctrine to keep their followers intellectually barefoot and pregnant—never asking any question except, Why is the world so unjust that farm prices are not higher? The parity movement has done a great deal to fuel farmers' contempt for the market, and thus to advance political control over farming and to destroy American exports. When farm lobbies talk of parity, they are usually either blinded by their own greed or are knowingly talking nonsense and attempting to delude their listeners.

Parity is simply a worship of ancient farm prices. Even though farmers' income is higher than nonfarmers' income, many farmers claim that they are still victimized because crop prices are lower now in real terms than they were in 1910. But so are prices for most commodities, farm and nonfarm. The only justification for parity nowadays is that farmers are treated unfairly because nonfarmers don't pay as much for farm products as their great-grandfathers paid. It appears that not only are farmers now entitled to an equal income, but they are also entitled to a deceptive measure of farm income that results in making farmers far richer than nonfarmers.

Farmers Are Entitled to Their Cost of Production

Representative Byron Dorgan respectfully quotes a farmer from his
district:

> When I produce wheat and sell it at the local elevator and get $3.40 a
> bushel for it, after it cost me $4.10 to produce, I have a hard time
> believing anybody is subsidizing me. I happen to believe I am sub-
> sidizing the person who is eating what I sold for much less than the
> cost of production.[32]

Since the earliest days of the New Deal, it has been proclaimed
that if a farmer cannot sell his crop for more than it cost him to grow
it, he has been robbed. The right to costs of production is treated by
some farm groups as a self-evident truth, perhaps number seven on
the list of the Ten Commandments. The notion is based on the idea
that if farmers grow a crop, taxpayers are obliged to pay for it and
give farmers a profit, too. In any other business, if a person can't sell
what he produces for a profit, he learns that he must either lower his
costs or leave the business. In agriculture, if a farmer can't sell for his
cost of production, it proves that taxes should be increased and the
choice of consumers restricted.

To pay farmers according to their costs of production is anticompetitive, since it discourages them from becoming more efficient. This
was obvious from the beginning of the New Deal farm programs.
Ralph Robey, a contributing editor of the *Washington Post*, observed in
1934,

> The New Deal program has frozen in the inefficient producer. It has
> made it profitable for him to stay on his farm. He is in as good a
> relative position in history to the total supply on the market as he was
> before the reduction program went into effect. The efficient, low-cost
> producer has had to make as much of a curtailment as the farmer
> curtailing the poorest land. All danger has been eliminated of the
> high-cost producer being crowded out of the market as a result of
> someone else being able to supply the public needs at a lower price
> with profit. All possibility of the public getting the benefits of con-
> tinued improvements in agricultural technique has been stalemated.[33]

The 1977 Food and Consumer Protection Act partly replaced
parity with cost of production as the basis for federal agricultural
intervention in the pricing of wheat, corn, sorghum, cotton, rice,

peanuts, and barley. But this only replaced a religious relic with a pseudoeconomic relic. Cost of production is measured by the costs to the average producer, not the average unit of production. J. Bruce Bullock observed in a Cato Institute study that

> Since 93 percent of the total farm products were produced by the 40 percent of the farms that had positive net incomes, farm prices must have been below the cost of production for only 7 percent of total farm production. . . . Thus we have a paradox: the average farmer loses money, but the average unit of agricultural product is produced at a profit.[34]

Payment according to the average farmer's cost of production is guaranteed to generate huge surpluses from successful farmers. Farming is a cyclical business. Prices set to guarantee farmers a profit every year will also guarantee huge surpluses in most years.

Congress mandates that cost of production will be measured in a way that exaggerates apparent costs and increases the farmer's entitlements. The cost-of-production formula is biased upward, which increases land values because of the expected future income; higher land values result in a higher apparent cost of production, which in turn boosts government payments to farmers, which further increase land values, ad infinitum.

The basis for the national cost-of-production estimate for each crop is irrational. The USDA might as well add apples and oranges and pears and prunes, and then announce that the proper weight of each piece of American fruit is 3.2 ounces. There is no way to calculate reasonable estimates of national production costs for farmers in a dozen different regions, with scores of different soil types and vast differences in weather. The variable costs of production for farmers growing soybeans in the Southeast is more than double those of corn belt farmers; efficient cotton growers produce cotton in California for far less what it costs some Mississippi growers. There are as many differences in farmers' costs of production as there are among fifty states and hundreds of thousands of farmers.

Congressmen warn that if farmers are not paid their costs of production, they will stop producing. But if the market is actually paying less than the farmers' costs of production, then some farmers will quit the business—which will decrease the crop supply and drive prices up for the remaining farmers. There was a common saying in the South in the 1950s: "The cure for ten cent [a pound] cotton is ten-cent cotton."

Aid to Farmers Helps Other Sectors of the Economy

Farm aid is based on the old superstition that "no money can set industry in motion till it has been taken by the tax-gatherer out of one man's pocket and put into another man's pocket," as Thomas Babington Macaulay observed in 1830.[35] The defense of agriculture programs is always based on the "multiplier effect"—the idea that there is some special force that turns federal payments to farmers into "magic beans" that make the whole economy grow up to the clouds. Franklin D. Roosevelt declared on July 24, 1933, that "for many years, the two great barriers to a normal prosperity have been low farm prices and the creeping paralysis of unemployment."[36] The original Agricultural Adjustment Act was titled, "an act to relieve the existing national economic emergency by increasing agricultural purchasing power, etc." The doctrine assumed that any price increase for any product was a good thing because it would increase the producers' income and create a multiplier effect that would make everyone else better off. (This doctrine is much more popular with producers than with consumers.)

Agricultural programs are based on the idea that some sectors of the economy are far more important than others—and that everyone benefits when government takes a dollar from a janitor and gives it to a tobacco farmer. According to Congressman Tom Daschle, "It has been said that every American farm-generated dollar translates to five dollars of economic activity throughout the economy."[37] According to Congressman Kika de la Garza, "If you kill the farm, you are killing the taproots of what America is. This illusory thing, that [lowering dairy price supports] will help the consumer [is wrong]. . . . the best way to help the consumer is to have jobs. It all begins on the farm."[38]

According to congressional logic, the higher food prices are, the richer America will be. If there were any such economic magic in high food prices, Congress has been criminally negligent for not pegging milk at $10 a gallon long ago. If plumbers, garbage collectors, or the National Federation of Female Streetwalkers proclaimed the same doctrine, people would laugh in their faces. But the more absurd the farm lobbies' arguments become, the more respect they seem to receive.

Congressmen and the USDA often defend agricultural programs for creating jobs and stimulating economic activity. This defense is based on the traditional theory of government benevolence—that a dollar in tax payments is no loss to the economy, while a dollar in government handouts is a great gain. Such theories would only make sense if the government could create wealth out of thin air or if the shuffling of assets automatically multiplied them.

When 70 percent of Americans were farmers, the health of the farm economy heavily influenced the health of the national economy. As fewer people are working on the farms, the less important farming has become to our national economy. Farmers now make up less than one percent of the American labor force, and on-farm employment is only 2.5 percent of the work force. Congressmen from farming states often proclaim that agriculture and food account for 22 percent of the gross national product (GNP), and are thus significant elements of the national economy. The vast majority of this 22 percent would exist regardless of federal farm aid. Most of the food and fiber sector of the GNP is made up of retail food businesses and grocery stores. Many agricultural programs reduce farm productivity, reduce employment, and squander resources. The economy will not decline if government stops paying farmers to kill their cows and idle their land.

Farms Are All Alike

Federal agricultural policy has always presumed that farmers are more homogeneous than members of the great majority of professions. Chester C. Davis, the Agricultural Adjustment administrator, said that "farmers should recognize that they are all in the same boat. All must be helped."[39] The doctrine that government should pay farmers according to an artificially determined cost-of-production formula implies that there are few differences in the competence or ability of the nation's farmers. Farm lobbies attempt to make people believe that it is only fate or bad luck that makes one farmer go bankrupt and another become a millionaire. But in farming, as in most other occupations outside politics, talent, ability, dedication, and hard work separate the wheat from the chaff.

Farming is a high-tech industry, and capital-per-farm-worker is now double capital-per-industrial-worker. No one would suggest that any man off the street could run a factory. Yet for some reason, politicians act as though they believe that anybody outside the city limits can successfully run a farm. There is as much difference in what a good farmer and an inept farmer can do with 500 acres of land as there is in what a good sculptor and a klutz can do with a block of marble. Efficient farmers routinely have twice the yield and half the cost of production of inefficient farmers. The more innovative agriculture becomes, the greater the difference in the costs of production between the most-advanced and the most-backward farmers, and the louder the screaming for a bailout by the less competent.

Congressmen and farm lobbies imply that all farmers are in the same boat in order to justify giving handouts to all farmers. If one farmer is prospering and another is on the verge of bankruptcy, politicians strive to represent the difference as due to factors beyond the farmers' control—unfair prices, heavy debt, or bad advice from some government official fifteen years before. Politicians have an incentive to give money to as many voters as possible—and by denying individual farmers responsibility for their own problems, politicians have a blank check to provide aid to everyone outside the city limits.

Farm Bankruptcies Are a Fate Worse than Death

If a small business provides miserable service to its customers, there are few tears when the banks foreclose. But if a dairy farmer mismanages his business so badly that many of his cows die, then the resulting bankruptcy is portrayed as a national tragedy. Federal farm policy is increasingly designed to provide "feel-good" experiences for existing farmers rather than to maximize productivity or efficiency.

Listening to some politicians, one gets the impression that when a farmer goes bankrupt, the land vanishes and a farmer dies. Congressman David Martin of New York warned in 1984, "When the farm goes . . . there goes the farmer, there goes the home, and there goes the family."[40] The occasional suicide of a farmer receives vastly more news coverage than that of a bankrupt small businessman. Politicians strive to perpetrate the notion that farmers can only leave farming in a body bag.

Politicians have knowingly tried to fan public fear by greatly exaggerating the number of farm bankruptcies. Congressman Jamie Whitten, one of the most powerful members of the House of Representatives and chairman of the House Appropriations Committee, declared on June 16, 1988, that since 1981, "the government policy forced the bankruptcy of 261,000 farmers."[41] This is a fabrication: Fewer than 50,000 farmers went bankrupt nationwide between 1980 and 1987. The General Accounting Office, reporting data from Dun and Bradstreet, mentions fewer than 3,000 farm business failures a year for 1985 and 1986, two of the most financially stressful years of the 1980s. The Farmers Home Administration, which lends to the financially least-stable farm borrowers, reported fewer than 3,000 bankruptcies a year among its borrowers since 1983. When prominent politicians intentionally attempt to mislead people about vital farm data, then it is no wonder that the American public's ideas on farm policy are often so muddled.

Hostility to farm bankruptcies stems partly from the notion that any clodhopper can be a good farmer, so it is a shame to throw one fool off the land and put another in his place. Federal agricultural policy implicitly presumes that the farmers currently on the land are the best of all possible farmers—and that we should pay any price to keep them in possession of their farms. This is why Congress forces the Farmers Home Administration to give new loans to farmers who cannot or will not repay previous Farmers Home loans.

The apocalyptic view of bankruptcies has deterred—or more accurately, provided an excuse—for Congress to treat farms unlike other businesses. Yet farm bankruptcies are simply turnovers. One farmer transfers the land to another farmer who, more likely than not, will use the land more productively. A recent survey of sales of foreclosed farmland in Minnesota found that 90 percent of the land was bought by neighboring farmers. Federal agricultural policy has massively impeded the transfer of good cropland from less-capable to more-capable farmers. With every inept or incompetent farmer kept in business, there is less good farmland available for a new farmer, or for a productive, competent farmer to expand. Land is a scarce resource.

The government cannot allocate land to inefficient farmers without lowering the productivity of the entire agricultural sector.

The normal failure rate for new small businesses is around 50 percent. In the 1970s, when the farm bankruptcy rate was only 0.1 percent, the commercial bankruptcy rate was twenty times higher.[42] Yet who would contend that only one farmer out of a thousand was incompetent and should have been forced out of the business? There were too few bankruptcies in agriculture to permit the industry to function at maximum efficiency. Repeatedly, the federal government provides billions of dollars of cheap credit to keep floundering farmers on the land for a few more seasons. The result: an increasing accumulation of relatively incompetent farmers.

The comparatively high farm bankruptcy rate of the 1980s has been taken as proof of pervasive depression in agriculture and the need to give more federal aid to all farmers. Yet over half the farmers in the country have had no mortgages; the increased federal aid was pure gravy. If 5 percent of the farms went bankrupt, it would say little about the profitability of the majority of farms. Few people would judge IBM's health by the bankruptcy rate in Silicon Valley, and it would be naive to assume that a 2 percent bankruptcy rate in farming meant that all farmers were in trouble.

Politicians' attitude towards farm bankruptcy ignores the fact that farming has become a high-tech industry requiring rapid adjustment. The more high-tech farming has become—the faster the farm economy and farm productivity factors are shifting—the greater the differences in people's ability to succeed at farming. But federal farm bankruptcy policy is based on the idea that if a farmer keeps doing what he always did, he should be allowed to stay on the land.

It is sad when a person is forced to leave the occupation of his choice. But millions of nonfarmers face the same life crisis each year without receiving tens of thousands of dollars of federal aid. Tens of millions of ex-farmers have successfully started new careers in recent decades—and there is no reason to expect that those farmers who leave farming in the coming years will be any less talented or successful than those who left the land before them.

Chapter 4

A USDA Honor Roll

Government programs are usually judged by their intentions, not their effects. Farm policy discussions usually begin and end with vague generalities and lofty rhetoric—with heavy emphasis on how government programs should ideally operate rather than a close examination of how government programs actually work. Farm policy is the sum of individual farm programs. Only by looking at the individual parts can we understand the whole of agricultural policy.

While many people speak of farm programs as if they were a homogeneous whole, there are as many differences among farm programs as there are among other government programs. Different programs have different rationales and goals, and have varying effects on farmers, consumers, and taxpayers. Some programs rely on voluntary measures and are direct handouts, while other programs impose strict controls over farmers. Some programs provide minimal benefits, while others provide selected farm groups with the key to the Treasury. Some programs are intended to double or triple food prices; others generously compensate farmers without affecting market prices. The differences among farm programs are not based on different traits of the subsidized commodities, but are largely the result of political accidents or of political clout.

Following are examples of individual farm programs—how they came to be and how they actually operate.

Sugar: Greed Has No Limits

Some people win the lottery; others grow sugar. The U.S. government
has been heavily protecting or directly subsidizing the sugar industry
since 1816. For nearly the entire history of the United States, American
sugar prices have been held at two, three, or more times the world
sugar price. Even in the 1930s, it was recognized that American sugar
growers were much less efficient and productive than their foreign
competition was; the U.S. climate is less than ideal for sugar production. President Roosevelt launched the existing sugar program in 1934
partly to "provide against further expansion of this necessarily expensive industry."[1] Because the sugar lobby makes generous campaign
contributions, politicians have resolved that consumers should pay
any cost and bear any burden for domestic sugar production.

Since 1980 the sugar program has cost consumers and taxpayers
roughly *$2 million for each American sugar grower*. According to the
Public Voice for Food and Health Policy, a Washington consumer lobby, "in the sugar beet industry, eleven processors receive 40 percent of
federal subsidy benefits while the balance is divided among about
10,000 farmers. . . . In the sugarcane industry, five corporations produce 98 percent of the Hawaiian crop (with less than 250 farmers
producing the other two percent) and two corporations produce over
half of the Florida crop (with about 125 producing the rest)."[2]

Congressmen justify the sugar program as protecting Americans
from the "roller-coaster of international sugar prices," as Congressman Byron Dorgan declared.[3] Unfortunately, Congress protects consumers against the "roller-coaster" by pegging American sugar prices
on the level of the Goodyear blimp, floating far above the amusement
park. The sugar program, like other farm programs, provides a price
floor but no price *ceiling*. Thus, the USDA prevents prices from falling
but allows prices to rise as high as the moon: Price supports are always a "heads, farmers win; tails, taxpayers lose" proposition. Since
government guarantees to buy unlimited quantities of the crop at a set
price, farmers will not sell sugar on the market at a price lower than
they can sell to the government. The government's support price
thereby becomes the minimum price for any sugar sold in the United
States. If world prices soared above U.S. prices, American sugar growers would export their harvest for the higher prices abroad, or U.S.

prices would also rise. U.S. sugar prices have been as high or higher than world prices for thirty-seven of the last forty years.

The sugar program is a great inflationary success: At a time when the world sugar price was only 4.5 cents a pound, sugar sold in the United States for 21 cents a pound (world sugar prices are now about 8 cents a pound). Each 1-cent increase in the price of sugar adds between $250 million and $300 million to consumers' food bills, according to Alfred Kahn, the Carter administration's chief economic adviser. A May 1988 Commerce Department study estimated that the sugar program is costing consumers up to $3 billion a year. This works out to more than $45 a year for the average family of four.[4]

The sugar program makes sugar producers an aristocracy among farmers. The average Minnesota sugar beet grower got almost four times the return from growing sugar in 1982 that he would have received from growing corn in; a Louisiana farmer received almost seven times as much per acre for growing sugarcane as he would have received for growing soybeans.[5]

High prices have resulted in sharply reduced sugar consumption. The average American consumes one-third less sugar now than he did in 1971. Lower-priced corn syrup and low-calorie sugar substitutes are rapidly driving sugar out of the market. The manufacturers of Coca-Cola and Pepsi-Cola no longer use sugar in their soft-drink formulas. Sugar's share of the sweetener market has fallen from 72 percent in 1972 to 43 percent in 1987, and the consumption of corn sweetener now surpasses that of sugar. The government can drive up the price, but it can't force people to use sugar.

Congress' generosity to sugar producers is victimizing other farmers and other American industries. In the Dominican Republic, former sugar growers are now producing wheat and corn, thereby providing more competition for American farmers. American candy producers are losing out to foreign competition, partly because foreign companies can buy their sugar at much lower prices. Since 1982, dextrose and confectionery-coating imports have risen tenfold and chocolate imports are up fivefold.

Sugar protectionism is also disrupting American commerce. In the early 1980s, when U.S. sugar prices were seven times higher than world prices, "entrepreneurs were importing high-sugar content products, such as iced-tea mix, and then sifting their sugar content from them and selling the sugar at the high domestic price."[6] In order to protect the domestic sugar program, the Reagan administration in 1985 banned all imported foods containing sugar. Hundreds of private contracts were nullified. An Israeli company that had sent 20,000 kosher pizzas (with a sugar content of 0.5 percent) to New York had its property seized and put in storage by U.S. Customs. A Minnesota company's Korean noodles were impounded because they contained a soup base that was 0.2 percent sugar. Because government insisted on being so generous to American sugar producers, other businessmen saw their enterprises paralyzed and consumers were denied imported goods. Federal restrictions made sugar smuggling immensely profitable; the Justice Department caught twenty different companies in Operation Bittersweet, a crackdown on sugar bootleggers.[7] The Justice Department was far more worried about businessmen bringing in cheap foreign sugar than it was about the sugar lobby bribing congressmen to extort billions of dollars from consumers.

The more costly a farm program becomes, the more politically viable it can be. If the sugar program only inflated prices half as much, it might have been abolished five years ago. Production of high-fructose corn syrup, which would be uneconomical if the government did not inflate sugar prices, has increased from 2 million to over 5 million tons since 1980. To keep sugar prices high, the corn-sweetener producers make campaign contributions to politicians who support the sugar programs. Nebraska congressmen are now among the most fervent defenders of high sugar prices. The sugar program has greatly enriched corn-sweetener producers such as Archer Daniels Midland, which now runs television advertisements to persuade everyone how terrible the farm crisis really is.

The sugar program has destroyed far more jobs than it has saved. America had an efficient sugar-refining industry with an excellent location near the Caribbean. Thanks to the forced reductions of imported sugar, since 1981 ten sugar refineries have closed down and thousands of nonfarm jobs have been lost. Eleven thousand sugar workers have lost their jobs in Louisiana since 1978. Keith Schneider, writing in the *New York Times,* observed that, "The growing use of more powerful and advanced machines has been encouraged by a Government price support program that has brought about a decade of prosperity."[8] Congress made producing sugar so profitable that the plantation owners could afford to lay off the sugar workers.

A few thousand sugar growers have become the tail that wags the dog of American foreign policy. Early in 1982, President Reagan announced the Caribbean Basin Initiative to provide U.S. aid to Latin America. A few weeks later, the President and the USDA slashed the amount of sugar Latin America could sell to the United States in order to protect the high price received by American growers. Sugar was Latin America's third-largest export in the early 1980s; today sugar revenues have almost evaporated. The State Department estimated that the reductions in sugar-import quotas cost our Third World allies $800 million a year. By reducing Latin America's dollar revenue from sugar sales, the sugar program has hurt American banks awaiting repayment of loans to Third World governments. The sugar program has indirectly become a full-employment program for the Drug Enforcement Administration, since many poor Third World farmers who previously grew sugarcane are now harvesting marijuana.[9] The communist insurgency in the Philippines is the strongest in the sugar-growing areas, thanks partly to unemployed sugar workers.

There are so many farm programs today because each farm policy failure seems to beget a new farm program. The Reagan administration responded to sugar import cutbacks by creating a new foreign-aid program, the Quota Offset Program, to give free food to countries hurt by reductions. In 1986 the United States dumped almost $200 million of free food on Caribbean countries and the Philippines. Clifford Krauss reported in the *Wall Street Journal*, "By flooding local markets and driving commodity prices down, the United States is making it more difficult for local farmers to replace sugar with other crops."[10] Richard Holwill, deputy assistant secretary of state, observed, "It makes us look like damn fools when we go down there and preach free enterprise."[11]

So Congress, in December 1987, came up with a Solomon-like solution. Sugar refineries would be allowed to import 800,000 tons of sugar from Third World countries, the refineries would refine the sugar and then export it, and Uncle Sam would compensate refineries for the difference between the high American sugar prices and the low world prices with certificates that entitled sugar refineries to millions of bushels of government-owned surplus wheat and corn. Thus the government would make our allies and sugar refineries happy, buy off the sugar program's most powerful critics, help get rid of some embarrassing grain surpluses, create jobs for maybe another dozen bureaucrats, and give new meaning to the word *inefficiency*. (The USDA refused to implement the program.)

Though many congressional agricultural bills are labeled agricultural adjustment acts, the sugar program, like most commodity programs, has done nothing to encourage farmers to adjust. Instead, the government continues to pay farmers extremely generous prices without regard to their efficiency or competitiveness. Though only a major climatic change would make American growers able to compete on world markets, high federal support prices have led to a boom in domestic sugar production, which has risen by 23 percent since 1982.[12] This is the perfect example of government generosity encouraging inefficiency in the private sector. The higher the sugar price guarantees, the more farmers begin producing sugar, and the louder the demand for government to continue driving up prices. There is no reason to expect that American sugar growers will ever be competitive with foreign sugar growers, or that the sugar lobby will ever stop demanding more subsidies.

The sugar program has always cost consumers far more than it benefited farmers. Sugar tariffs were raised sharply in 1930, and a 1933 study estimated that the tariffs cost consumers five times as much as they benefited growers—$268 million a year versus an estimated $53 million.[13] The USDA estimates that sugar beet and cane growers had roughly $300 million in net farm income in 1986, from a total sales volume of $1.7 billion. With the Commerce Department's estimate that the program cost consumers $3 billion, this means that the government was imposing almost $10 in costs on consumers in order to provide $1 in benefits for farmers.

The Shearing of the Taxpayers

The wool program is agricultural policy at its worst—ineffective, expensive, and incorrigible. Since Congress began subsidizing sheep farmers in 1938, wool production has fallen 75 percent, wool quality has slumped, and foreign producers have surpassed American producers in every measure. Last year Uncle Sam gave farmers $145 million to encourage wool production; wool farmers had their smallest harvest since 1909.

Four-fifths of the wool Americans purchase now comes from overseas. Imported wool is of higher quality than American wool and comprises most of the wool used by American textile plants. At least one American textile plant refuses to buy domestically produced wool because it is so cluttered with briars, hay, twine, and other rubbish. A 1969 USDA report concluded that American wool was inferior to foreign wool because of "insufficient incentives to improve the quality of the clip under existing marketing practices and costs."[14] By paying producers solely according to the quantity of their output, the USDA encourages farmers to produce low-quality wool. Taxpayers receive nothing from the wool program except the satisfaction of knowing that they have encouraged domestic production of inferior wool.

The wool program has a target price—the price Congress feels that sheepmen should rightfully receive for their clip. In 1987, the target price was $1.81 a pound—almost triple the market price of 67 cents a pound. The USDA paid sheepmen the difference, and labeled the handout an "incentive payment."

Last year the amount of federal wool "incentive payments" was far greater than the value of the wool produced, yet wool production continued to slide. Wool is a by-product of sheep production, and wool provides only 20 to 30 percent of sales revenue; sheep are raised primarily for their meat. A big increase in wool prices means only a slight increase in revenues from sheep. Bruce Gardner, an economist at the University of Maryland, estimated in a 1982 study that the wool program has increased sheep production by between 6 and 13 percent; the federal government therefore paid up to thirty times the market value for each additional pound of wool generated by the wool program.[15]

Wool has been a continuing source of humility for USDA officials. The 1949 farm act set a national wool output goal of 360 million pounds a year. Production in 1950 straggled in at 217 million pounds. The National Wool Act of 1954 increased government handouts and proclaimed a goal of 300 million pounds. Production is now barely 80 million pounds a year. The USDA has spent almost $2 billion priming the wool industry—and still the great sheep depopulation continues.

As one USDA official grieved, "Pretty soon we'll have to start worrying about stocking the zoos."

The 1954 National Wool Act declared that wool is an "essential and strategic commodity," vital to national defense. The primary reason: Wool is used to make military dress uniforms. In 1974 the Pentagon decided that dress uniforms weren't necessary for national emergencies and wool was taken off the list of strategic commodities. But in 1977 Congress justified extending the Wool Act because it contributes to "a positive balance of trade."[16] In other words, no matter how high the cost or how low the quality, it is better to produce a commodity in America than to buy it from foreigners. The National Wool Growers Association praises the wool program for enabling "farmers and ranchers to utilize marginal lands that were otherwise unsuitable for agriculture."[17] If Congress were willing to spend another $30 billion, the United States could grow cotton on the mountaintops of the Sierra Nevadas.

Many handouts to wool producers have no effect except to make the recipient smile. The USDA gives out many wool subsidy checks for $3 or less. The USDA tried to abolish these "chicken-feed" payments in 1977, but parents of youngsters conducting 4-H projects protested vehemently. The parents apparently wanted to instill the agricultural welfare ethic at as early an age as possible.

Many American sheepmen are losing money because they are just plain inefficient. A report by the New Mexico State University Extension Service concluded that "small flocks, from 10 to 50 ewes, are often not profitable because they tend to be poorly managed." Robot shearers are widely used in Australia, but not in the United States. The average Australian sheep produces over one-third more wool than an American sheep.

The wool program has a special provision to pay sheepmen if they sell their sheep unshorn. This provision supposedly exists "to avoid unusual shearing of lambs before marketing to obtain the payments on shorn wool." In reality, the program exists to insure that farmers get paid no matter what they do. Three different producers can get federal payments for the same sheep, with the amount of the benefit dependent on how many pounds the sheep supposedly gained while each producer owned him. The USDA admits that payments for unshorn wool are almost impossible to administer, but insists that if unshorn payments cease, then people who make a living tearing the hair off sheepskins will be out of work.[18] This is just the kind of job America should preserve into the twenty-first century.

The National Wool Growers Association (NWGA) claims that wool producers are entitled to subsidies because the industry was irretrievably damaged back in World War II: "In 1942, the [federal] Office of Price Administration froze the price of wool at 41 cents per pound because of the wartime, urgent need for wool." The NWGA claims that "sheepmen could not even come close to staying in business at this price." But the 41 cents a pound was more than double the federal support price of 18 cents of 1939.[19] Regardless of how flimsy such arguments appear to most people, they persuaded Congress to ante up a half billion dollars to sheepmen in the 1985 five-year farm bill. The NWGA also rants against its foreign competition: "If the [domestic] sheep industry is to continue, we must continue to make those who export wool to the U.S. pay for the disruptions they create."[20] The NWGA apparently believes that any country that sells American consumers a better product at a lower price is by definition guilty and must make reparations.

The NWGA and the House Agriculture Committee claim that wool payments are completely financed by a tariff on imported wool. The sheepmen's lobby even claims that taxpayers are better off because of the wool program; without it, the NWGA warns, the State Department would probably abolish the tariff on imported wool and lose revenue. Citizens might then be victimized by lower clothing prices. Since tariff revenues are not earmarked for domestic sheepraisers, it is easy to see that this propaganda is merely a sedative to put budget-watchers to sleep. The charade does seem to make farmers feel better about accepting government money. Clark Bredahl, Iowa sheepman, told the House Agriculture Committee, "Coming from an area of the country where self-reliance is a way of life, it is important for me to note that basically the wool act is a self-help program."[21] Apparently, any program that helps farmers get their hands into the Treasury is a "self-help" program. In 1985 a NWGA spokesman justified wool subsidies to the House Agricultural Committee with allusions to the Biblical importance of sheep.[22]

The value of handouts to sheepmen has exceeded the total value of wool produced in the United States every year since 1983. Wool subsidy payments vastly exceed the total profits of sheepmen. In 1985, sheep producers lost $73 million from their operations in a year when federal subsidies amounted to $97 million. Without subsidies, many sheepmen may have abandoned the business—and avoided losing tens of millions of dollars. In 1986, sheep producers had a net profit of $13 million while federal wool subsidies amounted to $99 million. Thus, the federal government spent over $7 for each dollar of income realized by sheep producers.

What would happen if the wool program were abolished tomorrow? Under the "Chicken Little" scenario offered by farm lobbyists, no more wool would be produced. Since the United States produces less than 2 percent of the world's wool, the loss would not topple the pillars of commerce. Instead of getting almost all of their wool from overseas, American consumers would get every bit of it from abroad. Instead of raising sheep at a loss, many ranchers would raise cattle at a profit. The Pentagon could easily stockpile all the wool it needs for less than current program costs. And even if the program continues, the Defense Department will still have to buy the wool at some point, because nearly $2 billion in wool payments has not entitled the government to a single handful of fleece.

The USDA also has a special program for mohair, the fleece of Angora goats used in expensive sweaters. In 1986 federal handouts to Angora goat keepers exceeded the value of all the goat fleece they could snip—$42.3 million in handouts versus $38.1 million in mohair sold. Traditionally the mohair program was not a burden on taxpayers; but between 1976 and 1986, Congress raised the mohair target price over 600 percent and costs exploded.

Goober Madness

The USDA has a distinguished half-century record of disrupting the peanut industry. The USDA has made peanut production far more expensive, undercut exports, driven up peanut prices, and repressed peanut consumption. Since 1941, Congress has managed the peanut industry almost solely for the benefit of existing peanut growers, or the sons and grandsons of farmers who grew peanuts in 1941. The federal peanut program is a model of the futility of feudalism in a modern economy.

In 1933 Congress began supporting peanut prices by buying farmers' peanuts at very generous prices. Farmers responded to the high prices by boosting production. Congress responded to large peanut surpluses in 1941 by slapping mandatory controls on peanut farmers and prohibiting any citizen from growing peanuts without a federal license, which specified to the hundredth of an acre how much land might be cultivated. The right to grow peanuts in the future was based on the number of acres of peanuts a farmer had grown in the past. In order to maximize government control, almost all peanut imports were prohibited.

Congress set peanut price supports very high over the years, thereby encouraging farmers to maximize production on their limited acreage. Relatively high peanut prices mandated by the government repressed peanut consumption, and the result was perpetual surpluses. In 1973 Secretary of Agriculture Earl Butz publicly declared that the peanut surplus was driving him crazy. In 1977, Congress, in an attempt to drive up domestic peanut prices, changed the peanut license system from a base of acres to a base of pounds, thereby allowing the USDA a much tighter control over peanut production. The federal government has reduced the domestic peanut supply since 1975, causing an artificial peanut shortage and shifting the cost of the peanut program from the government to the consumer.

Congress is resolved to keep the peanut licenses, or "quota allotments," in the same congressional districts at any cost. Quota allotments cannot be rented outside of the county in which they were originally allocated in 1941. Peanuts are a "soil-depleting crop," causing a decline in soil nutrients. Peanut yields in parts of Texas have long been declining. While many acres with yields below a thousand pounds have quotas, over a million acres with potential yields of 2,500, 3,000, or 5,000 pounds or more may not be used to produce peanuts for the domestic market. Even though the productivity of much federally licensed peanut land is slowly declining, Congress refuses to open up the system.

The peanut program is driven by the USDA's estimate of the costs of production. In 1980, peanuts were hit by drought, which sharply reduced yields and made the production costs per pound appear much higher. By basing its 1981 cost-of-production calculation on the 1980 drought year, Congress justified a 21 percent hike in price supports, from $440 to $555 a ton. Naturally, once price supports were raised because of the drought year, they could never be lowered afterwards, regardless of good rains or perfect weather.

The government-decreed cost of production is also deluding, because the peanut program itself adds as much as 60 percent to a farmer's cost of production. Approximately half of all peanut-growing licenses are rented by farmers from nonfarmers, with farmers paying a tribute of up to $240 a ton for the right to grow goobers. The cost of renting allotments is added into USDA's cost-of-production estimates, which then are used to justify increasing the peanut price supports, which then makes the licenses more valuable and thus more expensive, which drives up the peanut cost of production, ad infinitum.

In 1981 Congress decided that farmers without quota licenses would be allowed to grow peanuts (called "additional" or unsubsidized peanuts)—but with no real price guarantees from Uncle Sam, and only if the peanuts were not consumed within the United States. This muted some of the criticism of the program, but it has also revealed the absurdity of the status quo. Georgia farmers are profitably growing peanuts for export at $325 a ton at the same time that the USDA insists that farmers cannot afford to produce peanuts for less than $615.85 a ton. Foreigners can buy U.S. peanuts for half the price that Americans can. While total American farm exports plummeted in the 1980s, peanut exports more than doubled.

The USDA is so paranoid about controlling the domestic peanut supply that it actively hampers the export of unsubsidized peanuts. All "additional" peanuts must be sold before they are harvested. This stricture puts unsubsidized peanut farmers at a disadvantage in bargaining for the best export price, and is typical of how Congress and the USDA treat self-reliant farmers worse than government-dependent farmers. Wheat and corn farmers are given interest-free loans to ensure that they will not be pressured into selling before they think the market is right. There are other restrictions on the export of unsubsidized peanuts. Peanut butter made from quota peanuts may be exported to Canada and Mexico, but peanut butter made from additional peanuts may not. The additional peanuts themselves may be exported to Canada, and American peanut-butter manufacturers worry that Canadian companies might be using cheap peanuts to make peanut butter that is then sent back across the border to reap a windfall profit. The lower foreign peanut prices have also helped European candy manufacturers increase their imports to the United States. Senator Richard Lugar led a push to abolish restrictions on unsubsidized peanut exports in late 1987, criticizing the USDA for allowing only the export of raw materials and prohibiting the export of manufactured food products. USDA Undersecretary Pete Myers replied to Lugar, "We believe the elimination of this provision could result in substantial interference with the peanut price support program. We recognize this provision may seem to be inconsistent with the Department of Agriculture's overall export objective to increase the exportation of U.S. farm products."[23]

Congress gives peanut growers a far better deal than it gives other farmers. An American Peanut Product Manufacturers Institute (APPMI) study estimates that peanut price supports "have been set 80 percent above USDA-defined production costs when land costs are excluded, and 60 percent above when the inflated costs of land are included."[24] The APPMI estimates that net returns to peanut farmers are four to ten times higher than are returns from competing crops. Twelve peanut growers each received benefits exceeding a quarter-million dollars from the program. The bankruptcy rate among peanut farmers is far lower than the bankruptcy rate among all farmers.

Consumers get shelled by the peanut program. The USDA estimates that the peanut program boosts peanut-butter prices 13.5 percent. Thus, the peanut program mulcts consumers for $250 million to $300 million a year. The federal government would never drive up the price of caviar or pate, but the ruling elite sheds no tears over higher peanut prices.

In 1930, U.S. farmers planted 1.1 million acres each of peanuts and soybeans. In 1933, Congress decided to protect peanuts and leave soybeans to the ravages of the marketplace. By 1980, U.S. farmers were growing 1.4 million acres of peanuts and 68 million acres of soybeans. The peanut crop was worth about $500 million, while the soybean crop was worth more than $13 billion.[25] Though peanuts and soybeans have many common uses, soybeans have left the USDA-annointed crop in the dust.

Tobacco

At the same time that the U.S. government is spending millions of dollars a year on the tobacco program, it also spends millions each year convincing people not to smoke. While the Surgeon General runs a campaign portraying smoking as the root of all evil, Southern congressmen lead a campaign portraying the tobacco program as the only thing preventing an economic collapse of Kentucky, North Carolina, and Virginia. The tobacco program provides an extremely generous price to tobacco producers, but to grow tobacco one must own a federal allotment or license. Most of the benefits of the tobacco program have been capitalized into the value of these allotments. As a recent editorial in *The Flue-Cured Tobacco Farmer* declared:

> The benefits of the support program appear to be migrating largely into the bank accounts of the non-producing quota (allotment) owners, with you, the active producers, profiting at approximately the level you could be expected to without any program at all.

Most allotments are owned by people who are not tobacco farmers. For the privilege of growing tobacco, farmers must pay a tribute to others.

Tobacco congressmen love to point out that the tobacco program was approved by a margin of 90 percent in the last USDA-sponsored referendum. But allotment owners and farmers are both allowed to vote, and there are far more allotment owners than growers. Thus, the allotment owners had far more votes than farmers in deciding the question of whether farmers would continue to be forced to pay a tribute to allotment owners. This is like allowing slave owners and slaves to vote on whether to abolish slavery—and giving most of the votes to the slave owners.

The USDA is trying to be the OPEC of tobacco. But the United States has lost its dominance of world tobacco markets, thanks to Southern congressmen's blind devotion to enriching existing tobacco growers regardless of their efficiency or productivity. A 1984 USDA report noted that "the U.S. price support program has helped push U.S. tobacco prices to nearly double those of the major competing countries of India, Canada, Thailand, Malawi, Brazil, Zimbabwe, and Korea."[26] The American Enterprise Institute concluded in 1984 that the abolition of price supports and supply controls could easily double American tobacco exports.[27] A North Carolina State University study found that abolishing the tobacco program would reduce tobacco prices, "but by less than the total burden of assessments and allotment rents that would, with the abolition of the program, be lifted from the back of the tobacco farmer."[28]

The U.S. share in world tobacco trade has fallen sharply since the 1930s, to 18 percent by 1982. While world production has soared in recent decades, the USDA has forcibly slashed American production by over 50 percent since 1975 in an effort to boost prices. The USDA has frozen tobacco production in the same counties that were producing it in 1938. The result: heavy costs for taxpayers, huge losses in exports for tobacco farmers, and pervasive inefficiency in tobacco production. Thanks largely to the USDA, tobacco farmers have not adopted the large-scale farm machinery and high technology that have sharply lowered costs of production for other crops. The cost of renting allotments sharply reduces the competitiveness of American tobacco—and helps explain why tobacco imports have tripled since 1975.

In 1982, to quell public criticism about the tobacco program, Congress enacted a "no net cost" tobacco program, designed to boost tobacco prices and camouflage the program's cost. Because a majority of congressmen decreed that the tobacco program should not have any more direct costs, then, abracadabra!—it had no more direct costs. But as the General Accounting Office noted, the programs have still piled up huge government-owned surpluses that taxpayers will eventually have to buy, and the program's interest-free loans to farmers are not interest-free for taxpayers.[29]

The obvious solution to problems caused by government controls is tighter controls. When the USDA announced that, because of a falling market demand, it was cutting the 1987 allotment for certain types of tobacco, some tobacco farmers argued that the USDA "tobacco police" should instead measure the acreage of every tobacco farmer to ensure that no one was planting more than the quota to "prevent overproduction and protect the future of the dark tobacco industry."[30] Will Clark, manager of the Western Dark-Fired Tobacco Growers Association, warned that unless government provided more benefits, tobacco farmers' wives might have to get jobs. This would bring tears to the eyes of the 65 percent of American families in which wives are already working outside the home.

But the tobacco program has done some good: For a while, it provided Americans an opportunity to show their compassion for the Third World. The tobacco program has engendered huge government-owned surpluses over the years. Politicians found an easy solution: Distribute free tobacco to the Third World through the "Food for Peace" program, derided by critics as a "Smoke for Peace" program. If Africans were going to starve, at least they could smoke cigarettes to take their minds off their misery. The USDA ceased giving free tobacco to Third World governments in 1981.

Much of the land that produces tobacco is well-suited for other crops. Virginia Tech is leading a campaign in Virginia to help tobacco growers shift to broccoli, which is very profitable and in strong demand on the urban markets on the East Coast.[31]

And while politicians claim that tobacco cannot be grown without government aid, there is a similar crop that has prospered despite government hostility. Marijuana is, according to some estimates, America's largest cash crop, with an estimated $33 billion harvest in 1987. Yet farmers grow it without any price supports, target prices, or subsidized farm loans, and according to most recognized experts, the quality of domestic marijuana has increased sharply in recent years. But to be fair, the government does provide extensive protection for domestic growers by occasionally shooting down Cessnas flying in from Columbia, thereby boosting profits and providing a vital stimulant for the development of the domestic industry. And admittedly, a farmer is more likely to get arrested for growing tobacco without a license than he is for growing marijuana.

Honey

The honey program cost taxpayers $100 million in 1988, almost equal to the market value of all U.S. honey production. Yet less than 6 percent of the nation's 200,000 beekeepers received benefits from Uncle Sam.[32] Several beekeepers have received over a million dollars a year from the government for their surplus honey.

Until 1949, honey producers got along fine without any government price supports. During World War II, the government exhorted beekeepers to increase production to compensate for a temporary sugar shortage. When the war ended, a honey glut occurred and the obvious solution was a perpetual subsidy to encourage increased production. The cost of the honey price-support program was negligible so long as the government price-support level was below world market prices, since honey producers naturally choose to sell their harvest on the market rather than dumping it on the government. But USDA price supports for honey more than quadrupled between 1972 and 1984, from 14 cents to 66 cents, and are now far above world market prices. Congress sealed back honey price supports slightly in the 1985 farm bill, but American price-support levels are still roughly 50 percent higher than world prices.

Honey is not protected by stiff import barriers. Thus, when government drives up the price of domestic honey, foreign honey comes pouring across the borders while U.S. honey piles up in government storage. High U.S. price supports signaled foreign bee-keepers to increase production and to dump their surpluses on the U.S. market. In 1985, the USDA bought up about 130 million pounds of domestically produced honey, while Mexico, Argentina, China, and a few other countries sold 138 million pounds of honey to U.S. consumers. In 1985, Congress "reformed" the honey program to allow honey producers to receive large subsidies without forfeiting their harvest to the USDA.

The honey program contains the usual King Kong loopholes and engraved invitations to fraud. Some American processors in 1984 were reportedly buying foreign honey at 40 cents a pound and reselling it to the USDA for 59 cents a pound. Since there are no obvious differences between U.S. and foreign honey, this was an easy scam. As the General Accounting Office noted, "USDA generally does not perform tests on honey used for loan collateral to ensure that the honey is not imported or adulterated with corn syrup."[33]

The USDA has invested heavily over the years to build up farmer-owned cooperatives. Michael A. Hiltzik notes in the *Los Angeles Times* that high price supports are "deeply disruptive to the basic structure of the nation's insular beekeeping industry, the honey cooperative."[34] Until Congress changed the program in late 1985, members refused to sell honey to their cooperatives, preferring to sell it to Uncle Sam instead.

The honey program is built on the price-support level the USDA establishes. The USDA sets honey prices with a rigorous exactitude that is surprising even by Washington's standards. Price supports are supposed to be based on a combination of parity ratios and costs of production. The General Accounting Office found that "decisions regarding the price-support level are based on estimates resulting from telephone inquiries with a few beekeepers and industry officials."[35] The USDA disrupted a $100-million industry with a policy based on a few casual phone inquiries with little documentation or verification.

How does Congress react to this mess? Congressmen from honey-producing states propose a stiff tariff to keep foreign honey out. Because of low tariffs, the cost of high price supports shows up in the federal budget instead of being hidden in consumers' grocery bills; the farm protectionists now want to camouflage the honey subsidy.

Several congressmen insist that the USDA continue bankrolling beekeepers because pollination is vital to the agricultural sector. South Dakota Senator Larry Pressler declared in 1984, "With food costs in the U.S. at over $100 billion annually, it is clear that bees are vital to the American public. Without the honey bee to pollinate crops, the diet of American consumers would be limited to nuts, cereal grains, and meat."[36] This is the old fallacy that nothing would get done if the government didn't do it. Many beekeepers already rent out their bees for pollinating, and more could do so. Generous federal subsidies for honey production have undercut the development of a private pollination market.

At the same time that government works overtime to protect honey, there is no federal support for molasses or maple syrup. There has never been a persistent shortage of either product, prices fluctuate up and down, and consumers buy more or less accordingly. But congressmen do suffer from the lack of contributions from molasses and maple syrup producers.

The Cotton Mess

Thanks to influential Southern congressmen, cotton farmers have usually been treated far more generously by Uncle Sam than other farmers.[37] Unfortunately, Congress' passion for lavishing benefits on cotton growers has resulted in contradictory programs that skewered taxpayers while decimating cotton exports.

In 1985, U.S. cotton exports fell to their lowest level since the Reconstruction period after the Civil War, largely because federal farm programs imposed a de facto export tax on American cotton. The federal price-support program offered farmers a "loan" of 57.5 cents a pound for their cotton, while world market prices were significantly lower. Since the federal loan levels were higher than market prices, farmers chose to forfeit their cotton to the government and keep the loan money rather than sell their harvest at market prices.

When Congress was writing the 1985 five-year farm bill, there was a consensus that the cotton program must become more market-oriented. Congress lowered the price support slightly (though keeping it well above world price levels), and created a new cotton program, "marketing loans," primarily to boost exports. If the market price for cotton is below the federal price-support level, the "marketing loan" will give farmers the difference between the federal price and the market price. ("Marketing loans" is one of the great euphemisms of the 1980s, equivalent to calling welfare payments a cost-of-living loan.) Marketing loans sought to prevent the price-support program from encouraging farmers to store their cotton or forfeit it to the government instead of selling it.

Thanks to the marketing loans, cotton growers can totally disregard how low prices fall, since government guarantees their income. American cotton dumping sharply depressed world cotton prices in 1986, punishing relatively impoverished foreign cotton growers in Malawi, Cameroon, and the Sudan. But by driving down world cotton prices, the federal program made cotton exports less profitable than they had been in the early 1980s, when federal cotton program costs were only half as large.

Marketing loans have become a budgetary hemorrhage, and the cotton program will likely cost most than $7 billion between 1986 and 1989. Since there are only around 6,000 full-time cotton growers, this means the Agriculture Department will spend the equivalent of over $1 million per full-time cotton grower over four years' time. The Congressional Budget Office estimated in 1985 that the average full-time cotton producer was already a millionaire even before the current program began.

The generous marketing loans are being undercut by another cotton welfare program. As part of the cotton price-support program, Congress requires the Agriculture Department to offer cotton growers eighteen-month interest-free loans to hold their crop off the market, and the agency also pays for farmers' storage costs. The eighteen-month loan allows the farmer to speculate with his harvest, guaranteeing that the taxpayer will take any loss while farmers can keep any profit if market prices rise above federal price-support levels during the eighteen-month period. Neil P. Gillen, vice president of the American Cotton Shippers Association, observes, "The government has taken care of all the grower's risks in selling with the marketing loan, but all of this is contradicted by the eighteen-month loan which induces them to hold out for prices which are above the going market rates."

Even though the United States has had large cotton harvests the last two years, the cotton program is causing an artificial scarcity of cotton in domestic markets. Cotton shippers and millers must pay growers a bonus of 6 to 8 cents a pound above world market prices to persuade them to sell their cotton before the end of the eighteen-month loan period. But this 6–8 cent bonus has made American cotton uncompetitive on world markets: cotton exports are predicted to decrease 25 percent this year from 1987 levels. American textile mills that must rely on American cotton (thanks to strict import quotas on foreign cotton) must pay significantly more for their cotton than do foreign textile mills, thus handicapping them in competition against textile imports.

The cotton program is designed to export cotton at any price—as if exports had a metaphysical value in themselves. Yet the cotton program requires farmers not to plant on 25 percent of their cotton acreage—supposedly in order to help balance world cotton supply and demand. (Farmers who refuse to leave part of their fields idle are not eligible for cotton subsidies.) Set-aside programs, by leaving valuable resources idle, raise farmers' cost of production, thereby decreasing American competitiveness. The set-aside program is explicitly intended to drive crop prices up, while the marketing loans were implicitly designed to drive prices down. It would be a great breakthrough if farm policy-makers could decide once and for all whether to drive prices up or down.

The cotton program costs taxpayers far more than it benefits cotton growers. Cotton farmers' net cash income (total income before depreciation expenses) in 1986 was $1.3 billion—compared to total federal cotton program costs of $2.1 billion. Thus, each dollar of cotton growers' income effectively cost taxpayers $1.50, even including farmers' revenue from cotton sales. Cotton program costs could again easily exceed cotton growers' income in 1989—a good measure of the waste and inefficiency the government program engenders.

The cotton industry is roughly divided into those farms that need no government help and those farms that will remain inefficient regardless of government help. Large corporate cotton farms, such as J. G. Boswell, Inc., in California, produce some of the world's highest-quality cotton with extremely low production costs. (Boswell is not currently enrolled in the cotton program, and has lobbied Washington to curtail federal intervention in the cotton industry.) On the other hand, the USDA estimates that small cotton growers' cost of production is almost 50 percent higher than large cotton growers' cost, and thus small growers have little chance in a free market.

Rice

In 1980 the United States was the world's leading rice exporter. But the 1981 farm bill set rice loan supports for 1982 through 1985 far above world market prices—and Congress refused to lower the price-support levels even after it was obvious that it had grossly overestimated inflation. The price supports paid American growers to put their crops in government storage instead of selling them abroad. The result: U.S. rice exports nose-dived, rice imports quintupled, and the rice industry quickly became addicted to government welfare.

There are fewer than 4,000 full-time rice growers in the United States, and their average net worth was almost $2 million each in 1982, the last year for which detailed information exists.[38] The federal government has spent the equivalent of more than $1 million per full-time rice grower since 1985, at a time when the value of American rice exports plummeted. Yet the American Farm Bureau and many congressmen have praised the rice program as a model for "market-oriented agriculture." The rice program is market-oriented because the government drives down the market price and then pays rice producers the difference between the market price and the target price—the price that government wants rice growers to have. In 1986 the USDA target price was triple the world rice price. The United States paid four times the world market price for each additional hundredweight of rice exports.

The rice program is a case of government planning for planning's sake. As a USDA report notes, "Approximately 90 percent of the world's rice is produced in Asia. Thus, 40 percent of the world rice harvest depends on the critical timing of the Asian monsoon."[39] World rice production fluctuates sharply from year to year. Yet Congress and the USDA still insist on dictating what portion of an American rice grower's field he may plant in order to qualify for federal subsidies. Though the United States normally only contributes 2 percent of the world rice crop, the USDA and Congress insist on manipulating this tiny share of world production—sometimes cutting it back to 1.8 percent, or 1.4 percent, or, if the USDA is feeling especially adventurous, allowing American farmers to produce a full 2 percent of the world's rice harvest. No matter how small a percentage of a crop America produces, the USDA is confident that, with the right throttling and jiggling, it can make farmers richer by reducing their harvest.

In 1985 the rice program cost taxpayers $1 billion and rice growers had a total profit of $43 million. In 1986, the USDA spent $947 million on the rice program. Total profits—both from rice sales and government handouts—of rice producers in 1986 amounted to $236 million. The USDA spent more than $4 for each dollar of income realized by rice growers.[40]

◆ *Chapter 5* ◆

Paying Farmers Not to Work

In 1934 Agriculture Secretary Henry Wallace declared, "The present program for readjusting productive acreage to market requirements is admittedly but a temporary method of dealing with an emergency. It could not be relied upon as a permanent means of keeping farm production in line with market requirements."[1]

In thirty-three of the last thirty-five years, the U.S. Department of Agriculture (USDA) has tried to balance supply and demand by rewarding farmers for not growing crops on their land. Paying farmers not to work has always been the nuclear weapon in the USDA's policy arsenal. When worse comes to worst—when surpluses pile up, or prices fall, or exports vanish—the USDA comes to the rescue by spending billions to bribe farmers to take a vacation. Set-asides are based on the idea that politicians can solve farmers' problems by reducing farm harvests.

Set-asides have devastated the American farm industry, sharply increased farmers' operating expenses, reduced farm-related employment by up to 300,000 jobs a year in recent years, bankrupted fertilizer and farm suppliers, and crippled unsubsidized farmers with unfair competition and plummeting prices. Set-asides are based on the idea that the United States is the Saudi Arabia of wheat and feed grains, and that we can cut back our production, drive up prices, and increase our profits. If nobody else in the world had any farmland, this policy might make sense. But in recent years, while Uncle Sam has bled taxpayers to bribe farmers not to work, foreigners have planted fencerow-to-fencerow and are rapidly taking over world markets. Gary Myers, president of the Fertilizer Institute, noted that there has been a massive "deportation" of American farmland.[2] Foreign farmland in production has increased by over 70 million acres since 1980—largely in response to high U.S. price supports and set-asides.

The Early Days

The first great crop-destruction program occurred in 1933, when the government "rescued" cotton and pork producers by paying farmers to plow up 10 million acres of cotton and massacre 6 million baby pigs. The USDA got a black eye from this operation and learned an important lesson: It is better to pay farmers not to grow at all, rather than to destroy what they have grown, because that makes the waste much less obvious.

The idea of paying farmers not to work stemmed from the Roosevelt administration's decision to abandon the export market and restrict farmers to providing only enough food for domestic demand. Paid set-asides were the core of the "domestic allotment" program, whereby farmers were allowed to plant only a percentage of their property according to what the USDA planners estimated national demand to be. Set-asides cannot be understood except as part of the decision to abandon world markets and concentrate on boosting prices for American farmers.

The assistant secretary of the USDA, M. L. Wilson, announced in 1936, "Farm profit is no longer possible with uncontrolled production."[3] The USDA trumpeted the first set-aside program as the breakthrough of "the planned harvest." USDA officials were confident that by controlling the amount of land planted, they could control crop supply. Chester Davis of the Agricultural Adjustment Administration declared: "The long-term relationship between acreage and volume is very close."[4] Yet from the very first year, farmers evaded supply-control efforts by blanketing the remaining planted acres with extra inputs to boost yields. In 1933, railroad shipments of fertilizer to cotton growers increased fourfold even while the USDA was paying farmers to plow up much of their cotton fields; cotton yields soared.[5] "Paid diversions" were continued throughout the 1930s, even though they were only supposed to be a one-time emergency program.

Acreage-reduction programs have always been run in slipshod fashion. Senator John Williams of Delaware observed in 1961 that the USDA was paying farmers an average of more than $20 an acre to retire 53 million acres of farmland from production—at the same time that the government leased 4.8 million acres of its own cropland back to farmers at an average rent of less than $3 an acre.[6] At the same time the USDA felt obliged to pay farmers not to work, USDA fire-sale rental rates encouraged other farmers to boost production.[7]

In 1972 the USDA paid farmers to set aside more acres than ever before. The Soviets had suffered an especially poor harvest; they entered the U.S. market and bought a quarter of the U.S. wheat crop. The USDA's set-aside program helped quadruple wheat prices and create a worldwide inflationary atmosphere. The General Accounting Office (GAO) concluded in 1974 that the USDA's faulty estimates of grain demand had resulted in excessive set-asides that wasted over a billion tax dollars and reduced U.S. exports.

In 1973, in response to the high grain prices, the USDA ended all paid set-asides for feed grains and expected that the 62 million acres that government had paid farmers to idle would come back into production. Only 38 million additional acres were planted. The USDA was embarrassed to discover that it had paid set-aside allowances for 24 million acres that farmers had had no intention of planting anyway. A 1977 GAO report concluded that in the early 1970s the USDA had paid farmers $800 million to idle these phantom acres. The *Washington Post* reported the USDA's usual defense against accusations of waste: "The set-aside programs were also intended to help farmers' income, and . . . if they hadn't been paid for fallowed land, they would have received money—'a major portion of the $800 million'—in other farm benefit programs."[8]

Set-asides have often been simply an excuse to give money to farmers. As Bruce Gardner writes:

> One county [Agricultural Stabilization and Conservation Service] sent postcards out to farmers reading, 'You know that low area that you couldn't plow or plant? It may be used as set-aside if it contains

at least two acres. You know that field you are planning to idle? Why
not designate that as an area for set-aside. Be safe, not sorry.'[9]

Many farmers have both dry land and irrigated land. The irrigated
land has much higher yields. The USDA, at least until a few years ago,
paid farmers to idle their dry land—and based the payment rate on
the productivity average of their dry and irrigated land. Thus, farmers
were paid far more to idle their land than the dry land possibly could
have produced.[10] The USDA knew it was overpaying farmers, but did
not attempt to correct its generosity until the GAO publicized the
waste.

Set-asides are also made a mockery by USDA rules on summer
fallow. In dry land areas such as Oklahoma, Colorado, Nebraska,
Texas, Arizona, and New Mexico, land must be left idle every second
year in order to soak up moisture. This is the only way the land can
maintain minimal productivity. Yet the USDA's set-aside rules allow
farmers to count as set-aside acres land that would be left idle under
any circumstance. Both the Carter and Reagan administrations fought
hard to abolish this gaping loophole, but Congress ignored them. Bob
Bergland, the USDA secretary under Jimmy Carter, said that "the summer fallow situation is a scandal" and a major reason for the farm
program's leaking "like a sieve and . . . dying of its own weight."[11]

Don Paarlberg, formerly the chief economist of the USDA, observes, "It's not that farmers falsify records. But the laws and regulations are written by people who don't really believe in the programs.
They don't want things to work. They don't want farmers to actually
have to cut production in order to get federal money. And the rules are
administered locally by farmer-committees who don't want to move
against their neighbors and themselves."[12]

"The Most Successful Agricultural Program in History"

The best way to understand the set-aside programs is to examine in
depth the 1983 payment-in-kind program (PIK), which sought to
boost crop prices by rewarding farmers for idling 77 million acres of
cropland.[13] In return for idling enough farmland to cover the entire
states of Ohio and Indiana and half of Illinois, PIK gave farmers more
than $10 billion worth of commodities. The agriculture secretary, John

Block, declared in 1983, "Never in the history of agriculture has there been a farm program more successful than PIK."[14] USDA officials bragged about successfully shutting down some of the best farms in the world.

In Pennsylvania, Indiana, and elsewhere, PIK helped drive hundreds of egg producers out of business. In Oklahoma, Texas, Iowa, and other states, PIK devastated cattle and pork producers. Across the Midwest, hundreds of fertilizer, farm-equipment, and seed dealers had to close shop because PIK cut their sales by up to 50 percent. PIK-related losses to agriculture businesses totaled $4 billion, according to an estimate made by Abner Womack, an economist at the University of Missouri.[15] PIK also cost poultry, egg, pork, and cattle producers up to $7 billion due to higher feed-grain costs. At a time when unemployment was still at a postwar high, PIK slashed employment for laborers and among farm suppliers and other industries by up to 250,000 jobs.[16] When the economy was still struggling to recover from a severe recession, PIK intentionally reduced production and thereby decreased America's GNP by an estimated one-half percent. When American crop exports were already declining, PIK effectively raised a white flag in the world grain markets.

The story of PIK begins with the 1981 farm legislation, which called for automatic 4 or 5 percent increases in crop target and loan prices annually. But the USDA and Congress misguessed the rate of inflation, and government support and target prices were soon far above market prices. By the summer of 1982, farm programs were widely perceived to be a mess and sure to get worse unless repaired soon. Program costs had doubled from the previous year, exports were plummeting, farm income was declining for the third successive year, and government-owned surpluses were the largest in history. Congress responded by raising the federal support prices for corn and wheat still higher, justifying the boost—which would almost inevitably cause greater surpluses and fewer exports—by claiming that farmers needed the extra money to make a profit.

The *Farm Journal* branded the price-support hike "The Canadian Agricultural Development Act of 1982" because the higher prices would reduce American export and allow Canadians to capture our foreign markets.[17] There was no economic sense to Congress' move: It was only another election-year bone thrown to the farm lobbies.

Federal price supports that are higher than world market prices act as an export tax on American farm products. The "farm problem" was perceived to be caused by huge surpluses, yet at the same time Congress paid farmers to cut production, the higher support prices encouraged increased production and made it more difficult to sell American harvests abroad.

Reagan announced the PIK program in early December 1982. But from the beginning the USDA had little idea of what it was doing. It originally estimated that 23 million acres would be idled by PIK, but took no marketing surveys to see how farmers would react to its offer. When the returns were tallied in March 1983, farmers had chosen to idle 77 million acres in PIK and other programs—one-third of all the eligible cropland, and more than triple the USDA's prediction. Several private economists had made much more accurate estimates.

PIK offered to give wheat farmers 95 percent of their usual production, and offered 80 percent of the usual production to corn, cotton, rice, grain, and sorghum farmers in return for idling their land. PIK was extremely generous to farmers, since it gave them most of their output while farmers saved expenses for labor, seeds, fertilizer, and fuel. PIK often paid farmers two or three times what they could have earned otherwise. The *Washington Post* reported that the National Cotton Council estimated that a large California cotton farmer could get a million dollars from PIK; if he actually produced as much as he could, he would earn only $368,000.[18] The triple pay for California cotton growers is especially galling since the federal government also spent millions of dollars to provide free irrigated water to many of the same producers who idled their land in PIK. The government first spent a mint to set them up in business, then spent another mint to pay them not to work.

The USDA often administered PIK as though its sole purpose was to give farmers money by hook or by crook. PIK gave benefits in proportion to the number of acres farmers had planted in previous years and to their average yield per acre. Once PIK was announced, the reported acreage base for corn, grain, sorghum, cotton, and rice increased by over a million and a half acres overnight. This meant that many farmers lied about the amount of these crops they previously planted. Allowing farmers to claim as PIK acreage land that had previously been idle or planted with crops that were not eligible made a mockery of efforts to reduce production.

The USDA also gave farmers up to $391 million to store their free crops for up to seven months so that they could wait and sell at the most profitable time. Farmers received the storage bonus regardless of whether they planned to store their crops or sell them the next day. A survey by the USDA inspector general found that cotton farmers received an average of $1,500 more than they should have because local USDA offices manipulated or miscalculated their production statistics. Several farms that planted no cotton in the previous year were allowed to reap PIK windfalls solely because they claimed to have planted cotton in the 1970s. One corn grower was given free corn for almost twice as many acres as he had planted the previous two years because he had planted more corn in 1977, 1978, and 1979.

In California, the USDA allowed farmers to claim the empty space between rows in cotton fields as PIK-idled acreage, thus allowing farmers to boost their production while at the same time allowing them to claim half their acreage as idle and eligible for PIK benefits.[19] Six farms in the Tulane Lake Basin in California got $4 million from PIK even though their 14,000 acres of farmland were under nine feet of water and could not have been planted regardless of PIK.[20] President Reagan, to buy votes for Republican candidates in the 1982 congressional elections, announced in October 1982 that the USDA would give many farmers advance payments to compensate them for the low prices that were expected for crops to be planted in 1983. Then, when the farmers enrolled in PIK, the USDA let them keep over $100 million in advances, even though they weren't growing any crops.[21] The USDA paid up to a quarter of a billion dollars more than necessary for the crops it acquired to give to farmers, because it used a bidding process that was blatantly flawed and that prevented the agency from perceiving how much it was paying to acquire the crops.[22]

In its first announcements on PIK, the USDA promised that it would strive to take land out of production "without adversely affecting local agricultural economies."[23] But the USDA allowed up to 45 percent of the land in a county's farm base for each commodity to be taken out of production. Apparently the USDA believed that only a 45 percent loss of business would not adversely affect local agricultural supply dealers. Fertilizer dealers already had supplies in store for

spring planting when PIK was announced. The USDA originally estimated that PIK would decrease fertilizer sales by 3 or 4 percent. But
total fertilizer sales dropped 15 percent, and in some areas sales dived
by 50 percent. Dennis Jorgensen, owner of a fertilizer and pesticide
business in Ulysses, Nebraska, saw his business turn from a $53,000
profit in 1982 to a $75,000 loss in 1983.[24]

As PIK came to be seen as a boondoggle, the USDA kept finding
new justifications for giving billions of dollars' worth of crops to wealthy farmers. By June 1983, the USDA was claiming that the main
purpose was to raise farm income—a point little emphasized in January, when PIK was justified as reducing surpluses. By September, the
secretary of agriculture was defending PIK as "the best drought assistance ever offered," even though the USDA already offered farmers
heavily subsidized crop insurance, which would have covered
drought losses, and even though this so-called drought assistance
helped only farmers who chose to accept government handouts instead of growing their own crops.

The USDA also continually changed its estimates of PIK's supposed benefits. In January, the USDA claimed that PIK would save
$3.6 billion in the 1983 and 1984 fiscal years. In May, the USDA was
claiming that PIK would save $9 billion through the 1986 fiscal year. In
July, the USDA claimed that PIK would save $14.9 billion in the fiscal
years 1984 through 1986. By August, the deputy assistant secretary,
Dawson Ahalt, said that PIK would save $9 billion in the same period.
The USDA's claim that PIK would save the government money was
based on the assumption that its surplus crops were of no value because the crops had been paid for in previous years and the government had to dispose of them anyway. This would have surprised the
average shopper, who has to pay hard cash for a loaf of bread or a box
of rice. The GAO concluded that there was no way to accurately predict costs or savings from PIK in future years.

The effects of PIK were intensified by a severe drought in the
summer of 1983. The USDA quickly seized on the drought as an excuse for higher food prices. But the price of corn was already up 30
percent from its 1982 low before the drought became severe. The
USDA planned to slash crop production and assumed that the nation
would have normal weather—then, when "God signed up for PIK,"

as Earl Butz, a former USDA secretary, quipped, the USDA's plans were devastated.

PIK did its greatest harm to U.S. exports. When American producers cut their plantings, farmers in every major foreign crop-producing country increased their plantings by 60 million acres. One USDA official called PIK the "best friend Argentinean corn growers ever had." The former USDA secretary of agriculture, Clifford Hardin, observed, "Quantities of corn left in private markets were so small that a few export orders could not be filled and sales were lost."[25] Curt Leonard, vice president of Uncle Ben's Rice Company, said, "We haven't been able to compete in the world market for the last two or three years. PIK is adding fire to the flame."[26] G. Edward Schuh, chairman of the Agricultural Economics Department at the University of Minnesota, declared, "A better recipe for losing markets and market share would be difficult to design."[27] Don Paarlberg, former USDA chief economist, concluded, "One must deplore cutting our production of coarse grains by 26 percent while foreign output is expected to go up 5 percent."[28]

John Block, the secretary of agriculture, claimed that "nearly eighty million acres were set aside in conservation uses" under PIK, and that PIK improved "the quality of the environment." Peter Myers, the Soil Conservation Service chief, said PIK would be "the largest national conservation effort ever undertaken by farmers." But most farmers did little or nothing to conserve their idled lands. A Midwestern survey "found 20 percent of the idled land . . . unprotected from wind and water erosion and another 37 percent . . . protected only by last year's crop residue or weeds."[29] The *New York Times* reported that "state conservation surveyed a twelve-state area from Ohio to Colorado and found that only ten percent of the 43 million acres idled [in those states] were treated adequately to conserve soil and provide wildlife habitat."[30]

By lavishly rewarding farmers to shut down their businesses, the USDA threw many other people out of work. A study done at the University of California at Davis concluded that PIK cost California 60,000 jobs. When 10 million people were already out of work, the USDA launched a program that added to the unemployment lines. And many of these people and their families received unemployment compensation, food stamps, and other social services, thus adding millions more to the cost of PIK.

PIK was justified largely as income assistance for the struggling family farmer. The average small farmer got little or nothing from PIK. The Chemical Bank reported that PIK would "widen the income disparity among crop farmers."[31] Federal law prohibits the USDA from giving more than $50,000 a year to any single farm. The USDA evaded this law by claiming that, since it was distributing commodities instead of cash, no limit applied—as if giving a million dollars' worth of cotton were less inequitable than giving $51,000 in greenbacks. C. J. Ritchie Farms Corporation received over $5 million worth of government-owned cotton in return for leaving its farmland idle. In Nebraska, National Farms Corporation received over $3 million worth of corn from the government as a reward for not planting its own crops. A GAO survey found that large farmers received an average of $175,000 apiece worth of government crops nationwide to compensate them for planting less than in previous years. The agency ruled that the USDA violated the law by giving million-dollar windfalls to farmers, yet no USDA official was penalized. If the same breach of law had occurred in the defense industry, some federal officials may well have been awarded prison pinstripes.

Congress and the Reagan administration did little to change the government's fundamental incentives for farmers to overproduce or to produce only for government storage. As a result, in 1984 farmers again planted fencerow-to-fencerow, and congressmen mounted the ramparts to denounce the USDA for rewarding farmers to idle only 27 million acres. In 1986 the USDA paid farmers to idle 48.1 million acres; in 1987, 75 million acres; and for 1988 the USDA estimates that farmers idled 78 million acres in response to government programs. While the President preached the need for the United States to become more export-oriented, administration officials busied themselves shutting down the farms.

The Grim Reaper of Rural Jobs

USDA Secretary Henry Wallace conceded in 1934, "I am fully aware that acreage adjustment produces its unemployment problem just as the shutting down of factories in the cities."[32] Though USDA policy-makers occasionally concede this point in theory, the USDA shows little or no concern in practice for the people who lose their jobs when the USDA decides to boost farm income by reducing farm production. As William Amberson wrote in *The Nation* in 1935, "Once the basic error of production restriction has been made, it is no longer within the power of administrators, however humane, to prevent a train of vicious sequela."[33]

In a study published by the USDA in 1986, it was estimated that "a 30-million-acre reduction [of cropland] reduces final stocks $9 billion, on-farm activity $5 billion, input industry activity $3 billion, and downstream activities $1 billion. The program's effects on employment are also largely limited to those same industries: 315,000 jobs lost in farming, 162,000 jobs lost in upstream input industries, and very few jobs lost in downstream industries."[34]

According to a 1987 study by the Economic Research Service of the USDA, the 70 million acres that government paid to idle that year cost the U.S. economy 300,000 potential jobs, plus an estimated $4 billion in lost sales from farm input industries.[35] The Agricultural Policy Working Group reported that since 1980, the farm equipment industry has lost 86,000 jobs, while fertilizer and agricultural chemical industries have lost 16,000 jobs. Between 1979 and 1984, almost a quarter of all farm dealerships closed down.[36]

Set-asides are defended as saving farmers' jobs. There are roughly 300,000 full-time farmers of subsidized crops. Of these 300,000, perhaps 250,000 are in a sound financial position, with a debt-to-asset ratio of less than 40 percent. Of the other 50,000, perhaps half are doomed to sink eventually unless the Farmers Home Administration continues to forgive their bad debts each year. This leaves perhaps 25,000 farmers who might be kept in business partly by federal bonuses for idling their land. To save 25,000 farmers, the USDA rewards all subsidized farmers for throwing farm labor out of work. As a ballpark estimate, for every farmer saved, farm programs may have put twelve farm, farm-input, grain-export, and other workers out of a job. Because agricultural policy-makers are convinced that they need to control supply in order to protect agriculture from itself, they perpetuate policies that would not be tolerated in any other American industry.

But perhaps even this 12-to-1 ratio of jobs lost to jobs saved is too flattering to agricultural policy-makers. Good farmland will be farmed regardless of whether one individual farmer goes bankrupt or not. Insofar as set-aside programs decrease bankruptcy rates, their main effect is to keep financially unsuccessful farmers in possession of farms, rather than allow more competent farmers to buy and plant the land. Some of the land government pays farmers not to sow is of poor quality and would not be planted even if government did not pay farmers not to plant on it—or is planted only due to lucrative federal subsidies. There is no way of knowing precisely how much marginal land is included in the program, but it is unlikely to be more than half the total of 78 million acres idled in 1988.

Sideshow: Massacre of the Innocents

The USDA has long been the biggest source of unfair competition in American agriculture.[37] In most years when government pays farmers not to plant on their land, the USDA allows farmers to raise hay or graze livestock on their so-called "idle land," ruining the market for farmers who try to profitably raise hay in most parts of the country and giving some livestock producers a big advantage over other producers.

In the 1985 farm bill, farmers who were paid not to plant corn, wheat, and other crops were given a blank check to grow unsubsidized crops on their "unplanted" land. Farmers effectively were promised up to $200 an acre in government bonuses for any crop they chose to produce, which meant that they could afford to neglect supply and demand and glut previously balanced markets. Both Congress and the Reagan administration favored this provision in the 1985 farm bill as a way to encourage farmers to shift from subsidized crops in surplus to "non-program crops that are less likely to be [in] oversupply under current market assumptions and conditions," as Richard Stallings, a Democratic congressman from Idaho, phrased it.[38]

This new provision quickly devastated many farmers not on the government dole. As Byron Dorgan, a Democratic congressman from North Dakota, observed in March 1986, "The markets for edible beans have virtually shut down nationwide as processors wait to see how the provision is handled."[39] Harold Wilson of the Western Bean Dealers Association warned: "In Idaho, the pricing trend now is headed for destruction for the [unsubsidized] farmers."[40] Contract price offers for the fall popcorn crop fell more than 50 percent. Fruit and vegetable growers in Texas, California, and elsewhere were terrified. Doug Michael of the National Potato Council complained that "the Council has worked vigorously against any effort to include potatoes in government farm programs. The market is not calling for the production of additional potatoes."[41] Many of the independent growers who were victimized had fought over the years to avoid any federal "assistance" for their crops. A former assistant secretary of agriculture, Bill Lesher, declared, "You're talking about destroying people's livelihood when they never asked for anything. It really is un-American."[42]

The 1986 massacre of unsubsidized farmers was indicative of Congress' attitudes towards farmers. Congress always treats agricultural welfare recipient groups with more respect and consideration than it accords self-reliant farmers. Congressmen have little admiration or interest in farmers who don't need a handout—that is, who are not dependent on politicians.

The Republican representative from Michigan, Bill Schuette, a member of the House Agricultural Committee, said that the unintended impact of the farm bill provision "came as a surprise to many of us."[43] One staff member of the Senate Agricultural Committee told Ward Sinclair, a reporter for the *Washington Post*, "No one contemplated creating surpluses in other commodities when the farm bill was written, but it seems that every time you cure one problem, you create another."[44] Congress collected more than 10,000 pages of testimony on the 1985 farm bill, yet apparently never realized that providing massive subsidies to plant unsubsidized crops could devastate those markets as badly as government has devastated wheat, corn, and cotton markets. Congressmen's inability to perceive such a simple example of cause and effect raises serious questions about their ability to manage anything more complex than the House of Representatives barbershop.

Despite the 1986 debacle, the USDA still occasionally casually disrupts the markets for unsubsidized farmers. The Texas Agricultural Stabilization and Conservation Service (ASCS), which administers

USDA programs in Texas, announced in February 1988 that farmers would be allowed to raise hay or graze livestock on the so-called conservation-use acres that the government was rewarding them for idling.[45] Terry Harmon, the state ASCS director, declared, "The state ASCS committee determined that haying and grazing . . . will not result in adverse economic effect within the state of Texas." This is typical of how the USDA sees the farm economy: Bureaucrats look at the overall economic impact and disregard the adverse impact on individual farmers who are trying to raise hay for a profit or who are raising cattle and not receiving a federal subsidy for their grazing land. As long as "net farm income" increases, individual farmers are irrelevant.

Idiot Schemes

While the government is paying farmers not to plant on good land, it has spent billions to create more farmland and make existing farmland more productive. The Bureau of Reclamation of the Department of the Interior has spent more than $22 billion since 1905 to make the desert bloom, building new dams to make more farmland, even though the new farmland costs taxpayers far more than it is worth and the additional harvests often glut markets and depress farm income. According to a 1988 study by the Bureau of Reclamation, "The federal government is paying about $203 million a year in irrigation subsidies in the West for crops that also receive price supports or other farm subsidies."[46]

The federal government is spending $2 billion on the Garrison Diversion project in North Dakota to create new farmland. The Garrison project will divert the Missouri River and create a series of huge lakes in central North Dakota. Garrison will irrigate 250,000 acres— but the Fish and Wildlife Service of the Department of the Interior estimates that the project will destroy or damage 217,000 acres of wetlands, grass, and woodland. Garrison is an interesting case of political arithmetic: Many farmers will be flooded out by the new dams and only 800 farmers will benefit, at a cost of more than $1.5 million each.[47] The farmers who will receive the subsidy are already producing surplus crops. Thus, government will spend more than a million dollars each to boost the productivity of farmers to whom the USDA is already likely paying $50,000 a year each to reduce their production. Garrison makes no economic sense, but the contractors who build the project will make lavish campaign contributions to incumbent congressmen.

The Meaning of Set-Asides

Set-asides are a political response to what politicians perceive as excess capacity—too many acres producing a given crop. Yet a recent USDA study concluded,

> Excess capacity exists for . . . the commodities that have traditionally been given the most policy attention. . . . Excess capacity is a much more serious problem for the seven major crops (wheat, corn, oats, barley, sorghum, cotton, and soybeans) than for the rest of U.S. agriculture.[48]

Excess capacity has greatly increased since 1979, thanks to generous federal subsidies that encouraged farmers to produce more crops. USDA economist Dan Dvoskin estimated that in 1985, excess capacity for wheat in 1986 was 31.14 percent; rice, 24.12 percent; corn, 28.85 percent; sorghum, 25.61 percent; feed grain, 25.61 percent, and for cotton in 1985, 49.82 percent. Dvoskin concluded, "Excess capacity in agriculture is caused primarily by agricultural prices that are higher than market equilibrium prices."[49] The excess capacity of unsubsidized crops was less than 6 percent.

Supply controls are introduced only after politicians and bureaucrats have mismanaged price controls. We have had perpetual set-asides in agriculture largely because Congress insists on perpetually paying farmers more than their crops are worth. Government first artificially raises the price and then artificially restricts production. The higher Congress drives up the price, the greater the need for government controls on the amount produced. Set-asides are designed to make supply and demand meet at exactly the point that pleases the most politicians.

If a set-aside is a success, prices are higher; if it is a failure, surpluses are larger. Set-asides force taxpayers to bankroll a scheme intended to drive up prices for consumers. Every acre of set-aside land is an indictment of the failure of federal planning. Permanent set-asides mean that government perpetually attracts too much capital to agriculture and then, instead of allowing a natural adjustment and the capital to flow out, perpetually intervenes to keep some of that capital idle.

Each year the forecasts upon which USDA set-aside programs are based turn out wrong, and result in either temporary shortages of feed grains (1983 and 1988) or massive surpluses (1982, 1984, 1985, 1986, and 1987). Government forecasts of world demand are a joke, because demand is largely a factor of price. Insofar as the set-aside program succeeds in driving up the American crop price, it will decrease the world demand for American exports. Good or bad weather on any continent of the globe often determines short-term crop price swings. Shifts in currency exchange value also wreak havoc with export estimates. Since the USDA cannot control world prices, the government cannot know what the demand will be. Every major increase in crop yields is the equivalent to adding a million or more new acres. Since the USDA cannot forecast yields, it is completely incapable of accurately forecasting supply.

Set-asides mean unilateral United States disarmament in the campaign for world crop exports. Since the United States again became a major agricultural exporter in the early 1970s, every idle acre "bought" by the USDA means one less acre available to compete with Australian, Canadian, and European wheat. Every set-aside program is intended to drive prices higher than they would otherwise be. But every increase in American crop prices tends to decrease exports. Set-asides set up a vicious cycle: The United States cuts back its production, foreign farmers respond by increasing production, the United States loses market share, which leads to bigger U.S. surpluses, which lead to more acreage cutbacks, which further encourages foreign production, which further reduces American market share, which causes more surpluses. The "success" of set-asides becomes a question of how fast politicians can shut down American agriculture.

Set-asides are based on the assumption that foreigners will buy the same amount of crop exports at a high price as at a low price— that it is not necessary to maximize the efficiency of the American farmer since foreign buyers don't care whether American crops are high-priced or low-priced. If any single state attempted to drive up crop prices by restricting its farmers' acreage, that state would soon be the laughingstock of the nation as farmers in other states took up the slack. But the United States is trying to do exactly the same thing in world markets.

Since 1978 the U.S. government has paid farmers not to plant only seven of the more than four-hundred crops grown in the country. Politicians and bureaucrats always argue that because of the nature of agriculture, farmers cannot adjust by themselves to changes in market demand. Yet the arguments made to justify paid diversions of some crops either apply to all crops or they make sense for no crops.

Soybeans have been America's largest farm export for six out of the last seven years. Though soybeans have a price-support program pegged at 75 percent of the average of the previous five years' market prices, the price support is low enough that soybean farmers are not encouraged to produce endless surpluses. The secretary of agriculture is prohibited by law from imposing a set-aside program for soybeans. Soybean acreage has fluctuated in the 1980s from 51 million to 77 million acres—all in response to price changes. The success of soybean producers in rapidly adjusting to market signals proves that set-asides are not necessary to balance markets.

By paying to idle productive land, the USDA increases farmers' average cost of production. The Agricultural Policy Working Group estimates that set-asides increase the average cost of production for a bushel of corn by 33 cents. Since the variable cost of production in the most efficient corn-growing areas is only about one dollar a bushel, this has a huge influence on American competitiveness. The group observed:

> The 1987 wheat program carries an inefficiency penalty of 94 cents a bushel due to the 27.5 percent unpaid Acreage Reduction Program [requiring farmers to leave 27.5 percent of their wheat acreage idle in order to qualify for federal subsidies]. If the farmer were allowed to produce on all the land in his base acreage instead of just [on] 72.5 percent, the target price could be 94 cents lower and the farmer would still receive the same income above variable costs that he gets from the 1987 program.[50]

Set-asides are a triumph of enlightened land-use policy. Across-the-board acreage-reduction requirements mean that millions of acres of the best farmland in the world are left idle. Yet at the same time, due to high target prices, farmers increase production on marginal land because federal handouts make producing surpluses so profitable. Between 1976 and 1985, total farmland in the U.S. increased by an average of almost 4 million acres a year.[51] Politicians respond to the increased production from relatively poor farmland by requiring farmers to idle more of the best farmland.

While the government pays some farmers to reduce production, other farmers are free to boost their output. The GAO noted, "from 1982 to 1985, while participating U.S. wheat farmers idled about 55 million acres under Acreage Reduction Programs, nonparticipating farmers in the United States expanded wheat cultivation by about 35 million acres."[52]

Government efforts to manage supply result in far less efficiency and far higher production and adjustment costs than do the private sector's efforts. The government pays indiscriminately to idle the best and the worst land in the nation. If there were no set-asides and crop prices were low or failing, market incentives would result in the least-productive land being removed from production and the least-efficient farmers leaving the profession.

Many farm aid advocates believe that America's problems could be solved if only the United States could force other nations to set aside some of their farmland. According to Peter F. Deffly of the American Cotton Shippers Association, "The United States should warn other producing countries against increasing acreage when we cut back production."[53] The USDA has repeatedly tried to set up international wheat cartels, to no avail. Congressmen often denounce foreign farmers for expanding their acreage when the United States pays American farmers not to plant. Just because Americans do stupid things doesn't mean the world is obliged to follow our example.

Every set-aside program means a government-paid vacation for farmers. In 1988 the government paid to idle 78 million acres. Full-time farmers have farms that average just under 1,000 acres. Thus, the set-aside program was equivalent to paying for a one-year annual vacation for almost 80,000 farmers. Part of the reason we have heard so much about the "farm problem" in recent years is because, thanks to acreage-reduction programs, many farmers have a lot more free time on their hands; they join other farmers and holler about how they are suffering. Set-asides are increasingly becoming an indirect subsidy for the Florida tourist trade. Congressmen praise farmers for being hard workers, and then create program after program to pay farmers to live in idleness. If anyone proposed to raise Harlem's moral tone with a program to pay young blacks not to work, he would be ridiculed. If the beneficiaries are white farmers, the same arguments are met with respect.

Secretary of Agriculture John Block claimed that PIK was "the most effective acreage-reduction program in history." If PIK were a good thing, then why didn't President Reagan brag in 1982 when a recession succeeded in shutting down thousands of factories? If squandering resources is the key to success in agriculture, why shouldn't it work for all our other industries? Farm set-aside programs make as much sense as paying every kid in a city to mow one less lawn a week, or paying cab drivers to scorn every third person who hails them for a ride.

Instead of preventing farmers from growing crops on a third of their land, why not simply prohibit farmers from using tractors? This would encourage a return to traditional mule-drawn cultivation, thereby stimulating the demand for mules and creating thousands of new jobs in the mule-breeding business. It would stimulate demand for oats, thereby helping many hard-pressed oat farmers. Replacing tractors with mules would also help modern farming harmonize better with the nineteenth-century lithographs from whence most urban Americans derive their opinions on farm policy. Once politicians decide that productivity is an evil, who can say where the line should be drawn?

Conclusion

Richard Lyng, secretary of agriculture, declared in 1987, "We would hope that acreage reduction programs could be eliminated in the longer term. However, for the immediate future, as long as we have record surpluses and income and price supports that encourage excess production, the only way we can avoid even larger surpluses and enormous government outlays is with acreage reduction programs."[54]

It is easier for American politicians to shut down American agriculture than to straighten out the tangle of self-defeating federal farm policies. It is easier just to pay farmers not to work than to adjust farm programs so that farmers can produce and sell as much as they choose around the world.

Set-asides epitomize the USDA's view that productivity is a problem, not an asset, and that American farmers will be better off with lower productivity. Set-asides epitomize the view that the USDA can and should control the agricultural economy no matter how badly the plans work out. Set-asides were a temporary emergency measure that became institutionalized because politicians and bureaucrats could not think of any other way to control farmers.

How can the government be saving farmers when its method of saving them is paying them not to farm? At what point does a farmer become a nonfarmer? When the government pays him to take a one-year vacation—as it did in 1988 for thousands of wheat and corn farmers? When the government pays him to take a five-year vacation, as it has done for dairy farmers? Is a farmer someone who owns bib overalls and drives an old pickup truck, or is he someone who actually makes a living harvesting crops and not handouts? Should the goal of farm policy be to help real farmers—or only to maximize the number of individuals who can fill in a blank on a census form with the word *farmer?*

Set-asides are the clearest proof of the incorrigibility of agricultural policy-makers. The set-aside policy is one more example of the tendency of politicians to latch on to a policy tool—and then use it as if it were the only tool in existence. The only reason we have paid set-asides now is because we had them in the 1930s. If the United States had never paid farmers not to work and some politician came forward tomorrow and suggested them, he would be ridiculed. But because we have always done things that way, people assume that the policy cannot be as stupid as it appears.

Chapter 6

Redistribution via Cows

The dairy program is about as close to pure graft as farm policy gets. Since 1980, the federal government has spent over $15 billion buying and storing surplus dairy products, and consumers have been forced to pay over $40 billion in higher milk, cheese, and butter prices because of federal price regulations and trade barriers. The annual subsidy per American dairy cow exceeds the per capita income of half the population of the world.

Above all, the dairy policy is a caring policy. Congressman Tony Coelho, perhaps the most influential congressman on dairy issues, summed up the goal of federal dairy policy when he declared:

> There are many people who advocate that we get rid of some of the dairy farmers that we have, that this is the salvation to this industry. As one who was born and raised on a dairy farm and worked hard milking cows—and my family went bankrupt—it ain't the way to go. The scars that are left over are tremendous and they are long lasting.[1]

Thanks to Coelho's powerful position in Congress, the entire nation is still suffering due to the Coelho dairy-farm bankruptcy.

Since 1952 the number of commercial dairy producers has fallen from 600,000 to about 130,000—and, according to the Congressional Office of Technology Assessment, could fall to as few as 5,000 by the year 2000. The number of dairymen has decreased by an average of 4,800 every year since 1970. The federal government has fought a rearguard battle every step of the way, always trying to boost prices and find new ways to postpone adjustments. No price was too high, no burden was too heavy for taxpayers and consumers to pay to delay the retirement of a single dairy farmer.

Dairy policy has been the most expensive farm policy for consumers. With the excuses that politicians concocted for not reforming the program, the pervasive atmosphere of deception in the dairy dealings of the House of Representatives, the incredibly lame, self-defeating regulations that the U.S. Department of Agriculture (USDA) devises to administer dairy programs, and the federal government's blatant efforts to drive independent dairymen out of business, we have farm policy at its worst.

The dairy program has little or nothing to do with milk and everything to do with politics. Though the average full-time dairy farmer is worth far more than the average citizen, federal law still treats him as if he were a hardship case, with a right to a federal handout limited only by his ability to produce surplus milk. Campaign contributions from the dairy industry are among the most productive investments in America: Dairy lobbies give congressmen $1 million or $2 million a year in contributions; congressmen give dairymen *$1 billion or $2 billion* a year in subsidies and help dairymen fleece consumers for another $5 billion or $7 billion in higher prices. Everyone benefits—except for taxpayers and consumers.

Politicians have always seen dairy productivity as a nuisance rather than a blessing. Congressman Steve Gunderson of Wisconsin, the ranking minority member of the House Dairy Subcommittee, declared: "The dairy industry needs more productivity . . . about as much as the drunk driver needs another drink."[2] If a politician said the same thing about the steel or computer industry, he would be laughed all the way to the unemployment office. But the dairy industry is different.

The Mystery of Surpluses

Congressional discussions of dairy surpluses are replete with references to the need for the government to balance supply and demand, as though the dairy market were so incredibly complex that no one could expect it to function properly without intervention. The intervention itself is very simple: Congress sets high price supports, dairymen produce more milk than the public will buy at such high prices, and Congress spends a few weeks every year or two rushing to the rescue, concocting excuses not to lower the price support to a level at which farmers will produce only as much as consumers will buy even at politically approved prices. The milk market functions in the same way that any other market functions: As long as Congress sets prices above market-clearing levels, dairymen will continue producing surpluses.

Dairy price supports have always marched hand-in-hand with campaign contributions. Early in 1968, the Associated Milk Producers Inc. (AMPI), one of the largest milk cooperatives in the United States, made illegal campaign contributions of $104,000 to Lyndon Johnson's re-election campaign; Johnson responded by raising dairy price supports by 7 percent just before the Wisconsin primary. After Johnson dropped out of the presidential race, AMPI made $90,000 in illegal contributions straight from its corporate treasury to Hubert Humphrey's presidential campaign. On August 1, 1969, an AMPI representative gave $100,000 in $100 bills to Herbert Kalbach, President Nixon's personal lawyer. In the spring of 1970, Nixon raised milk price supports by 38 cents a hundredweight—the largest price hike in the history of the dairy program. On March 12, 1971, the secretary of agriculture, Clifford Hardin, announced that another milk price hike could not be justified. The dairy lobby was outraged and arranged a meeting on March 23 between dairy-farm representatives and the President, at which he praised the dairymen for their understanding of the importance of Washington and said that "a lot of businessmen and others I talk to around this table, they yammer and talk a lot, but they don't do anything about it. But you do, and I appreciate that. I don't need to spell it out." The dairymen then pledged $2 million in campaign contributions. On March 25, 1971, USDA Secretary Hardin announced a rise in the dairy price support from $4.66 to $4.93 a hundredweight. The dairymen's $2 million investment boosted their profits by $300 million.[3]

In 1976 Jimmy Carter needed desperately to win the Wisconsin primary to secure the Democratic nomination for the presidency. The obvious answer: Promise a big raise in dairy price supports. The result: a primary victory and, in 1977, a federal "safety net" for dairymen far more generous than that provided for most subsidized crops. Between 1971 and 1977, the milk price support increased by 82 percent, while the cost-of-living index increased by only 44 percent.[4] The milk support price rose from $9.00 to $13.10 per hundredweight between 1977 and 1980—a 47 percent increase.

By 1979, government milk surpluses were piling up at an alarming rate; in 1979 the Congressional Budget Office concluded that the federal benefits were so generous that they were keeping inefficient dairy farmers in business. In 1980 the USDA purchased 2 billion pounds of surplus dairy products, and the dairy program was widely ridiculed as an example of the incompetence of Big Government. By 1981, when federal spending on dairy subsidies had increased sixfold in two years, the government was sitting on top of a $3 billion surplus with mountains of rotting cheese and butter in storage. The Commodity Credit Corporation (CCC) was buying nonfat dry milk at 94 cents a pound and desperately selling it for 55 cents a pound to help provide hogs with their daily minimum calcium intake. *Barron's* reported the CCC's recipe for success: "Mix [dry milk] with an oil to discolor it and make it unpalatable to humans. Voila! Animal feed."[5] Despite the huge surplus, Congress refused to reduce dairy subsidies significantly, and the surplus continued piling up toward the heavens.

By 1983, the USDA was spending more than a quarter of a million dollars an hour buying surplus dairy products and spending more than a million dollars a day simply to store them. John Block, the secretary of agriculture, appeared in television advertisements drinking a glass of milk and telling viewers, "If more people would do this we could straighten this dairy program up overnight."[6] The chairman of the House Agriculture Committee, Kika de la Garza, conceded, "Let me say that we are producing, yes, maybe a little bit too much . . . [but] there are still hungry people in the U.S. There are still hungry people in the world."[7] Apparently, as long as anybody anywhere is hungry, the mountains of rotting cheese and butter are an illusion.

The Great Bossie Massacres

The dairy program is an entertaining study of the extremes to which Congress will go in order to avoid the obvious solution to a problem. Congress finally admitted in 1983 that there was a dairy surplus; its solution was not to reduce the price supports, but rather to maintain incentives for overproduction while rewarding some farmers for selling less milk. In 1983 Congress created a "guaranteed one-time only" solution to the dairy surplus: paying farmers not to produce milk and presumably, to kill their cows. In 1986 and 1987, the USDA ran a "guaranteed second-time-only" dairy buyout, again to pay farmers to kill or export their cows. Both programs are milestones in the history of efficient resource allocation.

Congress launched the first dairy buyout in November 1983, but insisted on paying farmers for any reduction in their milk production since 1982. Thus many farmers were handsomely rewarded by the government for cows they had already slaughtered before the program began. The House Republican leader, Robert Michel, called the dairy buyout a "kill a cow for conservation" program and ridiculed government buyout payments as "loafing payments": "This is a preposterous program setting supports too high, thereby causing a surplus, and then paying people not to produce that surplus."[8] The average California and Florida dairy farm participating in the program received over $100,000 for milking less.[9]

The 1983–84 dairy buyout program was designed to give away the most money while asking the fewest questions. The General Accounting Office noted, "The participants were not required to abide by their planned methods to achieve their contracted marketing levels."[10] In other words, if a farmer had promised to slaughter his cattle but did not do so, he did not violate his agreement with the government as long as the government could not prove that he sold the cows' milk. There are easier things in the world to devise than an audit trail for a gallon of milk.

While the government paid some farmers to reduce their milk production, other dairymen were not prevented from increasing their production. At the end of the program, after $995 million had been spent, there were only 10,000 fewer dairy cows in the United States than there had been at the beginning.[11] The USDA paid the equivalent of $100,000 for each net cow reduction of the total American dairy herd, even though a used dairy cow is worth only about $1,000. But the first dairy buyout program did succeed in postponing any painful adjustment for dairy campaign contributors until after the 1984 congressional elections. After the buyout program ended, dairymen added to their herds, and soon the nation had 11.2 million cows, the largest national dairy herd since 1975. Dairy production per cow had jumped by 25 percent between 1975 and 1985, and dairy production was higher in 1985 after the termination program ended than it had been before the program began in 1983.

When the 1985 farm bill was being debated, the USDA was sitting on billions of pounds of surplus dairy products. But congressmen stuck to their principles and continued protecting consumers against a shortage. Obviously, America needed another cow massacre. The House Agriculture Committee proclaimed that the one-time-only dairy buyout program had been such a big success that it made good business sense to have another. To honor the memory of cows who had died in recent years, the House voted to set the "base period" for the second dairy buyout program at 1982, in order that the government might pay the same farmers twice for the same milk cutback. (The House and Senate conference committee finally set the base period as 1985.)

Under the 1986–87 Dairy Termination Program (DTP), 144 dairy owners received a million dollars apiece, and one California producer, the Magic Valley Dairy Investment Group, received $10 million. New Mexico State University received $314,000 for selling off 280 cows it had used for research. The USDA paid up to $22.50 a hundredweight to reduce milk production, at a time when milk was selling for $11.00 a hundredweight. Thus, the USDA paid farmers far more than their milk was worth in order to persuade them to take a five-year vacation. The General Accounting Office noted that 26 percent of the DTP recipients reported that they "probably or definitely would have quit dairy operations without the program."[12]

During the 1986-87 DTP, the USDA's Agricultural Stabilization and Conservation Service (ASCS) allowed farmers who were only renting their barns to enroll, even with no assurance that the barns would not then be rented out to other dairy farmers once the original renter's cows were slaughtered. An official of ASCS, Earle Bedenbaugh, said that the exclusion of rented facilities from the program would have "seemed unusually harsh and unfair." ASCS' generosity obviously defeated the program's intent. When Congressman Charles Stenholm asked why the contracts to renters did not contain a deed restriction clause that would have prevented the abuse, Bedenbaugh explained, "I guess again it would have caused the program to be much more restrictive."[13] When it comes to a choice of wasting billions or imposing on farmers, the USDA always takes the high road. As Congressman Jim Olin complained, "You have [a] regulation here which says something is going to happen but you haven't the foggiest notion of how you can make that happen."[14]

The USDA did not even attempt to identify dairy farmers who were near bankruptcy or foreclosure before compensating them. One farmer in Virginia received government money and then lost his farm to the bank, which promptly leased it out to another dairy farmer. The USDA was generous in its interpretations of buyout: The USDA gave one farmer $585,000 to leave the dairy business even though his partner, a son-in-law, stayed in the business and kept the farm.[15]

A program designed to pay farmers to leave the business for five years is nearly impossible to administer without putting the participants under house arrest. The USDA ruled that a farmer could take his DTP money and invest in another dairy farm. Dairy farmers who had been bought out might work as managers of other dairy farms as long as salary was the only compensation.

Under the program, it was relatively easy to "export" one's cows, trading them for foreign cows, and then go right on producing. An advertisement in the April 10, 1987, *Holstein World* proclaimed: "Once in a lifetime opportunity. U.S. Dairy Buy-Out Herd with 800 Head of the World's Top Jersey and Holstein. I have an individual who would trade these cattle on a very favorable basis for Canadian cattle of equal quality that are eligible for entry into the United States." There were many reports of farmers "trading" their cows with other farmers so that only the oldest, least productive cows were slaughtered.

The USDA tried to rid America of some surplus dairy cows by providing export subsidies that often exceeded the cow's value. First the USDA forced taxpayers and consumers to pay farmers the full value of the cow and then forced taxpayers to pay up to 150 percent of the cow's value in export subsidies to persuade foreign countries to accept the American bovines.[16] It would have been cheaper to push the cows off the Brooklyn Bridge than to pay such generous subsidies.

The second DTP succeeded in creating artificial milk shortages in some areas of the United States. In Atlanta, the DTP resulted in local milk shortages that drove milk prices up 20 cents a gallon and butter up 20 cents a pound. Yet the shortages were temporary, since farmers expanded production in response to lucrative federal price guarantees. As *Successful Farming* reported in October 1987, shortly after the program's completion, "Texas, with a strong 16 percent buyout, has many new dairy herds moving in and is up 3 percent in production. Florida, with a 14 percent buyout, hiked production 3 percent."

As the General Accounting Office noted, "Total milk production did not decrease because nonparticipating farmers increased their production during the program period."[17] Shortly after the end of the program, in mid-1988, milk production was skyrocketing and once again heading for a record level. Between the first quarter of 1987 and the first quarter of 1988, government purchases of surplus milk doubled, reaching the equivalent of 4.2 billion pounds. Government purchases in the first half of the 1987–88 milk marketing year (July 1–June 30) exceeded the purchases of the entire previous year. Milk production increased 2.5 percent per cow in the past year, and dairy herds are rapidly expanding.[18] It is only a question of time until America needs another dairy termination program.

At the same time that congressmen tried one scheme after another to reduce dairy surpluses, the Farmers Home Administration (FmHA) lent tens of millions of dollars to farmers to boost dairy production. Farmers Home realized that dairy surpluses were glutting the markets, but since dairy subsidies were so generous, dairy profits were high, and thus loans to dairy farmers looked good on the FmHA's balance sheets. Or perhaps the FmHA only thought the ASCS needed more of a challenge.

Sideshow: USDA's Slaughter of the Cattle Markets

On March 29, 1986, the USDA announced that it would soon be sending 1.6 million dairy cows to slaughter—far more cows than anyone expected to be slaughtered under the dairy buyout program. The

USDA was surprised when this action devastated beef markets, costing ranchers scores of millions of dollars in losses and bankrupting some cattlemen.

The 1983–84 dairy buyout caused some disruption to the cattle industry, but less than had been expected, because fewer cows were executed than had been planned. When Don Butler, president of the National Cattlemen's Association, testified before the House Dairy Subcommittee in 1985, Congressman Coelho sneered, "Who created the impact [on cattle prices due to the 1984–85 buyout]? Who created the psychological impact? The point I tried to make with the cattlemen continuously was that you created it, because you kept on saying, 'the sky is falling, the sky is falling,' and the market believed you."[19] Coelho was hostile to the National Cattlemen's Association because cattlemen, who received no subsidies, complained that the dairy program was disrupting cattle markets—and Coelho loves dairy farmers.

Congress and the USDA share a dunce cap for wrecking the cattle market. Congress mandated in the 1985 farm bill that the USDA should dispose of at least 1.1 million dairy cattle, yet not adversely affect beef or pork prices. This is like ordering a soldier to fire a few rounds of his machine gun into a crowd while insisting that the bullets not hit anyone. The dairy buyout's effect on the cattle market illustrates how little the USDA understands the markets it dominates. Agriculture Secretary Richard Lyng said to Jim Moody, an agricultural lobbyist, a week after the USDA's announcement and the cattle market crash, "This is a terrible day. . . . My economists did not tell me this would happen." Since the USDA had run a similar dairy buyout program two years before that had also adversely affected cattle prices, one wonders about the department's learning curve. Perhaps the bureaucrats were simply following the USDA's eleventh commandment: Thou Shalt Not Learn from Thy Mistakes.

At the time of the USDA's announcement, many cattlemen had already sent their herds to market and could not pull them back. They had no choice but to accept the decimated prices. Beef-cattle prices in California plunged by between $100 and $120 a head—roughly 15 percent. Some ranchers were able to postpone selling their cows, but it cost them money for extra transportation charges, interest expense, and feeding costs, and endangered their credit rating. Pat Casper, an agricultural banker with First National Bank in Billings, Montana, declared two weeks after Lyng's bombshell that "from where I'm standing it looks like an absolute disaster. This has been the greatest injustice ever done to the cattle industry."[20] Max Thornton, a feedlot operator in Billings, Montana, noted, "What is strangling this industry is disruptions in the normal production flow, like this dairy buyout. Our prices are being made in Washington, and you never know what a politician is going to do next."[21]

One ranch that the DTP devastated belonged to Joe and Betty Buck, a middle-aged couple with a 589-acre wheat and cattle operation near Cherokee, Oklahoma. As the *New York Times* reported, the Dairy Termination Program drove down cattle prices just when Mr. Buck needed to pay a loan installment to the federal Farm Credit System. Buck "took an $84,000 loss just as [the] $61,000 land payment came due." Even though Buck said this was the first time in nineteen years he had not sent in his annual land payment, the Farm Credit System demanded immediate payment on his entire $542,000 debt. (Frank Naylor, the Farm Credit System administrator, admitted in early 1988 that it was the organization's practice to foreclose on any borrower who missed a single payment.)[22]

Both congressmen and the USDA responded by blaming the markets and the cattle industry. Several congressmen criticized the cattle futures market, implying that it was a conspiracy by traders rather than an act of government that wrecked the market. According to J. Darwin Carter, an ASCS official, "It is the Department's view and feeling that this market was an overreaction to the program." As usual, when the USDA and the market see things differently, the USDA announces that the market is wrong. Congressman Glenn English pressured Carter: "In recent history to your knowledge has USDA ever publicly admittedly they made a mistake?" Carter replied, "Not to my knowledge, Mr. Chairman."[23]

Daniel Amstutz, the undersecretary of the USDA, had an even more bizarre explanation, claiming that the USDA's plan was "to the extent possible, maintain normal seasonal marketing patterns of *dairy cattle*" (emphasis added).[24] The farm bill had clearly specified that the DTP should be designed to minimize "the effect of such program on the red meat markets," that is, for beef.

The USDA also defended itself by pointing out that it did eventually dispose of much of the extra beef it dumped on the cattle market. But Willard R. Sparks, president of Sparks Commodities, observed that the USDA "killed the [dairy] cattle for 8 weeks in a row, . . . before any beef was literally removed from the market. Reading the press releases . . . USDA seemed to say making a sale or talking to Brazil and killing the cattle, things balanced out, when there is a big time difference and the market is made by timing."[25] According to Chandler Keyes of the National Cattlemen's Association, the USDA "didn't try to know anything—they didn't try to find out the facts. Any number of those people from the top level down could have gotten the facts—but they didn't."[26]

Congressmen shrugged off the damage. Congressman James Jeffords commented at a House hearing in June 1987, "What happened the first three weeks [of the DTP] is very, very regrettable. . . . Twice I've been more than willing to bury the hatchet, but the cattlemen keep either printing articles, or doing things, which just raise the specter. . . ."[27] It was touching that Jeffords was "willing to bury the hatchet" after Congress and the USDA had buried a lot of cattlemen; some congressmen apparently feel it is very ungracious of the cattlemen to mention their wounds in public.

The slaughter of the cattle market illustrates that congressmen are far more devoted to campaign contributors than they are to the farmers per se. Though the USDA was giving many dairy farmers over a million dollars each to quit the business, most members of Congress opposed the payment of any compensation to injured cattlemen.

The Balkanization of American Milk Production

Federal dairy programs were launched in the 1930s, at a time when the road transportation network and refrigerated technology were comparatively backward. The goal of federal milk-marketing policy was to make each small geographical sub-area self-sufficient in milk: the balkanization of American milk production. The United States is divided into forty-four different milk fiefdoms, known as milk-marketing orders, and each fiefdom is restricted from selling milk to the other fiefdoms. Some parts of the United States are far better suited to dairy production than others; milk production costs roughly 50 percent more in Florida than in California. But in order to guarantee local self-sufficiency and maximize congressional support for the dairy program, the system mandates that Floridans must pay far higher dairy prices than Californians.

The milk-marketing orders constitute a massive, mindless apparatus designed almost solely to boost prices and prohibit competition. In 1977, the Justice Department called the orders "one of the most complicated arrangements that government has yet conceived." Senator Patrick Leahy quipped on milk marketing orders, "There are only three people in the nation who fully understand them, and they are not allowed to talk."[28] The Justice Department observed that, on the whole, "farmers all the way back to Wisconsin get a Florida price less transportation. . . . Consumers in the rest of the nation pay prices reflective of the most inefficient areas."[29] The General Accounting Office noted in March 1988, "As a result of legislative actions since 1980, marketing orders are playing an increasing role in influencing milk prices and attracting resources into milk production."[30] One USDA report notes that milk marketing orders exist "to assure the dairy farmer a reasonable maximum price for his milk."[31] Apparently, according to the USDA, farm prices are only "reasonable" if they are as high as possible.

The Capper-Volstead Act of 1922 exempted agricultural cooperatives from antitrust liability and made some parts of their operations tax-free. Milk-marketing cooperatives have a de facto license to monopolize milk marketing. The USDA has encouraged them, even helping to structure plans for a single nationwide milk-marketing cooperative. John Donahue noted in the *Atlantic Monthly* that the Capper-Volstead Act directs the USDA "to police the co-ops and forbid excessively high prices. But in the half-century since the law was passed, the USDA has never challenged a cooperative."[32] Milk cooperatives are not small businesses: Two milk cooperatives—Dairymen's Inc. and Associated Milk Producers Inc.—are large enough to be listed in the Fortune 500. In 1979, Congress prohibited the Federal Trade Commission from spending any tax dollars to prosecute dairy cooperatives for anticompetitive practices.

Congress and the USDA have increasingly sacrificed independent dairymen in order to protect and strengthen the huge dairy cooperatives who effectively write the marketing orders, which make it almost impossible for small dairymen to sell their milk directly to the public.

One small farmer complained, "We feed some milk to the calves. They say I have to weigh that every day and keep a record of how much. We buy small amounts of coffee cream and buttermilk as a service to our customers. They want me to account for every single half-pint of that." Another farmer complained that federal rules prevented him "from buying milk from his brother's adjacent farm as he has for years." When a *U.S. News and World Report* reporter asked a USDA assistant secretary, Richard Feltner, about marketing orders driving small farmers out of business, he replied, "That is always regrettable, but the real gut issue is whether you are going to have milk marketing orders or not."[33] In 1977, in a confidential report on dairy cooperatives, the USDA noted that "like the poor, rump groups and independent 'free riders' will always be with us."[34] USDA dairy specialist George Tucker told Phil Norman of the *Louisville Courier-Journal* in 1981 that, if it weren't for the USDA milk-marketing system, independents "would beat the dickens out of the dairy cooperative price," thereby supposedly creating an unstable market.[35] The USDA allows cooperatives to cast the votes for its members on marketing-order issues. Herbert L. Forest, the director of the Dairy Division, Agricultural Marketing Service, told the House Agriculture Committee in 1979, "Cooperatives justifiably do not want to place individual members under the pressure of . . . making frequent decisions as to whether an order program should continue, particularly when that vote is taken in the atmosphere of a controversial issue."[36] The USDA first pressures independents to join a cooperative—and then effectively rigs the voting rules so that the marketing order cannot be dissolved.

Milk marketing orders are replete with trivial distinctions designed to restrict competition and redistribute profits. For instance, on March 5, 1986, the Agricultural Marketing Service (AMS) announced it was terminating its restrictions on defining skim milk and butterfat used in milkshake mix as Class II milk in upper Florida (The USDA sets different prices for Class I and Class II milk).[37] On January 10, 1986, the AMS announced that it was changing the federally decreed price for milk used in infant feeding formulas that is not packaged in glass or all-metal containers in Georgia.[38] Rod Leonard of the Community Nutrition Institute notes, "The dairy division in the Agricultural Marketing Service believe that they can somehow play around with the nuances, they can manipulate markets, they can massage it, and because they are smarter than anybody else, they think they can get more income for dairy producers."[39]

Reconstituted Milk: The Essence of Agriculture Policy

Milk can easily be reduced to a powder that later can be reconstituted to taste almost exactly like fresh milk. *Regulation* magazine reported that "neither consumer taste-testers nor lab chemists can distinguish ordinary fresh milk from a blend of 70 percent reconstituted milk and 30 percent fresh milk."[40] Milk produced where costs are low can easily be dried, shipped to areas where costs of production are high, and reconstituted, allowing consumers to reap the benefits of America's most efficient dairy producers. Reconstituted milk is as nutritious as fresh milk, but is effectively banned by the federal government as a threat to the health of the U.S. dairy program. Milk marketing controls are supposedly justified by milk's perishability—and the government is fighting tooth-and-nail any innovation that would make milk less perishable.

In 1965, the USDA prohibited the sale of reconstituted milk for less than the price of fluid milk. Reconstituted milk had been selling for up to 30 cents a gallon less than the price of fresh milk. In Houston, "orders for regular milk increased 35 percent [almost overnight] after the reconstituted milk price rule took place."[41] Dairy industry officials defended the regulation in 1980 by claiming that, in the long run, "eliminating the rule would cost consumers more because it would damage the milk supply system and lower farm income."[42] The ban on reconstituted milk is a very expensive insurance policy in case earthquakes swallow up all of America's interstate highways tomorrow.

Reconstituted milk sacrifices the most-productive to the least-productive dairy farmers. If reconstituted milk were legalized, dairy farmers in the natural dairy regions of the United States could produce a surplus that would provide citizens in the South and elsewhere with much cheaper milk. But the dairy industry is based on having a strong dairy industry in as many congressional districts as possible—and thus reconstituted milk would weaken the dairy program's political foundation. Besides, the employees in the USDA's Agricultural Marketing Service are strongly opposed to reconstituted milk. Their jobs and careers are dependent on the USDA's continued restriction of free choice.

Alden Manchester, who is the USDA's leading expert on milk marketing orders and a senior economist in the USDA's Economic Research Service, warned that reconstituted milk "might well mean larger variations in retail prices than consumers are willing to accept. It would certainly not represent stability, as long as consumers did not regard whole milk and reconstituted milk as very close substitutes."[43] Dairy policy is based on the assumption that consumers are not smart enough or sturdy enough to handle fluctuating prices, and that high prices fifty-two weeks a year are better than prices that might fluctuate.

The USDA's Manchester also justifies banning reconstituted milk because the USDA must protect consumers against excessive innovation: "Too much innovation will result in markedly higher costs for a very large number of products, containers, and services, and costs would rise. Up to some point, lower marketing margins reflect efficiency and indicate better performance. Beyond that point, marketing firms would go bankrupt at such a rate that consumers could not obtain the product. In short, too much of anything is not a good thing."[44] Career civil servants who face almost no risk on their path to a generous pension at age fifty-five are the self-appointed judges of how much risk and innovation society can tolerate.

A USDA deputy assistant secretary, Karen Darling, wrote in early 1988 that legalizing reconstituted milk

> would result in negligible benefits to consumers, but would substantially reduce returns to dairy farmers. It was estimated that total consumer expenditures could decline by $186 million annually, that government purchases [of surplus milk] would decline by $165 million, and that dairy farmer returns would drop by $520 million, with the latter impact having a multiplier effect in terms of the economic loss to rural communities.[45]

This is a perfect example of how the USDA views the American economy: Consumers' and taxpayers' savings of $351 million are "negligible," while the $520 million loss to farmers of course has a "multiplier effect." The USDA seems to believe that no dollar can stimulate the economy unless it is first put into a farmer's pocket. Consumer savings would likely be over a billion dollars instead of $186 million, but if that proved to be the case, a USDA bureaucrat would likely announce that the losses to dairy farmers carried a "multiplier" of three, making the loss to the economy from reconstituted milk over $1.5 billion.

The ban against reconstituted milk is the essence of farm policy— prohibiting consumer choice and squandering resources solely to enrich relatively inefficient farmers. There is no argument justifying the ban on reconstituted milk that would not justify every state putting up a Maginot Line around its borders to keep out the products of every other state. There is no argument for being self-sufficient in milk that would not justify forcibly becoming self-sufficient in everything.

How would dairy marketing be different if the Mafia controlled the milk business? Independents who refused to pay protection money to the syndicate would be driven out of business. Carefully delineated local turfs would be carved out that had little or nothing to do with competitive advantages. Severe penalties would be imposed for violating a neighboring turf. Prices would be jacked up solely to boost profits. Politicians would be bribed to keep their mouths shut and to make sure that nobody interfered with the system. The only difference between the Mafia and the milk marketing system is that the Mafia operates for its own interest, while the USDA's milk marketing orders operate in the public interest.

Blockading Our Own Ports

The byzantine milk-marketing orders and the multibillion-dollar butter mountains are all designed with one goal: to protect consumers against shortages. This is a farce. Government first prohibits American consumers from purchasing cheese, butter, and nonfat dry milk from 80 percent of the world's dairy producers, and then concocts a system to "protect" consumers against a shortage generated by the remaining 20 percent.

Dairy imports are restricted under Section 22 of the Agricultural Adjustment Act of 1933, amended in 1935. Section 22 is described by one farm-subsidy advocate as "a device to allow domestic price support programs to function without the interference of unneeded and excessive imports." By closing the border to imports, Congress can drive domestic prices as high as dairy campaign contributions demand. It is absurd to speak of "the interference of unneeded and excessive imports" when many Americans cannot afford to buy milk. Imports are "unneeded and excessive" only because they would interfere with Congress' efforts to drive up dairy prices.

The dairy industry is one of the most protected in America. For some products, American farmers are among the world's most efficient and competitive. But most American dairy farmers are not competitive by international standards. Farmers in Australia and New Zealand can produce milk at less than half the cost for the average American farmer.

Nonfat dry milk and butter imports are banned, and cheese imports are limited by a strict quota to less than 2 percent of U.S. consumption. Even this level of protectionism—probably higher than that received by any nonagricultural U.S. industry—is not enough to satisfy the dairy lobby. Trade barriers keep American prices far above world prices, and federal support prices and marketing orders drive prices up even further.

The importation of casein, a dairy by-product used in pizza among other things, is one of the red herrings of the dairy lobby. The imports are valued at about $300 million a year—roughly 2 percent of the U.S. dairy market. Casein has been the great rallying cause of the dairy lobbies in recent years. Congressmen compete to see who can sound the most indignant about the "flood" of casein imports that are displacing the jobs of more than a thousand dairy farmers. Each year Congress has tried to abolish or at least restrict the trade. Somehow the debate never focuses on the fact that U.S. butter prices are triple those in the world market.

The dairy lobbies and many congressmen argue that it is important to insure that the United States be self-sufficient in dairy production. But there is really no more reason to protect the dairy industry than there is to protect any other industry. It makes no more sense to force Americans to pay triple the world price for butter than it does to force consumers to pay triple the world price for cars, computers, or coffee.

If a free dairy trade existed, many American dairy farms would survive and prosper, but the average costs of production would nosedive. Congressmen defend high U.S. dairy prices by pointing to the apparent high costs of production. Without the federal program, the average costs of production would be far lower, because more milk would be produced in areas suitable for dairy cows and less elsewhere.

The United States has become a leading dairy exporter in recent years, even though American dairy producers cannot compete on world markets. The USDA is spending three times the world dairy price to dump surplus U.S. butter, buying it from American farmers for $3,000 a ton and selling it overseas for $1,000 a ton. Dairy exports have tripled in the last three years. The huge dairy surpluses in the early 1980s were becoming embarrassing. It is in the dairy lobby's interest to export dairy products, even if U.S. taxpayers get eaten alive, so long as the result is a smaller dairy mountain in the United States. The dairy lobby pays none of the costs of dumping, and the resulting surpluses make it easier for the dairy lobby to raise the specter of imminent domestic shortages.

A War Against the Poor

Apparently, the more nutritious a food is, the more expensive politicians think it should be. Many state and local governments drive milk prices even higher than Congress demands. In New York City, as of early 1985, milk cost 84 cents a gallon more than it did in Connecticut and New Jersey. The New York State Department of Agriculture had severely restricted the right to sell milk at the wholesale level. Five milk processors dominated the Manhattan market, with its 3 million customers. According to Joseph Gerace, New York commissioner of agriculture and markets, "We want to make sure milk is available throughout the commercial network. . . . We don't want to go back to the same situation that we had when the law was put in place originally—milk shortages."[46] Because of isolated, temporary shortages of milk in the early 1930s, the New York Department of Agriculture and Markets is still driving up milk prices half a century later.

The *New York Times* reported that a dealer wishing to obtain a license to sell milk in New York City must undergo lengthy hearings run by the agriculture department, which decides whether the market is adequately served and whether the entry of another dealer would provoke destructive competition.[47] The state agriculture department's concept of "destructive competition" apparently includes anything that decreases dairy profits. New York's major milk distributors had been convicted two years earlier on charges of price fixing and conspiracy, and the New York Attorney General, Robert Abrams, discovered that milk dealers in New York City were meeting secretly to carve up the market and set wholesale prices. But the state agriculture department continued to insist that more milk distributors in New York would create "destructive competition."

In early 1987, after a judge struck down the New York milk-marketing controls, the price of milk on Staten Island fell by 60 cents overnight.[48] By July 1987 milk prices in New York City were 44 cents lower on the average than they had been in the previous year. The New York State Department of Agriculture and Markets retaliated by attempting to create a regional marketing system to provide farmers and cooperatives with a cartel that included heavy penalties for those who sold their milk for less than the approved price. In November 1987 Abrams struck down the regional marketing scheme as illegal, sending the agricultural bureaucrats back to the drawing board to devise new schemes to raise prices.

On a national level, the federal dairy program has spent over $15 billion since 1980, including the cost of buying surplus products, paying to kill cows, export subsidies, and so on. This works out to roughly $240 per American family. Thanks to import barriers and marketing order restrictions on internal dairy trade, dairy prices have been between 30 percent and 200 percent higher than they might otherwise have been. Rod Leonard of the Community Nutrition Institute estimates that federal policies, including price supports, marketing orders, and trade barriers, add $6 billion to $7 billion a year to the price Americans pay for dairy products.[49] This amounts to $50 billion dollars in higher consumer costs since 1980, or roughly $800 per American family. The combined cost of higher taxes and higher prices works out to more than $1,000—enough to buy a used dairy cow.

The dairy program costs taxpayers and consumers far more than it benefits dairymen. Subsidies have exceeded dairy profits every year during the 1980s. In 1985 the dairy program cost taxpayers and consumers roughly $8 billion, while dairy profits amounted to $3.6 billion. In 1986, with the Dairy Termination Program, dairy profits a-mounted to $5 billion; subsidies again cost taxpayers and consumers around $8 billion.[50] Unsubsidized cattle production, by contrast, was far more profitable. Total cattle profits were $6.4 billion in 1985 and $7.7 billion in 1986.

The USDA's Alden Manchester in 1982 dismissed criticism of the USDA policies by asserting that consumers are "in the aggregate, af-fluent," and thus capable of paying higher prices.[51] Though the "ag-gregate public" may be affluent, the USDA's policies have had a dev-astating affect on many low-income Americans. Federal, state, and local governments have done such a good job of preventing milk shortages that many poor people can no longer afford to drink it. By pegging prices so high, government helped sharply reduce milk con-sumption by the poor between 1960 and 1984. The poor, who spend a much higher percentage of their income on food, are hit harder by USDA-caused inflation.

Thanks largely to the dairy program, calcium has long been the nutrient that poor people lack most. A major study concluded in 1982 that the federal dairy program was the major reason for severe cal-cium shortages among low-income families.[52] Despite a hundredfold increase in federal food-assistance spending, the average poor person consumes less calcium now than he or she did in 1955.

Many congressmen are apathetic over the effect of high dairy prices on the poor, with a "Let them eat food stamps" attitude. In order that politicians can continue receiving campaign contributions, millions of low-income Americans are supposed to forfeit their inde-pendence and pride and go on welfare. Only 60 percent of low-income families eligible for food stamps accept them. Instead of ending wel-fare for farmers and making food cheaper for everyone, the govern-ment has launched repeated campaigns to pressure millions of low-in-come people to accept federal handouts. A 1975 USDA brochure an-nounced: "You are in good company. Millions of Americans use food stamps." Federally funded brochures distributed in Maryland in 1981 declared: "Did you know some people would rather STARVE than seek help . . . ?" On the inside, that brochure read: "PRIDE NEVER FILLS EMPTY STOMACHS. . . . Are you one of thousands of Mary-land residents who . . . have too much pride to consider applying for help? Then you need to know more about the Food Stamp program.

Food Stamps should not be confused with charity! In fact, food stamps are designed to help you help yourself."[53]

Congress has also attempted to buy off criticism of the dairy program by creating new programs to give away food. The Temporary Emergency Food Assistance Program (TEFAP) was created in 1982, and in many states it gave away free butter and cheese to anyone who asked for it. By 1984 more than $500 million pounds of dairy products were being given away each year. Since few TEFAP recipients were actually underfed, federal food donations simply displaced commercial food sales. For example, for every ten pounds of butter distributed, margarine sales fell by 7.7 pounds.[54] The National Association of Margarine Producers reported that the decrease in margarine sales displaced the use of 200 million pounds of soybeans, thereby sacrificing one farm group to another. But the program made Congress look benevolent, so a "temporary emergency" program is well on the way to becoming permanent.

Eggs share many of the market characteristics of dairy products, including perishability, yet there is no federal program for eggs—and no reports of egg shortages in the last ten years. Prices for eggs fluctuate sharply and consumer spending is adjusted accordingly. Over the past thirty years, the real price of eggs has fallen roughly 50 percent, while the price of milk has increased or stayed stable despite a sharp fall in its average cost of production.[55] As with eggs, the price of chicken meat has fallen sharply in recent decades, but the USDA's Manchester notes scornfully that the broiler industry "with its 150 contractors . . . [has] had no success in getting the production and price cycle under control."[56] Even though broiler producers are prospering and surviving without government handouts and retail chicken prices are falling in real terms, as long as the poultry industry does not have "the production and price cycle under control," the industry is apparently a failure according to the USDA.

The Coming Death of the Dairy Program

New technology could sharply lower the cost of milk production and thereby destabilize federal controls. According to the Congressional Office of Technology Assessment, new revolutions in dairy productivity will soon mean that 5,000 large dairy operations in California could provide all the milk the United States needs. Artificial insemination and embryo transfers are steadily boosting the productivity of the cows by between 2 and 4 percent a year. A new bovine growth hormone is improving productivity by up to 30 or 40 percent per cow. The Food and Drug Administration has concluded that there is no significant difference in milk from untreated cows and those treated with the hormone.[57] James Gramlich, the director of agricultural research at American Cyanamid, a leading developer of the hormone, observed that "the bottom line is that we ought to be able to sell milk a hell of a lot cheaper than we sell Coca-Cola."[58]

Many congressmen are mortified that the new technology could sharply lower the cost of milk production and thereby totally destabilize federal controls. Congressman Tony Coelho says, "Nobody has demanded that [dairy growth hormones] be developed. Consumer demand is not there; dairy industry demand is not there. It is 'progress' because of the potential tremendous profit. . . . It is all a question of greed. . . . My concern is that we are going to let the big get bigger." Coelho denounced corporate greed for discovering a new production method that could radically improve the quality of low-income diets. The Wisconsin secretary of state and the National Farmers Union are leading the charge against the bovine growth hormone.

The dairy program was created supposedly to provide stable dairy supplies, but the program has become a parody of its original intent. The dairy lobby's fight against increased dairy productivity is indicative of the mentality that federal protection induces. The dairy lobby is far more concerned about its welfare checks than its customers' needs.

As comparative advantage in dairy production in the United States is shifting, with California surpassing the traditional dairy states, Midwestern congressmen are now loudly advocating a supply-control system for dairy products, remodeling the dairy industry on the tobacco or peanut feudal model. This would mean far greater federal control, and would make it much easier to camouflage the program's cost—one more scheme to boost farmers' profits by destroying farmers' freedom. And it would prevent California from further expanding super-efficient dairy production. Congressman Patrick Leahy, chairman of the Senate Agriculture Committee, has proposed legislation to cut dairy price supports in specific areas that exceed their traditional surplus levels. This would be a direct assault on farmers with above-average production, and a de facto federal ban on higher productivity in the milk industry.

Congressman Steve Gunderson denounced a 1985 50-cent cut in dairy price supports by the USDA as "a blatant attempt to discourage the purchase of dairy products by the CCC."[59] If one believed that congressmen actually wanted to serve the public, Gunderson's comment would be pathological—since there is no public benefit in government-owned mountains of rotting butter and cheese. But since the dairy program is only redistribution via cows, Gunderson's comment makes sense. The dairy program is a blatant case of congressmen managing a large sector of the economy for their own personal benefit—as though the reason that God invented milk, cheese, and butter were to give deserving congressmen a tool to get themselves re-elected.

Chapter 7

The Conspiracy Against Competence

The Farmers Home Administration (FmHA) is a welfare agency that routinely destroys its clients' lives. Congress and the FmHA have effectively created tens of thousands of mini-Mexicos in rural America. By flooding America's least-competent farmers with easy credit and perpetual bailouts, Congress and the FmHA have spurred a boom-bust cycle in farmland values, helped bankrupt many farmers, created huge entry barriers for young farmers, driven up crop cost of production, and thereby undercut American exports. With each federal farm credit disaster, government dominance of agriculture credit has increased, and the federal government now effectively controls half of all farm debt.

Federal agricultural credit programs have been one of competent farmers' worst enemies. H. Allan Nation, editor of *Stockman* magazine, declared:

> These government [credit] programs have been the very thing that has killed the family farmer by raising the price of land, equipment and inputs to levels insupportable by honest farming. The influx of the millions of dollars of FmHA money had the same effect on honest farmers that the millions of dollars of "dope money" had upon small

businessmen in south Florida. There is no way to compete with a guy
playing by another set of rules.[1]

The Farmers Home Administration was created to help the struggling family farmer. It ended up bankrolling John DeLorean's deluxe
motor-car factory, providing $50 million to a single California farm
(now bankrupt), and giving almost a billion dollars in subsidized
loans to already-bankrupt farmers in 1985 alone. With the FmHA,
incompetence is an entitlement. Federal farm credit programs began
with politicians proclaiming that farmers are unfairly discriminated
against in the credit market, and mushroomed long after farmers
joined the ranks of the private sector's most-favored borrowers. The
result was a flood of credit and repeated disruptions of the agricultural economy. The General Accounting Office estimated in late 1988
that the FmHA had an accumulated operating deficit of $36 billion.[2]

Politicians have always viewed cheap credit for farmers as a magical, mystical panacea. Congressman Steve Gunderson observed in
1986: "If you want to increase [the] efficiency of a farm enterprise, give
them a low-interest loan and they'll be an efficient farmer."[3] No matter
how much money the FmHA squanders, Congress is never satisfied
and forces it to squander even more.

Federal agricultural credit programs are managed according to the
axiom that it is better for ten inept farmers to be kept in business at
any cost than that one incompetent farmer be forced to find a new
profession. Programs are based on the principle that need is the basis
of right—and that politicians are the best judges of need. Farm credit
programs are the most striking example of politicians' inability to allocate capital intelligently and productively to private enterprises. Politicians' inability to view farm credit rationally has devastated the
agricultural sector.

A Short History of Federal Credit Policies

Farmers and politicians have long mistaken the symptoms of farm
problems for the problems themselves. Since the 1880s, when many
farmers borrowed money at justifiably high interest rates to buy land
and put in crops, the political answer to every farm crisis has always
been more credit on easier terms. Farm-state politicians, anxious for

votes, continually proclaimed the terrible plight of farmers. But as Wheeler McMillen noted in his 1929 classic, *Too Many Farmers,* "Agriculture's credit was gravely injured by overemphasis upon the industry's difficulties."[4]

Before the turn of the century, farmers loudly complained because they had to pay high interest rates on their debts. But farm bankruptcy rates were higher then than now, so it was understandable that poor credit risks would have to pay relatively high interest rates. The problem often was not that the farmer could not get a loan, but that he had to pay back the loan that he got. Farmers spent part of their time demanding a federal bank to provide them with cheap credit and the rest of their time calling for free silver or a flood of paper money to spur inflation and wipe out their debts.

The Federal Land Bank was authorized in 1916—at a time when American agriculture was more prosperous than ever before and when ample private credit was available for creditworthy farmers. The Federal Land Bank pumped hundreds of millions of dollars of cheap credit into the farm economy at a time when farmland values were already booming. The Federal Land Bank helped send farmland into orbit, exactly as the federal government did in the 1970s. Cassius M. Clay, author of *The Mainstay of American Individualism,* wrote in 1934, "Farm debt is an evil consequence of too much credit supplied at the wrong time."[5] President Coolidge, in his 1927 State of the Union Address, suggested that bankers "reduce credit to farmers to avoid financing an acreage manifestly too large."[6]

In the early 1920s, as in the 1980s, crop prices declined from historic highs and farmland values crashed. Many farmers were stuck with loans borrowed on the value of farmland that was no longer worth as much as the loan. Farm lobbies persuaded the national media and a majority of congressmen that agriculture was fundamentally unstable and required massive federal assistance. The high bankruptcy rate resulting from the land-value decline between 1919 and 1926 helped pave the way for the federal takeover of agriculture between 1929 and 1933.

The Government and the Land-Value Crash of the 1980s

It is not possible to understand the state of agriculture in the 1980s without examining the massive expansion of government credit programs in the 1970s. The more capital that government has injected, the less stable agriculture has become.

By the 1960s, agricultural economists were complaining of the overcapitalization of agriculture that led to perpetual surpluses that perennially depressed crop prices. William Lesher, the USDA's chief economist, noted, "During the 1960s, an average of 55 million acres per year were removed from production [by USDA programs] while at the same time FmHA loans for real estate were increasing at a 20 percent annual rate."[7] Despite ample private credit available for agriculture, federal farm credit programs exploded during the 1970s and early 1980s—helping to create a huge artificial boom in the farm economy, which contributed to the agricultural recession of the early to mid-1980s. (Private banks also jumped on the bandwagon to provide easy credit to farmers.) It was simply, "Give a loan, buy a vote" agricultural economics. By injecting huge quantities of cheap credit into a sector of the economy that already had enough capital, the government helped cause a boom and eventually a crash in the land market.

Between 1971 and 1983, the loan volume of the Farm Credit System (FCS) soared from $14.8 billion to $82 billion, while loan volume of the FmHA increased fivefold. Jonathan L. Fiechter of the Office of the Comptroller of the Currency observed, "From 1976 to 1981, farm debt doubled. The bulk of this lending came from the Federal Government and the farm credit system."[8] Charles Riemenschneider of Chemical Bank (and currently staff chairman of the Senate Agriculture Committee) noted, "The share of farm lending supplied by government agencies rose to 48 percent by 1982 from 33 percent in 1972."[9] Between 1975 and 1984, total FmHA farm debt increased from $5 billion to $27 billion, and the FmHA's 1979 annual loan volume was fifty times greater than its 1960 loan volume.[10]

The Farm Credit System, a system of federally guaranteed, farmer-owned banks, continually lobbied Congress to allow it to lend more and more money to farmers based on less and less collateral. Until 1971, the FCS could lend to farmers an amount equal to 50 percent of the borrower's collateral. After 1971, loans were made for up to 85 percent of the borrower's net worth, at rates that were often 4 or 5 percentage points below those of commercial banks. As the *Washington Post* noted, all FCS borrowers were "charged the same interest rate in a given area regardless of their relative creditworthiness, with the rate kept as low as possible relative to the system's cost of acquiring funds to lend."[11] Thus, FCS policies favored uncreditworthy borrowers.

In 1978 the American Agricultural Movement descended on Washington and tore up the Mall with their tractors. Farmers let loose a herd of goats on the floor of the House of Representatives, while other farmers forced their way into USDA headquarters and reportedly chased the secretary of agriculture, Bob Bergland, down the hall. (Bergland escaped through a window.) Congress saw the light and passed the Emergency Agricultural Credit Act of 1978.

The FmHA began making "economic emergency" loans, at 5 percent interest, that could be used to repay other loans or for whatever else the farmer wanted. The official definition of the term *economic emergency* for FmHA loans was "a general tightening of agricultural credit or an unfavorable relationship between production costs and prices received for agricultural commodities, causing widespread need among farmers for temporary credit." The loans were limited to $400,000 per borrower and almost any farmer "in economic stress due to unavailability of credit or cash-flow difficulties" was eligible. The act's definitions of economic stress and unavailability of credit were such that almost any uncreditworthy farmer who had been denied federal credit in the past could now qualify. And once a farmer qualified, he was automatically eligible for subsidized loans for five years. The year 1978—in which Congress proclaimed the economic emergency in agriculture—turned out to be one of the most profitable in history for farmers.

The 1978 act prevented any adjustment from occurring in agriculture, and thus guaranteed that the eventual shakeout would be much worse. The FmHA lent more than $5 billion in "economic emergency" loans, and by 1980 more than half of the loans were already delinquent. FmHA employees were given lending goals to reach; their careers depended on how much subsidized government money they could foist on farmers. There was almost no examination of a farmer's ability to repay, since the FmHA assumed that land values would continue soaring forever. As Vance Clark, FmHA's administrator in 1988, describes it, FmHA officials would call up farmers and say, "Hey, do me a favor. Take $75,000."[12]

Until 1979, interest rates on FmHA loans to buy real estate were fixed at 5 percent, thus providing a huge subsidy to people who wanted to buy farmland. In the late 1970s, several states issued tax-free agricultural bonds to provide loans with interest rates below prime rates to farmers to buy more farmland. In Louisiana, the state government paid half of a beginning farmer's interest costs when he bought farmland. The FmHA vigorously endorsed and promoted Aggie bonds, and thus, by injecting more and more money for chasing the same amount of cropland, helped send farmland prices into orbit.

In 1980, at the height of the land boom, Congress authorized the Farm Credit System to make loans for up to 97 percent of the appraised value of a farmer's assets. Land values had already tripled in the previous decade, and this reform flooded the farm economy with even more cash. As a *Wall Street Journal* editorial noted: "The 1980 liberalization was lobbied for by extension services, land-grant colleges, the whole universe of farm-fed enterprises. It is no surprise that so much of that universe now sees it as a normal evolution for the system to be brought under pervasive national control."[13]

In late 1980 and early 1981, land prices began to fall—and eventually plummeted by over 50 percent in Iowa, Nebraska, and Minnesota. Yet throughout it all, politicians and the federal government continued signaling farmers to stay in the business, announcing one rescue plan after another, and kept promising that they could see the light at the end of the tunnel. FmHA loan volume increased every year until 1986. As a result, many young farmers who should have sold out early when the farm economy began to decline held on until their entire net worth was erased and they had no choice but bankruptcy.

The federal injections of credit into agriculture meant a huge accumulation of farmers' debt and a huge increase in their annual interest payments—but little increase in their productivity, because most of the debt was spent bidding up the price of farmland. The skyrocketing land values of the late 1970s were largely a result of massive injections of federal credit, government-caused inflation, and, though to a much lesser extent, unwise lending by commercial bankers. The USDA promoted and financed massive farmland speculation. Then, when the land market crashed, the only cure was more government power.

Farmers Home Administration: A Comedy of Errors

The Farmers Home Administration is perhaps the most inept agency in a very inept department. The FmHA usually never knows what it is doing until the General Accounting Office comes in and tells it. Much of the incompetence is due to congressional mandates, though the FmHA has contributed a great deal of its own.

The FmHA's motto is: "Through no fault of their own." Senator Patrick Leahy, chairman of the Senate Agriculture Committee, declared, "The FMHA is a bulwark in our defense against farm bankruptcy and foreclosure."[14] Many agricultural committee congressmen judge the FmHA simply by the farm bankruptcy rate: If farm bankruptcies are low, the FmHA is a success; if farm bankruptcies are high, the FmHA has failed. The easy solution is to give the FmHA enough money so that no one goes bankrupt except by divine wrath.

The FmHA exists as a lender of last resort to provide credit to farmers who were supposedly unable to obtain private credit. *Creditworthy* simply means that an individual is judged by at least one other human being on earth as being sufficiently competent, intelligent, and trustworthy to entrust with the temporary use of other people's money. A contempt of creditworthiness means that politicians believe that only they themselves, and bureaucrats, should determine who will have use of other people's dollars. Government rakes in people's dollars in taxes and then gives the money to farmers whom no individual would trust with his own money.

The FmHA's main achievement has been to redistribute farmland from creditworthy to uncreditworthy borrowers. The FmHA is based on the idea that taxpayers should effectively pay for giveaways of farmland to farmers who have not even proved that they can farm rented land successfully. The FmHA insures that uncreditworthy farmers get capital on better terms than do creditworthy farmers.

Since the FmHA provides heavily subsidized loans, it is the lender of first choice for many farmers. Many FmHA offices do not bother to determine whether borrowers can get money elsewhere—and many borrowers also receive credit from private sources. This makes a farce of the agency's purpose, but as long as the money flows, politicians don't complain. And after a person once qualifies for FmHA credit, the agency tends to continue financing him until the cows come home.

As a recent USDA study noted, "FmHA credit assistance to farmers has generally and gradually evolved toward providing credit to all farmers who for various reasons are unable to obtain credit elsewhere. The subsistence and large-scale operations are equally eligible for a loan if credit is not available elsewhere at reasonable terms."[15] The FmHA, though it was created to help family farmers, currently has subsidized loans outstanding to hundreds of corporations. Apparently, uncreditworthy corporations are as deserving as uncreditworthy individuals.

Mississippi has received more FmHA loans than any other state except Texas. Among the needy farmers who have received FmHA subsidies in Mississippi are the lieutenant governor, a former governor, a member of the National Republican Committee, nine state representatives, and two state circuit court judges. When the FmHA director, Pete Perry, tried to block a $657,000 loan to a politically powerful farmer who had already borrowed $7.4 million and fallen $4.3 million behind in repayments, he was quickly fired. The next FmHA director quickly gave the farmer two-thirds of a million dollars.[16] In 1984 the state's FmHA director also served as a private attorney for one of the agency's largest borrowers.

An excellent investigation in 1983 by Gannett News Service reporters Mark Rohner and Dennis Camire pointed out that the FmHA lent a million dollars to a rich Mississippi real-estate speculator who used the money to pay off his other debts; lent $11 million to an inept farm company whose top officer was convicted of defrauding the bank of which he was president (and then, with a Christian turning of the other cheek, lent the company another $3.7 million after the man had finished his six months in prison); and lent a million dollars to an enterprising individual who persuaded a FmHA loan officer that he could get rich by playing the commodities futures market—and lost it all.[17]

The FmHA's credit policies are totally divorced from financial reality. One Mississippi farmer was almost debt-free when he accepted a low-interest disaster loan for $41,300. This made him automatically eligible for subsidized disaster loans in the following four years. By 1983, the farmer owed FmHA $661,000, and had a negative net worth of more than half a million dollars. So the FmHA gave him another $204,000 to put in another crop and stay on the land for one more year.[18]

Rohner and Camire noted that in Washington County, Mississippi, one FmHA supervisor told federal auditors that he "was too busy making new loans to evaluate" how a farmer was using the $1.7 million he received from the FmHA. When the farmer went bankrupt, the FmHA supervisor told auditors that he was "too busy" to put liens on the farmer's equipment.[19]

FmHA "generosity" has disrupted many rural Mississippi towns:

> In the community of Drew, Mississippi, blunt-spoken Mayor W. O. "Snake" Williford thinks his area faces a desperate farm debt crisis today in part because of the liberal FmHA loan policies Congress has decreed. They have led some farmers "down the path to ruin," Williford said. "FmHA loaned some money they shouldn't have loaned to people that shouldn't have had the money. You're not doing them a favor when you lend them more than they can repay."[20]

The FmHA's generosity split the farming community. As farmer Alex Ramsay who farms in Mount Olive, Mississippi, complained,

> the program has split the farming community between the "FmHA farmers" and bank farmers. Those of us who worked for years to build equity in our operation and credit at the bank suddenly found the poorest managers—or those who had never farmed anything more than a pea patch—were overnight wonders with the biggest tractors, newest combines, fanciest trucks and bid up land rents far beyond their value, all paid for with money they had not earned and had neither the ability nor intent to repay.[21]

In 1983 the Inspector General of the USDA reported that FmHA official policy was to make loans to farmers who could not repay previous debts and had "little or no chance" of repaying new debts. FmHA Administrator Charles Shuman defended his action:

> If the Agency had taken a firm stand against all its delinquent borrowers and had forced large numbers of those borrowers out of business . . . it would have aroused political concerns which might very well have resulted in legislation mandating the Agency to temporarily cease all foreclosure actions, provide moratoriums on loan repay-

ments, forgive principals, or mandate other unsound credit management policies. . . . [22]

In other words, if the FmHA did not waste money voluntarily, Congress might pass a law that forced it to waste it. In order to prevent
Congress from dictating "unsound credit management policies" to the
FmHA, Shuman beat Congress to the punch and thereby saved the
honor of the Reagan administration. Shuman apparently resolved
never to let Congress take taxpayers' money alive. As one federal
expert commented, FmHA policy is, "You can't repay your loans—so
here's another one."[23]

One of the FmHA's more memorable successes involved a $50-
million loan to some California flim-flam men. Bob Cox and Ronald
Campbell reported in the *Bakersfield Californian* that the FmHA provided over $50 million to Tex-Cal Land Management, Inc., of Delana,
California.[24] In some ways, this loan project will turn out better than
other FmHA loans because the FmHA might recover as much as $10
million after Tex-Cal bankruptcy proceedings are completed. Though
FmHA borrowers are supposed to be incapable of borrowing in the
private sector, Tex-Cal had borrowed $7 million from Aetna Life and
Casualty Insurance Company only a few months before receiving its
first FmHA loan. The company owned little or nothing, though it did
have leases for 7,000 acres of vineyards and almond orchards. Much of
the land was in poor condition and much of the "agricultural" land
was bulldozed after Tex-Cal finished using FmHA money to "improve" it. Bud Steele, Tex-Cal's manager, commented at the company's trial: "I've always been amazed how FmHA could loan money
to a corporate shell with no assets."

Michael Asher, an independent appraiser, was employed by the
FmHA and then fired after he mentioned flagrant inaccuracies in Tex-
Cal's claims about the boundary of its land. In 1985 Asher said, "The
FMHA didn't give a damn whether we have good legal descriptions
or not. The agency's attitude was 'Don't confuse me with facts. Just let
me loan money.'" The FmHA office in Kern County did not even have
an accountant to check the farmers' figures. Cox and Campbell reported, "The agency told its appraisers not to bother calculating yield
per acre in their loan evaluations, appraiser Michael Asher said. The
FmHA also told its customers to complete repayment forms, a job
normally done by bank credit analysts. The FmHA brought in special

'loan experts' but one local farm finance expert commented, 'Some of them didn't know what a cotton plant was.'"[25]

The *Bakersfield Californian* reported:

> Tex-Cal Land management got its first three loans July 16, 1979. About five and a half months later, it missed the first installment of $504,000 and began pleading for more money. The FmHA didn't blink an eye when Tex-Cal Land Management first failed to pay.
>
> When Tex-Cal Land management returned for another $9.4 million in 1982, Administrator Shuman decided to crack down. . . . As conditions for a $5 million loan, he insisted Tex-Cal Land Management submit to an independent audit, stop using federal money to plant new vineyards and orchards, accept FmHA supervision of its bank account and crop proceeds and acknowledge that "this is the last loan FmHA intends to make."
>
> It is clear now that FmHA officials realized as early as 1983 that they had a problem on their hands. At that point, Tex-Cal Land Management had borrowed more than $30 million, and had paid back virtually none of it. But then FmHA Administrator Charles Shuman approved an additional $6 million in crop loans that year after laying down strict conditions, including an audit of the company's books. But no audit was done.
>
> And despite Shuman's earlier warnings, Shuman authorized what eventually would amount to $15.2 million in "protective advances" in late March 1982.[26]

The FmHA suffers from internal blindness. As Gannett's Rohner and Camire reported, "FmHA's internal procedures are so cumbersome that the guys on the firing line—the FmHA county supervisors who must okay the loans—often need a crystal ball to interpret headquarters' pronouncements. Recently, FmHA officials in Washington proudly told auditors that their loan officers in farm counties now stress managing loans already made, rather than handing out new ones. So the auditors asked the FmHA county supervisors. About half—81 of 172—hadn't gotten the word."[27] The FmHA draws up a Farm and Home Plan for every farm applicant to help them with their family finances. "But a 1983 audit found 102 of 202 plans surveyed were inaccurate or unrealistic—'worthless' in the auditors' words. Some plans, they said, were 'so obviously inaccurate or unrealistic [as] to appear deliberately manipulated to establish eligibility for additional loans.'"[28]

The FmHA is founded on the idea that everybody deserves one more chance to succeed—with someone else's money. But according to the agency's own records, by far the most frequent cause of bank-ruptcy among its borrowers is "poor farming practices, such as inade-quate care of livestock or crops."[29] For instance, the FmHA provided several loans to one Wisconsin dairyman. "FmHA file documents indi-cate [that] the borrower was not completing necessary farm work and not properly caring for the dairy cows. Many cows died. . . . "[30] Sur-veys by the General Accounting Office found routine cases of FmHA borrowers "planting crops on land too poor for good production" and "inadequate fertilization and weed and insect control."[31]

According to the FmHA's own records, almost a quarter of the bankruptcies among borrowers from the FmHA are due in large part to having received too many FmHA loans.[32] The FmHA makes one loan to a borrower, and then lends more and more, piling up the debts until the borrower drowns. It is likely that FmHA records seriously underestimate the number of borrowers it has sunk. The FmHA is encouraging struggling farmers to continue farming until they finan-cially destroy themselves. As of early 1986, the average FmHA bor-rower had a net worth of $73,000. Eighty-five percent of FmHA bor-rowers were losing money farming. Their average annual negative cash flow was $56,000. If the average FmHA borrower had sold out at the beginning of 1986, he could have left farming with a cash sum greater than net worth of the typical American family. But at the then-current average loss rate, had he kept farming, he would have been bankrupt within sixteen months.[33] The GAO surveyed FmHA bor-rowers and found that their average net worth declined by 62 percent between 1984 and 1986.

The average FmHA farm borrower in 1985 had a debt-to-asset ratio of 83 percent—compared to 26 percent for all farmers. A debt-to-asset ratio of over 40 percent is usually considered a danger sign, according to the Economic Research Service of the USDA. In 1986, new FmHA borrowers had a debt-to-asset ratio of 70.6 percent—which meant that, for most of them, instead of staying in farming until they had a negative net worth, they should probably have sold out while they still had titles to their houses.[34] Many farmers who might have survived if they had only rented farmland in the early 1980s instead received FmHA loans to buy their own farms—and then were wiped out when farmland values crashed.

FmHA borrowers face the same problem that Third World governments have when they borrow cheap money from the World Bank. The average uncreditworthy farmer is unlikely to be using the government money productively enough so that he can pay back the debt-service costs and the loans itself. If the farmer had put his cheap FmHA loan into a certificate of deposit paying high interest rates, he would be assured of profiting from the FmHA's generosity. A loan even at a low interest rate is of no benefit if the borrower cannot use the principal productively. Even a subsidized interest rate will require some increase in productivity if the debt is to be serviced. Debt-service payments for a large FmHA loan often equal half of a farmer's costs of production; thus, overnight, the farmer has a huge new cost.

Like Mexico, the farmer then faces endless debt reschedulings and repeated de facto defaults—always struggling, never able to get his head above the water, always postponing his financial doom. General Accounting Office analyst Brian Crowley notes that "some of these people are borrowing themselves into oblivion. They continue to borrow, and to borrow, until they burn up what little equity they have left. At that point they are forced to leave farming and have nothing to show for their years of hard work."[35] The FmHA does farmers no good by throwing them a lifesaver made of lead.

The FmHA has a "buy-back" program for farmers who have lost their farms. By law, the person who defaulted on his FmHA loan has the first option to buy the land again, and is eligible for additional subsidized FmHA loans each year. The FmHA sells the land back to the farmer who defaulted at a much lower price the second time—a price at which the farmer could supposedly generate a cash flow, that is, where the profits from farming will allow the farmer to service his debts. The FmHA's estimates of cash flow are notoriously inaccurate and usually err in the borrower's favor. Thus, many farmers are rewarded for losing the first farm that taxpayers gave them with another quarter million dollars of taxpayers' money to buy the farm and role the dice again.

The FmHA's delinquent-debt load is now decreasing, largely because the FmHA is writing off much of its borrowers' debt. As a Senate Agriculture report on the Agriculture Credit Act of 1987 noted: "To be eligible for FmHA debt restructuring, the delinquency must be due to circumstances beyond the control of the borrowers . . . [including] declines in farm prices, farm income, and farmland value."[36] Congress says: "We will give you this loan at a subsidized interest rate—but if farm prices decline, you don't have to pay us back." Do housing loans contain a clause that says borrowers don't have to pay banks back if housing values fall? Do car loans contain a clause that says the borrower's obligations are waived if the car has a flat tire?

Recipients of FmHA subsidies are chosen largely by local county committees of farmers. But according to the FmHA (in a response to a query from the Senate Agricultural Committee), "We have had, and still have, cases where a county committee has been coerced into determining an applicant eligible by the pressure the applicant can bring to bear in a community. As a result of this action, ineligible applicants receive FmHA assistance."[37] Congress, instead of reforming the county committee system, gave it much more power in 1987. Now, if a farmer is turned down for a loan by his local FmHA committee, he can appeal their decision to the state FmHA committee. But if the local committee certifies an individual as eligible for a loan, the state committee has no power to overturn the decision.

The Farmers Home Administration has a Farm Ownership Outreach Program directed to "socially disadvantaged individuals" and designed to persuade Hispanics, blacks, native Americans, Asian-Americans, and Indian and Pakistani immigrants to apply for subsidized loans to go into farming. A member of these groups can qualify for aid more easily because the government considers them to be "socially disadvantaged." With such criteria for loans, there should be no shortage of farm bankruptcies in the 1990s.

As administrator, Vance Clark made an honorable effort to clean up the FmHA's mess. Congressman Jamie Whitten recently rewarded Clark for his efforts by slashing Clark's personal office budget. As Clark observes, some FmHA applicants "don't even possess the basic farming ability—they are selling used cars and they decide to come to us and become a farmer."[38] Kathleen Lawrence, formerly a USDA deputy assistant secretary, noted, "In many other small businesses you start out working for somebody else, you salt away your money so that someday you can open your own business. When you do start your business, you lease your office space, you lease your computers and then eventually you buy your own computers and your own office buildings."[39] But farming is different—or at least Congress thinks so.

When the Farmers Home Administration proposed limiting loans to borrowers who defaulted on previous FmHA loans, the Senate Agriculture Committee condemned the FmHA for attempting the "disenfranchisement" of eligible borrowers. But to speak of disenfranchisement of uncreditworthy subsidized borrowers implies that the Senate Agriculture Committee believes some individuals have an innate right to waste other people's money by playing farmer. Bruce Van Sickle, a federal district judge, barred the FmHA from foreclosing on borrowers in 1983, claiming that one of the foreclosure forms was unconstitutional because it lacked enough information to satisfy "due process." Van Sickle's decision was a landmark in advancing the rights of welfare recipients to taxpayers' dollars. No judge will ever strike down an IRS tax form for lack of "due process," but government handout recipients apparently have far greater constitutional rights than do the taxpayers who provide the handouts.

The FmHA is still subsidizing more people to charge into farming even though it is obvious that parts of the industry are already overcrowded. But if the FmHA had stopped lending when agriculture became less viable, bureaucrats would have no excuse for a job. The FmHA has a rural-housing lending program. An audit conducted by the USDA inspector general concluded, "We found that many FmHA field personnel were reluctant to classify urban areas as ineligible due to the resulting decrease in loan making activity."[40] The programs come to exist for the benefit of FmHA employees rather than to achieve their intended goal.

The Farmers Home Administration acts as if tax dollars were made to be burnt. The USDA inspector general's report noted that the FmHA was making no effort to collect on almost a billion dollars in defaults on guaranteed loans because the FmHA's national office believed "that losses on guaranteed loans were too small to be concerned about." One defaulting borrower in Texas who wanted to repay his FmHA loan was told by the FmHA to repay the financial institution instead, and then made no effort to recover the payment from the financial institution.[41] Under one loan program, the FmHA makes loans to farmers who are not eligible for FmHA credit so that they can purchase farms in the FmHA's inventory. But the FmHA,

unlike a sober private bank, does not require the verification of financial information on loan applications. The natural result: massive losses and endless scams.[42]

The FmHA is now the nation's largest owner of farms, with an
inventory of almost 20,000 properties. Regrettably, the FmHA is
managing farmland with the same suave talent it applies to credit
programs. It is leasing out hundreds of thousands of acres of farmland
that it has acquired. The USDA inspector general found that 90 percent of FmHA county offices had no formal system of monitoring
leases and that many leases were unpaid "because county supervisors
forgot about the lease payments."[43] Property acquired by the FmHA
often deteriorates so badly that it depresses the value of its surround-
ings. The FmHA makes little effort to sell the properties it has acquired. Only 9 percent of FmHA surplus property was listed with
realtors, even though FmHA personnel admit that they have no time
to sell it. Often the only sales effort is a For Sale sign posted on the
property. Congressman Jim Lightfoot discovered that the FmHA was
refusing to take bids on property above the asking price—another
breakthrough in bureaucratic efficiency.[44]

The FmHA is based on the idea that nobody ever suffered from a
cheap loan. But many FmHA programs are fundamentally idiotic. The
agency offers rural families thirty-year loans to buy trailer homes,
even though most trailers die before age fifteen. Sheldon Rose, a real
estate developer in Michigan, notes: "Thirty-year financing for mobile
homes is totally unrealistic. Some trailer parks ban trailers older than
seven years because the older homes become so tacky looking."[45] The
FmHA has a dwelling-retention program to provide low-interest loans
of up to $300,000 for foreclosed farmers to retain their homes. In some
parts of the country $300,000 can buy a mansion—and thus taxpayers
are forced to pay for some farmers to live in houses far nicer than
those the taxpayers themselves can afford. The FmHA has a special
program to lend money at an interest rate of 1 percent to build housing for farm labor. But other USDA programs pay the same farmers to
idle their land and throw farm workers out of jobs—and the new,
FmHA-subsidized housing goes vacant.

Congressmen feel that it is better for an individual to be a failing
farmer than a competent carpenter, truck driver, or salesman. Politicians want the FmHA to keep farmers in business at any cost—

sometimes regardless of whether or not the individual should stay in farming. Congressman Byron Dorgan reacted strongly to reports that the FmHA had advised some farmers to quit farming: "What kind of a government is it that counsels agriculture's future to get out of agriculture? That says to young farmers, 'You ought to quit'? That is not a government that has its priorities right."[46]

The FmHA provides a homestead protection plan to insure that bankrupt farmers can keep their homes and up to ten adjoining acres. The Senate Agriculture Committee report on the 1987 Farm Credit Act amendments complained: "Many [bankrupt farm] borrowers left to look for work without realizing that to be eligible for homestead protection they must continuously occupy their homes."[47] Apparently the Senate Agriculture Committee believes that instead of going to find a job, the ex-farmer needs a bounty to get him started again. Senators apparently would prefer the ex-farmer to stick around forever so that Congress can continue buying his vote, rather than going out and starting a new life.

The FmHA has done far more harm than good for farmers. Most FmHA borrowers are losing money and heading for bankruptcy—and will be saved only by a general forgiveness of loans. Many other farmers have been hurt by the higher rents and higher land values caused by the FmHA, and all nonFmHA farmers have been hurt by the FmHA's subsidizing more surplus production.

The 1987 Farm Credit Reform

In the name of kindness, the future creditworthiness and productivity of American farmers is being sold down the river. Thanks to the Agriculture Credit Act of 1987, the FmHA and the Farm Credit System are now more welfare than credit agencies. Since these two government entities jointly hold over half of all farm debt, their policies will be a major impediment to the efficiency of American agriculture. The FmHA's stratospheric delinquency rate and the perennial mismanagement of the Farm Credit System should have been sufficient proof of government's inability to intelligently manage farm credit. Yet the 1987 farm credit bailout was designed to sharply increase government's dominance of agricultural credit, and will likely cost taxpayers at least $10 billion.

When the FmHA announced in April 1988 that it would be writing off almost $9 billion in loans to farmers, the news sparked a backlash from many farmers who had struggled to stay current with their debts. Bernard Cohrs, who farms in Dickinson County, Iowa, was outraged because while he struggled along with an old pickup truck and made his loan payments, the officers of Terafact Inc., a local corporation that had recently had its FmHA loan restructured, were driving brand-new Mercedes.[48] Jerome and Kathryn Berg, a farm couple in Sigourney, Iowa, complained in a letter to Congressman Joseph Dio-Guardia, who led a fight in the House of Representatives against FmHA debt forgiveness: "Many of those with debt write-downs are again buying more land and expensive equipment, cars, trucks, and living it up while the rest of us who paid our bills and lived within our means are now expected to help bail them out."[49] Robert A. Dreyep, a farmer in Fenton, Iowa, complained that the FmHA is "rewarding the poor managers who are also very inefficient farmers."[50] Robert B. Delano, the president of the Virginia Farm Bureau, observed: "The only reason I can figure [for the FmHA's debt forgiveness] is this is an election year."[51] Oscar T. Blank, the director of the FmHA in Indiana, declared: "As a farmer, I'm unhappy about it. We already have huge surpluses, yet here we are keeping farmers producing. We may have too many farmers in this country and this is just going to keep the inefficient ones on the land."[52]

Congressmen defend the multibillion-dollar FmHA loan write-off campaign by claiming that it is cheaper for government to write off the loans than to foreclose on delinquent farmers. The FmHA is only supposed to forgive loans when the gesture would save money for the government. But Congress has mandated a method of calculating costs that is heavily biased in favor of loan forgiveness. Local FmHA offices are notorious for greatly overestimating farmers' probable future income in considering them for new FmHA loans, and the same method is being used to justify the forgiveness of loans. Farmers whose FmHA loans are forgiven are effectively entitled to more subsidized FmHA loans in the future—yet Congress has forbidden the FmHA from considering the cost of future loans to the same borrowers in its comparison of the probable costs of foreclosure and debt forgiveness.

The 1987 bailout vastly expanded the so-called borrowers' rights enjoyed by debtors who do not pay back government-guaranteed loans from both the FmHA and the Farm Credit System. Congressman James Jeffords said: "We ought to give farmers a better opportunity than they would get from commercial banks in the event that they go through hard times. . . . "[53] At the same time that the government is taking more energetic steps to collect overdue student loans, the congressional agricultural committees are making it increasingly difficult, if not impossible, to collect overdue farm loans. "Borrowers' rights" essentially mean that farmers are entitled to other people's money with little or no obligation to pay it back. Kathleen Lawrence, former USDA deputy assistant secretary who supervised farm credit programs between 1983 and 1987, observed: "If you end up having the kind of lawsuits filed against the Farm Credit System and restraining orders to prevent foreclosures in place, then you will end up turning the farm credit system into another Farmers Home Administration."[54] Vance Clark noted: "We are the only agency in government that is prohibited from using private debt-collection agencies."[55]

To understand what effect the new federal laws will have, consider Minnesota, which enacted a farm credit bailout similar to the federal bailout in 1986. As Robert Bennett of the *New York Times* reported in 1987:

> James Vermilya, a struggling but profitable hog farmer, would like to buy a neighboring bankrupt farm, but his hopes are not high. The obstacle, he said, is not in obtaining the money or credit, but a new Minnesota law that is intended to help bankrupt farmers hold onto their land.
>
> Critics warn that efforts to help a minority of farmers might impose excessive costs on the majority.
>
> Some bankers and farm experts say that the financial system is already punishing successful farmers by making it more difficult for them to get loans. Lenders say, "We'll stop lending to agriculture or we'll charge higher interest," said J. Bruce Bullock, chairman of the Dept. of Agricultural Economics at the University of Missouri in Columbia.
>
> The result is that a farmer who borrowed heavily to buy land at $2,000 an acre in the early 1980s can default on his debts, and assuming he can raise the money, buy the land back at current prices, about $650 an acre. The loss is absorbed by the creditor, usually the Farm

Credit System. . . .

Because of this Minnesota law, some farmers turn their deeds over to their creditors to settle their debts. But the farmers can still stay on the land, work it, and collect payments from the Federal Government that average more than $15,000 in this region by agreeing not to farm part of the acreage. At the same time, the farmer has no rent, taxes or mortgage and insurance payments.

It usually takes about 20 months between the time a farmer stops making payments on loans and the time the property is offered for sale by the creditor, according to John S. Jackson, general counsel of the Minn. Bankers Association. And the process can be much longer.

During that period, a farmer can accumulate considerable money, which helps explain why almost 30 percent of the dispossessed farms sold by the FCS this year in Minnesota went to farmers using the right of first refusal.[56]

Congress revised the bankruptcy laws in 1986 in order to make it much easier for a farmer to default on his loans and still keep his farm. Naturally, this revision would cause bankers to be leery of farmers, since it makes farmers an elite class that has a lesser legal obligation to repay its loans. So to insure ample credit for farmers who could easily default on their loans, Congress in 1987 created a federally guaranteed secondary market for farm loans. This insures that, when farmers do default, it will be the taxpayers, and not the private bankers, who suffer.

The 1987 legislation created a new Federal Agricultural Mortgage Corporation (FAMC—colloquially, "Farmer Mac") to inject more capital into agriculture. The FAMC is authorized to guarantee loans of up to 80 percent of the value of assets, even though the USDA considers that any farmer with a debt-to-asset ratio above 40 percent is at financial risk, and farmers with ratios above 70 percent are usually considered lost causes. The FAMC will provide implicit government guarantees for loans of up to $2.5 million—a nice cutoff point between the needy and the greedy. "It is the Farmer Mac that is going to keep the commercial banking and the insurance industry in the agricultural sector," Kathleen Lawrence observes.[57] By forcing the government to cover the risk of bad farm loans, Congress insures that more capital will be squandered in inefficient agricultural investments in the future.

Politicians and Credit: A Bad Mixture

In 1980, during his tough battle for re-election, President Carter reportedly pressured Secretary of Agriculture Bob Bergland to inject more FmHA loans into Georgia. Bergland reportedly replied, "Jimmy, we already spent a whole billion dollars in Georgia. The whole state is not worth a billion dollars." As of early 1987, Georgia had the highest FmHA delinquency rate in the nation—73.4 percent.[58]

Federal credit programs are a farce because congressmen disguise a huge welfare program in the trappings of banking respectability. It is much easier politically to defend a million-dollar loan than a million-dollar handout. The result is a farm "credit" program that requires only that an applicant appear uncreditworthy to qualify, that is totally incapable of foreclosing on delinquent borrowers, and that hands out subsidized loans of up to $50 million per farm.

Politicians profit from government credit programs not according to the soundness of the loans but according to their generosity. In early 1987, the FmHA proposed new regulations to rate applicants for loans according to the riskiness of the loans. Congress was, as usual, outraged. Congressman Byron Dorgan exclaimed, "These regulations could effectively be used to destroy the mission of the agency, to disqualify from loans exactly the type of farmers Congress intended the agency to serve."[59] The FmHA loses money because Congress designs the program that way. You can't win votes with programs that don't do borrowers any favors.

Whenever subsidies are being distributed on the basis of vague or illogical criteria, political pull will soon determine who gets the handouts. Local and state FmHA offices receive numerous calls from congressmen's offices, pressuring them to lend to campaign contributors and other politically preferred borrowers. The FmHA thus becomes a petty-cash drawer for farm-state congressmen, and is notorious for its old-boy network.

In many agricultural discussions, there is the implicit assumption that if a farmer goes bankrupt, the land vanishes and the farmer dies. Bill Kerrey, an agricultural adviser to the governor of Nebraska, told the *Washington Post*, "I consider anything above 1 percent in farm and ranch turnover to be too high."[60] What actually happens in farm bankruptcies is that farms are simply turned over to other farmers—

the amount of land in production (or paid not to produce) stays roughly the same and some other individual or corporation then attempts to make a profit off the same turf. In Minnesota, 90 percent of the farms foreclosed on by the FCS were purchased by neighboring farmers.

Farm credit policies are usually legislated in an atmosphere of hysteria. Congressman Tom Daschle remarked in 1985 that "the single most impressive fact is our estimate that at least 20 percent of this county's farmers will lose their operations within eighteen months if nothing is done—soon."[61] On February 9, 1985, the front page of the *New York Times* noted that "2.37 million farmers . . . are struggling to pay interest on total liabilities that have soared 63 percent since 1979, from $132 billion to $215 billion."[62] This was a gross inaccuracy, since only roughly 400,000 farmers were struggling to pay their debts and the others were not in financial danger. Harold F. Breimyer, a professor at the University of Missouri long known for advocating more farm subsidies, warned, "Half of all full-time farmers are in jeopardy."[63] As usual, laws were passed because it was assumed that all the farmers would soon be homeless unless Congress immediately gave agriculture another major injection.

A Conspiracy Against Competence

Farm credit handouts present a classic case of self-defeating humanitarianism: Government cannot help the individual without hurting the group. "One farmer's good fortune is his neighbor's misfortune," as the old saying goes. The more the government helps an individual farmer to plant, the less all other farmers will receive for their harvest. Every time congressmen say that they are helping a farmer, they are subsidizing competition for all the other farmers. Every FmHA loan goes either to a creditworthy farmer who could obtain loans elsewhere—or to an uncreditworthy farmer who is kept on the land to the detriment of creditworthy farmers.

Congress has created a two-class system of farmers—welfare farmers and self-reliant farmers. But every dollar of aid the government gives to welfare farmers makes it more difficult for self-reliant farmers to prosper and survive. FmHA officials recognize that its loans have adverse effects on farmers who are not its clients. Vance Clark, the administrator, told the Senate Agriculture Committee last year when the committee proposed changes in the FmHA's credit regulations: "Land is bid up because the landlords know there's cash rent available through our program, and we find our borrowers bidding against other borrowers, and up goes the rent, which really works to [our borrowers'] detriment."[64] Some farmers have been technically bankrupt for more than eight years, but the FmHA keeps giving them new loans each year to "keep them in business," and thus keeps them producing surpluses and driving down prices for other farmers. Good farmers had to pay inflated prices to acquire more land because the government bombarded bad farmers with cheap money to bid up the price of farmland. In North Dakota in 1987, FmHA borrowers were getting operating and farm ownership loans at 4.5 percent; other farmers were paying up to 13 percent.

The government cannot bail out one farmer without preventing some other person from entering farming, or another farmer from expanding his farming operation. The government cannot give subsidized loans to one beginning farmer without creating higher entry barriers for all other beginning farmers. Every government-subsidized loan to buy farmland drives up the price and makes it more difficult for unsubsidized buyers to purchase land. In some states—such as Louisiana, where more than 50 percent of farmers are on the FmHA dole—the other farmers are at a huge disadvantage. And the higher land values become, the more the politicians and bureaucrats claim that this proves that more subsidized credit is necessary in order to pay for the high land costs.

FmHA policies in recent years have been a farmland anti-takeover policy—preventing competent farmers from buying less-competent farmers' land. Most land being farmed by FmHA borrowers would be farmed whether or not the FmHA had ever existed. The only difference that the FmHA makes is that the land is farmed by someone who cannot survive without another $100,000 handout from the government each year, rather than by someone who can make a profit and pay taxes instead of squandering tax money.

FmHA loans have made farming more capital-intensive. Many relatively small farmers who in the past would have hired laborers were able, with FmHA's help, to buy expensive new machinery instead. This machinery often sits idle much of the year because the farms are often too small to justify the purchase of large equipment. The idle machinery reduces the farmers' efficiency. Thus the FmHA has succeeded both in destroying jobs and, in many cases, reducing efficiency.

The Political Allocation of Capital

Perennially, two of the biggest complaints on Capitol Hill are that farmers are growing too many crops and that farmers cannot get enough cheap credit. Whenever a large number of farmers could not get big loans on easy terms, politicians proclaimed that agriculture had a credit problem. The evidence of overcapacity in agriculture— low crop prices—has always been misinterpreted by Congress as proof of a farm credit crisis, because not all farmers could get generous loans at easy rates. Thus, the response of Congress to the symptom of overcapacity (more cheap credit) has always had the effect of aggravating the problem of overproduction.

Farm credit policies conflict with other federal farm policies. The FmHA sets farms up in business, and then the Agricultural Stabilization and Conservation Service pays the farmer not to work each year. In 1987, when the government offered farmers 92 percent of their federal deficiency payment as a reward for taking a year's vacation, the FmHA loaned millions to farmers who then collected more millions as payment for not planting their crops. In 1983–84, when the dairy buyout program paid dairy farmers almost a billion dollars to slash milk production, the FmHA lent tens of millions of dollars to dairymen to help them increase production.

It is ludicrous to make a single subsidized operating loan at the same time the government is paying farmers to leave cropland unplanted. The FmHA currently has 168,000 farm borrowers on its rolls. Assuming that FmHA borrowers have an average-sized farm (455 acres), the FmHA is subsidizing production on 76 million acres. This is very close to the number of acres that the USDA has paid farmers not to plant the last two years (70 million and 76 million, respectively).

Where there is a surplus of production, there is no shortage of capital. There is only an agricultural credit problem in the sense that some farmers cannot get loans at interest rates they like, rather than a shortage of capital to be invested in agriculture.

In early 1986, the General Accounting Office announced that half of the FmHA's $28-billion farm loan portfolio was held by farmers who would probably default and that, in the first six months of 1985 alone, the agency made almost $2 billion in loans to farmers who were already technically bankrupt or near bankrupt, among them farmers who had not made a payment on previous FmHA loans in over four years. This extraordinarily high delinquency rate would be much higher if the FmHA had not forgiven part of the debts or rescheduled and reamortized the debts of about 45,000 borrowers. Farm-state congressmen responded to the report, not by seriously re-examining the charter of a government agency that could burn so much money, but by continuing to denounce the FmHA for not being more generous to its borrowers.

Farm credit policies are among the clearest refutations of the competence of politicians to manage the economy better than private citizens can. A rational capital-allocation policy directs capital to wherever its returns are highest and shifts capital away from lower-paying investments. But for decades, federal agricultural credit policy has consisted solely of jamming as many loans into agriculture as possible, regardless of the effects. For politicians, the solution to low returns in agriculture is always to provide more capital. The cheap credit provides an illusion of prosperity in agriculture and helps congressmen make it past another election.

Conclusion

Dwight Coleman, the North Dakota farmer who led the class-action lawsuit that forced the FmHA to cease foreclosures in 1983, recently reflected on his experience with government credit: "If you can't borrow money from the local banker, stay out of [farming]. Lease your land instead of borrowing heavily and don't borrow from the government at all."[65] Coleman recognized the dangers of the lure of subsidized credit. If only Congress were as wise. Wheeler McMillen, author of *Too Many Farmers*, observed in 1929 that "if a farmer doesn't have enough pride and business about him to keep his credit good, certainly no one in the world is going to be able to do much for him."[66] Though McMillen's sentiment may seem harsh in contemporary times, the record of bankruptcies and delinquencies by government borrowers supports his view.

If the Farmers Home Administration were a bank, would anyone of sound mind deposit his money in it? Would anyone allow the FmHA to use his own personal savings the way it uses the tax dollars of the American people? Farm programs are managed according to the politician's usual profound philosophy: Giving away money can only have good effects. It is obvious that congressmen feel no obligation to taxpayers in how they manage farm credit programs. The goal is simply to keep another farm voter around for another election. Congressmen have no sense of personal responsibility for the ways in which the programs malfunction and disrupt the farm economy.

Politicians love to play Santa Claus with other people's money. This is why the Farmers Home Administration was created, this was why it grew, and this is why it is prospering even though it has helped wreck thousands of farmers' lives and is creating unfair competition for every unsubsidized farmer in America. Credit is usually a euphemism in farm policy discussions—a code word for either a handout or a bailout.

There is a limited amount of capital in America. Every subsidized loan to a near-bankrupt farmer means fewer loans for other Americans to buy a house, pay for an education, or start an independent business. For each FmHA subsidized loan of $400,000, as many as eight families are denied the opportunity to get mortgages to buy their first houses. For each farmer who borrows a million dollars from the FmHA, twenty entrepreneurs are denied the capital to start their own businesses. Every loan that politicians give to a politically favored borrower means less credit available for other Americans. The government is increasingly crowding private citizens out of the credit market—meaning that politicians have more control over everyone's future.

Congress treats farm credit like a pusher treats a heroin addict—constantly assuring him that one more fix, one more injection will solve all his problems. Like the heroin pusher who cares only about profit, congressmen only know that subsidized loans are good for snaring votes and campaign contributions. Regardless of how many heroin users die or how many farmers' lives are ruined by the FmHA, the pusher and the congressmen march merrily on.

Chapter 8

Export Schizophrenia

Farm policy has been a sixty-year war between export taxes and export subsidies. Exporting is currently a hypnotic word in discussions on agricultural policy—something so wonderful that it is supposedly justified at any cost. But in recent years, only the massive dumping of American crops on world markets has prevented the United States from being a net agricultural importer. Thanks to decades of self-defeating farm policy, agricultural exports are increasingly a Pyrrhic victory for taxpayers.

According to the USDA, the United States in 1986 spent up to four times the world price for each additional hundredweight of exported rice. The United States is spending three times the world price to dump butter on world markets, and has paid up to four times the world price for sugar exports. In 1987, roughly 75 percent of wheat, 90 percent of soybean oil, and 100 percent of barley, cotton, and rice exports received federal export subsidies. Yet to those who look only at export statistics and neglect the cost, these are success stories.

Exports are the lifeblood of the American farmer. The harvest of a third of America's cropland is routinely sent abroad. For major crops, exports often make the difference between profitability and bankruptcy. Yet Congress and the USDA have generally shown little or no concern about selling American crops abroad profitably.

For almost sixty years the federal government has operated domestic programs to drive up crop prices while simultaneously providing export subsidies to give discounts to foreigners. The biggest failing of agricultural policy since 1933 has been the contemptuous attitude toward exports, prices, and foreign customers. For decades politicians have assumed that foreigners will buy our crops regardless of price—and that lowering the price to boost exports thus cheats the American farmer out of a higher profit. Politicians have always tried to conduct foreign agricultural trade with bribes and bluster, subsidies and threats, and rarely considered how farm programs undercut the American farmer. Politicians' disregard of exports has been the single greatest factor in increasing the dependency of American farmers on the government.

The Myth of Averages

In the 1920s, the USDA and many congressmen decided that American farmers could no longer compete with foreign farmers and so proceeded to sabotage American export markets. As noted in Chapter 2, after the federal Farm Board intervened to boost wheat prices, wheat exports fell by more than 75 percent while world wheat trade declined only 25 percent. Federal policy-makers saw the problem not in the decline in exports, but rather that exports had not yet been eliminated. In 1931, the chairman of the federal Farm Board, James C. Stone, complained, "Kansas is the heart of the territory that has been expanding its wheat acreage . . . and contributing most to the national surplus over domestic requirements. . . . We believe from the facts before us that the world-market level in the next few years will be unsatisfactory to the American grower."[1] The chairman begged Kansas farmers, in the national interest, to reduce their acreage, abandon their aspirations to sell to foreigners, and accept instead a "domestic allotment," farming only that percentage of their land required to produce enough for national self-sufficiency.[2]

At that time, Kansas farmers may have been the world's lowest-cost wheat producers. Even though farmers in Montana, North Dakota, and Oklahoma may have been losing money, Kansas wheat farmers were still profiting. The value of farmland in Kansas continued to rise until 1932, indicating the confidence Kansas farmers had in their own future. But the federal Farm Board wanted to control the domestic wheat price and sought to isolate American farmers completely from the world economy. The Farm Board wanted to take care of farmers—so it desperately attempted to persuade farmers that they could not stand on their own two feet.

The federal anti-export crusade was based largely on a misunderstanding of the farm economy. In 1932, Bernhard Ostrolenk noted:

> The successful farmer today makes a good living because his neighbor grows small crops at a high cost. The average yield of wheat in the U.S. is 13 bushels an acre. Those producing 20–25 bushels an acre get a satisfactory reward for their labor, investment, and management; but those producing 13 bushels or less clamor for relief.[3]

The Roosevelt administration adopted the Farm Board's anti-export crusade with a vengeance. M. L. Wilson, the assistant secretary of agriculture, declared in 1934, "Agriculture cannot be said to possess a foreign market if the business it does there is a losing business. . . . There was only one thing left to do—regulate the production of exports."[4]

Since the 1920s, experts have repeatedly looked at the average U.S. crop production cost and announced that the country cannot compete with foreigners, with their "cheap labor and cheap land." But those statistics simply show the average of the costs of the best and the worst farmers. Judging American farmers' competitiveness by average production costs is like averaging the speed of America's fastest and slowest runners, and then announcing that the United States does not have a chance of winning any medals in the next Olympics. When the level of farm subsidies is determined partly by estimates of the cost of production, there is overwhelming incentive to overestimate the cost of production in order to justify providing more aid to farmers.

In most countries, it is not the marginal or average producer who exports, but the superior businessman. The question of whether America should export depends not on the average cost of production, but on the variable cost of the most efficient farmers. Yet price supports and target prices are based explicitly on the idea that an entire industry should be regulated, compensated, and restrained according to the competence of the average producer. The federal welfare system for agriculture has blinded policy-makers and the American public to the ability of America's best farmers.

Large areas of the United States could always compete with any farm area in the world. From 1933 until the 1960s, Kansas farmers were heavily impeded from producing for export because some Montana farmers could not compete in world markets. Because some farmers were comparatively inefficient, other farmers were forced to reduce their production. In order to justify giving handouts to some farmers, Congress and the USDA had to claim that all farmers needed help.

Sixty Years of Mercantilism

Many congressmen are devotees of the Robinson Crusoe school of prosperity: If the nation produces an item itself, then Americans will become rich; if the United States buys the product from foreigners, then Americans become poor. Mercantilism, the dominant economic philosophy of the seventeenth century, is the foundation of our present-day farm policy. Mercantilists assume that a nation always suffers from imports and always benefits from exports, regardless of how much money it loses producing its own goods or selling to foreigners at a loss. As a result, consumers are burdened with import quotas and taxpayers are burdened with export subsidies.

Since domestic agricultural production capacity is so much greater than domestic demand, farming must be an export industry. Yet agricultural policy-makers are among the most xenophobic in Washington. Congressman Glenn English declared in 1985, "Without question, the American farmer, each time he steps beyond the boundaries of our shores has been getting mugged."[5] During the 1985 farm bill debate, Kika de la Garza, the House agriculture chairman, ranted for continued protectionism of the sugar industry: "Would you kill the industry which is defenseless? Are we going to buy American? If you vote [to reduce sugar price supports 3 cents a pound], you are not showing the flag. . . . This may well be the beginning of a war, and we are going to have a trade war. . . . We have to let the world know that we will protect American manufacturers, producers, jobs."[6]

Farming is perhaps America's most protected industry. The 1934 Jones-Costigan Act, with its strict quotas on sugar, was the first act in American history to use quantitative restrictions on imports. In 1935, Congress added Section 22 to the Agricultural Adjustment Act, providing authority for the secretary of agriculture to impose quotas on, or to ban completely, any import that threatened to disrupt a domestic price-support program. Since the USDA was setting domestic prices above world market prices, it was necessary to close the borders to lower-priced foreign goods. Congressmen could not plan the United States economy without at least partly closing U.S. borders to foreign goods.

Farm-state congressmen have rarely had any concept of honor or responsibility in their attitude toward world markets. Since the 1920s, farm-state congressmen have talked as if world markets exist almost solely for the use and abuse of the American farmer. In the 1920s, Congress twice enacted (and Coolidge twice vetoed) a farm debenture plan designed to guarantee farmers high prices and to dump any surplus above domestic demand on the world market at fire-sale prices. There was little or no provocation to justify such a scheme to disrupt world markets, only a conviction that American farmers should receive more for their harvest.

Export Taxes

The premier goal of most agricultural policy-makers since 1929 has been to drive up crop prices. Yet over the last fifty years, every effort to inflate crop prices has decreased long-term exports. Federal crop price supports higher than market prices are an export "tax." If an American farmer wanted to sell his crop abroad, he would have to take less—sometimes only half as much—as if he sold it to his government. Up until the early 1970s, federal price supports for most major crops were generally well above world market prices. Thus, it has almost always been more profitable for a farmer to sell his produce to the American government for storage than to sell to foreigners. Lyle Stallman, an Iowa commodity trader, observed, "The usual procedure was to put it in the bins for nine months and then let the government take over."[7]

Congressmen realized in the 1960s that high price supports were undercutting exports and gradually began decreasing support levels in the 1970s. Unfortunately, once exports began increasing in the 1970s, politicians assumed that they would increase forever. As Richard Lyng, the USDA secretary, commented, "An American belief in the 1970s that expanding exports were 'our birthright' led to farm programs that damaged exports in the 1980s."[8] Politicians responded to increased exports by rapidly increasing price supports in order to win farmers' votes. Unfortunately, higher federal support prices effectively wiped out the achievements of the market-oriented agricultural reforms of the late 1960s and early 1970s. Between 1975 and 1982 federal price-support levels increased in constant dollars 43 percent for wheat and 38 percent for corn.

Though by 1981 large surpluses had piled up, the 1981 farm bill decreed that American price supports would rise by 5 or 6 percent each year. American crop prices quickly became far higher than world prices, yet Congress refused to admit the problem and lower price supports to allow American exports to regain competitiveness. Between the 1981–82 and 1985–86 market years, American wheat exports declined by 50 percent, cotton exports by 75 percent, corn exports by 40 percent, rice exports by 33 percent, and tobacco exports by 40 percent. In one year, 1985, the U.S. share of the world wheat market fell to 29 percent, the smallest market share since 1953–54 (it had been 68 percent in 1979).[9] John E. Lee, Jr., the administrator of the USDA's Economic Research Service, stated in 1985 that "the most important source of our export problems, especially the loss of market share, has been the export tax effect of our commodity loan programs exacerbated by the high value of the dollar."[10]

By early 1985, American crop prices were up to 37 percent higher than competitors' prices.[11] Despite the precipitous decline of American exports in recent years, many congressmen still believe that they can drive up world prices with the same facility that they drive up U.S. prices. Congressman Harold Weaver, a member of the House Agriculture Committee, expressed the attitude of many of his colleagues in 1985 when he declared: "The truth is . . . that the United States makes the world price. We set the world price. We could raise the world price by $2 a bushel and we would sell just as much grain as we do today. We have been giving away our grain."[12] Congressman

John Bryant of Texas felt the same way: "If we raise our export prices, we might lose a little export volume, but the overall value of them would go up."[13]

Washington discussions on agricultural prices are usually dominated by moral notions rather than economic facts. Dan McGuire of the Nebraska Wheat Board declared: "For farmers and farm organizations to accept the fallacy of the loan rate/export relationship is to accept the unrealistic notion that farmers deserve lower prices and lower income so that other interest groups can benefit."[14] Congressmen consider not what a bushel of wheat is worth to foreign buyers, but what an American farmer is entitled to receive for his efforts. Unfortunately, every attempt by Congress to dictate morals to the marketplace has blown up in the faces of the farmers or the taxpayers.

Congress eventually conceded that high federal support prices were undermining exports in 1985, and reduced support prices while maintaining extremely high target prices to guarantee farmers a good income. But the reduction was still not enough to make American grains competitive on world markets. The Agricultural Policy Working Group noted that "at the [1987] loan rate, a ton of U.S. wheat is priced at about $110 in the world market today. Our competitors have consistently been selling a ton of the same quality of wheat anywhere from $20 to $40 below the U.S. price."[15] To hide the damage caused by high price supports, the USDA now provides billions of dollars of export subsidies.

Federal agricultural programs have reduced exports by destroying the competitiveness of American farmers with welfare. Every crop that the USDA has lavished benefits on has ended up with either strict controls or huge excess capacity. The USDA does not reward farmers for improving their capital base, but for idling their acreage, continuing to grow surplus crops, and playing by the government's rules. Every handout has encouraged farmers to look more toward Washington and less at the market. High target prices encourage farmers to boost their costs of production in order to maximize yield and thereby create the illusion that American farmers' cost of production is too high for the world market.

Federal benefits are capitalized into the price and rental value of farmland. Two acres of equally productive land in Iowa can differ by 50 percent in sales price or rental rate according to whether or not the land has a history as a "base" for USDA benefit programs—that is, whether farmers in the past enrolled the land in order to qualify for federal benefits. The more federal benefits for which the crops grown on the land are eligible, the higher the price of the land, and therefore the higher the farmers' cost of production. This system drives up the costs of production while doing nothing to increase farmers' productivity or efficiency.

If congressmen openly declared that high wages for union members made American manufacturing more competitive on world markets, or if they proposed to force factory owners to pay twice as much for their factories in order to help make American manufacturing more competitive, they would be ridiculed. But farm-state congressmen openly attempt to drive up farmland values to enrich farmers, disregarding the effects this will have on American competitiveness. Congressman Ed Madigan bragged in a speech on March 29, 1988, that farmland values in his district had increased by 25 percent in the past two years, offering this as proof of the success of the 1985 farm bill.[16] Yet higher land values increase the cost of production, increase farmers' debt load, and drive up farmland rents, thereby providing Australian and South American farmers with a big advantage over American farmers.

Federal generosity to the producers of some crops has undermined the exports of other crops. In 1986 the government offered extremely lucrative payments to farmers to grow (or not grow) wheat and corn. Sunflower products were one of America's fastest-growing exports. But because federal wheat subsidies were much more generous than anything a farmer could earn growing sunflowers, farmers planted wheat for government storage rather than sunflowers for foreign customers. The shortfall in sunflower production decreased farm exports and also damaged America's reputation as a reliable sunflower producer. The absurdity of this policy became especially clear during the drought of 1988. Sunflowers are much more drought-resistant than wheat. Many farmers whose wheat crops were burned up by the sun would have done much better if they had planted sunflowers instead.

Similarly, federal handouts to corn growers have created new foreign competition for soybean growers, who historically have received little from the federal till. Soybeans have been the great agricultural export success story of recent decades and the largest American crop export in 1986. In recent years the USDA has driven corn prices down sharply (while providing more than 10 billion dollars in handouts to corn growers) in an effort to boost corn exports. But by driving corn prices so low, this made growing corn far less attractive to Brazilian and Argentinian farmers, who shifted over 20 million acres into soybeans.

Foreign wheat farmers outside of the European Economic Community have likely received far more "subsidies" from the U.S. government since 1933 than they have received from their own governments. Every time the U.S. government paid American farmers to slash production, foreign farmers received a higher price for their harvest. Every time Congress set U.S. price supports higher than world market prices, foreign farmers benefited from the decreased supply and competition in the world market. Each program or regulation that has increased the American farmer's cost of production has been a de facto export tax and an indirect subsidy to foreign competitors. Congressmen denouncing foreign competition ignore a major source of the problem: the U.S. government's policies that repressed American productivity and indirectly rewarded foreign agriculture development.

Congress and the USDA are more interested in controlling domestic production than in maximizing exports. The USDA restricts the export of peanuts, lemons, and oranges to Canada in order to safeguard the USDA's domestic-supply programs. A North Carolina State University study estimated that the abolition of the tobacco program with its feudal restrictions on tobacco growing would double tobacco exports, from $1.4 to $3.0 billion a year.[17] American tobacco exports have fallen and tobacco imports are soaring, but so many powerful people are benefiting from the tobacco program that political paralysis prevents reform.

Several recent studies concluded that American exports would be far higher if all federal agricultural programs were abolished. A study by Purdue professors Thomas W. Hertel, former USDA chief economist Robert L. Thompson, and Marinos E. Tsigas concluded that the allocation of resources and capital to agriculture has depressed the productivity of other sectors of the U.S. economy and reduced American manufacturing exports by $7.5 billion and service exports

by $3.4 billion.[18] Andrew Feltenstein of Kansas State University es-
timated that the elimination of agricultural subsidies in 1986 would
have reduced America's trade deficit by $42 billion.[19]

Any Slop Will Do

The USDA's contemptuous attitude toward foreign buyers is perhaps
best illustrated in federal grain standards. The United States probably
exports the dirtiest, most infested grain of any major crop exporter.
U.S. grain-grading standards are roughly the same now as they were
in 1916, and permit grain exporters to add 3 percent "foreign material"
to their haulage. Exporters sometimes dump grain dust, dirt, or stones
into American grain before shipping it overseas, simply because
USDA standards make such trash profitable. John Ford, the former
deputy assistant secretary of agriculture, noted that "we raise the fin-
est wheat in the world—and then we send shit abroad—five bushels
of wheat and a bushel of dust."[20]

According to federal grain standards, if 2.5 percent of a bushel of
wheat consists of dead bugs, the grain is not infested, because the
bugs are dead and the foreign material does not exceed 3 percent. But
most bakery customers would not judge a loaf of bread clean if it had
only 2.5 percent cockroaches, dead or alive.

Roger Asendorf of the American Soybeans Association noted:

> The farmer can receive a premium of $12 per acre for delivering dirty
> corn. The system rewards farmers who do a poor job of harvesting
> and cleaning, and penalizes those who use extra time, effort and
> management to deliver top quality corn. We have designed a system
> to reward below average farmers and penalized better than average
> farmers.[21]

Cooper Evans, a former congressman, notes that the USDA's definition of a "whole" kernel of soybeans is "one from which not more
than 25 percent is missing, and that under USDA's lowest standards, a
mixture of 5 percent broken soybeans, 10 percent oats, and 40 percent
topsoil could still be classified as a load of soybeans."[22]

Most businesses pay attention to their customers. Not the USDA.
Congressman Berkley Bedell noted that "for 1986, the ten-month
report period shows thirty complaints [from foreign customers]—

'none valid.'" And how did the Federal Grain Inspection Service decide that none of the complaints was valid? It checked its files in Washington for reports on the quality of the grain when it left an American port—which said the grain was just fine. Such treatment is endearing to foreign customers.[23]

Federal price supports pay farmers only according to the number of bushels of wheat they produce. This has led to a shift to wheat seed varieties that produce high yields—and little else. Paul McAuliffe, an assistant vice president for Continental Grain, notes that "rising yields have been accompanied by decreasing protein levels, and this has allowed Canada to move to the forefront as the major provider of high protein wheat."[24] Asian countries have complained loudly of the decreasing quality of American wheat. The Japanese avoid buying U.S. corn now because its moisture content is low compared to Canadian and Australian corn. The USDA has opposed even basic reforms such as the requirement for more accurate measurements of crop moisture or damage. The General Accounting Office has long urged the USDA to shift to a measure that shows the crop moisture or quality to the tenth of a percentage point, or to at least half a percentage point. But the USDA continues rounding up (or down, if it helps the seller) to the nearest percentage point. This is simply a scam to favor sellers over buyers.

The Futility of Export Subsidies

American agricultural policy-makers appear never to have developed a political awareness of the difference between profit and loss in selling. The rule of thumb seems to be that if the United States exports something, it is fair trade; if a foreign country sells a crop to America, that is dumping. D. Gale Johnson, a professor at the University of Chicago, observes, "The United States embarks on policies that create excess capacity and then uses the power of the Treasury to find export outlets for the surplus production."[25] The government first pays the farmer more than a crop is worth to produce it—and then often sells it to foreigners for less than the crop is worth.

Congressmen defend agricultural export subsidies as being necessary to maintain America's "traditional share of world markets." This is indicative of how politicians view markets as a perpetual entitlement rather than as an arena in which producers must earn the dollars of their customers. The notion that America is morally entitled to a certain share of world markets has done wonders for boosting federal budget deficits.

The flood of export subsidies in recent years is creating absurd results. According to *Pro Farmer*, a farm-policy newsletter, the Mexican subsidiary of a U.S. corporation received subsidized U.S. white wheat, processed the wheat into crackers, and then sold it back to the United States, provoking an outcry from other American food manufacturers.[26] The United States sold wheat to Turkey at a big loss—and Turkey promptly re-sold the wheat to Iran and Iraq at a profit. The USDA's Foreign Agriculture Service admits that generous subsidies for wheat exports have displaced unsubsidized American corn exports.

Between 1986 and 1988 the Reagan administration provided over half a billion dollars in subsidies for sales to the Soviet Union, China, Bulgaria, Poland, Hungary, and Rumania to buy American crops. American wheat is cheaper in Moscow than it is in Kansas City, and traditional American customers such as Japan are being discriminated against in order to attract communist customers. The United States has provided a subsidy for Russia that is equal to half of the annual subsidy that the Soviets provide to Nicaragua. Even though Poland effectively defaulted on a billion dollars in previous USDA loans, Poland benefited from almost $100 million in USDA export subsidies in 1987. The USDA provided almost a billion dollars of credit to Iraq in 1988, thereby allowing American taxpayers to underwrite the Iraqi war machine.[27]

Some export subsidy deals are contortions to escape farm law. The U.S. government acquired 400 million pounds of sugar from American sugar growers who sold their crop to the government when the domestic sugar price fell below the government's support price of 18 cents a pound. Because federal law prohibits the United States from selling government-acquired sugar domestically for less than the price-support level *plus* 10 percent, the USDA sold the sugar to China for 4.9 cents a pound. The sale for far less than the world market price temporarily knocked the bottom out of the sugar market. World prices fell by 25 percent overnight.

Our agricultural export statistics are designed to mask reality. Surplus food dumped in the Food for Peace program is given the same statistical weight as the unsubsidized sale of a bushel of soybeans. This sleight-of-hand means that the more tax dollars are spent, the more competitive American agriculture appears to be. No matter how much the United States loses in export sales, the aggregated agricultural export statistics make foreign sales appear profitable.

The net U.S. agricultural trade balance in 1986 was $5.4 billion ($26.3 billion in exports, $20.9 billion in imports). In that year, the United States donated $2.2 billion (including cargo preference costs) in food abroad, spent $400 million for the Export Enhancement Program, $2.9 billion in marketing loans to boost rice and cotton exports, $4.6 billion in federal guaranteed subsidized loans for exports, and $235 million to pay off defaulted export credit loans. Thus, export subsidies easily exceeded the surplus of exports over imports. In 1987 the net agricultural trade balance rose to $7.3 billion. Food donations accounted for $2 billion, export enhancement bonuses for $1.6 billion, targeted export assistance for $110 million, rice and cotton marketing loans for $2.7 billion, government-guaranteed credit for $3 billion, and payments on defaulted export loans for $373 million.

On top of the direct export subsidies, the United States paid farmers a bonus for each bushel of corn or wheat that was produced and exported. This added over $3 billion a year in 1986 and 1987 to the total federal subsidies for exported food items. Such payments are usually considered export subsidies under the rules of the General Agreement on Trade and Tariffs (GATT). In 1987 the USDA paid farmers $4.38 a bushel for growing wheat, yet received only $1.60 a bushel net, after subsidies, from the Soviet wheat sale.

The premise of export subsidies is that U.S. profit margins are so low that American grain exporters cannot afford to cut prices in order to garner sales. Yet if the profit margin is so low, any subsidy higher than 5 or 10 percent would mean that the United States is selling at a loss. The average cost of the Export Enhancement Program subsidies has equaled 62 percent of the value of the exported product. It is tricky to earn a profit this way, but the USDA has a multiplier to prove that America benefits from every USDA boondoggle. According to the USDA's Foreign Agriculture Service, "USDA economists calculate that, at the very least, each dollar received from exports stimulates another $1.51 worth of business activity for the rest of the economy. Thus, our $27 billion in exports resulted in $70 billion in increased economic activity."[28] If every dollar of exports generated $1.51 of profitable business activity, why don't we just pay foreigners to take all our crops and make ourselves rich? If such a wonderful multiplier actually existed, the government would not need to provide subsidies for export sales. If the USDA is paying a subsidy of 62 cents to get a dollar's worth of sales, on which the profit may be only 10 cents, how can America possibly benefit? Such multipliers become a blank check for any foolish policy: No matter how much money the government loses, policy-makers can always contrive a number that "proves" that the nation gains. But most multipliers make no distinction between economic activity at a loss and economic activity at a profit—as long as government action churns the economy, it is assumed that it is profitable.

The Export Enhancement Program, the United States' largest export subsidy scheme, is mandated by the USDA to be cost-effective: "a net plus to the overall economy should result [from subsidies]."[29] But the notion that America can profit from export subsidies presumes that the USDA bureaucrats have the wisdom of Solomon, the patience of Job, and the speed of Mercury—that they can play a market with all the skills known to the best traders. If they had such skills, they probably wouldn't be working for the government. The General Accounting Office reports that the USDA does a shoddy job of calculating subsidies, that they are incapable of judiciously setting subsidy margins, and that they move too slowly to seize sales opportunities.[30] Government reports on agricultural exports are designed to show sales volume, not profitability. Thus, bureaucrats will always be biased in favor of boosting sales, regardless of costs. The Export Enhancement Program may have actually decreased American exports. The program provided generous subsidies to a few buyers, but when word got out about the size of the discounts that some customers were receiving, other customers were naturally very irate. The National Corn Growers Association demanded that the USDA not provide any Export Enhancement Program subsidies for corn exports, fearing that to provide subsidies to some buyers might antagonize the traditional customers for American corn.

Since 1985, cotton and rice growers have had access to special export-oriented "marketing loans." Spending for the cotton program has increased sevenfold and rice program costs are up threefold since 1984, yet the total dollars received from cotton and rice exports are now much lower than they were when the program began. The rice and cotton marketing loans were unlimited predatory pricing to drive down world prices in order to boost American exports.

Who were the victims? Thailand was the United States' main competitor in the world rice market; Thailand's average per capita income is $842. What proof did Congress have that the Thais engaged in unfair trade? The Thai government provides minimal aid and credit to its rice farmers; most receive nothing. To "compensate" for Thai government subsidies averaging less than $100 per rice grower, the U.S. government launched a program that spent an average of more than a million dollars for each U.S. rice grower. Thailand's subsidy justified the U.S. government knocking the price of rice down by more than 50 percent in 1986. The cotton program drove the world cotton price down by 55 percent in 1986—and butchered America's foreign competition, including Egypt, Chad, and the Ivory Coast. These countries are so poor that they could barely afford to subsidize their farmers even if they wanted to. Because the loans provide extremely generous payments to the farmers regardless of how much the U.S. government loses in exporting their crops, farm lobbies are anxious to extend marketing loans to other crops.

The Targeted Export Assistance program (TEA) is one of the more colorful farm export programs. The TEA was authorized in the 1985 farm bill largely to satisfy Senator Pete Wilson, who wanted to make sure that California farmers got some government benefits while farmers in other parts of the country were getting the key to the Treasury. TEA was designed to provide federal funds to commodity organizations to help them offset the effects of unfair foreign trade practices. The TEA program will spend $200 million in 1989.

The USDA is paying for brand-name foreign advertisements for Samuel Adams premium beer, Paul Newman gourmet sauces, Moyle Mink furs, Celestial Seasonings tea, Chateau San Michel wine, Kroger groceries, Blue Diamond almonds, and Sunkist oranges and lemons. Private companies keep the profits from sales generated by the increased advertising while American taxpayers pick up the tab.

Government-subsidized brand-name advertising is a flagrant violation of the General Agreement on Tariffs and Trade.

Some American groups receiving federal funds for foreign advertising are actively impeding American exports. The USDA gave $4
million to the California Almond Growers Exchange for foreign pro-
motions—even though the exchange controls the USDA's Almond
Board, which is prohibiting American farmers from exporting more
than 100 million pounds of almonds this year in an effort to drive up
world almond prices. Sunkist received $17 million from TEA, even
though Sunkist publicly urged Japan not to remove its import quotas
on American citrus. (Sunkist had a lock on the Japanese market and
did not want competition.)

The Targeted Export Assistance program is trying to boost exports
of products that other Agriculture Department programs sabotage.
TEA has spent $25 million to boost raisin exports, even though byzan-
tine USDA restrictions are today deterring the export of 100 million
pounds of California raisins. The National Peanut Council received
$11 million to boost peanut exports, while the Agriculture Department
prohibits the export to Canada of peanut butter made from unsubsidized peanuts. The USDA gave $5 million to the Chocolate Manufac-
turers Association even though chocolate exports are repressed because the government drives domestic sugar prices to triple or quadruple world sugar prices. The National Sunflower Council received $3
million, even though sunflower exports have plummeted largely because lavish federal subsidies encouraged farmers to grow fewer sunflowers and more surplus wheat. The Tobacco Associates received $1.3
million in tax dollars to boost American cigarette exports at the same
time that the Surgeon General was desperately trying to reduce domestic cigarette consumption.

TEA was supposedly based on countering unfair trade. But a
report issued by the General Accounting Office concluded that the
Foreign Agriculture Service (FAS)

> considers virtually any restriction on imports of U.S. agricultural pro-
> ducts an unfair trade practice. This broad definition allows partici-
> pants to qualify for TEA in virtually any foreign market for a variety
> of commodities. . . . FAS has chosen to concentrate its efforts on of-
> fsetting [compensating commodity groups for reduced sales in one
> country due to unfair trade practices by increased exports to another]
> because if a country's trade barriers are severely limiting, marketing

development in that country would have minimal impact. For example, to help offset the adverse effects of the EC's tariff preferences and Korea's import restrictions, the California Avocado Commission proposed using TEA funds to expand sales in Japan, where it has been successfully promoting avocados since 1977.[31]

Because one country may impede American imports, Congress and the FAS claim a license to engage in unfair trade practices in any country in the world. If the Japanese government began paying for Nissan advertisements in New York because Mexico banned Japanese car imports, Congress would go berserk. But it's okay if the United States plays such games.

TEA money is doled out primarily to large, established corporations and marketing boards that have good contacts on Capitol Hill and in the USDA bureaucracy. As usual, farm benefits accrue to groups with Washington lobbyists. The General Accounting Office noted, "FAS assists applicants in completing the applications and sometimes actually rewrites them to add information it needs."[32] It noted that "TEA applications were accepted throughout the last half of the [1986] fiscal year on a first-come first-served basis."[33] Yet the FAS did not even publicly announce the program until mid-1987, after it had already given $140 million to groups with inside tracks. The GAO found that "at the time, some participants stated that they had not determined how they would spend the funds when they received the advance."[34]

The FAS has been far more concerned with spending the money than with getting results. Initially, the FAS required virtually no evaluation of the funds spent. The GAO noted that "although FAS is requiring evaluations of most TEA participants, it has provided virtually no guidelines on what constitutes an independent third-party or on evaluation criteria, scope, purpose, or cost limitations."[35] The same problems have been diagnosed by the GAO in previous audits of other FAS export assistance programs. The FAS, when pressed by the GAO to require more evaluations, "warned against over-regulation and said that different commodities, markets, and activities demanded different evaluation techniques."[36] The FAS apparently considers it bad manners or an invasion of corporate privacy to inquire of grant recipients, "What did you do with the money we gave you?"

Food for Peace: Bankrupting Foreign Farmers

During the debate on the 1985 farm bill, many congressmen who favored high price supports implied that, with so many people a-round the world starving, the U.S. government could solve the American farmers' problems simply by donating surplus crops to hungry foreigners. Such self-serving charity is often the worst thing America can do for the Third World.

Food for Peace has probably been our most harmful foreign-aid program. Food for Peace was devised in 1954 to help dump embarrassingly huge crop surpluses. The primary purpose of Public Law 480 (in which the program is embodied) has been to hide the evidence of the failure of other farm programs: Although PL-480 sometimes alleviates hunger in the short run, the program usually disrupts local agricultural markets and makes it harder for poor countries to feed themselves in the long run.

Most Americans have the impression that U.S. food relief goes mainly to foreign areas hit by disasters or emergencies. Actually, only a small percentage does. More often, as one congressional staffer described it, a representative of the Agency for International Development (AID) goes into a country, finds an excuse for a project, and then continues it for fifteen years, regardless of need or results.[37] Many such programs have fed the same people for more than a decade, thereby decreasing permanently the demand for locally produced food and creating an entrenched welfare class.

In the 1950s and 1960s, massive U.S. wheat dumping in India disrupted India's agricultural market and helped bankrupt thousands of Indian farmers. In 1984, George Dunlop, chief of staff of the Senate Agriculture Committee, speculated that American food aid may have been responsible for the starvation of millions of Indians.[38] U.S. officials have conceded that massive food aid to Indonesia, Pakistan, and India in the 1960s "restricted agricultural growth . . . by allowing the governments to (1) postpone essential agricultural reforms, (2) fail to give agricultural investment sufficient priority, and (3) maintain a pricing system which gave farmers an inadequate incentive to increase production."[39]

U.S. food aid is still having devastating effects. A report by the AID inspector general found that food aid "supported Government of

Egypt policies . . . which have had a direct negative impact on domestic wheat production in Egypt."[40] In Haiti, food received free from the United States is widely sold illegally in Haiti's markets next to the crops of local farmers, thus driving down the prices received by the Haitians. A development consultant told the House Subcommittee on Foreign Operations that "farmers in Haiti are known to not even bring their crops to market the week that [PL-480 food] is distributed since they are unable to get a fair price while whole bags of U.S. food are being sold."[41]

Food for Peace has harmed Jamaican farmers as well. Scott D. Tollefson reported in the *SAIS Review*:

> An example of the disincentive created by PL-480 to Jamaican food production occurred in late July 1984 when Jamaica experienced a political near-crisis. The market mechanism worked with clocklike precision as small farmers, attracted by increased prices for rice substitutes, rushed their goods to the market. Days later, 4,890 metric tons of rice were imported under PL-480, the first parcel of an allotted 16,000 tons costing $5 million.[42]

The imported rice sent the prices of substitutes tumbling, thereby hurting local producers.

In Somali, a report made by an AID inspector general concluded: "Nearly all Title I [PL-480] food deliveries to Somalia in 1985 and 1986 arrived at the worst possible time, the harvest months, and none arrived at the best time, the critical hungry period. The consensus of the donor community was that the timing of the deliveries lowered farmers' prices thereby discouraging domestic production."[43] In Senegal, the Food for Peace program in 1985 and 1986 resulted in the government's closing down the local rice markets in order to force the Senegalese to buy American rice that their government had been given. The Senegalese are among the few peoples in the world who prefer broken rice to whole-grain rice, as they feel it better suits their sauces and national dishes. PL-480 does not offer broken rice. Since PL-480 proceeds went straight into the government coffers, Senegalese politicians had an incentive to prohibit the local farmers from selling their own rice in order to dump American rice on the market.[44]

The *Kansas City Times* reported that in 1982 the Peruvian agriculture minister begged the USDA not to send his country any more rice, fearing that it would glut the local market and drive down prices for struggling farmers. But the U.S. rice lobby turned up the heat on the USDA, and the Peruvian government was told that it could either have the rice or no food at all.[45]

Food for Peace is an administrative nightmare. Recipient governments often neglect for years to file reports on how food aid is used, but AID keeps shipping them millions of dollars of more free food every year. The Congo, instead of using PL-480 donations to feed its people, sold the food to buy a small arms factory from Italy. In March 1984 the *New York Times* reported that AID believed Ethiopia was selling its donated food to buy more Soviet weaponry. Mauritius insisted on receiving only the highest-quality rice—and then used it in hotels catering to foreign tourists. Cape Verde begged for more emergency relief aid and, at the same time, was busy exporting wheat donated by other countries.

At the same time that the United States has given handouts to a few foreign governments, U.S. agricultural policies have since 1933 been aimed at driving up world grain prices. Though it is easy for agricultural bureaucrats to point to pictures of smiling Third World citizens who received free American food, no one knows how many Africans and Asians have starved to death because they could not afford to buy grains that were more expensive as a result of the U.S. policy. While the United States gave free food to a small percentage of the world's poor, it made food more expensive for all the world's poor.

The Food for Peace program is a classic example of spreading the wealth so that the greatest number of congressmen will benefit. The 1985 farm bill requires that at least 75 percent of all donated commodities be shipped in American-owned carrier vessels. The cargo preference payments provide a windfall to the U.S. merchant marine. During the 1985 African famine, it cost five times more to ship emergency food aid to Zambia on an American merchant marine ship than under a competing foreign ship. In some cases, shipping charges cost almost as much as the food donated. Cargo preference payments were so generous that some businessmen reportedly shipped food in an old ship and then sunk it off the African coast after delivery.[46]

The cargo preference subsidies are allegedly justified to preserve U.S. merchant ships in case of a national emergency. A report issued by the Senate Agriculture Committee concluded, "Rather than encouraging the development of improved U.S. vessels, the program encourages the continued use of semi-obsolete and even unsafe vessels which are of little use for commercial or defense purposes."[47] As Congressman Virginia Smith noted, "Between 1963 and 1983, more than 350 seamen died in major accidents on old ships operating beyond their productive life."[48]

Farm Programs and Trade Reform

Farm lobbies nowadays often have a contempt for free trade because they perceive their own destiny not as a choice between selling abroad or sinking, but between selling abroad or getting a government handout. Federal subsidies and protection have turned the natural allies of free trade into rabid advocates of protectionism. During the 1986 debate on textile imports, the National Cotton Council threw its weight behind a bill that would have severely reduced textile imports and prompted retaliation against American exports by many countries. The cotton lobby assumed that it would gain in domestic sales more than enough to make up for other countries retaliating against the United States for textile trade barriers. And even more surprisingly, the National Corn Growers Association, to show its solidarity with the cotton lobby, also endorsed textile import restrictions, saying that farm lobbies should stick together in the fight against imports.[49] If farm lobbies believed that farmers had to earn a living in the marketplace, they would not support schemes that closed the borders and victimized American consumers and those American producers who do rely on exports.

Agricultural policy has long been an albatross around the neck of American trade negotiators. Though the United States had huge comparative advantages in agriculture, its policy since 1933 has been to create import barriers combined with export subsidies and to push through GATT amendments that allowed pervasive agricultural trade barriers. In 1955 the United States fathered a GATT exemption that declares that export subsidies are acceptable agricultural trade practices for a country to retain its equitable share of world markets. No two countries can agree on what is "equitable," and this provision has been a blank check for the proliferation of unfair trade practices. D.

Gale Johnson of the University of Chicago noted, "The U.S. paved the way for all agricultural subsidy sinners."[50] The United States thereby also gave every foreign country a good excuse not to buy American crops.

Conclusion

From 1919 to 1988, every political scheme to enrich farmers by driving up crop prices has decreased American competitiveness, subsidized America's competitors, and disrupted American agriculture. Government cannot drive American prices above world prices without also driving American farmers out of world markets. The best policy for exports is that policy which least disrupts domestic agriculture.

Much of federal agricultural policy can be explained only by Congress' naive belief that there is little relation between efficiency and competitiveness—that no matter how much government decreases farmers' productivity American farms will still be able to sell as much as otherwise, and that Congress can mandate that every wheat farmer leave 25 percent of his land idle without reducing the American farmers' ability to outsell Canadian and Australian farmers. Much of federal farm policy can only be explained by congressmen's naive conviction that if their intentions are good the programs they create cannot do farmers any harm.

In farm export policy, politicians cut the farmer's jugular and then promise him enough blood transfusions to make up the difference. But politicians have always done a better job of undercutting exports than of boosting farm income. The U.S. farmer is in danger of losing his strongest cards—some of the most productive land in the world and the best agricultural infrastructure—to politicians who are sure that the next set of controls and subsidies will fix the damage done by all the previous controls and subsidies.

Despite the clear role of federal agricultural policy in reducing American competitiveness, many congressmen perceive the export problem as solely a political problem. According to Congressman John Thomas of Georgia, "How well farmers do in those world markets does not depend on their farming skills, it depends on the skills of our American trade negotiators."[51] American politicians often talk of agricultural exporting as if it were a shoot-out at high noon with other agricultural producers. The agriculture secretary, John Block, declared on May 25, 1985, "We are going on the attack in the international marketplace."[52] Senator Bob Dole repeatedly urged the Reagan administration to "take a more aggressive approach" to agricultural exports. Congressmen see the answer as "bigger export weapons," when it would suffice to simply stop shooting ourselves in the foot.

American farmers have a choice between exporting and becoming permanent wards of the state. Farmers can bet their future either on their productive, competitive ability or on their political clout to perpetually shake down taxpayers and consumers. Farmers cannot abandon world markets without abandoning their productivity and efficiency—and eventually their public respect. But once agriculture abandons exports, it will lose much of its public respect. Once farmers become widely recognized as only another inefficient group of government dependents, handouts to farmers will plummet and the gravy train will dry up.

Throughout the 1980s, the proliferation of new seed varieties and other inputs has sharply decreased crop production costs around the world. Yet American policy is based on the assumption that the only reason that U.S. farmers are not exporting more is because of foreign subsidies, and that the only solution is to sacrifice more American taxpayers on the altar of agricultural exports.

American agriculture exports would likely be far higher and more profitable if the USDA had been abolished long ago. But the real issue is not the dollar amount of U.S. food exports or our food trade balance, but whether those exports and imports make the best use of scarce resources and capital. Exports of the vast majority of American foods and crops benefit the American economy, but the handful of items that the USDA spends a king's ransom to dump only make America a poorer place.

♦ *Chapter 9* ♦

Trampling Individual Rights

*Any people which must be governed according to [a Con-
stitution] which defines the spheres of individual and
group—state and federal—action must expect to suffer
from the constant maladjustments of progress.*

—Rexford Tugwell,
Undersecretary of Agriculture, 1934[1]

In 1940 the president of the California Fruit Growers Exchange, C. C.
Teague, warned that without federal marketing restrictions, only
"those who produce the best quality fruit" with "the greatest production per acre" would survive.[2] For forty-seven years, marketing orders
have fought valiantly to protect the inefficient and humble the
productive. Marketing orders are one of the most archaic and oppres-
sive sections of the Code of Federal Regulations.

Marketing orders are the clearest relic of the Mussolini school of
agricultural economics. Federal marketing orders are essentially
federal prohibitions against some farmers selling part of their harvest.
They were hatched in the same batch of federal programs as the National Industrial Recovery Act, and were based on the idea that prosperity can be assured if government gives each separate industry the
power to regulate and control itself so as to guarantee its own profits.
Marketing orders were based on the New Deal philosophy of

"managed abundance"—prosperity through "universal monopoly and universal scarcity."[3] People quickly realized that it was not in the public interest to give industry federal licenses for conspiring and price-gouging. But the government still gives dominant cooperatives and producers of fruit and nuts the power to outlaw competition, to force growers to abandon much of their crop, and to prohibit new entries into the field. To preserve federal control, the U.S. Department of Agriculture (USDA) effectively bans new technology that would boost fruit sales and benefit both growers and consumers. Marketing orders are based on the belief that whatever is bad for the rest of the economy is good for agriculture. With marketing orders, the government destroys harvests in order to prevent farmers from committing suicide.

The USDA's Annual Lemon Massacre

In the 1982–83 season, more lemons rotted on the trees in California and Arizona than were sold fresh to the American people.[4] Federal restrictions require California and Arizona growers to grow three or four lemons to earn the right to sell one fresh lemon on the domestic market. The USDA has driven up fresh lemon prices by as much as 40 percent, paralyzed the lemon business, blatantly sacrificed Arizona lemon growers to those in California, and helped drive thousands of growers out of the business. In 1929, before modern truck refrigeration, over 90 percent of the lemons grown in the country were sold fresh to the public. By 1955, thanks to the USDA, only 55 percent of the fresh lemon harvest was allowed on the market; by 1983, only 28 percent.

In the 1920s and 1930s, the California Fruit and Vegetable Exchange cooperative (the predecessor of Sunkist Growers, Inc.) tried to organize farmer boycotts in order to boost crop prices. But while some members agreed to withhold part of their crop, nonExchange growers continued selling their whole harvest on the market. Since some Exchange members were beginning to abandon the Exchange to play the market, the only solution was to have the government come in and effectively break any farmer's leg who would not follow the Exchange's decrees.

The USDA accepted the task of enforcing the Exchange's monopoly, effectively conferring upon the Exchange the right to regulate the lemon industry for its own benefit. For forty-five years the federal government has enforced Sunkist's cartel, attempting to freeze the lemon industry in its 1940 condition. Sunkist still controls 50 percent of the California-Arizona lemon crop, thanks mainly to federal restrictions on competition. Federal marketing orders allow Sunkist to sacrifice Arizona growers (who are not Sunkist members) to its Southern California members.

All lemons grown in California and Arizona are covered by Federal Marketing Order 910, created in 1941 ostensibly to help save the small family grower. But since 1954, the number of lemon growers has fallen from 8,012 to 2,079, according to the Small Business Administration. Order 910 is also supposed to stabilize lemon prices. But fresh lemon prices fluctuate far more than those of most fruit.

Marketing-order supply controls are based on the idea that USDA-sanctioned committees can maximize the revenue of growers by minutely controlling the supply allowed into the marketplace. Marketing orders prorate the amount of fruit that a grower can sell according to the number of lemons he claims to have available to ship. The prorate allows handlers in each of the four different districts affected by the order to ship the same percentage of their crop each week. The Lemon Administrative Committee (LAC) convenes in Los Angeles once a week and tells the USDA how many lemons growers in California and Arizona should be allowed to ship that week to the American market; the USDA then announces the number in the *Federal Register*. For instance, for the week of October 18–24, 1987, the USDA permitted 267,500 cartons of lemons to be shipped domestically. (Each carton contains roughly 100 lemons.) The following week, the USDA took a "riverboat gamble," opening the floodgates and letting lemon handlers dump 268,500 lemons on the market—an additional thousand cartons, equal to one extra lemon for every 2,000 American citizens. Luckily, the markets did not collapse, there was no panic at the Chicago Board of Trade, and the Republic survived. But the USDA quickly recognized the error of its ways and decreed the following week that only 265,800 cartons of lemons could be shipped to the market.

Parity is the foundation of lemon marketing orders. The success or failure of the lemon order is measured largely as the percentage of parity that government can drive prices up to. For marketing orders, coercion is justified to resurrect the price ratios of the good old days before World War I. Farmers' rights and consumers' choice are less important than the final price that government bureaucrats manage to finagle for a few.

Restrictions on domestic lemon marketing force growers to dump their crops at a loss on the export market. Japanese consumers often receive higher-quality American lemons for lower prices than Americans pay. This is one farm subsidy few congressmen brag about. Exports to Canada, on the other hand, are covered by federal restrictions, and growers need the LAC's permission to sell north of the border. Perry Walker, the vice president of Riverbend Farms, commented on the restrictions on exports in an interview with the author on April 23, 1988:

> Last week I sat in on the Lemon Administrative Committee meeting—and a representative from Sunkist announced that the industry has lost the eastern Canada market to foreign imports—and then she went on to give her market analysis without any comment or apparent chagrin. And then the Lemon Committee went on to tighten the regulations so that they could inflate the prices and make a lot of money. This has been the mentality of the industry for so many years—regardless of the facts of life.[5]

While the USDA restricts the rights of domestic producers to sell lemons to U.S. consumers, no such barriers exist for foreign producers. Inflated prices for fresh lemons in the United States have encouraged production increases in Spain, Chile, and elsewhere. Imports are pouring in while American growers gnash their teeth and watch their lemons rot. The *New York Times* reported in 1986 that California lemons cost 46 cents apiece while imported lemons from Chile cost only 31 cents.[6] And Chile is increasing its market share by leaps and bounds. In July 1987, two U.S. lemon growers imported thousands of cartons of lemons from Chile to supply their customers' demands. At the same time, the federal government forced the growers to let millions of their own lemons rot on the trees in order to preserve "stable markets."[7]

Order 910 is especially perverse because the three districts it covers harvest their crops to market at different times of the year. Lemon prices are sometimes twice as high in the summer as they are in the winter—thanks largely to the Lemon Administrative Committee, which is controlled by growers in Southern California. Northern California growers are not permitted to hold their fruit for sale during the summer, when demand is high. Arizona growers have had to stand by and watch their lemons freeze on the trees while waiting to receive government permission to harvest. The portion of the crop that must be allowed to rot (on the LAC's orders) is far lower in Southern California than it is in either Northern California or Arizona. A Small Business Administration study concluded that "there is a wide disparity in average net on-tree return between [Arizona and Southern California], as much as three to one in some years."[8] Even though Southern California lemons are the lowest-quality of the three districts, the LAC allows Southern California to sell culls while forcing other districts to let their top-quality fruits rot.

Lemon marketing orders are a case of planning for planning's sake. The *Federal Register* announcement of USDA policy for the 1987–88 lemon marketing policy declared, "The exact number of growers is not presently known, but estimates are that this number is in the range of 2,000 to 2,500."[9] The USDA insists on tightly controlling every single lemon grower even though the agency has little idea how many lemon growers there are.

The USDA marketing order disrupts all the lemon markets. Normally, growers sell their highest-quality fruit on the fresh market and then send the culls to the juice factory. But with prorate, farmers are forced to dump many high-quality lemons, glutting the juice market and making it impossible for farmers to earn a profit on lemons sold for lemonade. The net result of lemon marketing is that consumers buy fewer fresh lemons and more processed lemon juice, even though fresh lemons have more flavor and more vitamins. And since farmers lose money on their sales to the juice factories, this works out badly for both farmers and consumers.

Lemon prices were much higher in the 1987–88 season than in the previous year, and were far above parity. Yet the USDA continued to restrict lemon sales in order to drive prices even higher. As of April 12, 1988, lemon prices were 127 percent of the parity ratio. The branch chief of the marketing order administration, Ray Martin, told Charles Brader, the agricultural marketing service fruit and vegetable director, in January: "The LAC reports that the market for lemons is weak and unsteady, because of cold weather and excess inventory remaining unsold in the marketplace."[10] He was referring to the cold weather, not in the lemon-growing areas, but in the United States as a whole. According to most almanacs, cold weather is not an unusual condition for most of the United States during the winter months, but the Lemon Administrative Committee still offers that as an excuse to control lemon growers.

The USDA and LAC have some very entertaining arguments for continuing federal controls. The LAC claims that the demand for lemons is very inelastic, meaning that price changes would not increase demand for fresh lemons. The evidence: Demand for lemons has been very constant over recent decades.[11] In the same vein, a small business owner could say that he had no reason to open his shop after 5 P.M. since he had never had any customers after 5 P.M. in the past when his shop was closed. Since federal controls have prevented any real increase in demand, the LAC's argument is not exactly a model of persuasion.

In 1986 a severe frost destroyed much of the lemon crop, and the USDA temporarily suspended controls over its lemon growers. As Perry Walker observed, "Throughout the entire year, while the marketing controls were suspended, the industry moved more lemons than ever at higher prices, as measured by gross dollars to producers."[12] In the following season, the LAC asked the USDA to impose controls over lemon growers again, and the USDA obliged. Even though the growers were more prosperous without regulations, the Lemon Administrative Committee succeeded in reimposing its grip.

The USDA's Orange Crush

In 1980 Carl Pescosolido, a California orange grower, donated his surplus oranges to San Francisco churches to give to the poor. The USDA threatened to sue Pescosolido for $200,000 for disrupting the navel orange market by giving away oranges to poor people. Pescosolido claimed that his charity did not hurt anyone, since poor people could not afford to buy oranges anyway. So began a nine-year battle between one orange grower and the USDA, which has offered a flock of reasons to prohibit Pescosolido from selling all his oranges. But Pescosolido and lawyer-activist Jim Moody continue to make life miserable for USDA bureaucrats. Billy Pectal, the chairman of the Navel Orange Administrative Committee (NOAC), denounced Pescosolido, a Massachusetts immigrant, declaring that he had no business being in the citrus industry since he didn't get his college degree from Fresno State.

Pescosolido investigated the orange industry in 1980 and found that most of the family farmers the marketing orders were intended to protect were actually absentee owners, hobby farmers, or doctors and lawyers enjoying tax shelters. Russell Hanlin, the president of Sunkist, admitted that roughly 80 percent of the citrus farmers in California are absentee owners.[13]

Pescosolido declares, "When they say I can sell only 68 percent of my oranges, it's like someone taking 32 percent of my land."[14] Don Johnson of Johnson Farms in California complained in 1984 that he was only allowed to sell 6,000 boxes of oranges a day in the United States and Canada. "That's a half day's work," Johnson said. "We've got orders, but we can't ship them. I cannot sell more even if the buyer is willing to pay a premium price."[15] The USDA decrees the waste or squandering of up to half of the fresh orange crop each year.

Marketing orders are based on the idea that USDA-ordained committees know all and see all. Between 1980 and 1985 NOAC misestimated the navel orange harvest by 18 percent, 2 percent, 18 percent, 24 percent, 28 percent, and 12 percent respectively, but still insists on restricting orange sales. Donald Campbell, the chief judicial officer of the USDA and an ardent defender of marketing orders, noted in a January 1988 decision: "NOAC's weekly shipping schedules set forth in its annual marketing policies vary drastically from its later recommendations, which are reflected in the Secretary's volume regulations later issued. . . . NOAC's weekly schedules set forth in its annual marketing policies provided a 'helpful planning guide' that was better than nothing—but that is all that it was better than!"[16]

NOAC apparently believes that less is more, come hell or high water. For the 1986–87 season, NOAC hired an econometrician who stirred together some numbers and graphs and equations and announced that the growers' revenues would be maximized if they sold fresh only 43,600 train cars of a 77,500-car crop. (Each train car contains 1,000 cartons.) The committee decided to throw caution to the wind and ship 45,500 cars, declaring: "While this additional volume may result in less than maximum industry revenue as projected by [the econometrician], it is viewed by the committee as a future investment in market expansion of the fresh domestic market for navel oranges." But at the same time that NOAC was patting itself on the back for its "future investment in market expansion," it was slashing the domestic fresh navel orange supply by 15 percent from the previous year. This is a peculiar way to invest in future market expansion.

The USDA's insistence on throttling the navel orange supply is puzzling considering that, in announcing the 1987–88 navel orange policy, the USDA admitted that Florida orange production was increasing sharply, that Texas orange production was up by 50 percent in one year, and that there were big increases in apple and pear production as well as in imports of nectarines, peaches, and plums—all of which compete with navel oranges in the supermarkets.[17] The USDA still believes it can enrich growers by driving up orange prices. Florida growers are unhampered by federal supply controls and profit when the USDA stifles California orange sales.

There are four districts in the navel orange fiefdom. Reading the *Federal Register* notices on orange controls, one senses a peculiarity: Again and again, in every year from 1982 through 1985, the USDA restricted the amount of oranges that could be shipped from district 1, while allowing unlimited shipments from districts 2, 3, and 4. In order to control the orange crop the USDA has treated growers in different regions with gross inequity.

Because growers cannot sell their fresh navel oranges, they are forced to sell much of their crop to processors. As the 1984–85 marketing policy for California-Arizona navel oranges noted, "The processing market is unattractive as a major outlet for navel oranges since navel juice contains a bitter off-flavor which necessitates mixing it with other juices. This makes it unfeasible to compete successfully in the juice market," especially considering "negative grower returns from sales to processing outlets."[18] Growers have a choice between selling their fresh oranges and losing money. NOAC thinks that growers are better off losing money on much of their sales so that the prices they receive for fresh oranges may be artificially inflated.

The greatest absurdity of the citrus cartel is that it impoverishes consumers without enriching farmers. California farmers would be better off if they could sell all their crop, even at reduced prices. If the fruit were a few cents cheaper, consumers would buy all the oranges that California growers could produce. As Pescosolido says, "No USDA bureaucrat has ever been able to answer a single question: Can you tell me how my economic welfare is improved by your making it illegal for me to sell the product of my labor?"[19]

A severe frost occurred in Florida in 1985, creating the specter of a serious orange shortage. The USDA suspended supply controls on navel oranges for six months; there was a sharp drop in orange prices and a sharp increase in consumption despite the frost. A report by the USDA's Economic Research Service concluded that under deregulation in 1985, "grower income was about the same as it would have been under regulation."

A confidential 1974 study by the Navel Orange and Lemon administrative committees compared the return on investment in the three regulated citrus industries with that in thirty other comparable industries and found that, when regulated, citrus had the lowest return of all, and that returns were negative for navel orange and lemon producers. A *Journal of Law and Economics* study noted that "the inflation-adjusted, average per acre price of California valencia and navel groves fell by 17 and 24 percent respectively, between 1958, the first year for which data are available, and 1984. During the same period, the real value of farm acreage in the U.S. and in California more than doubled."[20] The loss in value of regulated farmland is the best measure of the farmers' vote of no confidence in marketing orders.

Both the orange and lemon controls have resulted in pervasive waste. A 1985 Justice Department study concluded that the lemon prorate caused "reduced consumption of fresh lemons, misallocation of resources due to chronic overproduction, reduced firm growth, and reduced price competition . . . and wasted $72 million a year.[21] A 1981 USDA report on the navel orange–marketing order concluded, "The result is that 'consumers pay for the production of much more food than they use.' Without supply controls, the USDA estimates, 20 to 30 percent fewer acres would be needed to produce the California-Arizona oranges currently reaching the markets."[22] In 1982, 83,000 tons of navel oranges were fed to cattle. Congressman George Miller, who led a fight against marketing orders, notes that 72,000 tons of those oranges "were produced by federally subsidized water brought to you by the taxpayers, a result insulting to the people of this country." One federal agency spends a mint to give farmers in dry or near-desert regions water nearly free—and another federal agency then prohibits the farmers from selling their crops.

Protecting Other Crops

Federal marketing orders provide benevolent markets for other farmers. The USDA's Raisin Administrative Committee forced California farmers to hold roughly a third of the raisin crop off the market in 1987 and restricted farmers from exporting their surplus raisins. The controls vary for each type of raisin: 33 percent of the natural seedless raisins, 27 percent of the dip seedless raisins, and 5 percent of the golden raisins are held off the market. The raisin surplus has become so large that the Raisin Administrative Committee is running a raisin diversion program, which gives growers old raisins in return for not producing new ones.

The filbert marketing order restricted farmers from selling 26 percent of their harvest in 1987. Ironically, while the USDA blocked the sale of 7 million pounds of domestic filberts, 7.5 million pounds of foreign filberts were imported.[23] The USDA restricted walnut farmers from selling 100 million pounds, or 28 percent, of their crop. The Spearmint Oil Marketing Committee prohibits farmers in California and Oregon from selling spearmint without a government license, though farmers in other states can produce and sell to their hearts' content. Each spearmint license specifies a set amount of production, called the producers' allotment. In 1987 the USDA allowed regulated spearmint producers to sell only 48 percent of their permitted production.

Under the Targeted Export Assistance program, the USDA has spent $5 million since 1986 to boost almond exports. Yet the almond marketing order is forcing producers effectively to abandon 18 percent of their almond harvest.[24] Over half of the U.S. almond crop is exported, but the quantities are strictly controlled so that the USDA can attempt to inflate world prices. One USDA program is spending millions to boost foreign demand for American almonds, while a second is prohibiting American farmers from exporting their almonds. Spanish and Italian almond producers are increasing their production at the same time that the USDA is stifling American exports.

The USDA's rationale for prohibiting almond sales is classic: "An oversupply of almonds could result in market instability and a downward spiral in prices, whereby buyers would be reluctant to purchase almonds until they were convinced that a bottom price had been reached."[25] This is typical of the bizarre assumptions underlying USDA supply-control programs: The USDA thinks it will not decrease demand for a crop by driving up the price, but fears that demand will fall if the crop prices falls. Perhaps if Mercedes Benz prices fell to $4,000 apiece, nobody would be interested in buying Mercedes anymore. The USDA apparently believes that consumers will only buy a product if the price is increasing or holding stable. If this were true, no business would ever have a sale, because consumers would all stay away expecting the next sale to offer even lower prices.

The USDA did terminate the hops marketing order in 1985. From 1966 to 1985 only licensed farmers were permitted to grow hops. The General Accounting Office noted that "there are no curbs on the import and export of hops. . . . Many brewers are willing to use domestic or foreign-produced hops interchangeably."[26]

The USDA had issued no new hops allotments since 1966. A grower either had to inherit, purchase, or lease allotments, which were based on how much a grower happened to produce in the years 1962, 1963, 1964, and 1965. Increased demand for hops was met simply by increasing the size of the allotments held by recipients. Noting that "a secondary market has developed which focuses producer concern more on allotment base trading than on the production and marketing of hops,"[27] the USDA found that the hops industry was characterized by a depressed market, large surpluses, and a severe disruption of the industry, and concluded: "All of these market conditions developed while the marketing order was in full operation."[28] "The salable quantity [of hops] recommended for the past several years has not accurately reflected market needs but rather has attempted to prevent

the allotment percentages from cutting across the contracts producers
have with dealers and to keep the price of lease base at reasonable
levels."[29] The same argument could justify abolishing all marketing
order supply controls.

Maximum Arbitrariness

Marketing orders are based on the idea that government can enforce
the will of an industry's dominant business on its competitors, and
that only good things will result. If this happened in any other industry, the Justice Department would sound the alarms; in agriculture,
the Justice Department is called in to punish violators of USDA cartels.
In 1937 the Supreme Court struck down a federally sanctioned cartel
in the coal industry. Marketing orders have survived court challenge
so far because the USDA claims that it is supervising the cartels to
insure that they function in the public interest.

But as the General Accounting Office concluded, "USDA relies on
industry-led marketing order committees to initiate all marketing
order actions and attends industry education meetings only when
specifically invited by industry groups."[30] Even a judicial finding of
fact that "there is no active supervision nor meaningful oversight by
the United States Department of Agriculture over the decisions by the
Nectarine Administrative Committee, the Nectarine Sub-Committee,
the Plum Commodity Committee, and the Plum Maturity Sub-Committee" fell on deaf ears.[31] The federal government promises to use its
full criminal prosecuting power to enforce the decisions of a private
business group the USDA does not even monitor. A 1986 study in the
Journal of Law and Economics observed: "So great is the Navel Orange
Administrative Committee's power that Secretary of Agriculture John
Block was forced to abandon his announced investigation of the degree to which his own administrative committees may have unduly
constrained the supply of California-Arizona fresh oranges."[32]

Marketing orders have been very profitable for the cooperatives
who control the committees. Sunkist has dominated the Navel
Orange, Valencia Orange, and Lemon administrative committees ever
since their creation. On the Lemon Administrative Committee, six of
the twelve voting members are Sunkist affiliates. Sunkist can thus veto

proposals it doesn't like. The Small Business Administration concluded that, "in effect, the LAC's annual marketing policy statement originates at Sunkist, which has far more data processing capacity than any other marketing entity represented on the Committee. . . . The inescapable conclusion is that prorate allows Sunkist to maintain its market dominance."[33] The employees of the Navel, Valencia, and Lemon Order administrative committees are members of Sunkist's pension plan—which surely does wonders to preserve their objectivity. There is even a direct phone line from the Navel Orange Administrative Committee to Sunkist's headquarters.

In 1987 a USDA administrative law judge found that

> the USDA official in Washington to whom all reports concerning NOAC's meetings were first screened before being sent upward, admitted that he "would exclude information such as alternative motions for volume regulation," on the basis of a judgmental decision that information concerning alternatives to volume control should not be upstreamed. . . . No effort was made to ascertain, analyze, or consider contrary views or objections to the marketing policy submitted by NOAC. . . . The consistency of the regulations with NOAC's recommendations was, in fact, asserted as a justification for their issuance without meaningful, independent analysis of the underlying considerations upon which they were based.[34]

In other words, because USDA regulations had always followed NOAC requests, that proved that NOAC requests were in the public interest.

Quality Control as a Weapon

Many federal marketing controls also restrict the *quality* of fruit that may be sold to consumers. While this may seem reasonable, such controls are easily manipulated to restrict supply. James Gattuso of the Heritage Foundation noted that "by adjusting quality standards on an annual basis, many industry associations attempt to limit the supply of their product going to market in order to maximize their income. The NOAC, for instance, has often varied its size limitations for oranges from season to season, and sometimes during a season, to control the supply of that crop."[35]

Federal quality controls are based on the idea that a free market has no incentive to regulate the quality of products—that consumers are too stupid to judge good fruit from bad. The federal government has a beef-grading system that informs consumers about the quality of beef—Grade A, Grade B, Choice, etc. If the federal beef-grading system worked like the marketing order system, the government would condemn 10 billion to 15 billion pounds of hamburger each year in an attempt to drive up T-bone steak prices. But federal quality controls, which are changed at the drop of a hat, are often only a de facto expropriation of the grower's property.

The Nectarine Administrative Committee (NAC) has used so-called quality controls to restrict the varieties of nectarines the public can buy. The NAC invented fourteen color chips and declared that fruit that did not match the required color chip could not be sold. When the chips were first invented, nectarines had to match the color chip "G" to be sold; now, nectarines must meet the more restrictive color chip "M"—even though there is no evidence that consumers' preference in nectarines has changed. The NAC never did any research to see if its color chips accurately measured the nectarine's condition at the time it was received by the buyer or grocery chain. A USDA administrative law judge, Dorothea Baker, observes: "At no time when the color chips change or when the specific maturity standards change has said change been published in the *Federal Register*, or been open to notice, and an opportunity to comment. There has been no showing of a substantial basis and purpose for said changes."[36]

The same color standards apply regardless of whether the nectarine is heading for a store shelf two miles away or to New York City, 2,500 miles away. Since nectarines continue to ripen after being picked, federal quality controls often cause the fruit to be overripe by the time it reaches its final destination. The NAC has done no research on how many cartons of fruit were rejected by buyers for being overripe.[37] Elliott, Inc. in Fresno, California, lost $347,000 in 1986 alone due to the committee's standards. Elliott was the only grower producing Tom Grand nectarines—a variety popular on the East Coast that does not turn as yellow as some others. The NAC prohibited Elliott from shipping his Tom Grands until they had passed the color-chip test. Elliot, Inc., received many complaints about overripe fruit.

The NAC prohibits handlers from allowing fruit to ripen after being picked in order to meet the color-chip standards. The nectarine harvest now requires six or seven pickings per orchard; it used to be done in two or three. This greatly increases labor costs, yet does nothing to boost fruit quality.

The NAC's enforcement of its color-chip standards is arbitrary. Nectarines often become so ripe that they fall off the tree, while the nectarine committee is insisting that the fruit is not ripe enough to pick.[38] The committee has raised color standards at the last minute in order to prevent some farmers from harvesting their crops, so that farmers who are members of the NAC can have an advantage over their competition. None of the farmers who are member of the Nectarine Administrative Committee has ever been harmed by the maturity standards; nonmembers have. USDA judge Baker notes, "There is evidence on record that the Nectarine Administrative Committee, the Nectarine Maturity Sub-committee, the Plum Commodity Committee, and the Plum Maturity Sub-committees . . . have engaged in favoritism with respect to dealings with handlers and growers. . . ."[39]

One nectarine grower, Kash, Inc., had to abandon much of its nectarine crop in 1986 because of the NAC's stringent color standards. Still obliged to fill outstanding orders for nectarines, Kash purchased some nectarines from the company owned by the chairman of the Nectarine Administrative Committee. These nectarines had passed the color test at the chairman's warehouse, but, the inspectors ruled, they failed to pass the color standard after they had been bought by Kash, Inc.[40]

The Plum Marketing Committee has also created quality-control standards that are easily abused. In 1985 the committee decided to protect the public from buying any plums that did not have "spring" at the time they were harvested. Fresno, California, attorney Brian Leighton observes, "Spring is nothing more than the inspector holding the plum in the palm of his or her hand and squeezing it, and if it does not depress then there is insufficient 'spring'—but this is so subjective, since one inspector may not squeeze it as hard as some other inspector."[41] Elliott, Inc., had to throw away $50,000 worth of plums because the inspector said they had insufficient spring. None of the members of the Plum Marketing Committee has lost a cent from a springless plum.

The Almond Board appears to have blatantly abused its power. The California Almond Growers Exchange (CAGE) controls most almond production, and thus controls the USDA's Almond Board. In 1983 the Almond Board passed a rule to force all members to spend 2.5 cents per pound of almonds produced for brand-name advertising. Since almond profits are often around 10 cents a pound, the advertising fee eats up roughly 25 percent of the normal profits.

The vast majority of domestic almonds are either exported or sold to food processors as candy-bar or cereal ingredients. Brand-name advertising is a waste of money for most almond growers, since their sales are determined by industry contracts rather than advertising. One company—the California Almond Growers Exchange—sells 92 percent of all almonds sold in U.S. grocery stores under its Blue Diamond label. By forcing other companies to advertise, it essentially forced all almond companies to subsidize Blue Diamond sales. And the Almond Board specifically prohibited companies from doing brand-name advertising that would direct the consumer to a specific store that stocked the company's almonds instead of Blue Diamond.

The Almond Board has also abused its set-aside power. Almonds that are set aside can be either sold for cattle feed, which brings in less than 10 cents a pound, or for almond butter. But nuts destined for almond butter may not be sold for less than 65 cents a pound. CAGE is one of the few companies in the United States that makes almond butter.

Nineteen eighty-five was a good year for almond production, and the Almond Board forced growers to hold 20 percent of their harvest off the market. The Almond Board set a September 1986 deadline for almond handlers to dump at a loss all the set-aside almonds from the 1985 crop year. In March 1986 the Almond Board became aware that the 1986 almond crop would likely be much smaller than traditional demand, thus driving almond prices up sharply. Most of the almond handlers had disposed of their almond surplus at a loss by July 1986, when the Almond Board announced that, due to changes in the almond market, growers and handlers could sell their set-aside reserves on the open market. CAGE still had almost its entire reserve, and thus made millions of dollars selling its set-aside almonds for over $2 a pound after the CAGE-controlled board had pressured CAGE competitors to dump their almonds, often for less than 10 cents a pound.

The Almond Board has also been accused of using confidential business information to steal customers. According to Robert Saulsbury of Saulsbury Orchards:

> The CAGE-controlled Board has had access to Saulsbury Orchards' almond receipt and sales records and all other handlers' records and, upon information and belief, uses those records to its competitive advantage . . . by observing to whom Saulsbury Orchards sells its almonds and with what growers Saulsbury Orchards contract for handling of the growers' almonds, which records CAGE then uses to undercut Saulsbury Orchards' sales price, and uses to solicit Saulsbury Orchards' growers away from Saulsbury Orchards.[42]

The USDA claims that the marketing orders are supported by more than two-thirds of all growers. But the USDA's elections are enough to make Richard Daley, the late mayor of Chicago, envious. In a recent referendum on nectarines, growers representing only one-third of the nectarine harvest voted. The USDA asked nectarine handlers for a list of the growers and left it at that. Many of the growers who did receive ballots were confused about what they were voting on. The USDA's official press release declared that the growers would be voting on whether to continue the USDA marketing-order regulations "to provide a flow of quality fruit to market."[43] The USDA defended itself against charges that it failed to publicize the election by claiming that it had announced the coming referendum in the *Federal Register*. But not many nectarine growers read the *Federal Register*, as Brian Leighton points out.[44]

Marketing orders are apparently so vital to public safety that Congress increasingly prohibits any discussion of their merits. Congress has explicitly prohibited the Federal Trade Commission and the Office of Management and Budget from spending any money studying the effects of marketing orders. If Congress will not fix the program, at least it can prevent government agencies from needlessly upsetting people about it.

The USDA's Star Chamber

One might expect the usual American response to all this manipulation: Sue the bastards! Growers often do sue the USDA. But disputes between the Agriculture Department and farmers, handlers, and others affected by USDA regulations are under the jurisdiction of the USDA's own administrative law judges. The USDA, in writing and administering the rules and passing judgment on accused violators, serves as legislator, executor, and judge. This is a perfect recipe for tyranny. Brian Leighton, formerly an assistant U.S. district attorney, declares: "Thieves, murderers, and rapists have far greater legal rights—far greater right of due process and far greater right of speedy appeal—than do farmers regulated under USDA marketing orders."[45]

The USDA's Administrative Law Judge system is notorious for arbitrariness and politicization. In the case of *Utica Packing Company v. John R. Block*, a USDA judicial officer made a decision with which USDA officials "violently disagreed," according to the USDA's own testimony. A top USDA official removed the judge who made the "wrong" decision from the case, announced that the case would be re-opened, and then appointed a deputy assistant secretary who had no legal experience to preside over the second trial. Surprise! The defendant was found guilty the second time around. The United States Court of Appeals, Sixth Circuit, overturned the USDA's conviction and condemned the USDA's judicial process: "There is no guarantee of fairness when the one who appoints a judge has the power to remove the judge before the end of a proceedings for rendering a decision which displeases the appointer. Yet this is exactly what happened in this case." The court concluded, "All notions of judicial impartiality would be abandoned if such a procedure were permitted."[46]

Growers and handlers suffering under marketing orders have been caught in a Catch-22 bind. On the one hand, the USDA's own administrative law judges will provide no relief—or if they do, their decisions will be overturned by their superiors. On the other hand, federal courts insist that growers first exhaust their administrative remedies and are extremely deferential about the Agriculture Department's "expertise." As the Supreme Court ruled in 1984, "The regulation of agricultural products is a complex, technical undertaking. Congress channeled disputes concerning marketing orders to the Secretary of Agriculture . . . because it believed that only he has the expertise necessary to illuminate and resolve questions about them."[47] Farmers are thus left with no escape. The USDA's alleged expertise in farming thus becomes a blank check to oppress individual farmers—for the supposed good of farmers as a class.

The ongoing Saulsbury–Cal-Almond case against the almond marketing order is a typical example of how growers get caught in a legal crossfire. On October 13, 1985, Cal-Almond, along with Saulsbury, filed a suit in the USDA's administrative law system to end their forced payments for advertising under the almond plan. USDA lawyers filed a "Motion to Dismiss or in the Alternative for a More Definitive Statement" on December 5, 1985. Saulsbury filed an amended petition on February 24, 1986. On March 28, 1986, USDA lawyers filed a "Motion to Dismiss Petitioner's First Amended Petition"; on August 6, 1986, Cal-Almond filed a request for a hearing. On September 30, 1986, Administrative Law Judge Victor Weber dismissed the first amended petition. On November 3, 1986, Cal-Almond filed an appeal protesting the dismissal. On November 24, 1986, the USDA requested additional time to file its "Opposition to Cal-Almond, Inc.'s Appeal Petition" because "due to other legal work currently pending Respondent's attorney will be unable to prepare a response by November 24, 1986." On April 13, 1987, the chief judicial officer of the USDA, Donald Campbell, denied Cal-Almond's appeal, declaring that "whatever legal or factual merits may exist in Petitioner's views, they are submerged in sweeping opposition to the Marketing Order."[48] In other words, because the almond handler did not like marketing orders in general, he was not entitled even to a hearing of his grievances.

While Saulsbury was repeatedly denied relief through the USDA's glacier-like bureaucracy, the USDA and the Justice Department were both prosecuting the company in a federal court at full speed for failing to comply with the marketing order. Then, when Saulsbury attempted to raise "affirmative defenses" in the federal court, both the USDA lawyer and the Justice Department declared that such issues could only be raised in a USDA administrative law hearing, since they were outside the province of the federal court.[49] Federal courts would not provide relief because the bureaucracy was supposed to provide relief; the bureaucracy would not provide relief because the grower was hostile to its marketing orders.

The more the government attempts to control the economy, the less respect it can afford to show for individual rights. This is epitomized by the USDA's refusal to allow citizens to comment on its weekly regulations restricting citrus sales. As Donald Campbell, the chief judicial officer, declared: "It would be as practicable to require the weatherman to engage in notice and comment rulemaking before issuing a weather forecast as to require the Secretary to engage in notice and comment rulemaking before issuing the weekly volume limitation regulations."[50] But the weatherman is not seizing anyone's property; the secretary of agriculture's regulations are often de facto condemnations of a grower's harvest.

Carl Pescosolido's case against marketing orders required six years to get a ruling from the USDA. And when one judge vindicated Pescosolido, saying that NOAC supply controls from 1979 to 1984 violated federal law, Campbell promptly overturned that decision. His 284-page decision, replete with exclamation marks and warnings of a "bloodbath" if government ended controls, offers valuable insight into the USDA's paternalist mentality. Campbell proudly described himself "as a careerist who has been involved with USDA's regulatory programs since 1949." Growers must seek relief from a man who has spent his whole life working in and building the existing system; they have little chance of getting an objective hearing.

Campbell struck down the vindication partly because:

> It is well settled that the lawfulness of a marketing order must be judged by the facts contained in the promulgation hearing record rather than the facts petitioners would seek to introduce at a § 8c(15) (A) proceeding. The Order must stand or fall upon the basis of the evidence before the Secretary adduced during the promulgation proceedings, and additional evidence is not relevant or admissible in the 8c(15) (A) proceeding.[51]

Campbell notes, "All interested persons had the opportunity to testify at that [promulgation] hearing, file briefs, and file exceptions to the recommended decision." But the hearing Campbell refers to was held in 1953! Because the USDA decided it made sense to expropriate farmers' harvests thirty-six years ago, the sons and grandsons of farmers have no right to complain about the loss of their property now. (Pescosolido's lawyer, Jim Moody, apologized that he was not yet born in 1953 and thus missed the hearings.) Campbell even declared that the USDA administrative law judges "should not permit petitioners to subpoena or introduce evidence relating to the wisdom of the program, or purporting to show that petitioners have been damaged by activities in accordance with the provisions of the order."

Campbell then declared that it was very important that people not expect the USDA to act on the evidence presented at a hearing on marketing orders:

> Moreover, even at an "ideal" hearing where all sides of the issue were presented by the witnesses, if the Secretary were required to adopt every proposal supported by the evidence, this would drastically curtail or eliminate the value of the Department's expertise derived from thousands of hearings. The witnesses at the hearing, rather than the Secretary, would actually determine whether an order or an amendment should be adopted to effectuate the Congressional policy. This could easily lead to the disruption of the Federal regulatory program through the adoption of unsound proposals.[52]

Campbell declared, "The purpose of the hearing is to allow interested parties to present their views and evidence in order to 'educate' the secretary as to the issues involved," and any expectation that the USDA would act strictly on the evidence "would make a farce of the hearing process, and would prevent it from being an important educational tool for the Secretary."[53]

This is an enlightened-despot theory of justice: The hearings are not intended to result in any action, but only to "educate" the ruler who might use the information to grant relief to the suffering peasants. Farmers have no right to expect any action based on the evidence; they can only hope that their appeals and efforts to "educate" the secretary will persuade His Excellency to alleviate their plight.

Campbell was also upset that the administrative law judge had allowed C. W. McMillan, a former assistant secretary of agriculture, to "testify voluntarily with respect to his mental processes" in the hearings on the orange marketing orders. The judge had issued a subpoena to John Ford, a deputy assistant secretary, to testify, which Campbell said "violated the principle against issuing subpoenas to high-ranking agency policy-makers. Indeed, it would even have been improper to require these officials to give a deposition." Campbell concluded, "This is a matter of substantial import to the Department since there are at present eleven cases now pending in the Department involving challenges to Fruit and Vegetable marketing orders, in which subpoenas may be (or have been) requested. (If any subpoenas have already been issued under circumstances not consistent with this decision, they should, of course, be quashed.)"[54] Campbell thus invoked executive privilege for almost anyone related to the marketing orders—including the administrators of the Navel Orange Administrative Committee. "For the foregoing reasons, the testimony of the Department's officials and former official should be disregarded in this proceeding, and, in future proceedings, such witnesses should not be required or permitted to testify."[55] Thus, the Department of Agriculture has the right to control minutely a farmer's business operations, passing economic life-and-death decisions over them, and yet has no obligation whatsoever to explain the grounds of its decisions. Because the USDA's regulatory mission is so important, the regulators have no obligation to the regulated.

Crucifying Consumers

The Supreme Court ruled in 1984 that American citizens have no voice in federal regulations that restrict their food supply. In a decision on the effort made by the Community Nutrition Institute to rescind federal regulations that sharply increase the price of milk, the Supreme Court ruled: "Handlers and producers—but not consumers—are entitled to participate in the adoption of retention of market orders. . . . Allowing consumers to sue would severely disrupt this complex and delicate administrative scheme. . . ."[56] Marketing-order supply controls are one of the most overtly anti-consumer laws in the Code of Federal Regulations.

Congress claims that marketing orders are not not anti-consumer because there are provisions in the law to protect the consumer. What exactly does the law say? According to CFR §602, "It is declared to be the policy of Congress. . . . To protect the interest of the consumer by (a) approaching the level of prices which it is declared to be the policy of Congress to establish . . . and (b) authorizing no action under this chapter which has for its purpose the maintenance of prices to farmers above the level which it is declared to be the policy of Congress to establish. . . ."[57]

This is wonderful: The consumer will be protected because the program will establish prices at the point where Congress wishes prices to be—hence, the consumer is protected. As if the consumer were automatically protected because the prices are driven up to the level Congress wants them to be—as if any price Congress chose automatically protected consumers, simply because Congress said, "abracadabra"!

According to the USDA's chief judicial officer, Donald Campbell, the secretary of agriculture's "statutory duty is to protect the interests of the producers. . . . The essential purpose of the [Agricultural Marketing] Act is to raise producer prices. If a marketing order can double producer prices in a particular year, without exceeding parity, that is exactly what Congress had in mind when it passed the Act. . . ."[58] Congress amended the Agricultural Marketing Act in 1954 to allow supply controls to drive food prices far above the parity level, thus making a shambles of the argument that marketing orders are only intended to provide farmers a fair price.

Marketing orders have driven up prices and slashed consumption of many regulated products. Since 1960, average per capita citrus consumption has dropped by 29 percent, from 32.5 pounds in 1960 to 23.0 pounds in 1985. When a journalist confronted Ben Davis, a USDA official, with evidence that the USDA was driving fresh citrus out of the average citizen's life, Davis responded, "Oranges are not an essential food. People don't need oranges. They can take vitamins."[59]

Anti-Marketing Orders

Federal marketing order restrictions have destroyed farmers' and handlers' incentive to sell their crops vigorously. Creating a permanent, artificial scarcity guarantees that the seller needs to make little or no effort to dispose of his product. Prorate for oranges and lemons has destroyed competition throughout the grocery industry and lowered the quality of fruit received by American consumers, because with so little fruit available, it is far more expensive for grocers to throw away fruit of poor quality. As a University of California study concluded, "The system protects the growers of inferior fruit, but only by removing the major incentive to improve fruit quality."[60] Another reason for low quality is that the orange prorates tend to make the marketing season longer than it would have been under a free market, "so that more oranges deteriorate on the tree." As professor Roy J. Smith of the University of California at Riverside noted, "essentially what the prorate has done is eliminate in marketing the contributions of the American competitive free enterprise system. Growers with the poorest of fruit quality now under prorate can sell just as much fruit as growers with the best of fruit."[61] Robert Herrick, the vice president of Citrus Company, notes, "The technology of growing, packing, marketing and distribution of agricultural products is much more sophisticated than the system that existed in the mid-1930s. . . . In spite of major modifications and improvements the [government administrative committees] . . . have never taken one positive step toward improving marketing."[62]

Marketing order committees have been actively hostile to new technology that could increase sales of restricted crops. A new techology—shrink-wrapping—greatly decreases the perishability of lemons. Lemons shrink-wrapped in a plastic coating do not dry out as fast as unwrapped lemons do, and can be stored for six months or more. The Small Business Administration noted that shrink-wrapping would give the lemon industry "greater ability to assure an orderly, dependable flow of lemons to meet shifting seasonable demand. . . . Market survey tests indicate that shrink-wrapped lemons would displace plastic container lemon juice, thus bringing higher returns to the fresh market."[63] The National Association of Convenience Stores vigorously supports the legalization of shrink-wrapping and expects that it would sharply increase lemon sales.

But so far the USDA has effectively blocked shrink-wrapping.[64] Lemons must be sent to market within a few weeks of harvest, regardless of market prices or demand. The number of fresh lemons a grower is allowed to sell is determined by the weekly prorate. The grower can automatically sell his prorated share, but any shrink-wrapped lemons he sells reduce his quota, so he has no incentive to spend the extra penny per lemon to wrap his crop. The new technology would disrupt government control; in order to save their jobs, USDA employees effectively ban the new technology.

Marketing orders have reduced the farmers' share of the consumer's food dollar. For the average fruit and vegetable, the farmer receives 28 cents of the retail dollar. For citrus from California and Arizona, farmers receive only 15 cents on the dollar. Marketing orders, by creating de facto monopolies, greatly increase the power of the middlemen—the fruit handlers and packers. Marketing orders divert much of the crop to the processors (of orange juice, lemon juice, almond butter, etc.) at fire-sale prices. Often the same cooperative that forces farmers to sell their harvest to processors at a loss owns the processing plants.

To be fair, marketing orders have engendered many creative marketing techniques. Hops producers resort to "rolling bales," in which the owner rolls a bale of hops off his truck into the ditch and a friend drives by afterwards and retrieves the contraband. Orange growers resort to "right-hand–drawer sales" or "Mexican exports," a charade in which a grower would claim exemption from prorate for a crop because it was being sold to Mexico. Orange exports to Mexico would soar, even though no Mexican ever received the oranges. Almond growers are allowed an exemption from controls if they sell their almonds for cattle feed. One almond grower launched a cattle-feeding business on the side, painted a yellow line down the middle of his warehouse, and then moved his almonds from one side of the warehouse to the other. (The Almond Board was very unhappy.)[65]

Marketing controls assume that farmers are lemmings and will plunge into the sea unless government keeps them on a short leash. Marketing order controls are based on the idea that farmers are inevitably victimized by a free market and cannot make a profit unless the USDA intervenes to knock both farmers and consumers on the head. Most fruits and vegetables are marketed with no restrictions, yet somehow their producers avoid collective suicide. While the federal government spends tens of thousands of dollars a year imposing restrictions on spearmint farmers, peppermint farmers are allowed to grow and sell as much as they choose. As James Gattuso notes, "Growers of pistachios, macadamia nuts and pecans, for example, produce crops freely, while walnut, filbert, and almond growers are regulated. Sweet cherries are uncontrolled, while tart cherries are subject to marketing orders."[66] The USDA forces farmers to abandon most of their fresh lemons, while the entire fresh lime crop is sold on the market without any disruption. The USDA keeps a death grip on navel oranges, but there are no controls on the sales of Temple oranges grown in California—and no market disruptions.

Avocados were under strict marketing orders until 1973. After marketing controls were lifted, the real price of avocados fell by 23 percent and avocado consumption increased fourfold: Both producers and consumers were better off.

Farmers of many crops routinely contract ahead of time to sell their crops at a set price, a procedure that provides security to farmers and stability to markets. California grapefruit growers routinely sell their entire crop to Safeway and other grocery chains before the harvest. The market is orderly and there is no need for the federal government to force the growers to waste half their crop.

The USDA's Know-Nothing Economics

The USDA builds its policies on a foundation of meaningless terms and nonsense definitions. The annual waste of citrus fruit has provoked much controversy. But as the General Accounting Office reported:

> The only written analysis the USDA provided us in regard to the controversial lemon marketing order was a September 1983 position paper that concluded that the lemon order should be reaffirmed because the program "tends to minimize intraseasonal price instability and result in higher season average grower returns than would be realized without regulation." No analyses were provided regarding such factors as the competitive nature of the lemon order, . . . whether consumers were paying higher prices for prorated lemons than would occur in the order's absence, or whether the order allows for individual incentives and product innovation. In brief, the position paper did little to respond to basic concerns that have been expressed by consumers about the market performance of the lemon marketing order.[67]

As usual, the USDA kept its eye on the big picture—higher prices for farmers. It doesn't matter how tiny a fraction of his harvest a farmer is allowed to sell; as long as he gets a good price for a single carton of citrus, the marketing orders have succeeded.

Marketing orders are "abracadabra" economics—with a bureaucrat picking numbers out of thin air and then praising or damning reality according to how it corresponds to his fancies. When asked what orderly marketing was, the USDA assistant secretary for marketing, C. W. McMillan, admitted, "I have no idea what that is. I have never heard anyone define orderly marketing."[68] The USDA recently commissioned a study on marketing orders that concluded, "Orderly marketing is . . . a matching of supply with potential demand at prices reflecting the costs of producing and marketing the commodity by typical well-managed firms in the industry."[69]

This definition sounds plausible, but such a regulatory goal is like searching in a dark room for a black cat that isn't there. Who can know what potential demand is at any given price except by seeing the market move to that price and watching how buyers and sellers react? If the producers' profits are 2 percent, does that mean the market is disorderly, but would be orderly if profits were 4 percent? And who is to say which firm is "typical" and "well-managed"? Congress has made it very profitable, for tax purposes, to lose money in agriculture. Should tax-loss profits be considered or disregarded? And if they are disregarded, how can the rest of the analysis make any sense?

Marketing orders are intended to produce higher prices. Higher prices inevitably lead to increased production and drive down consumption, which increases the amount of apparent surplus at USDA-decreed high prices. The USDA has forced California and Arizona lemon and navel orange growers to throw away more and more of their crop as the years go by. Marketing orders tend to make markets progressively more and more unbalanced. The more successful the USDA is in inflating prices, the greater the need for government supply controls.

Marketing orders characterize the USDA's paranoia toward price fluctuations—typical of any bureaucracy where stability is the highest value and risk and uncertainty are among the greatest evils. With marketing orders, the USDA thinks it is better to have high prices every year than a low price one year and a high price the next year. The USDA's preference is contrary to the inherent nature of agriculture according to records dating back to 8000 B.C.

Even if the government could perfectly control the supply of a single product, marketing orders would fail. If the government drives up the price of navel oranges, people will buy more Temple oranges, apples, or grapefruit. If the government drives up the price of nectarines, people will buy more peaches. If government drives up the price of almonds, people will buy pistachios and cashews. Marketing orders only make sense with captive customers. Until the USDA can dictate to consumers like it dictates to fruit and nut farmers, marketing order controls are an exercise in futility, and suicide for the controlled farmers. The USDA is paying hundreds of bureaucrats to plan, regulate, restrict, and balance American supply and demand at the same time that imports are pouring in and making a farce of the entire process.

Marketing order supply controls are based on a philosophical foundation that is antithetical to other farm programs. For the Farmers Home Administration, the individual farmer is a sacred entity worth any cost to preserve. The concept of marketing orders blatantly disregards the interests and survival of individual farmers. The Regulatory Flexibility Act requires that federal agencies take special consideration of any federal regulation that could have a significant adverse impact on small businessmen. Each week during orange and lemon seasons, the *Federal Register* blithely announces that "the Administrator of the Agricultural Marketing Service has determined that the issuance of weekly volume regulations will not have a significant economic impact on a substantial number of small entities."[70] While many lemon growers are screaming that federal restrictions are sinking them, the USDA smugly repeats that its regulations do not have a significant impact on a substantial number. The political reason for this is clear: Marketing orders are designed to benefit cooperatives rather than independent farmers, and cooperatives have more political clout.

Conclusion

De minimis non curat lex—"the law does not concern itself with trifles," the Romans said. While murder, robbery, and rape rates in the United States have soared, the United States government is devoting more and more resources to haggling over the diameter of navel oranges to the hundredth of an inch, contemplating whether plums have enough spring, and entertaining itself by decreeing how many lemons American farmers will be allowed to sell each week. If the government cannot maintain law and order in American cities, at least it can make its wrath felt in the nation's citrus groves. The more the government fails in its basic duties to the citizens, the more obsessed government becomes in attempting tasks for which it has no competence.

There are two astonishing things about marketing orders. The first is that the USDA ever believed that it could enrich farmers by strangling their market and destroying their incentive to actively market their crops. The second is that the USDA has kept doing the same thing for almost fifty years, regardless of the overwhelming evidence of failure. Government begins by making an economic mistake and then is obliged for political reasons to repeat the same mistake every year. Once government intervention disrupts a market, those who benefit create political pressure to prevent the government from ever allowing the market to regain equilibrium. Eventually the bureaucrats who administer the program come to believe the politicians' own rhetoric about the public interest.

Marketing orders exemplify the principle that underlies almost all agricultural policy: The USDA can make America a better place by wasting and misallocating resources and by forcing people to do what no individual in his right mind would do. There is no excuse for restricting supply of one commodity that should not apply to restricting supply of all commodities. And since most commodities do just fine without supply restrictions, supply restrictions are unjustified for any commodity. As Jim Moody notes, "If oranges were condoms, [there] would be no problem with selling them. If government tried to restrict the number of condoms like it tries to restrict the number of oranges, judges would go berserk in minutes."[71] But agriculture is different.

♦ *Chapter 10* ♦

Uncle Sam, Super Sodbuster

Federal agricultural policy has sacrificed the land in order to buy farmers' votes. Conservation is one of the biggest smokescreens in agricultural policy, and is routinely invoked to justify giving money to almost anyone living outside the city limits. Conservation has always been one of the cups in the shell-game defense of farm policy.

Federal agricultural policy-makers have long proclaimed that the private sector is inherently destructive to the environment. In 1934 Henry Wallace, secretary of agriculture, declared: "Probably the most damaging indictment that can be made of the capitalistic system is the way in which its emphasis on unfettered individualism results in exploitation of natural resources. . . ."[1] In 1936 Agricultural Adjustment Administrator H. R. Tolley declared, "Farmers were pushed—or if you pleased, coerced—by sheer competition into ruthless exploitation of soil fertility. Destruction of the remaining good lands of the country appeared to be the goal of rugged individualism."[2] The New Deal and subsequent federal agricultural policy have been based on the idea that the more the government fetters individuals, the better off the farmland will be.

Yet though the free market has produced many environmental abuses, the federal agricultural system has produced far more systematic and pervasive land damage. While the U.S. Department of Agriculture (USDA) has spent over $25 billion on so-called farm conservation programs, other USDA programs and policies have financed almost every environmental abuse the Sierra Club can think of. The government's bonuses for land abuse have been far more effective than government programs to prevent or curtail erosion. Agricultural conservation is a classic study in self-defeating government policy—and of politicians' faith that one more handout or one more regulation will counter the damage of all the previous handouts and regulations.

Conservation programs have been pseudoscience at its worst. Bureaucrats arbitrarily chose a number that was supposed to represent the dividing line between good and bad soil practices. Yet there was no scientific foundation for the standard: Bureaucrats made a guess, and then wasted billions of dollars on the belief that their guess was worth more than half a page of print in the *Federal Register*. And now that new research proves that the bureaucracy's guess was extremely inaccurate, politicians and bureaucrats have refused to reform programs to conform with new evidence. Conservation programs are a classic example of a handout program's inability to stop giving handouts after it is proven that it serves little or no public purpose.

A Humble Beginning

Soil conservation became a big cause for the USDA when the Supreme Court struck down the Agricultural Adjustment Act (AAA) in 1936. The AAA was the USDA's main engine for giving money to farmers—and without a good funnel to distribute money, government control of agriculture was doomed. So a few weeks later, the Soil Conservation and Domestic Allotment Act was enacted to pay farmers for reducing their acreage of "soil-depleting" crops—which by amazing coincidence turned out to be exactly the same crops that government planners were anxious to restrict.

To boost public support for farm programs that were widely derided for paying farms not to work, the USDA greatly exaggerated the danger from soil erosion, warning of imminent national disaster unless soil erosion was immediately controlled. Political scientist Charles Hardin noted in his 1967 report for the President's Commission on Food and Fiber, "The nation repeatedly was told that '100 million acres' [of soil] had been 'ruined.' On one occasion, Dr. Bennett raised the figure to a billion acres, whereupon one of his aides hastened to correct his slip, but added that when men of the SCS [Soil Conservation Service] spoke of the 'ruin' of virgin soil they did not necessarily mean 'lost beyond any future use,' but rather they used the word 'ruin' as it would apply to any virgin."[3] This was the usual political scam of creating a crisis in order to justify an expansion of government power. In 1936 President Roosevelt even suggested that erosion was so devastating that the United States should consider abandoning all agricultural exports, since it really amounted to "shipping our soil fertility to foreign nations."[4] This was very convenient, since FDR's agricultural policies had already decimated crop export markets.

Hardin concluded in 1967, "The alarms over soil erosion went so extravagantly beyond the facts."[5] A 1936 study by the Brookings Institution concluded that "the program seems on the whole to take on more definitely the character of financial aid for everybody and less that of specific implementation for a planned system of efficient farming."[6] Joseph Davis of Stanford University's Food Research Institute observed, "The [soil conservation] payments . . . tend to create vested interests which will stand in the way of sound economic development of the industry in the future."[7] But paying farmers to conserve soil was much more politically defensible than paying farmers not to work, so government paid farmers to conserve soil.

After the 1930s, soil conservation was a secondary goal of the farm program until 1956, when the Eisenhower administration launched the Soil Bank to pay for long-term acreage reduction because huge crop surpluses were straining the federal budget. The Soil Bank eventually enrolled 30 million acres. Paul Findley writes in *Federal Farm Fable*:

> An Illinois farmer showed me a patch of ground earning [conservation] payments that most recently was a heavily graveled parking lot. . . . An oil man in Houston bought a 300-acre wooded farm as an investment and as a place for hunting, fishing, and vacationing. All he had to do to qualify for [conservation payments] was to erect a cattle guard to keep the cattle of the neighboring farms from grazing on his non-existent crops.[8]

The Soil Bank was extremely generous—based on the idea that since conservation was a good thing, the more the government spent for conservation the better off everyone would be. As Findley notes, "a North Dakota farmer bought a 280-acre farm for $5,000. After a five-year contract in the Soil Bank, the farmer had received $6,400 from the government, or $1,400 more than he paid for the farm."[9] By calling a program that paid farmers not to work a "soil bank," the USDA was apparently killing two birds with one stone—protecting the land while balancing supply and demand. In reality, the USDA missed both targets—but at least the farmers were happy when the checks arrived.

In the 1970s, when farmers were producing fencerow-to-fencerow for export markets, conservation was swept aside as a farm policy goal. But by the early 1980s, congressional mismanagement had eroded American exports, and the USDA needed a good reason for massive acreage-reduction programs. In 1983 the USDA secretary, John Block, announced that the payment-in-kind (PIK) program was "the most successful conservation program in history." All the 77 million acres that the government paid farmers not to plant were officially defined as conservation-use acres. The USDA's policy-makers seemed to believe that if a program were called a conservation program it automatically conserved something. But the PIK program probably resulted in more erosion than would have occurred if farmers had planted the land to the hilt with corn, wheat, and cotton.

Pork Barrels and the Friendly Neighborhood Sodbuster

Politics has always been more important than the environment in the USDA's conservation programs. The driving force behind every farm program is to find a reason to make farmers grateful to politicians. Congressman Jamie Whitten, the chairman of the House Appropriations Committee and the so-called Permanent Secretary of Agriculture, has always had a soft spot in his heart for the government conservation programs, especially for programs that blindly shovel out money to farmers. When Secretary of Agriculture Bob Bergland tried to reform some of the abuses in so-called conservation programs, Whitten slashed the budget for Bergland's office staff. When the assistant secretary for Natural Resources and the Environment, George Dunlop, fought to reform the programs in 1987, Whitten, with his line-item control of the agriculture appropriation bill, abolished Dunlop's job.

Agricultural conservation programs have routinely been administered with a contempt for conservation. In 1966, Arkansas farmers complained to the USDA that its inspector general had been out investigating how they were actually spending government conservation payments. Mr. Charles Cox, the assistant deputy administrator of the Agricultural Stabilization and Conservation Service (ASCS), assured the farmers that they "do not have to be too much concerned" about the inspector general interrupting their benefits.[10]

Erosion is a serious problem in some places in America partly because of the failure of the agricultural conservation programs. An evaluation of agricultural conservation programs made by the General Accounting Office (GAO) in 1977 found no significant difference in the erosion rates of the vast majority of land receiving federal assistance and similar land not receiving federal assistance.[11] Most federal conservation payments have gone either for conservation measures on land with little or no erosion or to increase farmland productivity. Bruce Gardner, an agricultural economist at the University of Maryland, says that conservation programs "cannot hope to distinguish production-promoting practices from conservation practices...."[12]

When the General Accounting Office examined the USDA's Resource Conservation and Development program, the auditors found that "conservation" money was being spent for producing food dishes for a dog pound, building a gun rack for a sheriff's office, constructing an indoor swimming pool, and constructing a replica of an 1836 fort for historical interest. The GAO concluded in its usual purple prose, "Benefits realized for the federal investment in the Resource Conservation and Development program are difficult to pin down."[13]

Federal conservation dollars are doled out according to political clout, not environmental need. A study published by the USDA in 1981 found that if conservation spending were better targeted to problem areas, three times as much erosion could be prevented at no additional cost. The General Accounting Office concluded that "about 25 percent of all erosion occurs on about 2 percent of the cropland. About 43 percent of the water-related erosion occurs on 6 percent of the cropland."[14] Yet while congressmen clamor for more money for conservation, they refuse to target existing spending on the problem. The National Association of Conservation Districts is a powerful lobby that ensures that federal money is sent to every conservation district.

Much of the conservation aid and advice that the government provides is of little value. The General Accounting Office reprimanded the SCS in the 1970s for providing overly complex, elaborate conservation plans that the farmers disregarded. The GAO noted that accomplishments for conservation programs "have been [listed] in terms of activity levels—how many wells were dug, miles of fence installed, or acres of land place under permanent vegetative cover—instead of the conservation result of those activities."[15] Government agencies sometimes confuse counting with achieving.

The GAO also chided the USDA for neglecting research into the cause and effects of soil erosion. A USDA Economic Research Service report noted that, until recently, soil program evaluations "implicitly assumed that the eroded soil had the same value in all situations. An inch of soil off a thin soil in Missouri was assumed to be worth the same as an inch of soil from the deep loess soils of Iowa. A ton of soil affecting a salmon fishery in Maine was assumed to inflict the same damages to society as a ton of soil eroding into a farm pond."[16] If the case for a conservation measure were better documented, there would be no excuse to bribe farmers to protect their most valuable asset.

Since so much of a farm's profits stem from the government nowadays, many farmers pay more attention to Washington than to their own soil. Farmers qualify for federal handouts partly according to how many acres of each subsidized crop they planted in previous years. In 1982, H. Krauss and R. Allmaras found that some farmers till highly erosive land at a loss to avoid losing acreage credit for future farm subsidies.[17] Even John Block, then-USDA secretary, conceded that the USDA "encouraged farmers to tear up the cover crop on erodible soil ahead of schedule to provide a crop history."[18] By planting on a field for a few years, farmers can qualify for federal payments not to plant a crop there in the future or to give them higher prices for the crops they do plant. Richard D. Siegel, USDA deputy assistant secretary, says that "there is a direct connection between the degradation of the fragile soil and the wheat price supports."[19] Were it not for federal subsidies, farmers would be growing less wheat—and less land would be eroding. This is not a new problem: As far back as 1965, researchers Burnell Held and Marion Clawson observed that "one major [conservation] problem in recent years has been caused by the federal price supports for wheat, and the value arising out of acreage allotments for wheat (which every farmer was loath to risk losing). Land for wheat production has acquired a value which it is impossible to sustain if the land is used for grazing. . . . "[20] Even when land is seriously eroding, government subsidies make it profitable to continue planting wheat on many acres that otherwise would not be in production. Though the problem was obvious for decades, Congress until 1985 refused to address it. (As we shall see, the 1985 solution was mostly one of blue smoke and mirrors.)

Federal aid is targeted to farmers with the worst conservation practices. A study by the USDA Economic Research Service found that high-erosion areas tend to have more acres in USDA commodity programs than less-susceptible areas, and that farmers dependent on Farmers Home Administration loans have higher erosion rates than farmers who borrow from commercial sources.[21]

Federal disaster payments and subsidized crop insurance reduce the costs of crop failure, thereby encouraging farmers to produce on low-quality, highly erosive land. In the 1970s many farmers sodbusted poor-quality grasslands solely to qualify for federal disaster payments when their crops failed—as was expected. Some farmers plow worthless land, seed from an airplane, and collect government payments when the crop fails.[22] No one knows exactly how many fragile acres have been plowed up because of perverse federal incentives. Between 1977 and 1982, almost 4 million acres of relatively low-quality land were sodbusted. Many of the newly plowed acres are born-again cropland that the USDA paid farmers to retire into grassland in the 1940s, in response to an earlier Dust Bowl.

Highly erosive land is usually less productive than low-erosion land, and provides less return on investment (labor, seeds, fertilizer, etc.). Without high federal crop payments, the total acreage planted in the United States would decrease, and the least-productive, most-erosive land would tend to be the first idled. The soil-erosion problem is partly the result of government's excessive generosity to farmers.

The USDA's programs have undercut normal crop-rotation practices. In order to keep his "program base"—that is, his eligibility for future farm handouts—a farmer must plant the same subsidized

crops on his land almost every year. But most of the subsidized crops
are highly erosive. This de facto conservation tax makes conservation
practices far more expensive than they otherwise would be. To compensate for the lack of normal crop rotation, which would naturally
revitalize the soil and boost its productivity, farmers often flood the
land with fertilizers and pesticides. The extra chemicals are then
washed off the land into groundwater, thereby contributing to the
billions of dollars of off-farm damages from agriculture. Ken Cook of
the Conservation Foundation notes that "we've had fifty years of bias
against sound conservation policy in the commodity programs. . . .
Some of the best practices for dealing with that land that is highly
erodible is to use conservation tillage and crop rotation. But if you
rotate your crops, then you lose part of your basis for getting federal
subsidies."[23]

The justification that federal intervention in agriculture protects
natural resources is specious. A property owner has as much incentive
to take care of his land as he does to take care of his house. If the
government started routinely passing out checks in Westchester County, New York, to help millionaires repaint their mansions, the public
would be outraged. But as long as the checks are going to millionaire
farmers for routine upkeep on their farms, there is no problem.

Federal conservation programs have always been defended on
the grounds that cropland erosion is a serious threat to America's
future ability to produce crops. Two recent studies by the National
Academy of Sciences and Resources for the Future show that erosion
has far less effect on cropland productivity than had previously been
suspected. The USDA's *Agricultural Outlook* concluded that, "if the
present levels of wind and sheet and rill erosion continued for another
100 years, productivity on the soils with the biggest erosion problems
nationwide might decline only about 4 percent."[24] Since the soil conservation panic of the 1930s, increases in crop yields due to new fertilizers and seed varieties have greatly exceeded the loss of soil
productivity from erosion, and there is no reason to expect this trend
to reverse in the future.

A 1986 USDA study concluded, "The benefits of erosion control
measures exceed the costs involved only on land eroding at about
fifteen tons per acre per year and above."[25] The accepted standard and
the guiding light of federal conservation programs since the 1930s has

been that any erosion above five tons per acre a year is excessive, which makes over 100 million acres of land eligible. Only about 25 million acres of farmland would qualify for aid if the fifteen tons–per-acre standard were followed. This study concluded that USDA conservation programs had cost taxpayers more than they have benefited society.

Actually, while government programs have literally thrown billions of dollars to the wind, many farmers have voluntarily adopted conservation measures. The American Farmland Trust reports that most farmers choose a conservation measure "with the clear expectation that it would lead to lower operation costs."[26] Only 21 percent of farmers polled said that federal aid was the primary reason for adopting one conservation practice instead of another or none at all.

Many farmers are now relying on "regenerative agriculture" — concentrating on natural fertilizer, crop rotation, and the minimum of chemicals to lower their costs and to take better care of the environment. These practices have given many farmers excellent yields at a low cost. Unfortunately, despite its rhetoric about the need to reduce the amount of groundwater pollution from farming, the USDA has provided very little research money for any alternative to heavy-input, heavy-chemical farming. The 1985 farm bill mandated that the USDA begin allocating more for research into organic farming. The USDA dragged its feet, and finally gave its first grant for organic fertilizer in early 1988—roughly a dozen years after many farmers had already proven the viability of organic fertilizer. Orville Bentley, a USDA assistant secretary, announced in his press release on the $3.9-million low-input agricultural research grant that low-input farming was "an idea whose time has come."[27] The Fertilizer Institute, a Washington trade association whose members sell chemical fertilizers, denounced the USDA research grant as "an unprecedented move by the USDA to advocate one farming system at the expense of another."[28] (Yet this is exactly what the USDA had done for decades by neglecting research into low-input agriculture.) The *Washington Post* reported that deputy agriculture secretary Pete Myers "apologized to [the Fertilizer Institute] after Bentley's February announcement."[29] Mr. Bentley prepared a sharp reply to the Fertilizer Institute's criticism of the grant, but someone in the USDA showed the Fertilizer Institute a draft of it, and Bentley's reply was spiked. It appears that politicians are more worried about offending interest groups than about advancing new research that might radically improve the environment.

Uncle Sam, Swampbuster

Government regulation often creates more problems than it solves. In the 1985 farm bill, congressmen implicitly admitted that farm programs were encouraging farmers to plow up fragile prairieland and wetland in order to produce more surplus crops and qualify for more benefits. The 1985 farm bill mandated that in the future, farmers who plowed up fragile land or converted wetland to cropland would lose all eligibility for federal benefits. The conservation lobbies danced in the streets when the bill was passed, confident that America had entered a new era of maturity and responsibility in the use of land.

At the same time that the government is spending billions of dollars to idle cropland, farmers have converted millions of acres of wetland to cropland, primarily because of lucrative federal subsidies that make otherwise untenable farmland profitable.[30] After the wetland is converted and cropped for a few years, it often is left idle, because the USDA is paying the farmer each year in perpetuity not to grow crops on it. In the late 1970s and early 1980s as many as a million acres of wetland a year were converted into cropland, according to estimates made by the 1982 National Resources Inventory. (The inventory, made by the Soil Conservation Services of the USDA, is a national survey of the condition of soil, water, and other resources.) Wetlands provide an invaluable habitat for many species of fish and wildlife, store floodwaters and reduce flooding, and act as a natural filter to improve water quality and help moderate local temperature and precipitation. Many hunters have been denied a decent chance to shoot a duck because of our vanishing wetlands—an important breeding ground for waterfowl.

Since farm programs often pay benefits of up to $200 or more an acre, the conversion of wetland added hundreds of millions of dollars a year to farm program costs. Much of the grain glut of the 1980s is due to new acreage brought into production since 1973, and federal government incentives discourage farmers from taking this land out of production.

North Dakota is one of the states most heavily affected by "swampbuster" regulations. In September 1986 Senator Mark Andrews, who was in a tough re-election fight at the time, managed to secure a "new interpretation" of the preliminary regulations from the USDA that created a major loophole for converting tens of thousands of acres of wetlands to croplands. After Mr. Andrews was awarded early retirement by voters in November 1986, the USDA issued a "clarification" of its preliminary regulation, moving back toward a stricter definition.

The new federal regulations to protect wetlands may actually cause a sharp increase in swampbusting as farmers rush to get projects started before stricter regulations come into force. In one county in North Dakota, the Department of the Interior noted seventy-one suspected swampbuster violations in the fall of 1986, and in a confidential memo complained of "the interpretation of everything to the drainer's benefit," saying it was "causing the destruction of thousands of acres of wetlands."[31] In the whole state of North Dakota, the Fish and Wildlife Service reported 150 potential swampbuster violations to local ASCS offices in 1987. Amazingly, not a single farmer in North Dakota has been found guilty of converting wetland and declared ineligible to receive benefits. Nationwide, only two farmers have been taken off the federal dole for violating wetland regulations.[32]

Swampbuster regulations leave huge discretion to local USDA employees. Swampbuster regulations say that a conversion project could be exempt from penalties if "substantial funds" had been expended before December 23, 1985. But as Lloyd Jones, the supervisor in the North Dakota Wetland Habitat Office of the U.S. Fish and Wildlife Service in Bismarck, North Dakota, notes, "Our first question is, what is substantial funds? We heard anything from $1 up to $5,000."[33]

Senator Andrews' replacement, Senator Kent Conrad, is working overtime to gut the regulations. The *Fargo Forum* reported in February 1988 that

> Conrad boasted he had the swing vote on an amendment to [block oil leasing in an Alaskan wildlife refuge] and that he would use his position to force modifications in the Swampbuster program which is supported by environmental groups. The amendment passed Wednesday despite Conrad's opposition. However, representatives of the Sierra Club and the National Wildlife Federation told Conrad before

the vote that they would support "reasonable changes" in the regulations to make them more palatable to farmers, he said.[34]

(Jan Goldman Carter of the National Wildlife Federation hotly denied that the Federation had made a deal with Conrad.)[35] One U.S. congressman declared, "Swampbuster was never intended to apply to the wetlands we have in our state."[36]

Nor is it clear exactly what are and aren't wetlands. There is no universally accepted definition that can be easily applied. Different USDA programs have different definitions of wetlands. And there will be disputes about whether land that was cleared and cropped fifteen years ago, but has since reverted to wetland, can be reconverted to cropland without penalty. Since farmers can annually harvest as much as $50,000 apiece or more in federal benefits, these technical questions will become very important. The regulations could provide a full-employment program for lawyers.

Another problem is that the program will be supervised in part by local ASCS committees, which are composed of local farmers. No one is predicting that they will be "hanging judges." The National Wildlife Federation used the Freedom of Information Act to search ASCS documents in North Dakota, and discovered a letter from the chairman of the Ramsey County ASCS, Terry Borsted, warning that "Fish and Wildlife Service better back down on their power of authority before farmers 'power up' their authority with gunpowder." Jerry Harris, chairman of the ASCS state committee in Texas, commented on enforcing conservation programs on farmers, "Whether we are elected, appointed or employed, we have to remember who the program belongs to—the producer."[37] Since the ASCS has taken the lead in the past in paying farmers to convert wetland to cropland, this program is paying the fox to guard the chicken house. One Senate aide was even less diplomatic and noted that the ASCS was more interested in "slopping money out to farmers [and] couldn't care less about conservation."[38] Lloyd Jones notes, "We have seen a lot of conflicts come up where we have individuals who are less than supportive of what swampbuster is trying to do."[39] It will be very difficult for the farm on the ASCS committees to rule that their neighbors have violated the regulations, when such rulings could easily mean bankrupting the violators.

Conservation Reserve

The Conservation Reserve Program (CRP) is the biggest agricultural conservation boondoggle of them all. The USDA is now paying farmers to idle 25 million acres of farmland—equivalent to shutting down the entire state of Ohio—and will eventually spend more than $20 billion on this program by the time it is complete. But this farm conservation program is destroying jobs, reducing exports, and squandering billions of dollars on a pseudoproblem. The CRP is a case of politicians misunderstanding a problem and then concocting a program that is guaranteed not to provide a solution.

The Conservation Reserve Program gives farmers ten extremely generous annual payments not to plant on farmland with above-average erosion rates. In New Mexico, the USDA is paying three times the going rent for land put into the CRP, and in Colorado the USDA often pays double the going rent. In Missouri, the CRP has so disrupted land values that rocky, craggy ground is now worth more than good farmland.[40] Though farmland mortgages are routinely stretched out over thirty years, the USDA's ten annual CRP rental payments will exceed the total value of the land for more than half of all the land enrolled in the program. Some real-estate firms specialize in marketing farms put in the CRP. Richard Wood, owner of Spencer Farms in Kansas City, described the CRP as "a perfect vehicle for investors who have wanted to buy farm land. . . . They can put 30 percent down and let the government pay for the rest." In newspaper advertisements, Spencer Farms claims that CRP investments pay a yield of 10.77 percent—far higher than yields available from bonds or stocks.[41]

The 1985 farm bill specified that the Conservation Reserve Program should reduce erosion, protect wildlife, reduce sediment in water, reduce crop surpluses, and boost farm income. The proliferation of goals became a license to achieve nothing. When a farm program has multiple goals, the dominant goal—the ultimate litmus test—is almost always whether the program boosts farm income. As long as the farmers receive their checks, the program is a political success.

A 1987 USDA study found that erosion-control measures could reduce erosion on highly erosive farmland for roughly 47 cents a ton saved;[42] the CRP, in contrast, is paying five times as much—$2.50 per ton on average—for erosion foregone. Farmland erosion is like a factory with pollution: The choice is to put scrubbers in the smokestacks to reduce emissions or to shut down the entire factory. The USDA decided to shut down the factory.

Pierre Crosson of Resources for the Future noted that "soil erosion is highly concentrated in a few crop-growing regions of the United States. Yet soil conservation funds are and always have been widely dispersed."[43] The USDA now asserts that one-quarter of all cropland has such a serious problem that the government is justified in taking it out of production. The USDA has repeatedly broadened the definition of the term *highly erosive* in order to justify bringing more acres into the CRP. But each expansion of eligibility diminishes the average rate of erosion that determines eligibility.

The CRP has already driven some young farmers out of business because the payments are so generous that many landowners have found it more profitable to put their land in the CRP rather than rent it out for crop production. Even where rental farmers have not been thrown off the land, the CRP has driven up rental rates in many parts of the nation, thereby increasing the cost of production and making American farmers less competitive with foreign farmers. The conservation reserve has claimed over 25 percent of harvested cropland in 170 counties, thereby creating an artificial shortage of farmland in many areas.

The Conservation Reserve Program is generously paying farmers not to plant on 1 million acres of land that are already planted with grasses, legumes, or other conservation crops. Eight-million acres of the reserve were previously planted to crops that were not in surplus—a dead loss for consumers.

The CRP is also reducing American crop exports. The *Cargill Bulletin* estimates that up to 3 million acres of soybean land have gone into the CRP.[44] Soybeans are in short supply—domestic production has fallen sharply as lavish USDA benefits have persuaded farmers to grow corn instead of soybeans. Kenneth Bader, the chief executive officer of the American Soybean Association, concludes, "The CRP may be adding to the damage the present soybean program is inflicting on the soybean industry."[45]

The CRP has destroyed tens of thousands of jobs for farm workers. A study made by the USDA estimated that shutting down 31 million acres of farmland would destroy 150,000 jobs on and off the farm.[46] A study made by the University of Missouri estimated that the CRP will trim "$80 million annually from Missouri's agri-business economy."[47] Gary Devison of the University of Missouri told the *Kansas City Times* that "grain marketing and storage needs will be lower. Many firms will go out of business or at least curtail operations."[48]

The CRP is based on "soil-loss tolerance" or "T-value," which is the amount of erosion that would not adversely affect soil productivity over the years. Charles Benbrook of the National Academy of Science noted that "T-values simply do not reflect the relative susceptibility of soils to erosion-induced productivity loss."[49] Pierre Crosson of Resources for the Future agrees: "There's plenty of scientific evidence that the T-value standard is weak . . . the T-values as standards for judging when erosion reduces soil productivity are largely arbitrary."[50] The USDA is essentially pulling numbers out of a hat to provide the basis of the program, and has repeatedly changed its numbers on how much soil erosion farmland can tolerate.

The soil-loss tolerance standard simply measures whether any productivity loss occurs at all, and is thus biased in favor of blindly spending money to reduce erosion regardless of whether it is a wise investment. The SCS has an incentive to set T-values as low as possible in order to maximize the demand for SCS aid, thus making the SCS a more important agency in the future of American agriculture. The greater the public perceives the threat from soil erosion, the bigger the budget the SCS will receive.

The CRP is based on the idea that government can accurately measure the extent and effects of soil erosion. But as Mack Gray, special assistant to the chief for congressional and public liaison of the Soil Conservation Service, notes, "There is no way that any of us can go out and measure the wind erosion or water erosion that's occurring and tell others that we were very precise. If we measure ten tons per acre, it may be anywhere from five to fifteen tons, or even three to eighteen tons. We just don't know."[51]

Proponents of the CRP claim it reduces water pollution, but it is not targeted to areas where soil erosion affects watersheds. A Resources for the Future study found that the CRP has had little effect on improving water quality.

The CRP assumes that the cost of erosion-caused productivity foregone is higher than the cost of government payments plus the immediate production foregone—that it is worth more than $20 billion to have farmland erode in the future rather than in the present. But studies by the National Academy of Science, the USDA, and Resources for the Future concluded that erosion is reducing crop productivity by less than a tenth of a percentage point a year. The USDA is providing a return of over 10 percent a year on the value of more than half of the land enrolled in the CRP; the value of foregone production might be equal to 4 or 5 percent of the land's total value. With the current large budget deficits, taxpayers will be paying 7 or 8 percent interest on the deficit spending used to finance the program. Thus, the CRP is likely to be costing over a hundred times more than the value of the soil productivity that it saves.

Most damage from farm erosion occurs off the farm, in the form of polluted groundwater and silted dams, for example. The Conservation Foundation estimates that farm-caused pollution causes $6 billion a year in off-farm damage. Seven states now have regulations governing the runoff from farmers' land. Yet since the CRP is more interested in boosting farm income than protecting the environment, the "polluter pays" principle is reversed, and farmers with the worst environmental practices receive bounties from the Treasury.

At the same time that the government is paying to idle 27 million acres under the CRP partly in order to reduce pollution, the huge set-aside requirements for other crop programs are resulting in increased pesticide and fertilizer use on the remaining acres as farmers try to compensate for fewer acres planted by burying planted acres in inputs. The Conservation Foundation estimated in 1986 that farmers used 7.4 billion pounds of fertilizer and 110 million pounds of pesticides to produce surplus crops—equal to 28 percent of the fertilizer and 40 percent of the pesticides used for corn and wheat.[52]

The CRP is a gem of farm program logic. The Reagan administration supported the CRP largely because it was cheaper to pay to retire land for ten years than to pay to retire the same land ten times for one year. Programs are judged not by whether they make any sense in themselves, but by whether other farm policy options are more or less imbecilic. There is not the political will on Capital Hill to resolve the contradictions among farm programs, but there is always the political will to create another pork barrel for farmers.

Federal conservation programs may soon become even more tangled. Under the 1985 farm bill, every farmer with farmland that local SCS bureaucrats think is eroding too quickly must have a conservation plan for his land approved by the local Soil Conservation Service by 1990, and must implement the program for his land by 1995 in order to continue receiving handouts. It makes good sense to require farmers to follow conservation practices in return for federal megabillions; as the Supreme Court ruled in 1941, the federal government has a right to regulate that which it subsidizes. But for most farmland in the United States, the "soil-loss tolerance value" will be set at five tons per acre—not because there is any evidence that this is an appropriate amount, but because five tons per acre has been the amount the SCS usually claims. Farmers would be required to take corrective action on soil that is "eroding faster than it can regenerate," a formula that expresses the SCS's belief that any loss of soil productivity is to be avoided at any price. People would laugh if the federal government prohibited factory owners from allowing factories to depreciate more than one-tenth of one percent a year—but that is effectively what farm law dictates.

If Congress and the administration return to programs such as those in 1986 and 1987 that drove market prices through the floor and virtually forced all farmers to go on the federal dole or perish, the conservation compliance provisions will greatly increase government control over farmers' property. The natural tendency of government handouts to be followed by government control will be fulfilled with a vengeance, which would be something close to poetic justice for the farm lobby. But it is likely that the congressional agricultural committees or the Agriculture Department will find a way to gut this regulation long before it becomes a burden to farmers.

Conclusion

The Soil Conservation Service and congressmen have been warning loudly for more than half a century that erosion will destroy the productivity of American cropland, while crop yields have continued to increase year after year. The USDA's conservation policy history is largely a series of hoaxes: shouting "Fire!" and then taking the water elsewhere, maximizing hysteria in order to maximize budgets and handouts, and providing one subsidy to wreck the land and a second subsidy to insure that the land is not wrecked too badly. Unfortunately, federal subsidies to disrupt the environment have been more effective than federal programs to repair farm program damage.

If congressmen really gave a damn about conservation, they would design conservation programs that achieved what they promised. Agricultural conservation programs are as poorly designed now as they were in the 1930s. As University of Wisconsin sociologist Peter Nowak notes, "In the past, there has been very little attempt made to understand why a program has failed and why some farmers don't practice conservation. Rather, when one policy hasn't worked there has been a tendency simply to look for a new policy. . . ."[53]

Government aid to take care of private farmland is based on the assumption that land owners themselves are too poor to afford the upkeep. But the average full-time farmer is worth more than half a million dollars, and most farmers have great incentives to protect their investments. The truth of the matter is, politicians feel that they cannot afford *not* to give farmers money.

◆ *Chapter 11* ◆

The Congressional School of Economics

One should not look too closely at how sausages or laws are made.

—Bismarck

Farm programs will never be better than the congressmen who create them. It is impossible to understand agricultural policy without examining the thinking of farm-state congressmen. The nature of politicians is far more important to federal agricultural policy than is the nature of farming. Agricultural programs have far more to do with political deals than with planting and harvesting. As Wheeler Mc-Millen observed in 1929, "The farm problem for politicians is how to get the farm vote."[1]

Agricultural policy is usually spoken of as though it were made by a group of experts calmly discussing various economic possibilities, then judging with Solomon-like wisdom and striking the perfect balance. In reality, agricultural policy-making is more like throwing a handful of candy into a crowd of six-year-olds, or a roll of C-notes into an elevator full of MBAs, and watching the fur fly. Agricultural policy-making has little to do with economic planning and everything to do with deal-making.

The market sets the price of American wheat according to domestic and foreign demand, the wheat's quality, weather conditions around the world, the strength of the dollar, and other factors. Congressmen set the price of wheat according to the number of donations received from the wheat lobby, the paranoia over budget deficits at the time the farm bill is debated, the number of Urban Development Action Grants for which Dakota congressmen have traded their votes, the media climate at the time the farm bill is enacted, and so on.

Pearls of Agricultural Wisdom

Anyone who has faith in the ability of Congress to manage the economy should read the congressional debates on a farm bill. Each hour of congressional discussion pioneers new depths of creativity, with awesome leaps of logic that would make any country lawyer green with envy. The House Agriculture Committee chairman, Kika de la Garza, best summed up the spirit when he declared in 1985, "I heard a quotation once that said, 'Facts are the enemy of truth.' So forget all the facts and listen to the truth."[2]

Farm-state congressmen often act like religious devotees with a sacred right to fabricate for a good cause. Congressman Jamie Whitten declared in December 1987, "About half the farmers are either bankrupt or on the verge of bankruptcy."[3] In fact, U.S. Department of Agriculture (USDA) statistics show that less than 20 percent of the farmers were under severe financial stress at the close of 1987. Whitten declared on June 16, 1988, that "government policy [in the 1980s] forced the bankruptcy of 261,000 farmers."[4] This is a blatant fabrication by one of the leading farm-policy "experts" in Congress—an attempt to frighten listeners by overstating by fivefold the number of farm bankruptcies. In reality, only 200,000 farmers left agriculture between 1980 and 1987, and less than 40,000 of those went bankrupt.

Congressman de la Garza defended the peanut program in 1985 by saying, "We cannot send the wrong message out there to the farmers that are dying on the farms—and make no mistake, the peanut growers are in the same position as corn and wheat farmers."[5] In fact, the bankruptcy rate among peanut farmers was far lower than the rate among other farmers, and peanut growers were enjoying far higher returns than were corn or wheat farmers. When the chairmen of the House Agriculture Committee and the House Appropriations Committee resort to such wholesale twisting of the facts, it is no wonder that congressional agricultural policy often seems divorced from reality. Congressman Byron Dorgan declared in 1987, "The prices that the farmers are now receiving are so low that the majority cannot make a living."[6] Yet in that same year, farmers' net cash income set a record—and the income of the average farm families exceeded the median income of American families by 39 percent.

Many congressmen show a virulent hostility to the market. This is not surprising: East Germany feels the same hostility toward West Berlin—an island of free-market prosperity in the middle of an ocean of central planning—for revealing the failure of East German communism. De la Garza denounced a proposal for free-market agriculture: "What market clearing means is that you sell at the dump price, regardless of your cost of production. When someone says market clearing, that means that it is detrimental to the producer because market clearing has no respect or regard for the cost of production."[7] Congressman Tony Coelho warned, "The free market can be very destructive" at a House hearing a few months after the government's Dairy Termination Program had wrecked the cattle market.[8]

De la Garza and many other congressmen believe that there is some inherent defect in the economy that prevents farmers from getting a fair return on their labor. Congressman William Natcher of Kentucky said, "Agriculture is the only industry I know of where a seller must accept the price offered or else return home with his commodity."[9] Actually, farmers are not unique at all: Any person who grows or builds or paints something without an agreed-upon price will often be given a take-it-or-leave-it offer. Congressman Charles Stenholm, the chairman of the House Livestock Subcommittee, declared, "You can't get farm income up without production controls."[10] Most crops get no subsidies and no protection, yet somehow they are produced by farmers who are not held at gunpoint. There have been no outbreaks of intellectual curiosity on Capitol Hill about the fact that most crops can be raised at a profit while others supposedly cannot be grown without a $5 billion government kickback.

"If it ain't broke, don't fix it" is the motto of congressmen guarding super-generous farm programs. Congressman John W. Flannagan

declared in July 1945: "The tobacco program has been the most successful agricultural program ever inaugurated in the country. It works.
If this House will continue to leave the tobacco [program] to the tobacco growers and their Representatives in Congress, it will continue to
work."[11] Thirty-eight years later, Senator John Warner declared: "The
tobacco program is the least costly, most successful farm program ever
operated in our country."[12] Congressman Bill Emerson observed, "I
support the sugar program . . . for one very simple reason: it works.
The sugar program is one of very few commodity programs that isn't
broken; it therefore should not be fixed."[13]

Farm congressmen usually view any program that raises farm
income, no matter what the cost, as a success. Southern congressmen
are bragging about the 1985 farm bill's marketing loans for rice.
Senator David Pryor said, "Our [rice] program is working . . . the program is beginning to put money in the farmers' pockets. . . . now the
buyers are calling the farmers and they are being mighty nice, and
that's a change."[14] But the rice program's cost has tripled since 1984,
while export revenue has decreased. The rice program has cost the
equivalent of more than one million dollars per full-time rice farmer
since 1985, yet many farm congressmen see the rice program as a
model for other programs. Congressman Jim Slattery observed, "The
dairy diversion program does work. It will increase the price for
farmers and help the farm income problem that we are all concerned
about in rural America."[15] Congressmen judge farm programs not by
what nonfarmers pay, but by what benefits farmers receive.

Ethanol is a good example of congressional economic thinking.
Ethanol is the epitomy of farm policy—costing society $4 for each
dollar of benefits to farmers, according to a 1986 USDA study.[16]
Gasohol is produced by distilling corn, sugar, or other products into
ethanol. One part ethanol is then mixed with nine parts gasoline to
make gasohol. Ethanol can corrode the metal in car engines, and even
gas stations in Iowa have begun posting signs reading, "We do not sell
gasohol" to reassure motorists. Gasoline was wholesaling for 60 cents
a gallon at the same time that federal and state governments were
providing $1.35 per gallon in subsidies for ethanol production.[17] The
USDA estimates the average cost of producing ethanol to be $1.60 a
gallon, which means that ethanol will likely never be able to compete
in the free market with gasoline.[18]

But because ethanol is a covert way to provide handouts to farmers by boosting the demand for crops and thereby driving up crop prices, ethanol is very popular with the farm lobby. In the December 1987 Budget Reconciliation Act, Congress announced that "increasing the quantity of motor fuels that contain at least 10 percent ethanol from current levels to 50 percent by 1992 would create thousands of new jobs in ethanol production facilities," and urged the Environmental Protection Agency to require greater use of ethanol in the nation's gas tanks. It is typical for congressmen to talk of creating "thousands of new jobs in ethanol production facilities"—a scheme that is guaranteed to make America poorer. No matter how much ethanol costs the American public, House and Senate agricultural committees would still profit from increased campaign contributions from ethanol producers. Congressman Jim Leach even proposed a "strategic ethanol reserve"—as if there were any reason in Hades for the government to stockpile ethanol instead of stockpiling oil at half the price.

Congressmen talk about the need to ensure parity between farm and nonfarm income, when all they are truly interested in is new ways and excuses to boost farm income. Congressman Arlan Stangeland declared in 1985: "Our attempt in this farm bill is to freeze farm income so that it does not go down."[19] This is typical of every congressional "freeze" in agricultural policy: always providing a floor and never imposing a ceiling. Payments to farmers are not allowed to fall 2 cents a bushel below the federal support price, but if the market price soars to double or triple the support price, then that is just fine and dandy.

Farm-state congressmen devote themselves to driving up food prices—and then warn that, if it were not for farm programs, food prices would be much higher. Congressman Harold Volkmer declared in 1988, "If we do not have . . . a food policy in this country we could very easily find that in the next year or two we would have a loaf of bread at $5 a loaf, if we want that. You could have a gallon of milk out here at $10 a gallon if you want that."[20] According to Volkmer's logic, if the government stopped paying farmers to kill a million cows and idle more than 70 million acres of farmland, shortages could result and consumers would suffer. Congressman Norman Sisisky praised the peanut program because the "stable supply of peanuts is important to the nutrition of our young children."[21] But the peanut program exists to create a permanent artificial scarcity of peanuts that inflates peanut prices.

Farm-state congressmen have a dozen explanations for why subsidies to farmers are not really handouts. Congressman Pat Roberts of Kansas defended federal subsidies for farmers in 1985: "This is direct income to farmers, yes, but also [compensation] for . . . the high [federal budget] deficit."[22] Congressman Volkmer denies the existence of subsidies: "It has been the American farmer that has been basically subsidizing the consumer because he has been getting lower prices."[23] Congressman Robert Davis said: "$25 billion out of a $1 trillion [budget] certainly can't be considered welfare or any kind of a handout to the food and fiber sector of our country."[24] Congressman de la Garza declared that subsidies are "not going into the farmer's pocket. The farmer does not hold that dollar. It goes for rent, for taxes, for feed, for equipment, to Main Street USA."[25] This is another garden-variety defense for handout programs: The recipient's customers benefit more than the recipient himself. The farmer may no longer have the $50,000, but he may have 100 more acres, courtesy of U.S. taxpayers. If the government gave every American writer $3,000 to buy a new computer, who would have the chutzpah to insist that it was actually the computer industry that received the subsidy?

The more wasteful and abusive the program, the more inspired the defense becomes. The sugar program is widely recognized as subverting U.S. foreign policy by impoverishing the people of Latin America and the Philippines. But de la Garza easily refuted these criticisms in 1985: "To say the sugar program has undermined the foreign policy of the United States is completely erroneous. On the contrary, you do not bolster democracy abroad by killing American jobs."[26] According to the logic of the chairman of the House Agriculture Committee, the more protectionist the United States becomes, the safer democracy around the world will be.

The sugar program, by slashing U.S. sugar consumption, threw thousands of sugar-refinery employees out of work. But de la Garza easily proved that there was no conflict between sugar farmers and sugar-refinery workers: "Do you think the workers at the McCormick plant in Baltimore get the bulk of the money McCormick makes? No, it is the corporate stockholders and the president of the company. So [complaining that refinery workers are sacrificed to sugar farmers] is not a valid argument."[27] Workers who only lose their jobs (but don't lose stock dividends) actually lose nothing and thus have no right to complain. On the other hand, if a farmer loses his livelihood because he is inefficient, it is a national catastrophe.

Congresswoman Virginia Smith, who represents Nebraska corn growers who benefit from high sugar prices by selling their corn for high-fructose corn syrup, asserted: "The [sugar] program is a responsible, income-generating program. The program has generated an annual income of over $75 million."[28] Because the sugar program provides tariff revenue of $75 million a year from taxes on imported sugar—while mulcting consumers for $3 billion a year, according to the U.S. Commerce Department—congressmen praise it for "producing income." If the government could only launch a couple of thousand sugar programs, the budget deficit could be eliminated.

The tobacco program, which forced farmers to slash production by 50 percent in fifteen years, is defended by Congressman Tim Valentine: "The issue here is whether tobacco will continue to be grown by American farmers or by overseas growers."[29] This is the Big Lie defense—defending a program by making assertions so completely opposite to the facts that the listener is simply confused. The tobacco program is the only thing preventing more American farmers from producing far more tobacco, and U.S. government policies that drive up world tobacco prices are encouraging foreign farmers to boost production and take over the world market.

Congressmen sometimes create an artificial shortage and then congratulate themselves because there is no surplus. As Congressman William Dickinson describes the peanut program, "By limiting the amount of peanuts that can be grown for use in the U.S., we have closed the gap between supply and demand."[30] A program is a success when the shortage is so severe that consumers will buy the available supply at prices high enough to satisfy politicians.

Two metaphysical impossibilities dominate congressional farm debates. The first impossibility is that taxpayers could ever benefit if Congress were to reduce payment levels for farmers. The second impossibility is that consumers could ever benefit if the USDA stopped driving up food prices.

For generations farm-state congressmen have warned that cuts in government price supports always force farmers to produce more crops. Congressman Tom Daschle in 1985 denounced the argument "that by cutting the price support, we may be cutting the cost of the program. No one should fall for that argument. . . . One could guarantee that if we cut the [dairy price support] by another 50 cents, we will increase the cost of the program to the federal government. . . . Producers are going to be making up in volume what they cannot in unit price."[31] According to Congressman Harold Volkmer, "When support prices go down, production goes up and therefore the cost to the government goes up."[32] Congressman Jamie Whitten notes: "To meet decreased prices, the farmer has always increased volume. It's the only way to offset a drop in price."[33]

Many congressmen seem to believe that farmers, unless they are stopped, will keep producing until they destroy themselves. But farmers tend to be more rational with economic decisions than politicians are. The less profitable farming is, the less farmers will eventually produce. There is no evidence in American history of commercial farmers as a class perennially producing a crop at a loss. The "lower prices, bigger surpluses" charade justifies paying farmers to continue overproducing—and the resulting surpluses provide an excuse for continued political control over agriculture. As a USDA study found, the only crops with major "excess resources" are those that Congress promises to protect against surpluses.[34]

About once a month, some congressman warns that if Congress cuts crop subsidy levels, taxpayers will suffer. Senator Howell Heflin opposed a $50,000 payment limit for rice growers in December 1987 because he claimed it would make it more difficult to reduce government spending for the rice program.[35] Congressman Bob Traxler warned that if sugar price supports were cut, beet sugar farms in Michigan would cost taxpayers more because they would shift to growing corn and wheat.[36] Such arguments would be laughable if they were not so well received on Capitol Hill.

Nor will a change in federal policy reduce Americans' grocery bills, according to farm-state congressmen. In 1985, thanks to federal import quotas and price supports, U.S. peanut prices were roughly double world peanut prices. Yet Congressman Don Fuqua confidently declared: "There is absolutely no evidence that lower peanut prices to farmers will result in lower cost of peanut products."[37] The House

Agriculture Committee easily vindicated the peanut program in a few sentences in its report on the 1985 farm bill:

> While it has been alleged that the elimination of the peanut program would result in decreased prices for consumer products, this argument can be readily dismissed by a careful consideration of the facts. Comparing the increases in prices paid to the farmer for his or her peanuts, with the increases incurred at the wholesale level, it is apparent that the real culprit in escalating peanut prices is not the price received by the farmers, but "other" costs . . . increased advertising costs, profits associated with the chain of distribution, increased marketing costs with name brand versus generic products, and various other marketing expenses.[38]

Even though Congress forces Americans to pay far more for American-grown peanuts than foreigners pay, the only reason peanut prices are high, according to the House Agriculture Committee, is middlemen's profits and advertising costs. This is the "innocent bystander" theory of high prices: Just because federal policies inflate peanut prices, it would be unfair to blame the government for high peanut-butter prices.

Farm-state congressmen spend half their time trying to drive up crop prices and the other half of their time denouncing the government's "cheap food policy." Senator David Pryor declared: "I am one who believes that the farmer today has become the prisoner of a system and a policy. Cheap food has become a policy of our government."[39] Senator James Abdnor bewailed: "To claim that we might drive up the price of food is really discouraging to me. I hate to think that is going to be the attitude of congressmen to condemn every proposal that would cause food prices to go up just because the farmer happens to be getting more for his product."[40] When U.S. peanut, dairy, and sugar prices are two, three, and four times world price levels, Pryor and other congressmen still blame all the farmers' problems on the cheap-food policy. When congressmen complain of a "cheap-food policy," they are only admitting their incompetence: They tried their best to drive up food prices and failed. Most farmers are being paid according to federal target prices anyway, not according to the market price, so that even though market prices may appear to be low by historical standards, net farm cash income set an all-time high every year from 1984 through 1987.

Congressmen claim that farm programs are a success because Americans spend less of their income on food than do the inhabitants of any other country in the world. In reality, American food prices are not low; American incomes are high. As countries become more prosperous and as incomes rise, citizens naturally spend a smaller *percentage* of their income on food and more on other items. Congressman Jim Slattery of Kansas asserted on June 16, 1988: "I would observe that for the taxpayers in this country to have to contribute $200 a year [each] . . . when it comes to the federal government's involvement in agriculture is not very much to pay for that cheapest, best, most reliable food supply in the history of the world."[41] Actually, food is cheaper in Australia than it is in the United States, but because the average American income is higher than the average Australian income, Americans spend a lower percentage of their income on food than do the Australians. Congressmen often use statistics for the low percentage of income that Americans spend on food as an excuse to justify not reforming farm policies that drive up food prices.

If a study showed that Americans spent a lower percentage of their income than any other nationality to buy cars, would that justify Congress slapping a $3,000 tax on all new cars? If a study found that Americans paid the lowest prices for furniture, would that justify a federal intervention to pay chair factories to produce one-third fewer chairs in order to drive up chair prices? Just because American businessmen produce a product cheaply does not give politicians an excuse to intervene and drive up the price. American agriculture is relatively efficient in spite of—not because of—federal intervention.

In one breath congressmen argue that farmers are the stars of the economy, America's most productive citizens, and in the next breath warn that if farm subsidies are reduced, all the farmers will end up on the dole. Congressman Harold Rogers defended the tobacco program: "What shall these farmers do? Go on welfare? Draw food stamps?"[42] Congressman James Jeffords, leading a floor fight for more subsidies for dairymen, asserted in 1985: "The dairy industry of this country ought to have the unanimous support of everyone. It is the most productive industry in this country, bar none."[43] Apparently, the more productive a farmer is, the more he should receive from the Treasury as an honorarium for his amazing economic achievements.

Ever since farmers began receiving federal aid, congressmen have been obliged to portray them as hardship cases in order to justify continuing the gravy train. There has been a pervasive and perpetual inflation of need: The more farmers received, the more necessary it was to represent them as destitute. Then, of course, the more destitute they appeared, the more federal aid they deserved. If Congress is considering major farm legislation, it is a certainty that all farmers will be portrayed as being on the verge of bankruptcy. In 1977, when Congress was writing a four-year farm bill during a relatively prosperous time for farming, the National Farmers Union announced that farmers were suffering from the worst depression since the 1930s. In 1981, as the House passed the most generous farm bill in history, Kika de la Garza insisted, "This is only a blood transfusion." In 1985, Congressman William Thomas warned: "The stage is set for what will be a literal holocaust in rural America. . . . "[44] Congressman Thomas Foley, the former chairman of the House Agriculture Committee and the House majority whip, warned: "This farm bill was constructed in an environment of greater farm and farmer financial difficulty than at any time since the Great Depression. . . . The farm income in the United States has been steadily dropping." Yet according to the USDA, the average farm family's income in 1985 was 20 percent higher than the median American family's income, and 28 percent higher in 1984.

Farm issues are usually portrayed on the floors of Congress in the most hysterical, sensationalistic terms. De la Garza warned in 1985, "We are running out of time. Time ran out yesterday for Dale Burr of Iowa, who shot himself, his wife, his banker, and a neighbor. If he would have had the word that the Congress cared . . . perhaps . . . Dale Burr would be alive today."[45] A farmer goes on a shooting spree, murdering his wife, neighbor, and banker, and he is treated as a martyr for the farm crisis, his violence cited as a cause for giving more billions to farmers. No matter what farmers do, it is taken as proof that they need and deserve more aid. The farmer is almost always portrayed as a victim of forces beyond his control.

Once congressmen give farmers handouts for a single year, the question becomes not whether government subsidies are effective or wasteful, but whether government should "pull the rug out from under farmers." Congressmen always justify more handouts on the grounds that government gave farmers handouts in the past. Congressmen argue that the American people sent farmers a signal via subsidies to increase production—and now that production is increased, the American people are obliged to take care of the farmer. In actuality, it is always Congress who sends the signal—usually the wrong signal—to farmers to boost production. This is the "tar baby" method of benevolence, pushing aid through Congress for one year and then claiming that since taxpayers touched the farmers they can never let go without doing farmers a grave injustice.

Congressmen who favor more benefits for farmers generally claim a monopoly on compassion. Agricultural policy debates tend to be smearing contests. Disagreements on agricultural programs are almost always represented as a conflict between the decency of someone who wants to give more to farmers and someone who favors a general massacre of farmers and their families. The few debates in the House and Senate that do occur on farm policy tend to focus on motives rather than facts, as if the speaker's feelings toward farmers were more important than the effects of whatever policy the speaker was advocating.

Congressmen usually mistake the symptom for the problem. One great issue in congressional agricultural policy-making is the problem of surpluses. Many congressmen are certain that if they can only eradicate surpluses, the Golden Age will be restored in rural America. A crop surplus is usually seen as a metaphysical problem in itself with little or no connection to the federal policies that encourage farmers to overproduce. As Congressman Byron Dorgan declared in 1985, "For more than a decade, federal farm programs have forced America's farmers to overproduce in a hopeless effort to meet rising costs in the [face of] disastrously low crop prices."[46]

The Great Surplus Problem is the main excuse for the House of Representatives' decision in 1985 to allow some farmers to impose mandatory production controls on other farmers. The House bill would have allowed 60 percent of farmers to decree the creation of a national "wheat police" to regulate and restrict production on all farms in a massive effort to drive up prices by slashing production and closing the borders. Congress appropriated $10 million in July 1987 for more USDA studies and preparations for mandatory controls. According to the late Senator Ed Zorinsky, mandatory controls "would eliminate surpluses, which depress prices currently which have caused the entire problem. . . . The end result is that you end that cycle of overproduction which will continue under any other variation that we have."[47] Congressman Bill Alexander argued, "Production controls would even out the boom and bust cycles that have plagued our farmers."[48] But perpetual surpluses occur only because Congress perpetually rewards farmers for overproducing. Due to Congress' inability to manage prices, many congressmen want to effectively nationalize farming.

In July 1985 the House Agriculture Committee voted to outlaw an egg-breaking machine. This may have been the first time in history that a congressional committee targeted a machine for prohibition. A California businessman had invented the Egg King, a machine that broke up to 300 eggs a minute and was being used by the Pentagon, Disneyworld, and major hotels. The Egg King allowed its users to rely on fresh eggs instead of powdered or frozen eggs; this meant better taste and huge savings, since powdered or frozen eggs cost 50 percent more than fresh eggs. As Richard C. Gohla, vice president of the Retail Bakers Association, noted, "The higher percentage of eggs in a product, the more the quality suffers by using frozen eggs."[49] But the Egg King was hurting the business of the United Egg Producers, whose members supplied most of the powdered or frozen eggs. So the Agriculture Committee came to the rescue.

Congressmen justified the ban on grounds of concern about the safety of the Egg King, even though there were no reported incidents of health problems connected with it. The California Department of Health concluded that the Egg King "appears to be superior to the present hand method of cracking and straining eggs." The Food and Drug Administration had received no complaints of health problems involving the Egg King. The only people who complained about the new technology were the Egg King's competitors. The House Agriculture Committee—voting with almost no discussion of the issue—resolved to raise artificially the cost of food preparation, worsen the quality of food, and bankrupt a successful businessman. (The House of Representatives refused to go along with the Agriculture Committee, and the Egg King was saved.)[50]

Pick a Price, Any Price

The key to federal agricultural policy is how Congress sets prices. Every congressionally set price is covered with grease, through log-rolling, favor-trading, "pick a price, any price" political deals. For politicians, the effects of each handout begin and end at the ballot box. They can't run for re-election with a learned dissertation on market forces, but they can run with high prices for farmers. The fair price for congressmen is always that price that produces the most votes and campaign contributions for the greatest number of politicians. Votes and campaign contributions are more important than supply and demand. Letting politicians set prices is like giving an alcoholic the key to a brewery. If politicians wanted market-clearing prices, they would let the market set prices. Politicians want votes. Politicians set prices to fill ballot boxes, not to balance markets. All the disruptions and contradictions in agricultural policy follow from this self-evident truth.

Politicians' management of agriculture is based on the notion that the higher prices are, the better off farmers will be. Congressmen see only the price and neglect other factors, such as the volume of sales or the cost of production. Congressmen have perennially tried to enrich farmers by pricing their products out of the market. The short-term benefits of a high price are seen immediately by farmers, while the longer-term costs are seen only after the next election. Politicians get the benefit of a high price but rarely have to pay the cost of disrupted markets and declining exports.

Ron Phillips, press secretary of the Senate Agriculture Committee from 1983 to 1987, described how the Senate set prices in the 1985 farm bill: "You're sitting around a table and everyone is throwing out numbers. You've got this jumble of numbers that has no meaning."[51] Reading the record of the House Agriculture Committee farm bill markup sessions in 1985, one sees congressmen throwing out prices by the bushel, juggling prices to see which feels best to the most congressmen. The prices included in the final bill were only those that appealed to a sufficient number of relatively ignorant congressmen.

The congressional agricultural committees have usually been chaired by Southern Democrats. As a result, cotton, rice, and tobacco farmers have been treated far more generously by the government than have corn or wheat farmers. Cotton and rice received super-generous marketing loans in the 1985 farm bill, not because there was any reason to have marketing loans for one crop and not for another, but because Southern congressmen had more clout. Most of the Farmers Home Administration's largest loans and worst abuses have been made in the South.

Congressmen routinely vote on major agricultural bills without even reading them. The Senate's 1985 farm bill contained contradictory target price supports for future years for wheat and corn: One section of the bill mandated a freeze; another section mandated a slight cut. The Senate passed it anyway.

At most congressional agriculture committee hearings, the members either do not attend or step in and out, making ceremonial appearances for the record. The *Washington Post* reported on the 1985 farm bill deliberations, "The Senate Agricultural Committee has been plagued by absenteeism."[52] The committee staff carefully choose witnesses who will tell congressmen what congressmen want to hear. The same question is routinely asked by three or more congressmen, showing how little attention they are paying to the witnesses. (Congressmen often ask the questions from a list made up by aides. Often different aides think of the same questions.) At most hearings, congressmen spend much of their time asking recipients, "Are we giving you enough?" and hounding administration officials by asking, "Why aren't you giving more?" In congressional hearings on agricultural credit programs, the questions are never, "Is there too much capital in agriculture?" or "Is agriculture being destabilized by too much money being artificially pumped in?" but rather "How many farmers did not get a government loan—and why the hell not?"

At times, farm policy-making looks as if it should be regulated under the federal antiracketeering statutes. In late 1987 the Senate passed a plan that it claimed would save $1 billion in farm programs. Corn farmers who receive federal handouts would be prohibited from planting corn on as much land in 1988 as they had planted on in 1987. To compensate the farmers, the Senate planned to allow them to grow soybeans on the acres that the government had paid them not to grow corn on. This works out to a subsidy of up to $200 an acre for growing soybeans. Of course, the soybean market could have been devastated, so to placate soybean farmers, the Senate wanted to launch a new guaranteed-income program for soybean producers, traditionally among the most independent of farmers. The Senate wanted to wreck their market and compensate them by putting them on welfare. Since the soybean program would not incur higher costs until fiscal year 1989, it would have been a big "savings" for the fiscal year 1988.

Congressional attitudes toward waste and fraud are sometimes exemplified in open hostility to the General Accounting Office (GAO) or the USDA's inspector general. In 1987, Congressman Steve Gunderson condemned the USDA inspector general for a report on the Dairy Termination Program because the report put the program "in a very bad light."[53] Auditors from the GAO who wrote an audit report on the high cost of the tobacco program were called up to Capitol Hill to endure an hour of shouting from the congressional aides of congressmen representing tobacco interests.

Congressional hearings sometimes make it obvious that congressmen don't understand some programs that they have created. As the Washington Post reported, "Occasionally a senator turns to the committee staff for an explanation of a bill he himself introduced. . . . Senator David Pryor . . . counseled committee members not to confuse themselves by reading details of a pending bill."[54] On March 26, 1987, the Senate Agriculture Committee held a hearing on the use of generic payment-in-kind (PIK) certificates, the USDA's new funny money. (A detailed explanation of PIK certificates follows in the next chapter.) This program was one of the key changes authorized in the 1985 farm bill and had been in operation for almost a year at the time of the hearings. Yet from the questions asked, it was obvious that most senators didn't have the foggiest idea of how PIK certificates operated. Senator Rudy Boschwitz finally got indignant and insulted a member of the General Accounting Office's staff for trying to explain the program to him.[55] Senator Patrick Leahy, the chairman of the Senate Agriculture Committee, concluded: "I don't think anybody will be able to understand it sufficiently to cut [the budget]."[56]

Congressmen are often anxious to repress evidence of the failure or absurdity of agricultural policies. Not only do congressmen themselves not understand farm programs, they also want to prevent anyone else from understanding them. Congress prohibited the Federal Trade Commission and the Office of Management and Budget from studying marketing orders in 1984, and banned the Federal

Trade Commission from investigating abuses by milk marketing cooperatives in 1979. In the 1940s, Congress gutted the budget of the USDA's Bureau of Agricultural Economics after the bureau suggested that some poor Southern farmers might be better off if they abandoned farming. And in 1931, Congress banned the USDA from making any crop price forecasts, since Congress believed that the USDA's predictions were depressing the prices.

Government control of agriculture is based on the idea that the rulers are wiser than the ruled—or at the very least, that the rulers know what they are doing. But according to a 1978 study by the House Administration Committee, the average congressman spent only eleven minutes a day reading at work.[57] Congressmen don't even have time to read the new bills that are introduced each day Congress is in session, and are often less informed about public affairs than the average reader of the *New York Times* or the *Wall Street Journal*. Congressmen now routinely work only three days a week in Washington, conducting legislative business Tuesday through Thursday and flying to fundraising sessions on weekends. The *New Republic*'s Fred Barnes, in an article entitled "The Unbearable Lightness of Being a Congressman," concluded that "the daily routine of house members is mindlessly hectic and stupefyingly dull. . . . "[58] Congressmen's days are an endless stream of cocktail receptions, meetings, visits spent begging lobbyists for campaign contributions and listening to lobbyists beg for political favors. Congressmen are trying to do so many different things in so many different areas that it is almost impossible for them to be well informed. The more Congress' power has expanded in recent decades, the less the average congressman understands what he is doing.

Many congressmen and senators receive benefits from federal farm subsidies. Senator Mark Andrews received $20,000 a year for producing the crops for which he helped legislate subsidies on the Senate Agriculture Committee. If a government employee authored a policy and then collected a windfall, it would be a federal crime. But Congress effectively exempted itself from the Ethics in Government Act, which prohibits conflicts of interest for government policymakers. Regardless of how much money farm-state congressmen receive from farm programs, they will never have a conflict of interest in voting to give themselves more money.

"Consistency is the hobgoblin of mediocre minds" appears to be most congressmen's motto on farm policy. Most congressmen either don't realize or don't care about the contradictions among agricultural programs—they measure each program separately on a vote-buying scale. For congressmen, there is no contradiction between giving money to two different voters or giving two government checks to the same voter for conflicting programs. It does not conflict with congressmen's fundamental interest in agricultural programs—their re-election—so why all the fuss? There may be an economic contradiction, or a budget contradiction, but there is no political contradiction: Politicians benefit from each additional handout to farmers, regardless of its consistency with other handouts to farmers.

Most congressmen are believers in the Omnipotent Intention school of legislation—a blind and incurable faith that laws will have the effect that congressmen intend them to have, simply because Congress is mighty and wise. "We intend, therefore it will be" is the implicit preamble for most acts of Congress. As Congressman de la Garza declared in 1985, "This is the most important thing we do here today, telling American agriculture that we care."[59] This mentality helps explain the disdain many congressmen have for the details of programs; many congressmen believe that all they need to do is to make their wish known and it will miraculously become reality. It also explains much of the blitzkrieg legislation enacted without hearings and often with little or no floor debate.

Self-doubt is rare on Capitol Hill. There is a pervasive arrogance of power that often is intellectually blinding. Congressmen spend their lives being told by lobbyists and aides how powerful they are; eventually they come to believe it themselves. This superstition of the efficacy of power has been especially debilitating in congressmen's efforts to dominate world grain markets. Refusing to doubt themselves, congressmen usually respond to each farm program failure either by denouncing the administration or by proclaiming that more federal spending would solve the problem.

Many commentators on farm policy have pointed out the failures of present programs and exhorted congressmen to reform them with all due haste. But farm programs are chock full of waste, fraud, and abuse because that is how influential congressmen want the programs to run. The problems with farm programs have long been obvious, and Congress has long resented the General Accounting Office and the USDA's inspector generals for announcing where the bodies are buried.

Helping Truly Needy Congressmen

There are two different standards for agricultural policy: policies that make sense in themselves, and policies that make sense in an election year. In 1984 the Senate Agriculture Committee was considering an extremely generous farm-aid bill. Ward Sinclair reported in the *Washington Post* that when one senator "asked why farmers would be given money in 1984 for next year's farm program," Senator James Exon replied "elections" and "laughter engulfed the room."[60]

The most consistent goal of federal agricultural policy is the re-election of incumbent politicians. Defenders of government agricultural planning stress the need for a wise government to balance supply and demand—and then Congress and the administration in election years throw everything out the window in a desperate attempt to perpetuate their stay in Washington. Kathleen Lawrence, a former deputy assistant secretary of agriculture (1983–87), observes, "It is very difficult to achieve sound farm policy in even-numbered years, especially even-numbered years divisible by four."[61]

In almost every election year since 1928, politicians have engineered farm-bailout packages. Incumbent presidents routinely use last-minute boosts in farm benefits to attempt to buy themselves another term in office. President Ford increased wheat and corn price supports by 50 percent in the summer of 1976; President Carter sharply raised price supports again in August 1980. In 1982, Congress raised price supports and provided more generous payments for farmers storing their crops, while the Reagan administration postponed a cut in dairy price supports until after the November elections. In 1984, Congress enacted a special farm-credit bailout and Reagan went out on the campaign trail to announce that the Farmers Home Administration was forgiving the debts of many of its borrowers. In 1986, Congress enacted two separate farm bailout packages and Reagan announced advance payments to farmers for crops they might grow the following year.

Conclusion

How much of this is ignorance, and how much is conscious dishones-
ty? This is the Riddle of the Sphinx in judging farm policy-making.
After years of hearing their own speeches, congressmen often lose
touch with reality. The longer a politician stays in Washington, the
more that political reality becomes the only reality.

Some congressmen have worked hard to reform agricultural
programs. Senator Jesse Helms has strived to reduce wasteful spending in farm programs (except for tobacco and peanuts), and Congressman Jim Olin has struggled to make the dairy program less absurd. Congressman Barney Frank has been the most outspoken
against farm boondoggles in recent years. Congressman Joseph Dio-
Guardi tried to reform the Farmers Home Administration, Congressman Silvio Conte has repeatedly tried to remove the honey
program's sting, and Congressman Charles Schumer has exposed the
failures of export programs.

Members of the House and Senate Agriculture committees receive
de facto campaign contributions of tens of thousands of dollars a year
for maintaining the current interventionist system. If agriculture were
market-oriented, with no payoffs, one of the biggest losses would be
in the clout and campaign contribution of congressional agriculture-
committee members. By maximizing government intervention in agriculture, members of the agriculture committee's maximize their own
power and wealth.

$\blacklozenge$ *Chapter 12* $\blacklozenge$

Our Agricultural Industrial Policy

Federal agricultural bureaucrats couldn't run a watermelon stand if we gave them the melons and had the Highway Patrol flag down their customers.

— Jim Hightower
Commissioner of Agriculture, Texas

Secretary of Agriculture Henry Wallace announced in June 1934: "What we are doing is stop-gapping. We don't know where the further shore is."[1] Now, fifty-six years into the agriculture emergency of 1933, the USDA is still stop-gapping. When Franklin D. Roosevelt first sent the Agricultural Adjustment Act to Congress, he admitted it was a "trial and error" plan. In fifty-six years, the federal government has learned almost nothing from its trials and still repeats most of its original errors.

At the core of farm policy is a blind fixation on using coercion and handouts to raise short-term farm income. Agricultural programs are based on the idea that government can make America better off by restricting production and inflating prices. Spending tax dollars for agriculture presumes that government can use a dollar more productively than if that dollar were left in the private sector—even if government spends the dollar to pay someone not to produce anything at all. Current agricultural industrial policy is based on the assumption that America benefits more from federally mandated inefficiency and waste than it would from allowing farmers to operate at maximum productivity.

The Great Stabilizer

The *New York Times* of March 12, 1933, reported that Henry Wallace and a group of farm lobbyists had told President Roosevelt to ask for "farm dictator powers" to solve the farm crisis.[2] Today, fifty-six years later, the secretary of agriculture is still effectively the czar of agriculture. He can, with a sweep of his pen, drive crop prices up or down, spend $50 million to buy up almost any farm commodity he chooses, change the regulations governing the profitability of a hundred businesses, overturn decisions of the U.S. Department of Agriculture (USDA) administrative law judges, shower benefits on favored states and congressional districts while starving other areas, change the rules a farmers operates under each year, cancel a farmer's right to sell his tobacco or peanuts, or give away $29 million in government commodities to a personal acquaintance. So Alexander Hamilton observed, "Power over a man's subsistence is power over a man's will." And the secretary of agriculture has vast power over hundreds of thousands of farmers' subsistence.

One day in 1986, Agriculture Secretary Richard Lyng had a breakfast meeting with Dwayne Andreas, the president of Archer-Daniels-Midland (ADM), one of the nation's largest agribusiness corporations. Lyng and Andreas apparently had a very pleasant breakfast: Two days later Lyng announced that the USDA would give Archer-Daniels-Midland $29 million worth of free corn in order to make ethanol.[3] There is no public interest in giveaways for ethanol, any more than there would be if the secretary of energy gave the Mobil Corporation a million barrels of oil to refine into gasoline. The ADM bonanza was the biggest single handout in USDA history—yet because the subject was agriculture, the corporate welfare received little attention in the media.

New Deal–era planners assumed that giving practically unlimited power to the secretary of agriculture would allow him to stabilize markets. Farm programs are based on the New Deal distrust of markets and blind faith in politicians—on the idea that the more un-restrained power politicians have to dictate economic events, the bet-ter off America will be. Unfortunately, the USDA "stabilizes" markets like the U.S. Army "liberated" villages in France in World War II—planting an American flag on the rubble after the battle. As G. Ed Schuh, the chairman of the agricultural economics department at the University of Minnesota, observes, "Ultimately it is the instability of government policy and government intervention that cause the in-stability in commodity markets."[4]

Government treats agriculture far more arbitrarily than any other industry. Because government gives so much to farmers, politicians and bureaucrats often act as though they have a license to treat agri-cultural markets however they choose. In 1986 and 1987, the allegedly free-market Reagan administration effectively imposed federal price controls on wheat and corn. Crop prices were driven down with al-most total disregard for the livelihood of those farmers who were not receiving government handouts. If the government had manipulated steel or computer prices the way it whipsawed wheat prices, editorial pages would have exploded in indignation. But since the industry was only agriculture, few people paid attention.

In recent years, farm markets have had hanging over them the largest crop surpluses in history. The government effectively control-led most of this surplus, through the Farmer-Owned Reserve and price-support loans, and held most of the surplus off the market. Crop prices in recent years have largely been determined by how much of the surplus the government will allow into the market. Congressman Dan Glickman declared in November 1987, "We see the Commodity Credit Corporation controlling domestic, and arguably world, grain markets on a daily basis. . . . "[5] Congressman Glenn English said, "It appears now that the government is more deeply involved in setting prices and sales for farmers than at any time in the history of this country."[6] Since crop market prices were below the federal non-recourse loan rate, farmers could not sell their crops under loan to the Commodity Credit Corporation (CCC) without losing money. With payment-in-kind (PIK) certificates, farmers could sell their crops at the market price and get paid by the government the difference between the market price and the loan rate. And the USDA controlled prices by announcing posted county prices (PCPs) each day in each county—the price that pegged the value of the PIK certificates.

The creation of PIK certificates—coupons redeemable for government surplus crops—has allowed the USDA to dominate crop prices to a degree not seen since the New Deal. The government controlled the supply of crops allowed into the market by the number of PIK certificates it gave to farmers at the same time that the demand for crops was dominated by the amount of export subsidies the USDA provided for foreign sales. If the CCC flooded the market with PIK certificates and did not stimulate crop demand, prices would fall. When the USDA decided to drive down crop prices in order to spur exports, corn prices fell to $1 a bushel in Iowa in 1986—the lowest inflation-adjusted price in decades. PIK certificates epitomized the basic inequity of farm programs: Farmers who signed up for government farm programs to qualify for subsidies were completely protected against price declines and many enjoyed record incomes, while farmers who did not were sacrificed to the USDA's master plan for saving agriculture by temporarily driving down prices in order to boost exports.

The *Pro Farmer* newsletter, observing how the USDA was manipulating markets with PIK certificates, claimed that one USDA official described the agency's policy, "We follow prices in the direction we think they should go."[7] The USDA manipulated grain prices in order to camouflage the cost of other USDA policies. Under the headline, "USDA Dictates Wheat Collapse," *Pro Farmer* reported on May 23, 1987:

> The price of Texas Gulf wheat on Wednesday (5/19) was quoted by USDA's Agricultural Marketing Service at $3.17. But USDA . . . declared that for PCP [Posted County Price] purposes, the Texas Gulf price was not $3.17, but $2.95—a 23 cent discrepancy! It becomes a self-fulfilling prophecy because cash grain merchandisers are well aware they'll be deluged with grain if they hold cash bids at sharp premiums to PCP. Thus, cash bids tend to follow USDA's PCP quote as if hand-cuffed to it. . . . The motive is obvious. The lower the market prices, the less subsidy USDA must pay to meet terms of the recent Export Enhancement Program offer to the Soviets.[7]

Late on the afternoon of Friday, October 30, 1987, the USDA announced that it would begin making available for auction up to 10 million bushels of wheat each week. This unexpected announcement devastated markets: Wheat prices on the Portland, Oregon, exchange were 39 cents a bushel lower on the following Monday. As Congressman Pat Roberts declared at a House Agriculture hearing on November 17, 1987, "Our producers spend weeks and weeks watching the markets and trying to decipher the constant shuffling of the PCP at the county elevator price."[8]

According to federal law, the USDA is prohibited from selling government-owned wheat for less than the loan rate plus 10 percent. This would have prevented the USDA from selling wheat for less than $3.12 a bushel, more than the $2.87 market price at the time of the USDA's announcement. The USDA claimed that its redeeming the wheat for PIK certificates was not a sale but an exchange. Thus, almost 10 million bushels of wheat were exchanged at an average price of $2.38 a bushel. Not surprisingly, market prices went into a tailspin.

On November 3, 1987, the USDA announced that it would sell 80 million bushels of wheat to the Soviets under the Export Enhancement Program. The USDA had driven wheat prices down in order to decrease the apparent subsidy the Soviets received. Independent farmers were clobbered so that politicians could camouflage the costs of subsidizing the Soviet Union. The USDA's Ray Goldberg reassured the House Agriculture Committee, "We have the option, of course, to discontinue the program [of putting 10 million bushels of wheat a week on the market] at any time or to make it smaller or larger."[9] This is an excellent way to stabilize markets—to have a USDA official announce that the government will dump as much of its holdings as it likes on the market any time it chooses.

At the hearing of the House Agriculture Committee on November 17, 1987, Congressman Robert Smith asked Mr. Goldberg, "Did you anticipate that the price of wheat would drop after your announcement of October 30?" Goldberg replied, "Congressman, we did not anticipate that the market would drop but we know that that type of activity . . . would impact the market if no other factors entered into the market in various positions."[10] Either the USDA was incredibly unrealistic—thinking that such an announcement would not drive down prices—or Goldberg was less than forthright.

The USDA's arbitrariness continues to dominate domestic wheat prices. As the *Wall Street Journal* reported on March 11, 1988, "The USDA's campaign to unload its wheat stockpiles on the market continued to depress wheat-futures prices."[11] Some traders "are throwing in the towel," said Katharina Zimmer, a grain analyst at Merrill Lynch & Co., New York. "The USDA has pulled out all the stops in the last two weeks to dump its wheat. . . . Wheat prices have also been undercut by a lack of new export business. In February [1988], the market was boosted by anticipation of a rumored barrage of new offers by the Agriculture Department to subsidize wheat sales to targeted countries. Those offers, however, haven't materialized. . . . "[12]

The Illusion of Competence

USDA headquarters has never been accused of being a hotbed of intellectual dynamism. Until recently a sign in the USDA headquarters library in Washington said: "No eating, drinking, or sleeping." The sign is not there any more because the the library was shut down and moved to Maryland. This should improve the USDA's productivity, since policy-makers will be less inclined to waste time reading about the successes of past farm policies.

The red tape is mind-boggling. In the USDA's headquarters building, employees are required to fill out a form each time they make a photocopy. Instead of spending their time trying to better understand the economy they are ruling, USDA headquarters employees busy themselves filling out forms for photocopying one copy of a memo.

Congress has passed more than twenty different agricultural laws since 1980, but the USDA has little or no perspective on these policies. One cannot understand the current situation without looking at the shifts and reversals of policy since 1981. The author called the USDA's budget office and general counsel office in late 1987 to get a list and summary of each agricultural law enacted since 1980. After the phone calls were bounced around a dozen times, I was told no one had such a list. Jackie Patterson of the USDA's general counsel office said, "We just don't have a publication with a summary of all those laws listed for the last five years—not even for the last year. We used to do that, but it is such a tremendous project."[13] The USDA has more than

100,000 employees, but they can't keep track of the agricultural laws that Congress makes. This blindness reaches the highest echelons of the USDA. The author interviewed Secretary of Agriculture John Block in early 1984 for a story on the 1983 PIK program. When asked about a major farm-law change in late 1982 that had raised grain price supports, directly undercutting the PIK program, Block first denied that such a change had occurred. A USDA press aide who was present for the interview corrected him.

Federal farm programs are administered by local Agriculture Stabilization and Conservation Service (ASCS) committees elected by farmers. Local ASCS committees often complain that they are over-whelmed by all the changes in rules and regulations that descend upon them from Washington. In 1963, during the scandal over the activities of Billie Sol Estes, the chairman of the Texas ASCS committee admitted that "as chairman, he had read virtually none of the rules and regulations himself."[14] Each year, the ASCS headquarters sends out hundreds of regulations, revisions, and amendments to its program manual. Local administrators are supposed to keep up with each new program change and to understand all the different programs. Different local ASCS offices often give farmers different advice and apply rules differently.

The ASCS committee system appears as if it was designed to maximize giveaways. Local ASCS committees are a farmer-run farmer welfare system. Charles Hardin, political scientist, observed: "The ASCS committees have been largely infused with the ideal of parity as the farmers' due which it was their special mission to see that the farmer received."[15] Charles Brannan, a former USDA secretary, commented in 1963, "Many a taxpayer would welcome the opportunity to elect the IRS agent for his community."[16]

Local committees have been accused of showing favoritism in deciding which farmers shall be penalized or exempted from USDA regulations. It was a common complaint in the 1960s, when the USDA doled out allotments to produce grain, that "the man who boosts the program will get a bigger crop allotment than one who's against it."[17]

The USDA's annual plans for directing the agricultural economy are based on the accumulated statistics from 2,800 local USDA county offices, but the building blocks of national policy are usually unsound. For instance, many government payments and loans are based on the farmers' crop yields. These statistics are vital to the USDA's judgments on the health and productivity of American agriculture. But different divisions of the USDA routinely disagree profoundly in their estimates of the yields of the same cropland.[18] For one farm, the ASCS estimated a wheat crop at 31 bushels an acre, while the Farmers Home Administration (FmHA) claimed that the same land was producing 60 bushels an acre. (The FmHA has an incentive to exaggerate land yields because that allows FmHA to justify giving farmers more money.) How can the USDA fine-tune the agricultural economy when it cannot even agree on what is happening on the farms?

The USDA has many competent staff economists, but its policymakers make little use of them. The 1986 Dairy Termination Program sale of 1.5 million cows was handled almost solely by the dairy experts in the ASCS. Plenty of people in the USDA bureaucracy could have told the ASCS or the secretary's office that an announcement of the imminent butchering of that many cows would devastate cattle prices.

One of the greatest costs of farm programs is the rural brain drain: farmers spending weeks struggling to understand farm programs and to predict the USDA's or Congress' next surprise. Larry Johnson, vicepresident of the National Corn Growers Association, complains of "farmers standing in line [at the local committee offices] often times spending as much time there as they would to be putting the crop in on set-aside acres."[19] As University of Maryland economist Bruce Gardner observed, "The considerable entrepreneurial skills that farmers possess have undergone a substantial shift from outsmarting nature and the markets to outsmarting government."[20]

The USDA is a loose cannon on the deck of the agricultural economy's ship. Often the USDA and Congress have not agreed on a farm program by planting time. In recent years, farmers have repeatedly been stunned as Congress enacts legislation in March or April that radically changes the economic factors dominating that year's harvest. Congressman Bill Emerson complained in November 1987 that "what has farmers . . . upset the most is the uncertainty of what the USDA and the CCC is going to do next."[21] Congressman Byron Dorgan observes, "It just drives farmers crazy year after year to see us lurch in one direction and lurch back in another direction and then zig here and zag there."[22] Larry Johnson notes, "There is no predictability and we don't know what is going to come down on us next, and our local ASCS offices do not either."[23] Dean Kleckner, the president of the American Farm Bureau Federation, observes, "When it comes to farm programs, one Congress hardly gets done writing what the next one wants to rewrite or completely erase."[24] At a hearing on the USDA's delay in announcing details of its 1988 wheat program, House Agriculture Committee chairman Kika de la Garza groused, "We don't want to blame the Department for the inefficiency of the system, which leaves us without any answer except 'I will try and find out what the hell happened.'"[25]

The USDA's ability to successfully manage the agricultural economy depends on its ability to successfully predict future developments. One of the clearest measures of the failure of the USDA's ability to foresee the future is the inaccuracy of its budget forecasts. The 1981 four-year farm bill was expected to cost $12 billion; instead it cost $60 billion. The 1985 five-year farm bill was predicted to cost $52 billion; instead, it has already cost more than $90 billion, and will likely cost more than $120 billion total. Though some inaccuracies are not surprising in long-range forecasts, even the USDA's annual budget forecasts are grossly inaccurate—yet the USDA has made little or no effort to improve its forecasting methodology. A report by the General Accounting Office concluded, "USDA's budget estimates were substantially incorrect in most years."[26] In the years from 1972 to 1986, the USDA's actual annual spending was 78 percent higher than the amount it predicted it would spend each year. Between 1981 and 1986 the USDA misestimated the annual federal expenditure on the corn program by an average of 154 percent.[27] The General Accounting Office noted that, "except for 1984, the analysts generally underestimated total supply and overestimated total demand."[28] The USDA persistently underestiamted dairy production forecasts and overestimated expected consumption of dairy products, thus perpetually underestimating the size of the dairy surplus. As the General Accounting Office observed, "We found that USDA had not performed any evaluation to determine the extent to which economic assumptions account for the misestimates in the commodity budget estimates. . . . Although USDA recognizes that it has had accuracy problems with the budget estimates, no one management structure could act to see that improvements are made."[29] The USDA "has not maintained records of input data used to make supply-and-demand forecasts . . . USDA analysts generally have not documented their methods in producing forecasts. . . ." Despite perpetual gross inaccuracies in budget forecasts, the USDA made little or no effort to evaluate its budget forecasting system: "USDA has not systematically attempted to identify the source of these errors, nor has it related them to either uncontrollable or controllable factors."[30]

The USDA sometimes distorts its budget estimates in order to make people believe that floundering programs have been reformed. The budget forecasts of the Federal Crop Insurance Corporation (FCIC) in the 1980s have been exercises in wishful thinking. FCIC administrators pick their numbers out of thin air, choosing numbers that sound impressive and make politicians happy; every year, FCIC's expenses are far different from its predictions. The General Accounting Office noted, "Although FCIC has had a loss in each year . . . it has never forecast a loss."[31] How can the USDA plan the agricultural economy when it cannot even admit to itself what is happening?

Though agricultural policy-makers insist that farmers could not survive without federal subsidies, the unsubsidized part of agriculture has generally done as well as, or better than, the subsidized part. A Republican minority report to a farm bill in January 1956 noted that "the average price of [unsubsidized] commodities has been higher (as measured by parity price relations) in every year since 1940, except one, than the price of so-called basic crops."[32] The *Wall Street Journal* editorialized in 1967, on looking over the results of the farm program in the 1960s, "Producers of livestock, poultry, and such uncontrolled crops as potatoes and soybeans enjoyed rising incomes while producers of crops—wheat, feed grains, and so on—under governmental control programs saw their income decline."[33] In the 1970s, farm programs were comparatively inactive, and there was no clear difference between the incomes of subsidized and unsubsidized farmers. Bankruptcy rates in the 1980s have been higher among farmers of subsidized crops than among farmers of unsubsidized crops, and farmland values fell twice as much as in the corn belt as they did in areas where farmers produced unsubsidized crops.

If comparisons between the incomes of subsidized and unsubsidized farmers excluded government payments, the unsubsidized crops would appear vastly more profitable, and it would become apparent that many subsidized crops are being produced at a loss. Farm program costs routinely far exceed the farmers' entire profits. For 1986 the wheat program and wheat export subsidies cost $4.0 billion; the wheat producers' total net cash income (before depreciation) was only $2.0 billion. In 1985 the wheat program cost the federal government $4.6 billion; the wheat farmers' net cash income was $2.3 billion. In 1986 the corn program cost $11.2 billion; corn growers' net cash income was $4.4 billion.[34] As noted in Chapter 3, the rice program cost taxpayers $2.7 billion in 1986 while rice producers received $236 million in income; the cotton program cost $2.1 billion while cotton producers' net cash income was only $1.3 billion; and the sugar program cost consumers $3 billion while sugar producers realized roughly $300 million in income. A study made by the USDA in 1985 estimated the effects of extending existing farm-support programs through 1990 and concluded:

> For every dollar of net cash income transferred from consumers and taxpayers to farmers, an extra $4.25 would be incurred because of program provisions that inhibit the efficient operation of farm markets. Much of the $21 billion consumer and taxpayer expenditure would go not to farmers but would be dissipated throughout the agricultural industry in the form of higher input prices (including land) and increased profits to suppliers of materials and services to farmers.[35]

Politicians and bureaucrats have mismanaged agriculture so badly in recent years that government subsidies for a small percentage of farm products have approached or exceeded net farm income every year since 1983. In 1983 net farm income was $12.7 billion. Federal outlays for agriculture were $23 billion and, according to an estimate by D. Gale Johnson, an economist at the University of Chicago, consumers paid $13 billion more than they would have for American food had federal subsidies and trade barriers not existed.[36] In 1984 net farm income was $32 billion, with federal outlays at $16 billion and an additional consumer "farmer tax" of $13 billion. In 1985, farmers' income equaled $32.3 billion, federal outlays were $26 billion, and consumers paid over $13 billion extra because of federal agricultural policies. In 1986, net farm income was $37.5 billion, while federal farm programs cost taxpayers $31 billion and consumers $13 billion. In 1987, net farm income was estimated at $46 billion, while federal farm programs cost more than $30 billion (counting the $2 billion that the FmHA wrote off for bad debts) and higher food costs added an extra $13 billion.

Government cannot continuously increase farm income because the value of federal aid is inevitably capitalized into the prices of farmland. The more generous the subsidies, the more expensive the farmland. The more expensive farmland becomes, the higher the cost of production and the lower the profits from sales. The 1986 Economic Report of the President noted:

> Programs that increase land values and rental rates benefit most landowners holding the land at the beginning of the program. Farmers acquiring land after program institution may pay up to the entire capitalized program benefit to acquire the right to receive the payments. Thus, by enhancing land values, deficiency payments also augment landowner wealth relative to nonlandowners.[37]

A development report published by the World Bank in 1986 observed: "It is doubtful that high product prices have raised farm incomes in the long term although the rental value and price of land have been supported."[38]

It is difficult to fathom how the government could spend so much money to so little benefit. But when one accounts for salaries for a hundred thousand civil servants, the higher costs of production, the inflated land values, the tens of millions of idled acres, and the civil war of farm policies, one begins to see where the money goes. Even though the United States has a comparative advantage over other nations in producing wheat, the federal government has turned wheat production into a burden on the American taxpayer.

A study by Thomas W. Hertel, Robert Thompson (formerly the USDA's chief economist), and Marinos E. Tsigas of Purdue University shed some light on the true cost of farm subsidies. Having analyzed all the factors influencing agricultural policy and the economy, the researchers estimated that each job saved in agriculture was costing the U.S. economy and the taxpayers more than $100,000 each year. Their study concluded, "These costs include the following (measured in 1987 dollars and expressed in terms of farm jobs saved by current policies): (i) reduced non-food output ($107,000/year per farm job saved), (ii) increased Treasury outlays ($80,500/year per farm job saved), and (iii) lower real domestic income ($28,700/year per farm job saved)."[39]

The USDA runs farm programs with a contempt for taxpayers' money that is often mind-boggling. In 1986 the USDA ran a Cotton Warehouse Payment program to compensate cotton warehousers for a fall in the price of cotton. The USDA simply asked the warehousers how many bales of cotton they had—the warehousers sent or phoned a number in to the USDA—and then the USDA wrote out checks for more than $700 million. Until the General Accounting Office complained, no effort was made to verify that the warehousers actually owned the cotton they claimed. A USDA inspector general found the same enlightened administration of the rice program: "A general lack of program controls permitted rice producers to obtain special rice loans with any type of written documentation from persons handling rice without explanations as to how the quantity and quality were determined. Verifications were not required or made to ensure the validity of the written documentation submitted by producers. . . . "[40] The USDA repeats the same sloppy administration in its handout programs year after year, almost never learning from its mistakes.

In 1984, with the Reagan administration hungering for a bountiful harvest of votes, the ASCS announced that farmers who had received advance payments in 1982 for corn they planned to grow in 1983 but then did not grow because of PIK did not have to repay their 1982 windfall until 1985. This provided farmers with a six-month interest-free loan and cost taxpayers nearly $13 million. Though this is a drop in the ocean of farm program waste, it is a good example of how the USDA makes policy. There was a rumor at USDA headquarters that some local ASCS county offices had sent letters to farmers informing them that the 1982 unearned payments would have to be repaid on March 15, 1984, instead of on April 1, 1984, when the loans were actually due. But it turned out, after an investigation by the General Accounting Office, that only one county office in the nation had inadvertently told farmers that they would have to repay the handouts a few weeks early for crops they never grew, and that the office had sent farmers a correction notice a few days after the original letter.[41] Yet the rumor was sufficient justification for a mid-level USDA bureaucrat to authorize another multimillion-dollar windfall for farmers.

USDA's Federal Crop Insurance Corporation is famous for its "wind-shield" crop inspections, in which the crop insurer drives by the field, waves to the farmer, goes back to the office, and reports that 680 acres of cotton were damaged beyond recovery. The FCIC paid insurance claims for drought losses on 17 million acres of irrigated land—which makes about as much sense as compensating a shipowner for a boat sinking on dry land. Congress has launched numerous special disaster bailout programs in the last few years. In 1987 the USDA announced that the FCIC would not release names of its beneficiaries to other USDA agencies that provide farmers with disaster relief. This effectively guarantees that many farmers will get paid twice for the same crop loss.[42]

The USDA allows farmers to qualify for disaster payments according to the average county yield, not the yield that the land actually produces. This gives farmers the incentive to buy crop insurance, throw a few seeds on the land, and receive a huge federal bonus when the crop fails. Farmer Wesley Sandall explained the procedures to George Anthan of the *Des Moines Register*:

> "Now this field here is about 120 acres, and they just plant it and leave it. It's got a history of cropping and a government-established yield of 100 bushels to the acres [the county average]. So, they come into the ASCS office and get deficiency payments (currently at about $1.90 a bushel on corn) based on that yield." Sandall estimated that the operators of the field . . . will receive outright federal cash payments of some $12,000. "Also," he said, "the operators had bought crop insurance on that field and could be expected to get more than $21,000 for 'crop failure.'" He said, "After they plant it, they may run the irrigation rig through it once or twice to show that they're 'working' it. They have to look like they're making an effort. In the process, they've ruined this land for a long, long time. The government programs did this."[43]

Congressmen and USDA representatives defend farm programs as "economic democracy," but in practice this often means no more than giving the majority the right to seize the minority's property. The USDA's concept of economic democracy is best exemplified in farm program referendums. In the tobacco referendum, most of the votes are cast by nonfarmers to whom the farmers must pay tribute for the right to grow tobacco. The dairy cooperatives are allowed to cast the votes of their members, which is a lot like allowing a landlord to cast a are cast by nonfarmers to whom the farmers must pay tribute for the right to grow tobacco. The dairy cooperatives are allowed to cast the votes of their members, which is a lot like allowing a landlord to cast a vote for all his tenants. In the nectarine referendum, the USDA made only a feeble effort to distribute ballots to farmers who might not support continued government control. With the proposed mandatory acreage controls, two-thirds of the small farmers would be allowed to shut down the remaining one-third's largest farms. In all USDA referendums, the consumers and taxpayers who will be forced to pay the ultimate costs are never given a voice, and only the farmers who are already producing the crop are allowed to decide the future of that crop.

The mentality of federal agricultural planners was captured in the first annual report of the Agricultural Adjustment Administration (AAA) in 1934: "Anything which increases business activity actually increases the production of wealth. . . . The Agricultural Adjustment Program has made an important contribution toward increasing business activity, and thus the production of wealth."[44] This is the cat-chasing-its-tail model of economic development: Anything that causes activity will automatically increase society's well-being. The same line of thinking in the AAA annual report led to the Works Progress Administration (WPA) job program of the 1930s, popularly referred to as "We Poke Along," which gave leaf-raking a bad name, and to the CETA job-creation program in the 1970s that resulted in the building of artificial rocks for rock climbers to practice on. This view presumes that government intervention is like a shot of caffeine for the economy, always able to energize a sleeping giant.

Agricultural policy is defended by showing that artificial relative shortages of food can raise the farmers' short-term income. But why would artificial scarcity in one sector be good for the entire economy? Farm policy is based on the idea that consumers should be sacrificed to make farmers richer, because the richer farmers become, the better off consumers will be. In this view, the health of the American economy is dependent on making a few hundred thousand farmers even richer than they already are. Agricultural policy presumes that society gains more from transferring a dollar from 115 million workers to a few hundred thousand farmers than it loses from shutting down 78 million acres of farmland, destroying hundreds of thousands of farm-related jobs, wasting hundreds of millions of fresh oranges and lemons, and driving up production costs for all major crops. And how does society gain from all this waste and inefficiency? Farm income increases. In the final realm, farm policy can only be defended by magical multipliers.

The Cult of Planning

Federal agricultural policy presumes that government can better balance agricultural supply and demand with regulations, decrees, daily arbitrary interventions, and five-year plans than can individual farmers and their customers with voluntary agreements. Yet almost all the numbers on which agricultural policy is determined have little or no meaning. Predictions of future supply and demand are often not worth the paper they are printed on; parity is an ancient joke; cost-of-production estimates are a racket; farm income estimates are misleading; the official number of farmers is a ruse; and budget estimates usually miss by a country mile. Yet from a combination of misleading and meaningless numbers, a solid policy is supposed to result. "Garbage in, garbage out" is the proper characterization of the USDA's planning process.

Federal agricultural policies can only be justified with the blanket assumption that planned economies are superior to market economies, that government coercion is inherently superior to individual agreements, and that politicians and bureaucrats understand farming better than farmers do. Assistant Secretary of Agriculture Rexford Tugwell, a leading member of Roosevelt's Brain Trust, expressed the spirit of the New Deal in 1934:

> Russia has shown that planning is practical. . . . The challenge [of the Soviet model for America] lies rather in the idea of planning, of purposeful, intelligent control over economic affairs. . . . With Russia as an example, intelligent people in America will become less and less willing to seek remedies for economic evils in inactivity. . . . The organization of the Soviet system seems to have many advantages in efficiency and directness. . . . We have developed efficiency and science in the art of government. Our administrative, executive, and judicial bodies have proved competent to handle the most difficult matters.[45]

Tugwell did concede that a major impediment to planning in the United States was the "unreasoning, almost hysterical attachment of certain Americans to the Constitution."[46] (Even as Tugwell lauded the Soviet regime, Stalin was solving the Soviet farm problem with an artificial famine that killed up to 9 million peasants in the Ukraine.)[47] The original director of the Agriculture Adjustment Administration proclaimed in 1933 that the solution to the farm problem was the "planned harvest." The Kennedy administration's chief agricultural economist, Willard Cochrane, declared that government "had to save agriculture from itself." Subsequent USDA administrators may have abandoned the 1930s rhetoric, but they have retained the 1930s programs and goals.

The USDA spends tens of billions of dollars trying to balance supply and demand, even though it does not and cannot know what supply and demand will be. In order to protect its reputation, the USDA almost never sets quantitative targets for its interventions. In 1985, Richard Goldberg, the USDA acting undersecretary, defended this vagueness:

> The establishment of quantifiable goals confronts program administrators frequently. Specific quantity goals, while laudable in concept, must be viewed in terms of their value to the public. In the case of farm programs . . . the vagaries of weather, the U.S. economic situation, and world farm commodities production and markets make accurate and reliable estimation virtually impossible.[48]

Goldberg is to be commended for his honesty, but he essentially admits that the USDA cannot pick a clear target because there are so many outside factors that the USDA cannot predict. Though USDA officials deny that they have clear goals, they still insist on spending between $20 billion and $30 billion a year shooting at targets they claim they can't see. The USDA claims that it can plan the agricultural economy, yet cannot state any of its planning goals in hard numbers because the agricultural economy is so unpredictable. A 1936 Brookings Institution study described federal agricultural policy as "forward striving toward a flying goal," and little has changed since.[49]

Federal agricultural policy assumes first that government can perceive the general economic interest, and second that politicians and bureaucrats would follow it if they knew it. Planners tend to perceive economic progress as a moral issue—the problem is that people are too greedy or selfish to follow the public interest—and thus the simple solution is to give some people the power to force other people to do the right thing. Tugwell viewed the central problem of economic progress as "subordinating the profit motive to social welfare. . . . the most economical utilization of industrial capacity for the welfare of the people as a whole is inconsistent with private profit seeking. . . ." There is also a blind faith in technical expertise—in accumulating the most experts, who will form committees and then arrive at the right answer.

Government planners act as if directing the economy were largely a question of pushing people in the right direction, rather than knowing in which direction to go. But uncertainty is the essence of future economic activity. Prices fluctuate because conditions change. That is why there are stock markets—because people disagree on the expected future value of every company and commodity in existence. Congress and the USDA create programs as if there were or should be little or no uncertainty—that all that were necessary was to have government decide what the correct value for a product is and then impose it on buyers and sellers.

The market is simply the collective judgment about a product's current and expected future value by all individuals engaged in producing, trading, and consuming that product. When bureaucrats or politicians say that the market is wrong, they mean that they believe they are better able to judge the real value of a product than are the individuals actively engaged in buying and selling it. Every price is a subjective value judgment, and prices fluctuate because value judgments naturally change.

For government, planning means trying to dictate to the market where it should go. Both individuals and governments plan, but governments use heavy penalties and billions of dollars of handouts and taxes to try to make its plans effective. Agricultural Adjustment Administrator Chester C. Davis praised federal farm handouts in 1934 as "an instrument of hopeful experimentation in the direction of economic and social control."[50]

Yet the federal government's catastrophic misperceptions of markets have repeatedly devastated farmers. In 1920 the USDA thought the World War I grain bubble would never burst; wheat farmers were devastated as a result. In 1929 the federal Farm Board tried to corner the U.S. grain crop; it destroyed exports and helped wreck the world trading system. In 1974, after two droughts in the Soviet Union, the USDA announced that a new export era had arrived and U.S. farmers should plant till they drop; this led to massive, price-depressing surpluses. In 1980 the Carter administration expected that the embargo on crop exports to the Soviets would cow the Russians; instead, American taxpayers were the victims. In 1981 the USDA was confident that an era of world food shortages had arrived and accepted a farm bill that rapidly destroyed the competitiveness of the American farmer.

While farm policy remains in the Stone Age, many farmers are already in the high-tech age. At a time when more and more farmers are using computers to adjust their daily schedules and operations, the USDA is still plodding along with five-year plans. At a time when farmers are shifting crops on a few days' notice, the USDA is still devoted to maintaining the dominance of the crops that happened to be popular in the 1930s. At a time when computer systems and microsensors are radically changing the use of irrigation and pesticide systems, USDA conservation programs continue blindly blanketing the land with federal dollars for outdated conservation practices.

Agricultural policy has been economics as if price didn't matter, based on the belief that government can drive up prices without disrupting or paralyzing markets. Agricultural planning has usually assumed zero or minimal price elasticity—that demand would not be affected by price. This is nonsense, as almost any nonmillionaire will realize during a visit to the grocery store. But because this notion has been necessary to justify the USDA's fixing prices above market-clearing levels, it has retained a prominent place in the agricultural policy Hall of Delusions. Don Paarlberg, formerly chief economist for the USDA, noted that economists generally used the same coefficients of elasticity for exports as for domestic markets, despite evidence that they differed.

The USDA's fixation on stable prices simply means that buyers and sellers should be prevented from seeing or feeling shifts in supply and demand—the "ostrich" method of dealing with unpleasant economic facts. USDA policies are based on stability at any cost, but it is a blindman's vision: Everything looks fine because he can see nothing. In agricultural markets, artificially stable prices are usually false prices. Prices convey information; the more price controls government imposes, the less information prices convey. Every government-set price is a value judgment—a declaration that politicians' and bureaucrats' values are preferable to producers' and consumers' values.

Politicians and bureaucrats set prices with far less information, understanding, and concern than do markets. Such prices will be out of touch with the real world, either on the day they are set or a week afterward. Agricultural markets fluctuate. Prices go up and down in response to a hundred changing circumstances. Mike Bowles of the Texas Cattle Feeders Association observed, "Why does USDA not understand how fragile free markets are? The answer is because they don't go out and sit in the market on a day-to-day basis. Free markets are built on supply and demand and they can't be interfered with by outsiders that have no feel for the pressures of supply."[51]

The issue is not whether markets are all-knowing, but whether market processes are more likely than bureaucratic processes to produce efficient, rational results; whether the voluntary agreements of millions of individuals are more likely than the dice of bureaucrats to produce efficient results. Markets always react faster than politicians. The only case for having politicians and bureaucrats veto the market would be if it were better to act on outdated information than on current information. Every price sends a signal to every producer. Is there a good reason for government to continue sending farmers the wrong signals on production?

Federal farm planning presumes that the government can successfully control one crop without controlling all crops. As Calvin Coolidge observed in vetoing a bill to boost farm prices in 1927, "The truth is that there is no such thing as effective partial control. To have effective control we would have to have control of not only one food product but of all substitutes."[52] Ezra Taft Benson observed, "Farm prices are linked up with each other. What we fail to do, or overdo in one part, of the farm economy—we must try to make up for in another, and another, and another."[53]

Farmers' productivity has always advanced faster than politicians' understanding. The agricultural policy of the last half century is simply the history of politicians' misunderstanding of technological developments, fear of economic change, and religious belief that any price decline is evil and justifies the full force of the federal government to combat it. The political process has proven incapable of adjusting to economic and technological change, and thus has both impeded the economy and prevented citizens from benefiting from new technology.

The Character of Government Intervention

To visualize how farm programs are made, think of an engineering team building a single machine with every engineer thinking his gear or lever is the only one that matters. Each engineer is obsessed with inserting the largest, gaudiest, heaviest gear he can concoct into the machine, with no concern about how it all fits together. If the rest of the machine does not function, that is no problem as long as each engineer can brag about his contribution. Farm policy-makers are a team of engineers with little incentive to work together, since there is no individual responsibility for collective failure. Agricultural economist B. H. Hibbard suggested in 1934 that the guiding rule of federal policy-makers was, "Let not thy left hand know what thy right hand doeth."[54]

All the theories on the benevolence of government economic intervention assume that the government will carefully and wisely select its economic target. But farm policy reveals the illusion of government as an economic sharpshooter. Like the Philadelphia police department, government economic intervention wipes out a whole block of houses in order to flush out a few snipers. As the Council for Agricultural Science and Technology reported in 1983, farm programs are "blunt instruments" lacking the necessary precision to do the most good.[55] When the USDA or Congress decide farmers have a problem, they usually favor the "carpet bombing" solution: If one farmer needs a bailout, then to be safe it is necessary to bail out all farmers of the same crop and those in a vaguely similar situation. Congress mandated in 1984 that the USDA must provide disaster handouts to farmers in counties adjacent to counties that are officially declared disaster counties. Each farm program seeks to solve a "problem" while providing the most money to the greatest number of farmers.

Once the government intervenes, the question becomes not whether the intervention is achieving its aim, but whether politicians and bureaucrats approve of the intervention's goal and whether the intervention creates good public relations. The intervention's goal quickly becomes more important than its effect. The bigger the intervention becomes, the more job opportunities bureaucrats will have and the more votes politicians can harvest. There is no self-correcting mechanism in government intervention, there is no bankruptcy court for foolish bureaucrats or shady congressmen. Politicians and bureaucrats have an incentive to deny their mistakes; markets and individuals have every incentive to correct their mistakes.

FmHA Administrator Vance Clark suggested that after an avalanche, it takes government bureaucrats months to just go out and buy snow shovels to begin the cleanup. Government economic intervention will usually be playing a losing catch-up game with reality—always trying to direct the market while being far behind the pace of events. Government industrial policies will generally be based on ignorance of the key factors that should determine the precise intervention. The economy changes every day, and decision-makers are often still planning to intervene in an economic situation that no longer exists. Bureaucrats have no overwhelming economic life-and-death incentive to keep up with the fast pace of events as private business managers do. And so the solution becomes government freezing the industry to better control it, as happened with tobacco and peanuts.

The more the government intervenes, the less effective each intervention will be. Hungarian economist Janos Kornai observes, "The greater the bureaucratic intervention, the more each intervention weakens the effects of the other."[56] The government eventually catches the economy in a crossfire of its own interventions, an endless battle between bureaucracies and congressional subcommittees, a war of competing handouts. Government begins by aiming to save farmers and ends up fighting itself, entangled in its own rescue nets, tripping over its own fire hoses, lost in the maze of its own benevolence. The more balls government tries to juggle, the greater the odds that it will drop them all.

The number of existing farm programs is the clearest proof of the failure of farm policy over the last half-century. The USDA has grown largely because of its failures. Each new program is a confession of the failure of existing programs: the dairy price-support program begetting the Dairy Termination Program, the sugar program begetting the sugar quota–offset program, the crop surpluses begetting the Conservation Reserve Program, the high price–support programs begetting the Export Enhancement Program.

Political Profits versus Economic Profits

The question of whether or not to respect the market is always a question of whether politicians will have more or less power—whether they will have more or less pork to distribute to friends and voters. The only thing most politicians know about most government interventions is the name of the intended beneficiary. Interventions are almost always judged from a perspective of "more versus less," rather than "why?" Politicians measure the success of an intervention with two questions: Was a benefit given, and was the recipient grateful? An economic intervention is a failure only if its supporters are defeated for re-election. For politicians, the effect of each handout begins and ends at the voting booth.

Understanding the calculus of votes better than the relationship of supply and demand, politicians look at the economy through a prism of self-interest. They intervene in the economy to maximize political profits, not economic efficiency.

Government planning will always be hobbled because the incumbent party always has an interest in representing things as better than they are, while the opposition party has an interest in representing things as worse than they are. For politicians, it is more important that forecasts be popular than accurate. As Henry Adams observed, "Practical politics consists of ignoring facts." Since politicians have little incentive to portray reality, what likelihood is there that their schemes will deal with reality accurately?

The political concept of waste is almost diametrically opposed to the economic concept of waste. In politics, if a program garners votes, campaign contributions, or power, it is successful; in economics, if an activity produces something of value to someone, it is successful. What is useful for politicians and what is useful for producers and consumers are two entirely different things. This dichotomy is the black hole into which the benevolence of many government programs vanishes.

Government programs are designed to waste money because politicians benefit from an inefficient spendthrift program as much or more than they would benefit from an efficient, well-targeted program. Politicians benefit from the government's giving away money, not by government programs that achieve their stated goal with the least expense. Congressmen brag about the amount of federal money spent in their district, not about whether that money was spent wisely or wasted.

The High Cost of a Captive Profession

The habitual errors of agricultural policy-makers have only been matched by the habitual errors of agricultural economists, most of whom have always been on the government payroll, either in USDA-financed land-grant colleges or in state or federal bureaucracies. Agricultural economists as a group have been biased in favor of government intervention. H. C. Taylor, an agricultural economist and the former chief of the USDA's Bureau of Agricultural Economics, declared in 1929 that the duty of agricultural economists was to find ways to boost farmers' share of the national income. W. O. Jones, writing in 1952 in the *Journal of Farm Economics*, observed that "the agricultural economists . . . have a much greater tendency to identify the welfare of the entire society with that one economic class than have any other group, unless it be the Marxists."[57] Theodore Schultz, probably the most prominent agricultural economist in the 1940s and 1950s, observed, "One has to appreciate the profound unfriendliness which these organized political forces, both inside and outside the government, can feel for agricultural economics research that does not provide the 'right' answers."[58]

Even though the idea of parity has long been a laughingstock among most economists, many agricultural economists still cling to it. A group of agricultural economists headed by the well-respected Luther Tweeten announced that in 1978 "the long-run balance between supply and demand in the milk market is maintained with prices about 75 percent of parity."[59] The agricultural economists were committing themselves to a long-dead economic relationship that had briefly existed almost seventy years earlier, implying that the same relationship would provide a policy guide into perpetuity.

Agricultural economists have generally been either statisticians or lobbyists. Agricultural economists took the lead in creating measures of farm income that made it appear that government intervention was necessary to solve an illusory problem. The question of farm income was rarely discussed in terms of a surplus of farmers; instead, the agricultural economists designed measures that effectively passed moral judgment on the economy. In other areas economists strove to understand the market; agricultural economists led the attack to bury the market. In the 1920s, agricultural economists attacked the futures markets and helped undercut their public credibility—thereby undercutting the farmers' ability to purchase insurance against price fluctuations.[60]

In the 1930s agricultural economists eloquently debated the new federal agricultural programs, clearly perceiving the underlying foundation upon which the skyscraper of intervention was built. Today one could read half a dozen issues of the *American Journal of Agricultural Economics* before realizing that politics dominates farm program decisions. Agricultural economists nowadays spend far more time crafting elegant supply-and-demand curves than looking at government programs. But one campaign contribution is worth a thousand supply-and-demand graphs.

Even today, despite pervasive boondoggles, many agricultural economists are still timid about criticizing the USDA. Agricultural economics is only viable as a separate branch of economics as long as the government continues mangling agriculture. Agricultural economists tend to favor government intervention perhaps because it means vastly more power and opportunity for themselves. In the same way, most Soviet economists support the Soviet system—not because it works, but because the endless planning is good for Soviet economists. There have always been many economists who bucked this trend and provided clear, courageous, and uncompromising criticism of failed programs, but most agricultural economists have spent their careers asking the wrong questions.

Conclusion

Federal agricultural policy-makers have seized on the doctrine of market imperfections in the same way that Third World juntas point to a few ragged demonstrators to justify imposing martial law. Because the market is imperfect, government must rule all.

In every nation in the world where private and public sectors compete, state farms have been shamed by the private farmers. In Russia, China, Poland, Ethiopia, Tanzania, and Mexico, independent farmers with far less capital have danced circles around plodding government agricultural systems. In America in the 1930s, the Resettlement Administration's cooperative farms rapidly collapsed because of their sheer inefficiency. In North Carolina, the state prison farms are notorious for their high cost of production. Maybe this is a clue.

Bureaucrats, even with the best of intentions, will judge by bureaucratic standards, not by the needs and demands of an ever-changing market. Should government have the power to control private farmers when all the evidence proves that private farmers are far more capable than government bureaucrats? Should private farmers be held down to the level of the average bureaucrat? Is "good enough for government work" the standard we should impose on American agriculture? Should American farmers be held down and held back until American bureaucrats decide it is safe to let farmers take a step on their own?

It is not a question of good intentions. Many USDA employees and congressmen sincerely wish to benefit American farmers. The former secretary of agriculture, John Block, though frequently vilified as an enemy of farmers, was widely commended by those who know him as a fine human being who desperately wanted to help farmers. Yet when someone is controlling a $30 billion budget and possesses vast arbitrary powers, the question is not what he intends to do, but what effect his actions actually have. Good intentions are no excuse.

Chapter 13

The Morality of Agricultural Policy

The final questions on agricultural policy are moral questions. Federal agricultural policy assumes that it is morally appropriate for the government to treat farmers better than it treats the rest of the citizenry, that agricultural programs treat farmers morally and equitably, and that political machinery is a proper tool for achieving moral ends. Farm programs can only be defended on the basis that the economic waste is exceeded by the moral bounty.

But instead of being the strongest defense, the moral case is actually the most damning indictment of farm programs. The essence of agricultural policy is hollering about poor farmers and giving handouts to rich farmers. Patriotism is the last refuge of a scoundrel, and a "just price" is the last refuge of a demagogue.

Political debates on agricultural policy are characterized by the morals of a shell game—with politicians talking fast and always trying to prevent the listener from ascertaining the real motives and the real beneficiaries of any program. Just as one moral defense for farm programs collapses from the weight of its own absurdity, politicians concoct another. No matter how many times the moral justification for a government program is shown to be ludicrous, politicians repeat the claim like an incantation to dull the listeners' senses.

The moral foundation of our agricultural policy is a pervasive, perpetual denial of reality, a gross inflation of need, and a misrepresentation of how programs actually operate—of who benefits and who pays. Preserving a "moral" agricultural policy requires constant deception and sacrifice of the relatively poor to the relatively rich.

Most farm programs have always been justified based on farmers' need—and have always refused to target benefits according to need. This is the perennial fraud at the center of farm policy—a deliberate deception repeated in every farm bill, in every session of Congress, in every handout to farmers. It is amazing that Congress would be so persistent in this deceit—and that the public would remain so ignorant and complacent in tolerating it.

A Moral Dictatorship

Ever since the New Deal, farm programs have assumed that government coercion produces fairer results than does voluntary agreement between individuals. Agriculture Secretary Henry Wallace scorned "laissez-faire economists" and "the special interest which they have served under the guise of the 'individual liberty.'"[1] Rexford Tugwell, undersecretary of agriculture, declared in 1934, "We succeed . . . in harnessing a selfish motive for the social good."[2]

While scorning the fairness of voluntary exchange, farm policymakers found a much surer guide to justice. The morality of farm programs has been based on the principle that whatever used to be is just—whatever it was. Every quota or allotment system that has determined a farmer's "equitable share" of government benefits has been based almost solely on how much the farmer—or his father, grandfather, or great-grandfather—happened to produce at the time when federal controls and benefits began, or when benefit rules were last revised. There is no equitable way to arbitrarily distribute licenses to produce, so the government has simply declared that whatever existed before the program began was the apex of justice—and proceeded to restrict, regulate, and direct agricultural production to try to perpetuate the production patterns of decades ago. Federal policy assumes that it is more just to allocate the right to grow peanuts and tobacco according to the occupation of one's grandfather or great-grandfather than according to an individual's own ability to produce and sell in the marketplace. "To him that hath shall be given" has always been the moral guide of farm policy-makers.

Politicians decreed that the market was unfair because crop prices were not as high as they used to be, and then proceeded to coerce hundreds of millions of taxpayers and millions of farmers to recreate a moral golden age. Parity assumes that justice was achieved once in the age of our great-grandfathers and that public policy should be used to forcibly return modern society to the price relations of our ancestors. According to agricultural policy-makers, the present economy can only be moral and just insofar as it corresponds to the moral golden age of 1910–14, when farmers received high prices. The measure of justice becomes not what buyers and sellers can agree on, but what some politician or bureaucrat can force on both parties in order to benefit the party with the most political clout.

Farm programs assume that decreed prices are inherently fairer than agreed prices—that prices are set more fairly in the halls of Congress than in the grain elevators, grocery stores, and commodity exchanges of America—that America is better off when the dog-eat-dog competition of the marketplace is replaced by begging, groveling, and bribing competitions on Capitol Hill. The moral foundation of agricultural policy is the Just Price—and it is here that the Scales of Justice on Capitol Hill become most vivid. As we saw in Chapter 11, Congress sets prices according to political pull, not according to how much wheat is available and how much is demanded. Farm program "justice" is based on the idealization of political processes and the state.

For the U.S. Department of Agriculture (USDA) and Congress, good and evil in farm policy are simply high crop prices and low crop prices. Coercion is fairer than voluntary consent because coercion will produce a higher price. For the USDA, the bureaucratic goal of higher prices for farmers justifies any and every bureaucratic means. The USDA acts at times as if anything that increased farmers' income were moral, and anything that decreased farmers' income were immoral. The USDA's milk-marketing regulations perceive price-cutting competition as immoral and price-gouging, government-sanctioned private cartels as just fine and dandy. If milk, lemon, orange, or almond prices are high, the USDA considers its policies a moral success. The measure of justice becomes solely the final price, rather than the process by which the price was reached. The USDA believes that a farmer has no right to do business, and no right to his property, if he sells his fruit or milk for a price less than that which the USDA approves.

Senator Tom Harkin wrapped up a pitch in 1987 for mandatory controls over farmers by saying, "We are only asking for the same price that the farmer got ten years ago in the marketplace."[3] Grain prices in the mid-1970s were extremely high by historical standards, and the cost of production has fallen sharply in the past decade. Yet Harkin apparently believes that because farmers got a certain nominal price for wheat or corn one year, they are entitled to at least that much forever. Much farm policy debate is simply a moral deification of ancient farm prices—sacrificing today's farmers, consumers, and taxpayers on the altar of yesterday's farm prices.

Congressman James Polk, on March 22, 1933, praised the Agricultural Adjustment Act, saying that the secretary of agriculture "will have at his command a weapon to whip into line selfish interests who decline to cooperate in helping to bring up the price of these farm commodities."[4] Senator Tom Harkin sounded a similar theme in 1987 when he explained why most farmers did not support mandatory controls to slash production and raise prices: "There are a lot of selfish farmers out there, just a lot of selfish people all over the world. We have had the kind of a program for the last several years, not just in agriculture but in other parts of our economic life in this country, that promotes greed."[5]

According to farm program morality, the good farmer is the one who wants high prices and demands government coercion of other farmers to boost prices, and the bad farmer is he who is willing and able to produce and sell for lower prices. This is a world-turned-upside-down view—and the perfect example of how badly agricultural policy discussions have become divorced from reality. The evil farmer is not the farmer who wants pervasive federal controls to sacrifice consumers to boost farmers' profits, but the farmer who wants only to sell his harvest at a market-clearing price. The selfish farmer is not the one who wants politicians to shake down every consumer and taxpayer in the country for the farmers' benefit, but the farmer who asks only to be left alone. This is the de facto statutory definition of "selfish farmer" for marketing orders. A farmer's goodness thus becomes antithetical to his desire for independence and his tolerance for other farmers' freedom.

Yet even though politicians claim parity is sacred, Congress applies different percentages of parity to different crops. Farm lobbies proclaim that parity is divine, and Congress announces that the sacred ratio for this crop is 70 percent; for that crop, 55 percent; and finds that oranges and lemons are so blessed that they are worthy of 110 percent holiness. Farm-state congressmen have repeatedly changed the legal measure of parity in order to benefit selected groups of farmers. Parity has come to mean almost any price comparison that can show that farmers are being treated less fairly now than they were at some point in the twentieth century. One is reminded of the prophet Muhammad and the Koran: When Muhammad had three wives, God told him that he should declare in the Koran that only three wives were allowed to any man. Each time Muhammad found another woman he wanted to marry, God obligingly told him to revise the Koran. Parity is sacred, and parity is whatever the farm lobbies and farm-state congressmen say it is—this week.

Farm-state congressmen have managed to turn crop surpluses into a moral issue. The fact that farmers are producing too much means that society is immoral, because farmers cannot get what politicians think they should have for their efforts. Farm policy is based on the idea that no farm surplus is the farmer's responsibility—that taxpayers should be held liable for every extra bale or bushel that the farmers produce. Congressmen decree high prices that in turn generate crop surpluses. Then, when prices decline because of glutted markets, congressmen denounce society for its unfairness to farmers.

The Nation, observing the government's catastrophic efforts to raise crop prices in 1930, declared, "That price is a right price, in the sense of a necessary price, which will move the crop."[6] Economist M. R. Benedict observed in 1936, "The farther given prices are held above their competitive levels, the greater the problems of control, evasion, land speculation, and injustice as between individuals."[7] Farm markets worked quite well until politicians decided that politicians were fairer than buyers and sellers, and thus that politicians should have power over markets.

Some people imply that government should control food prices because food is vital to life, and thus farmers should be well compensated for providing a necessity. Medicine is often necessary for health; does that justify forcing rural Americans to surrender part of their paychecks to doctors? Gasoline is a necessity for modern society; should the people of Boston be sacrificed to boost the profits of Texas oil drillers? Clothing is a necessity; does that justify forcing the citizens of San Francisco to boost the profits of Carolina textile mills? The fact that something is a necessity is the best reason for government *not* to set its price. If the government sets prices below the producers' cost of production, there will be a shortage; and if the government sets the price well above the cost of production, there will be a surplus. Either way, consumers lose.

Agricultural Policy Morality

Agricultural policy morality is typically two parts fraud and one part farce. The key terms in agricultural policy seek to provide an economic camouflage to cover a moral judgment to take money from nonfarmers and give it to farmers. "Income protection for farmers" is a joke: The government does not protect incomes by taking one man's dollar and giving it to someone else. "Parity" is simply a series of internal trade barriers designed to sacrifice city folks to farmers. "Price supports" are always designed to drive prices up. "Deficiency payments" and marketing loans are simply tools for giving farmers as much as congressmen want them to have. "Marketing order" is simply a federal order to farmers not to market their crops in order to inflate food prices.

The $50,000 limitation on how much each farmer can receive in federal benefits each year nicely illustrate the ethics of agricultural policy-making. The main purpose of payment limitation is to deceive nonfarmers about how much the government is actually giving to individual farmers. In the cause of "equalizing" farm and nonfarm income, the government explicitly can give each farmer an amount far exceeding the average nonfarm family income. Farmers are entitled to receive more in handouts each year than the typical American family's net worth.

The $50,000 limitation only applies to benefits received from one program—target price–deficiency payments. A farmer could receive millions of dollars a year in subsidized loans and price-support benefits, not one cent of which would count against his $50,000 limit.

The $50,000 limit does not apply at all to dairy or wool producers, and cotton and rice growers are explicitly entitled to collect up to $250,000 a year each. The $50,000 limit did not apply to honey producers in 1985—Congress applied the $50,000 limit in 1986 and then repealed the limit in 1987, after receiving appropriate campaign contributions.

Finally, even for the narrow area where the $50,000 limit does apply, Congress concocts King Kong loopholes that allow almost any farmer who can sign his name to receive more than $50,000 legally by restructuring his farm. Occasionally, reacting to public criticism, Congress "tightens" the $50,000 payment limit. In December 1987, Congress decreed that each farmer could receive only three $50,000 payments each year—unless he hired a lawyer and shuffled his assets carefully, after which he could receive more.

The General Accounting Office annually reports a flock of abuses of the payment limitations law, and Congress annually scorns its advice on how to make the system do what Congress claims it wants the system to do. One California farm with 1,600 acres was leased by the landlord to fifty-six tenants; as a result, one farm received almost $1.5 million in farm program payments.[8] Many farmers' ten-year-old daughters and sons are getting very generous payments from the USDA to stay in fourth grade instead of planting crops. The USDA regulations require a substantial change in a farm operation in order for it to qualify as two separate farms for benefit purposes, but this requirement can be satisfied simply by reducing the amount of land planted. As the *Des Moines Register* reported, "In Arizona and Arkansas, lawyers are advertising in newspapers, offering to help farmers set up partnerships with children, grandchildren, spouses, cousins, friends, in-laws, anybody—just as long as they can be made to qualify . . . for the $50,000 maximum payment."[9]

Some farm lobbies admit that there are problems with the $50,000 payment limitation. Mary Ann Ritter Arnold, president of the Agricultural Council of Arkansas, complained, "Many Arkansas [farmers] suffered tremendous anxiety from the Inspector General audit of payment limitations during the past few months."[10] Women Involved in Farm Economics (WIFE), is suing the USDA to allow wives to qualify for a separate $50,000 payment after their husbands have collected their own $50,000. WIFE thinks that since USDA rules allow a gay couple living together to qualify for two individual payments, a husband and wife should each be able to collect $50,000 from the Treasury. Because one or two gay couples in the nation may get an extra $50,000 in welfare, WIFE wants more than a million farm couples to be eligible for another $50,000 apiece.

Agricultural programs have always sought to sacrifice consumers to farmers. The Agricultural Adjustment Act was denounced in 1933 as "class legislation"—a government intervention explicitly intended to sacrifice the general population to benefit a minority. Secretary of Agriculture Orville Freeman told the National Farmers Union in 1967, "I want to assure you that I am taking every action I can to raise dairy prices." In 1980, the National Association of Wheat Growers made a formal protest to President Carter after Carol Tucker Foreman, a USDA assistant secretary, received a $20,000 bonus for her "proconsumer efforts."[11]

For more than a hundred years, farmers have been complaining that crop prices are unfairly low. Farmers have offered a hundred different reasons to show that the economic system unfairly conspires against them: the tyranny of railroads, the deviousness of middlemen, the eternal cost-price squeeze, the Federal Reserve's deviancy, Jewish conspiracies, etc. Politicians and farmers have been complaining for a hundred years that farm prices do not cover the cost of production. But if farm prices have been so low, how did farmers get so rich? The gap between the net worth of farmers and nonfarmers has continued to grow despite the proclamation of a hundred farm crises. As early as 1962, it was four times higher than nonfarmers' net worth; now, full-time farmers are worth an average of almost ten times more than are nonfarmers. One of our largest antipoverty programs is creating a class of millionaires, a hereditary landowning class. Since around 1900, it has been a common saying that "farmers live poor and die rich." Apparently, Congress decided that it was unfair that farmers only died rich and that they should live relatively rich as well.

If the economic arguments for federal intervention to boost crop prices made sense, farmers would have long since abandoned every unsubsidized crop because of unfair markets. For some peculiar reason, the markets are fair enough for 400 crops produced in the United States, fair enough for the farmer to invest his capital and sweat in producing them. But there is some perversity that afflicts the cotton, rice, wheat, corn, dairy, and sugar markets that requires tens of billions of dollars in handouts and trade barriers to rectify.

The moral and economic arguments for government aid to agriculture either make sense for all crops or no crops. How can pecan growers prosper in the marketplace, but peanut growers require a feudal system and hundreds of "peanut police" to earn a fair profit? And why is it that peanut growers producing for export can produce their crops with no federal subsidy, while those producing for the domestic market need every protection and handout that career bureaucrats can think of? The more the government decides to help a particular crop, the more helpless that crop's farmers become.

A Thousand Inequities for Equality

Farm policy has perennially sacrificed real liberty for an illusion of equality. Farm policy has long been the home of sham egalitarianism. Government ensures equality by allowing farmers to sell an equal percentage of the harvest of fifty and five thousand lemon trees, by allowing one farmer to qualify for handouts by idling a hundred acres of sandpits and ravines while a second farmer must idle a hundred acres of the best cropland in the world, and by giving one uncreditworthy farmer a million dollars in subsidized loans and another uncreditworthy farmer $5,000.

New Deal farm programs were born of the assumption that farm income was unfairly low compared to nonfarm income. And the USDA's "remedy" has always been to give small amounts of money to small farmers and large amounts of money to big farmers, and no handouts to the producers of most farm products. Farm handouts are justified by farmers' need, but the main programs are designed to pay farmers solely according to the amount of their production—in other words, in inverse proportion to a farmer's likely need. A farmer who grows 10,000 bushels of wheat gets a hundred times more handouts than a farmer who grows 100 bushels of wheat.

Every scheme to reduce inequity between farmers and city folks has increased the inequality among farmers themselves. Every handout has increased the advantage of some farmers over other farmers. In 1986, the class of biggest farms received almost 150 times as much in benefits per farm as the class of smallest farms.[12] Federal farm programs have helped the big fish swallow the little fish. By handing big farmers $50,000, $150,000, $200,000, or more each year, the federal government has provided a war chest to allow big operators to "cannibalize" little operators, as University of Minnesota professor Phil Raup observed.[13] Farm workers receive pink slips while farm owners are paid billions of dollars for shutting down their farms.

Equality between farmers and nonfarmers has been a one-way street—regarded as a grave injustice if farmers are receiving less income than nonfarmers earn and a non-issue if farmers are receiving more. Parity has functioned as price-support loans function: It provides a price or income floor, but no price or income ceiling. Federal farm programs are designed so that farmers earn at least as much as nonfarmers—and if prices soar and farmers earn far more than nonfarmers, there is no injustice. What is the ethics of promising one group an income "equal or more than" that of all other groups? Equality is only a flag of convenience for the farm lobby.

None of the advocates of parity has suggested that government forcibly equalize income among farmers. But what sense is there in imposing a pseudoequality among groups if you don't do the same for individuals? If equality is good among groups, then why isn't it good among individuals?

In the past, politicians needed only a good capacity for spouting nonsense to demand parity. But now that farmers are worth far more than nonfarmers, politicians must also be adept liars. If congressmen's claims on farm programs were not exempt from federal laws on false advertising, the Washington, D.C., jails would have many distinguished guests.

The Moral Tithe

Kika de la Garza, chairman of the House Agriculture Committee, declared in 1987,

> We shouldn't—purely for the sake of the budget—disrupt policy or legislate solely for that reason, because if American agriculture is not deserving of no more than 3 percent of the total budget of this, the greatest country in the world, I don't know who is. That's all we are dealing with. . . . I think we may even have a basic right to a larger share of the national budget. . . . [14]

As he sees it, because America is "the greatest country in the world," the government should force taxpayers to pay the equivalent of more than $50,000 in tribute to each full-time farmer. Farmers are the only occupational group entitled to federal handouts by law, yet they routinely feel as though they are not getting their fair share. Because federal spending in general has exploded in recent decades, farm-state congressmen often imply that it would be petty to think twice about giving scores of billions of dollars to America's agrarians.

What does government owe farmers? What does one citizen owe another citizen? The dollars that politicians lavish on farmers must first be taken from other citizens. Do farmers have a right to a moral tithe—to get a big boost on food prices and handouts based solely on their moral worth? On what basis can politicians rightfully seize one man's earnings and give it to another man? In a free society, what gives one citizen the right to another citizen's paycheck?

A handout is a handout regardless of whether the recipient uses it to buy groceries or fifty acres of black gold. The occupation of the handout recipient does not change the nature of the handout—or the nature of the tax used to seize the redistributed dollar to be redistributed. The Supreme Court declared, in the case of *Savings and Loan Association v. Topeka*, "To lay with one hand the power of the government on the property of the citizen and with the other to bestow it upon favored individuals to aid private enterprises and build up private fortunes is none the less a robbery because it is done under the forms of law and is called taxation."[15] To take one man's wages to boost another man's profits is a proper policy for an oligopoly, but not for a democracy. In order for government to control agriculture, the poor must be sacrificed to the rich. Thus, in order to protect nearly nonexistent poor family farmers, millions of real poor people are sacrificed to a few hundred thousand rich farmers. What theory of government benevolence justifies taxing the poor to create more millionaires?

Farm handouts are defended due to farmers' moral goodness—as a moral tithe. But the more the government has given to farmers, the less respectable subsidized farmers have become. Farmers are lauded as hard-working, and then government pays them to take a year-long vacation. Farmers are touted as more honest than other Americans, yet every farm program provides another litany of farmers discovering new ways to pilfer the Treasury. Farmers are respected as independent, yet they are increasingly spending their winters, when there is little work to do on the farm, in tractorcades and marches on Washington and the state capitols, begging for more handouts.

Congressman de la Garza declared on November 9, 1983: "One farmer on the land is worth more than one missile in Europe or anything else we could do."[16] His comment epitomizes the way in which farm-state congressmen see the world: Every farmer is worth saving at any price, even if the price is the heavy taxation of twenty, thirty, forty, or one hundred other citizens who are providing money to keep that one farmer in business.

Congressmen speak of the sanctity of the family farm, but blithely create program after program that sacrifices cattlemen to dairy farmers, soybean growers to corn growers, and unsubsidized farmers to subsidized farmers. Politicians repeatedly reveal that they believe that some farmers are more equal than others—and that a farmer's moral nobility appears to depend strictly on how much he receives from the Treasury—as if the only farmers America should worry about losing are those who are a heavy burden on their fellow citizens.

If the same concept of need were applied to farmers as is applied to other federal beneficiaries, then virtually no farmers would qualify for federal aid, and most of the ones who did would be standing in line outside bankruptcy court. Almost every measure of "truly needy" in agricultural programs is based on a concept that is ten or twenty times more liberal than that used for other federal aid programs. To receive food stamps, a person cannot own more than $2,000 in assets. But to receive a subsidized Farmers Home Administration loan equal to a lifetime of food stamp benefits, a person can have a net worth of over a million dollars.

In agriculture, there is a big overlap of the "truly needy" and the truly incompetent. If a person can't feed himself, society may justifiably help him. A person who can't farm is not truly needy in the same sense. Just because a person isn't a good farmer doesn't entitle him to other people's money. I can't sing, but that doesn't entitle me to $50,000 a year in tax dollars for voice lessons. In a great many cases, a farmer "needs" help because he made bad business decisions. Farm aid is not a question of helping a needy individual but of bailing out an inept businessman, or of making a rich farmer richer. Every businessman who is losing money needs help, but none of them have a right to their fellow citizens' paychecks. Agricultural aid means giving tens of thousands of dollars a year either to successful businessmen who don't need it, or to unsuccessful businessmen who need it but who cannot use other people's assets productively.

In the Middle Ages, peasants were obliged to spend a certain number of days each year working for the king without pay. If the National Guard rounded up farmers, put them in trucks, and forced them to fill city potholes for a week, there would be an armed uprising in rural America. Yet the average family is paying around $500 a year for farm subsidies; the average American head of household must see his or her paycheck for almost one work week a year go to pay some farmer not to work, or to kill his cows, or to provide subsidies for the Soviets or Iraqis. Over the course of a person's working life, if farm subsidies stayed in the range of the mid-1980s, the average American family head would be forced to do almost one year's forced labor for the benefit of wealthy American farmers. Though being a "tax serf" is less humbling than being a feudal serf, the worker is still deprived of the product of his labor. The only reason there is no outrage is that the process is sanctioned by Congress and the money is laundered through the Treasury.

Many liberals criticize existing programs, but insist that farm aid would be moral if it were targeted to small farmers. If government aids the small farmers, it is taking the wages of full-time workers to pay a bonus to part-time workers. And even the small farmers (those with less than $40,000 a year in sales) have a net worth several times greater than that of the median American family. If a farmer is so small that he is worth less than the average American, it would require a huge loan to make his farm large enough to be financially viable. By loaning such an amount, the Farmers Home Administration (FmHA) saddles the farmer with such a huge debt load that his debt-to-assets ratio is untenable. The FmHA has ruined many people's lives by drowning them in debt. Nor does giving money to small farmers to get larger make moral sense, since even that is a transfer from relatively poor taxpayers to relatively rich farmers. Besides, government cannot give aid to some farmers without making it more difficult for other farmers to make a living. Government cannot help some farmers boost their output without diminishing other farmers' profits.

The viable size of a farm now requires far more capital than the average American family possesses. The industrialization of the American farm has destroyed all moral defenses for transfer payments based on farmers' low income. If farm programs are to be economically effective, they must be transfers from the relatively poor to the relatively rich; and if farm programs are to be morally viable, then they must be transfers from the average citizen to small, economically irrelevant farmers. If farm programs target small farmers, they are largely a sentimental indulgence and should be handled by the National Endowment for the Humanities.

The moral issues of farm aid become much clearer if we replace the word *farmer* with the word *landowner*. One percent of the landowners in America owns 33 percent of farm and ranch land. The *National Agricultural Forum* reported in 1984 that "8 percent of the households in America own the vast majority of the land, excluding public ranges and forests owned by corporations. . . . 63 percent of U.S. households own no land . . . "[17] Don Paarlberg, formerly the USDA's chief economist, notes, "In the north central states in 1978, three-tenths of one percent of the owners own 23 percent of the land."[18] At the same time that farmers have become richer and farmland ownership has become more concentrated, fewer and fewer Americans are able to afford to purchase a home. Most of the benefits of farm programs go to the landowner; farm program benefits are capitalized into land values, which means that farmers who rent their land are forced to pay higher rents because of government subsidies. Throughout history, governments have had policies designed to sacrifice serfs, peasants, slaves, and tenants to landowners. American agricultural policy follows a hallowed tradition.

Farm subsidies will always tend to be redistribution from the landless to the landowners. Historically, owning land has always been one of the clearest measures of wealth. Farm lobbies justify farm programs as helping some farmers to purchase land, but every tax dollar that is taken from nonfarmers to allow farmers to buy land decreases the nonfarmers' ability to buy land (or a house) for themselves. This is simply a redistribution of opportunity to buy land— and thus is guaranteed to make society less equal.

Though public opinion polls show strong support for farm aid, few people seem to be willing to spend their own money helping out farmers. The first FarmAid concert raised less money than the USDA spent paying a single dairy farm to slaughter its cows. John Cougar Mellencamp, a popular singer who made a mint off of a sentimental song about a foreclosed farmer, captured this paradoxical attitude when he testified before the Senate Agriculture Committee, "I have had [farmers] call and wanted me to loan them money. . . . And it's like, what is this? You know, why now is so much importance put on the private sector? Why is it being passed on to us to be concerned with these people when, in reality, we voted for you guys to do what was morally right, and I think that is what the people of America expect."[19] Apparently, social justice in the 1980s means that private individuals need not squander their money, but the government should squander everyone's money.

The Morality of Arbitrary Power

Agricultural policy morality rests on the assumption that government is entitled to control farmers in order to benefit them. Politicians and bureaucrats exercise arbitrary power over farmers and consumers supposedly to create a fairer society. Politicians' good intentions toward farming in general have become a license to sacrifice one farmer for another farmer's benefit. A vague desire to help farmers has become a license to give millions of dollars to one person while helping bankrupt another person (as the payment-in-kind program did).

The Supreme Court's ruling when it originally struck down the Agricultural Adjustment Act in 1936 provides insight into the moral caliber of current farm programs:

> The regulation is not in fact voluntary. The farmer, of course, may refuse to comply, but the price of such refusal is the loss of benefits. The amount offered is intended to be sufficient to exert pressure on him to agree to the proposed regulation. . . . It is clear that the Department of Agriculture has properly described the plan as one to keep a non-cooperating minority in line. This is coercion by economic pressure. The asserted power of choice is illusory.[20]

The Supreme Court's description is as appropriate for 1989 as it was for 1936. The only thing that has changed is the Supreme Court's interpretation of the Constitution's protection of individual rights.

Federal benevolence requires a huge increase in the power of government officials over the intended beneficiaries. The federal government cannot plan the agricultural economy without controlling farmers. Because politicians claim they want to help farmers, politicians claim the right to arbitrarily drive the value of the farmers' crop up or down, to prohibit the farmer from using his land as he chooses, and to decide which farmers will receive massive advantages in competition against other farmers. From tobacco and peanuts to marketing orders to corn and wheat restrictions on planting, agricultural policy aims to boost the income of some farmers by prohibiting others from using their land as they choose.

While congressmen make endless speeches on the sanctity of each family farmer, they show little or no concern for the farmers' individual rights. The avid support in Congress for allowing 60 percent of farmers to forcibly restrict all farmers' plantings proves that many, if not most, congressmen don't give a damn about farmer self-reliance or independence—any sacrifice of liberty is justified in a desperate scheme to boost farm income. Allowing the majority of farmers to vote to shut down their neighbors' farms is as fair as letting the majority of computer companies vote to shut down IBM. Yet because farm prices have become the sole measure of rural justice, the National Council of Churches of Christ, Catholic Rural Life Conference, and Union of American Hebrew Congregations have come out in favor of mandatory controls.[21]

Congressmen defend their farm policies by claiming their good intentions—as if good intentions were a political waiver for all subsequent damage. The question is, do good intentions toward someone give you a right to rule and ruin their business? Politicians tend to be economic drunk drivers: Does it make any difference to their victims that the head-on collision between the individual and some harebrained federal program may have been unintentional? "I didn't mean to hurt anyone" is the excuse offered by both drunk drivers and politicians who disrupt the economy, but is there any moral difference in their guilt—since both abused power that they should have known they could not control?

How can a policy be either moral or benevolent when it has contempt for the rights of the supposed beneficiaries? Farm policy morality is an appropriate moral theory for a parent with young toddlers—but what relevance does it have for economic acts among consenting adults? "Enlightened despotism" was the phrase used to justify arbitrary paternalism in the 1700s—but is there anyone who would suggest that either Congress or the USDA is enlightened?

Unnecessary coercion is always a moral issue. Government must engage in a limited amount of coercion in order to preserve law and order. But when the coercion multiplies unceasingly and government bureaucrats are dictating what farmers are allowed to plant, destroying markets with their surprises, and subverting the independence of dairymen and fruit growers and hay producers, where is the justice? If government is entitled to coerce in order to boost some farmers' income, what limit is there on coercion?

The Character of Politics and Politicians

H. L. Mencken observed, "A good politician is almost as rare as an honest burglar." Federal farm policy will never be any more honorable than the congressmen who make the policies. The bottom line for farm policy morality is trusting a politician in a crowded, smoky room late at night to do the right thing. Farm policies that are so vague and contradictory will only be as moral as those politicians themselves. It is naive to expect federal programs to be more honest and trustworthy than the typical politician's campaign speech. The building blocks of politics are not the stuff that moral utopias are made of. Agricultural policy is ripe for corruption because of its myriad meaningless definitions, vague goals, and nonsensical measures. The more complex and indecipherable the programs become, the more their moral caliber depends on the few dozen congressmen who have a direct stake in them.

There is a paradox in public thinking on government programs. When people think of politicians, honesty is usually the last attribute that comes to mind. The humorist Kin Hubbard joked a hundred years ago, "Now and then an innocent man is sent to the legislature." Yet even though politicians are widely perceived as deceitful, inconsistent, or untrustworthy, the public often seems to expect government coercion to produce a more moral result than the voluntary agreement of private individuals. Federal agricultural policy is based on the idea that politicians are more ethical than markets, and that it is better to trust politicians to cut the pie rather than the people who actually bake and eat the pie.

There is a fundamental dichotomy in politicians' right to seize the workers' paychecks and their duty to spend the workers' money wisely. President Grover Cleveland observed in 1886, "When more of the people's sustenance is exacted through the form of taxation than is necessary to meet the just obligations of government and expenses of its economical administration, such exaction becomes ruthless extortion and a violation of the principles of a free government."[22] Farm programs appear to be based on congressmen's sacred right to dispose of workers' tax dollars as they please. Congressmen sometimes show an open contempt for honesty in their grabs to hand out more money to their constituents. One more example will suffice: Congressman David Obey pushed hard to get a constituent farmer compensation under the Dairy Termination Program (DTP), even though the man did not qualify.

The barn of Kenneth Byers of Grantsburg, Wisconsin, caught fire and burnt down on February 6, 1986, killing his dairy cattle.[23] On February 10, the local Agricultural Stabilization and Conservation Service (ASCS) officer urged Byers to seek compensation from the DTP. Byers had previously been paid by the government to reduce his milk sales by 34 percent during the 1984–85 Dairy Buyout Program, and was also being subsidized by the Farmers Home Administration at the time of the fire. The farmer received a large check from the insurance company to compensate him for the cows killed.

The Wisconsin ASCS denied Byers' claim, so he appealed the decision to Washington—and changed the date of his fire from February 6 to February 17. Though the DTP signup began on February 10, the local ASCS office did not receive signup forms until February 19. Byers claimed that he had gone to the ASCS office to sign up on February 12, but had not been able to sign up because there were no forms; and then his barn burned down. Even though Obey's office publicized Byers' original letter to the ASCS stating that his barn burned down on February 6, Obey wrote to Agriculture Secretary Richard Lyng protesting Byers' denial of payments, claiming that the fire was on February 17. Obey thought Byers' case so meritorious that he included twenty-nine pages of correspondence on it in the appendix of a House Agriculture Committee hearing.[24] It is difficult to say whether Obey's office did not know what it was doing or knew and did it anyway, but the incident is typical of how congressmen treat tax dollars.

Government has a right to imprison people for not paying their taxes, but has no duty to spend citizens' tax dollars wisely. This is the fundamental contradiction at the foundation of the welfare state. When the worker's dollar reaches the U.S. Treasury, it becomes, de facto, politicians' property, to use and abuse for political purposes. The federal government apparently has diametrically opposed standards for collecting money and spending it: People get sent to prison for not paying taxes, and politicians get re-elected for wasting money.

Congressmen cannot escape responsibility for farm program waste and abuse by denying they knew what they were doing. Ignorance of the law is no excuse in court, and ignorance of waste, fraud, and abuse should be no excuse in the halls of Congress.

There are laws against embezzlement; corporation officers who convert business assets into their own personal property get sent to prison. But what about political embezzlement? It is well recognized by soldiers that some officers willingly send their troops to be slaughtered in order to win a medal or a promotion. In the same way, congressmen willingly sacrifice legions of taxpayers in order to win themselves another term in Washington. There is no penalty for politicians voting for a billion-dollar dairy giveaway solely in order to get $10,000 in campaign contributions or 500 votes. It would be amusing to inject congressmen with truth serum and ask them where their cutoff point is and how much government money they would be willing to waste in order to buy re-election—and to see how many congressmen would admit that there was no limit to the number of taxpayers they would sacrifice. This would be the surest test of congressmen's fitness to dispose of a trillion dollars a year of their fellow citizens' property.

Every intervention has its victims. Government cannot economically reward one group without directly or indirectly punishing other groups. Government cannot announce that some group is entitled to some benefit without effectively announcing that some other group is not entitled to their paychecks or to their livelihoods or to some opportunity they otherwise could have earned. The illusion of the welfare state is that government could ever give to the citizenry more than it takes away.

Conclusion

Franklin D. Roosevelt declared on September 28, 1935, "I like to think of the Agricultural Adjustment Act not as a temporary means . . . but as an expression of principle." To idealize agricultural policy morality is to idealize coercion. The moral canons of agricultural policy are in direct opposition to the principles of a free society. The only reason that our economy has not been paralyzed and that society has not been rent by the internal warfare of clashing interest groups is that government has not attempted to treat all groups with the same generosity that politicians claim some farmers are entitled to.

Agriculture Secretary Henry Wallace declared in 1934, "To have to destroy a growing crop is a shocking commentary on civilization. I could tolerate it only as a cleaning up of the wreckage of the old days of unbalanced production."[25] For half a century, agricultural policymakers have been claiming that society, "civilization," or markets necessitated the USDA policies that destroyed food, idled land, boosted prices, and worsened the diets of the poor. In fifty years we have made great progress: Now, instead of paying farmers to kill pigs, the government pays them to kill cows; instead of paying farmers to plow up their crops, the government pays them not to produce any at all. Waste has become institutionalized on a massive scale, and secretaries of agriculture still brag about their success in shutting down American farms.

Most moral defenses of agricultural policy are actually only sentimental responses. If you remove the sentimental element from the family-farm discussion, all that is left is a capitalist and his business—and a politician and a handout.

◆ *Chapter 14* ◆

The Solution

One way to evaluate federal farm programs is to consider them as objects of private charity. Suppose some private foundation were to set up a voluntary fund to collect donations for farmers, giving prospective donors a laundry list of agricultural programs and policies to which they could contribute. How many people would voluntarily pay farmers to leave more than 70 million acres idle? How many people would pay to help administer a system that forced farmers in California to abandon a billion fresh lemons and oranges a year? How many people would contribute to a $100,000 fund to keep one incompetent farmer farming for one more year? How many people would contribute to a pool to pay bonuses to millionaire rice, cotton, and sugar growers? How many people would voluntarily pay for export subsidies so that American wheat would be cheaper in Moscow than it is in Kansas City? How many people would voluntarily pay for the salaries of government employees who go around and measure each one-hundredth of an acre of a tobacco farmer's field? How many people would voluntarily make a contribution to a businessman whose net worth was ten or twenty times greater than their own? To ask these questions is to answer them.

People have a natural prejudice against change. But how badly must federal agricultural policies fail before we abandon them? Will the USDA have to throw half a million people out of work a year instead of only 300,000? Must it squander $50 billion in taxes a year rather than only $30 billion? Will it have to prevent all poor people from buying milk rather than only a substantial percentage?

The best solution to most agricultural problems is to abolish the USDA program that causes the problem. Most of American agriculture is healthy and relatively uncontrolled by politicians. The key to a prosperous agriculture is to stop disrupting the unhealthy sector so that it can become as strong as the uncontrolled sector. The solution to the farm program is simple: First, abolish contradictory programs; second, abolish programs that don't work; and third, abolish programs that raise farmers' costs of production. There is not a single commodity program that can stand on its own merits.

The debate on farm program reform is usually conducted in a haze of good intentions and vague fears—always looking at government control as a whole, avoiding analysis of the individual parts. To speak of "farm programs" as a whole implies that all farmers are dependent on the government—and that all farm programs are alike. The clearest way to consider "solving" the agricultural problem is by looking at the individual programs. What sacrifice would be required to wean the one-third of American farm products that are on the government teat to the same free-market conditions under which the other two-thirds currently survives? How should reform be approached?

It is vital that President Bush set the terms of the farm debate— that he avoid being boxed in by the farm lobby's usual scare tactics— and that he avoid at all costs getting locked into a Reagan-style "rope-a-dope" defense, in which he spends all his time either denying that a farm crisis exists or asserting that farmers are responsible for their own problems. The President should focus the debate on the high cost of farm programs to both consumers and farmers, and the consistent failure of federal agricultural policy to achieve its goals. A frontal assault on the program is the only way to achieve meaningful reform. The President must place the farm lobbies in the position of defending the indefensible. If the President can set the terms of the debate, he should be able to win.

Following are five reforms that President Bush should initiate immediately to solve the farm policy fiasco. The President should:

1. Send a special agricultural message to Congress calling for the abolition of the sugar, tobacco, peanut, honey, wool, rice, and cotton programs. Each of these programs affects only a small number of farmers. The sugar program provides windfalls to 11,000 farmers, the rice program provides benefits to 4,000 full-time farmers, and honey program benefits go to fewer than 10,000 honey producers. The wool program has achieved nothing except to flood a dying industry with tax dollars. These programs could all be abolished overnight with little impact on rural America. Every sugar beet grower could switch to other crops, many rice producers could survive in the open market, and honey producers did just fine before the explosion in federal handouts in the early 1980s. The average sugarcane and rice growers are millionaires. They can either sell out or survive a short adjustment period. Since wool provides only a small part of the revenues to sheep producers, abolishing the wool program will not have a devastating effect.

Tobacco program allotments (federal licenses to grow tobacco) have been renting for much higher prices than their capitalized sale value in recent years, which indicates that allotment owners anticipate the abolition or gutting of the tobacco program. Since 80 percent of the allotments are owned by nonfarmers, the growers themselves would be little affected. The average tobacco farmer can survive without paying a doctor, dentist, or lawyer for the privilege of growing tobacco. In the past fifteen years, the federal government has forced farmers to slash tobacco production by 50 percent. When the program is abolished, tobacco production will skyrocket, creating thousands of new jobs, boosting exports, and invigorating the economies of North Carolina, Virginia, and Kentucky.

The peanut program is already a laughingstock, with the U.S. Department of Agriculture (USDA) declaring that American farmers cannot produce peanuts for less than $615.85 a ton while thousands of American farmers produce them for the export market for between $300 and $400 a ton. The success of unsubsidized peanut growers proves that the government subsidies are unnecessary. Domestic peanut prices will fall sharply after the USDA intervention ends, but the Republic will not be endangered by lower-priced peanut butter.

Cotton prices are not depressed right now.—.which means this is a good time to end handouts for America's 6,000 full-time cotton growers.

Many American cotton growers are among the most efficient in the world, and the inefficient don't deserve welfare for another decade. There may be some painful adjustment, but since the average full-time cotton producer is a millionaire, most producers will have the option of selling out and living comfortably.

2. Terminate the federal prohibition on the sale of reconstituted milk. The most absurd dairy regulation is the de facto prohibition against shipping milk powder from areas with low dairy cost of production to areas with high cost of production. Once the President frames the dairy debate in terms of whether the federal government should use its police powers to prohibit the remixing of dry milk and whether federal agents should spend their time guarding against dry milk crossing state lines, the issue will be won. Once reconstituted milk is legalized, dairy marketing orders will collapse, because local administrative committees will no longer have monopoly power over local milk supplies. At the core of the dairy lobby is the powerful milk cooperatives that have benefited the most from the byzantine marketing orders. Once the marketing orders collapse, the cooperatives' income will plummet and the dairy lobby will be crippled.

Even though the federal government will buy billions of pounds of surplus milk from farmers this year because of high federal dairy-support prices, Congress in July 1988 prohibited the USDA from reducing the dairy support price in 1989 and even mandated a temporary increase in dairy prices (equivalent to 8 cents a gallon retail) from April to June 1989. If President Bush desires fundamental agricultural reform, the dairy lobby has given him a golden opportunity. Even if marketing orders are abolished, the government's mountains of butter and cheese and dry milk will likely grow in 1989. The surplus will provide the rationale for phasing out the dairy program.

The dairy program's days are numbered regardless of how many congressmen the dairy lobby buys. The use of bovine growth hormones will cause milk production to explode in the next three or four years as its cost plummets. Even if the hormones are not used, breakthroughs in cloning, artificial insemination, and milk production technology will drive production costs down. The federal dairy program will be greatly destabilized, and the only solution will be either to ban the new hormone or to abolish or gut the dairy program. The dairy import quota, which limits foreign cheese imports to 2 percent of the U.S. domestic supply, should be abolished today as a symbolic gesture of America's commitment to farm trade reform. If other countries attempt to dump subsidized dairy products on American consumers, U.S. laws on unfair trade provide adequate remedies.

3. Terminate all marketing order supply controls. These federal regulations that prohibit some farmers from selling their entire harvest are a crime against Mother Nature, and farmers will be better off being allowed to sell all their oranges, lemons, almonds, and raisins. The end of federally decreed waste in the fruit and nut business will not weaken the American economy. A few cooperatives such as Sunkist and the California Almond Growers Exchange that have used federal controls to cartelize their industries will suffer, but most farmers will be better off. Farm animals may miss the mountains of fresh oranges, lemons, raisins, and almonds—but humans will benefit.

4. After the first wave of agricultural reforms, propose the abolition of all federal programs that reward farmers for not working. Paying farmers not to work will always make America a poorer place. Set-asides have been based on the notion that the USDA has a special ability to foresee the future and plan accordingly. Yet the assumptions of the USDA's set-aside program are ridiculed each year by Mother Nature, by scientific breakthroughs that give higher yields, and by the ingenuity of farmers in circumventing the USDA's regulations. Nonetheless, because set-asides are the foundation of our entire Rube Goldberg agricultural contraption, they have continued regardless of how badly the USDA misguesses supply and demand. Once set-aside programs are abolished, there will be no effective way to limit wheat and corn production. This will effectively destroy politicians' ability to set price supports above market-clearing levels. Once politicians take their foot off the brake, they will quickly be forced to take their foot off the accelerator. Once politicians abstain from supply controls, price controls will also have to be abandoned.

Ending government subsidies for crop production would solve the problem of surpluses. Perpetual surpluses occur only because government perpetually pays farmers to overproduce. Remove the perverse incentives, and the great demon of the last half-century's agricultural policy will miraculously vanish. The government does not pay soybean farmers to overproduce, and there is no soybean surplus. The government sets corn target prices far above efficient

corn producers' variable cost of production, and there is a corn
surplus almost every year.

The farm lobby will fight this proposal tooth-and-nail. Busloads of
agricultural economists from USDA-subsidized land-grant univer-
sities will appear on Capitol Hill with complex econometric models
that have little relation to reality. The most ingenious rationales will be
offered for perpetuating a wasteful policy. To counter this attack, the
President could propose a national referendum on whether taxpayers
wish to continue paying producers of seven of the four hundred crops
grown in America *not to work*. Set-asides are a common-sense issue,
and as long as the President can keep the debate in common-sense
terms, he will win.

Once government stops driving up American crop prices, it will
no longer need to provide export subsidies, many of which are created
to compensate for those programs that raise U.S. prices above world
market prices. The main achievement of export subsidies is to camouflage the damage federal agricultural policy does to American
farmers' competitiveness. It makes no sense to produce and sell at a
loss. If American farmers can't sell at a profit, they should not be
producing.

5. Propose the abolition of all credit subsidies to agriculture. The
abolition of the Farmers Home Administration (FmHA) would reduce
unfair competition in farming and rationalize American agriculture.
Since easy credit drives up land values and rental rates, the elimination of FmHA loans would make it much easier for beginning farmers
to acquire farmland on their own, and for unsubsidized farmers to
survive and prosper. The FmHA should cease making new loans and
transfer its authority to collect old loans to private collection agencies.
The more incompetent farmers the FmHA keeps on the land, the less
stable American agriculture will be. Instead of losing $100,000 a year
farming, many FmHA borrowers should be earning $25,000 a year
painting houses, selling cars, or repairing vacuum cleaners.

Federal guarantees should be canceled for the Farm Credit System. The Federal Agricultural Mortgage Association should be abolished tomorrow. "Farmer Mac" is a time bomb waiting to explode.
The average American worker should not be held liable for government guarantees on $2.5 million in loans for farmers. There is no point
in sacrificing taxpayers to finance credit programs that drive up

farmland values and thereby drive American farmers out of world markets. After massive federal cash injections in recent years, the Farm Credit System should be able to stand on its own feet now. If it can't, it doesn't deserve to exist.

The Politics of Rational Economic Policy

What about politics? What chances are there for an outbreak of economic common sense on Capitol Hill? The key to political victory is to attack farm programs at their weakest points. Once the dam is broken, the rest of the *ancien régime* can be swept away bit by bit.

The only real defense of farm programs is, "They exist, so we should keep them." The only reason not to abolish farm programs is political lethargy—because the nation has become so paralyzed with the weight of big government that it can be longer raze even the most absurd program. It is easier for congressmen to continue wasting tens of billions of dollars each year than to break political gridlocks.

Abolishing farm programs is not as impossible as it may seem. The sugar program was abolished in 1974, but rose from the grave in 1977. The House of Representatives voted to abolish both the peanut and sugar programs in 1981 and the Senate came within a whisker of abolishing the tobacco program in 1983. The Senate voted to phase out the honey program in 1985. The dairy program has been on the ropes several times. The general hysteria surrounding farm issues in 1985, fanned by a few Hollywood movies, saved the farm programs when the last major farm bill was being debated. If urban and suburban congressmen understood the program better, their tolerance would be greatly reduced.

Farm programs have survived largely thanks to the lies of farm-state congressmen. Congressional farm policy debates are dominated by the tall-tale contests of congressmen, each warning of the apocalypse and shaking the rafters with visions of the imminent disappearance of rural America. There is no reason to expect that some of the more creative farm-state congressmen will be any more honest about farm programs in the future than they have been in the past, though in the future more farm-state congressmen may realize the damage that farm programs are doing to farmers. Farm-state congressmen have managed to get away with their deceits because urban congressmen were too busy or too lazy to care about farm programs or were trading their votes on farm bills for higher welfare benefits, or for a bridge or a new right-hand turn lane off a highway in their districts.

Public ignorance is the farm lobby's greatest ally. Every individual who understands farm programs is a tiny nail in the coffin of the programs. While the American public may have a general, vague sense that farmers are virtuous individuals and that the government should help them, once people realize how farm programs actually operate, support will evaporate. Once farm programs lose their aura of fairness and benevolence, they will be doomed. A deluge of angry letters and phone calls from constituents could spark a revolt among urban congressmen.

Many who admit the failure of existing programs propose that they be eliminated gradually over a ten-year period. But the longer Congress spends winding it down, the less likelihood there is that the program will actually be abolished. The U.S. farm economy was close to a free market for major crops in 1974, but then Congress and Presidents Ford and Carter went on repeated vote-buying binges. The farm economy was again comparatively close to a free market in 1981—and then Congress opened the Treasury's floodgates.

New Zealand recently eliminated almost all of its farm subsidies—the first major country to go "cold turkey." In 1984 a new Labour government took office and was confronted with disastrous budget deficits and high inflation. Farm subsidies were equivalent to 14 percent of the government's budget and 6 percent of the nation's gross national product (comparable dollar figures for the United States would be $155 billion dollars in subsidies and more than $300 billion of the GNP). In 1985 the New Zealand government wiped out almost all farm subsides. The Federated Farmers of New Zealand, the largest farm organization in the country, supported the move because the farmers had become convinced that government dominance of the economy was making the entire nation poorer. The federation pushed for sweeping cuts in government spending, elimination of protectionism, and tighter controls on the money supply. Peter Samuel reported in *Reason* magazine that the federation is still not satisfied with the Labour government because, although farm subsidies were cut overnight, government spending is still too high and many of New Zealand's corporations still enjoy trade protection, which forces farmers to pay higher prices for their machinery.[1] Land values fell after the government ended subsides, but bankers have worked with most of the affected farmers to restructure their debts. Farmers are diversifying. Many have switched from sheep farming to deer and goat farming. Despite the disruption caused by the reforms, the Labour Party recently won a second term from the voters.

The Effects of Abolishing Farm Programs

Environmental Benefits. Once federal subsidies ended, farmers would naturally begin rotating their crops and reducing their use of expensive pesticides and chemical fertilizers. The government's effective ban on crop rotation (because of the requirements to continue qualifying for federal subsidies) does far more harm to the environment than all the soil conservation programs achieve. The abolition of government programs that encourage environmental destruction will greatly reduce the need for other government programs to give aid and advice on reducing soil erosion. Soil conservation programs have been wasteful, poorly targeted, and ineffective. Since they have accomplished little, their abolition will have little effect. Once the government stops promising to solve the problem of soil erosion, farmers will have a stronger incentive to take care of their own land. Agricultural pesticides and fertilizers will continue to cause substantial damage off the farm, but the effects can be judged far more objectively by the Environmental Protection Agency than by the USDA.

Research. One area in which the USDA has made valuable contributions to American agriculture is in research. The research budget is less than a billion dollars, which usually amounts to less than 3 percent of the annual federal spending on farm programs plus consumer taxes. Much of the money for current agricultural research is dished out in agricultural appropriations bills: $300,000 for a food-marketing policy center in Connecticut, $8.5 million for a National Food Center at Ames, Iowa, $500,000 for curriculum improvement at Mississippi Valley State University, $285,000 for a study on milk consumption in Pennsylvania, and so on.[2] Politicians have generally been more concerned about who gets the money than about the results of the research. As one senior USDA aide observes, congressmen are more interested in building brick-and-mortar monuments to themselves in their home districts than in anything else.[3] Though agricultural research has pioneered better seeds and better methods of production, federal agricultural policies have often prevented consumers from getting the benefits of taxpayer-financed research. The USDA has an excellent research network that should continue to receive limited federal support.

Increased Efficiency. The biggest effect of the abolition of subsidies would be an enormous increase in the efficiency of American farmers. Without the massive set-asides, the productivity of American farmers could increase by 15 or 20 percent overnight. Farm programs greatly increase farmers' costs of production. The loss to farmers from abolishing the programs would be far less than the savings to taxpayers, consumers, and farmers. Roughly half of all farmland is rented, and farmers who rent land will lose little. The USDA drives crop prices up, and then landlords raise the rent. This is clearly the case in tobacco and peanut farming, where farmers who don't own allotments must pay nonfarmers for them. But it is also true for corn, wheat, and other crops for which there is only a limited amount of good farmland. Rental rates in the corn and wheat belt are established by the target price—$4.10 a bushel for wheat and $2.86 a bushel for corn in 1989. Because target prices determine the rental rates, it is extremely difficult to rent land and make a profit at market prices. Federal programs have made it much harder for the farmer who doesn't own land and doesn't want to rely on the government to survive.

Employment. It is an open question whether the abolition of farm subsidies will mean more or fewer jobs in American agriculture. Handouts have kept many inefficient farmers on their tractors, while USDA set-aside programs have destroyed hundreds of thousands of jobs. The Congressional Office of Technology Assessment predicts that 50,000 large farms could produce 75 percent of all the food and fiber in the United States by the year 2000.[4] Huge cotton and dairy farms in California could set the pace for far higher productivity in American agriculture. Some states, such as Nebraska, have reacted to this trend by severely restricting the purchase of farmland by corporations. But the result of such a reaction would be to consign American agriculture to the junk heap of economic history. There is debate among agricultural economists about the optimal size of a farm unit for maximimum efficiency and productivity. The place to settle that issue is in the market, not in the halls of Congress and in state legislatures. According to the most recent Census of Agriculture, less than than 10 percent of America's farms are owned by corporations.

The abolition of federal farm programs could actually help the family farmer stay on his land. Without federal price guarantees, farmers will worry less about maximizing their yields and more about minimizing their out-of-pocket expenses. Farmers would rely less on chemical inputs and expensive machinery and more on their own labor. Dennis Avery, formerly a State Department chief agricultural attaché and currently an analyst for World Perspectives, a consulting firm in Washington, observes:

> Federal farm programs have led to an overcapitalized agriculture with less actual employment than what it otherwise would have. It turned farming into a yield contest, and the farmer that could wring the highest yields out of the acre could afford to bid the most for it. The medium-technology farmer who could wring average yields from his land got a buyout offer he couldn't refuse. The trend was limited only by the amount of land that the high-tech farmer could handle with the largest equipment available. If you took out the support price, and prices varied again, farmers would not want to have high debt loads—they would not want to buy more machinery. I think the biggest farms would find themselves with a capital cost structure that would be too large to [enable them to] compete.[5]

(Avery is one of the most astute agricultural economists in the business, and was one of the few farm experts to predict the decline in farmland value in the early 1980s.)

Once subsidies are abolished, farm families with free labor will have an advantage. Farmers who are content with an average American income—instead of the $115,000 a year that many full-time farmers now receive—could survive and compete with much lower crop prices. Once the government stopped shutting down more than 70 million acres of farmland each year, there could be far more work available planting, harvesting, and transporting crops. Set-aside requirements, by forcing farmers to plant on a smaller amount of land, encourage reliance on fertilizers, pesticides, and heavy machinery. A more extensive farming system would encourage more reliance on labor and management rather than chemical injections.

But the health of an industry cannot be judged by the nominal number of people working in the industry—or being paid by the government not to work. The real measure of success or failure is the profitability of farm production. Farmers have become far wealthier than other Americans largely because there has been a huge exodus from the farms to the cities during the twentieth century. It would be naive to declare that the current number of Americans employed in agriculture is the right number, just as it is naive to say that $4.10 a bushel is the right price for wheat. No one can know what technological developments or market opportunities will occur in the next few years. The best way to ensure that agriculture provides employment for the right number of people is for politicians to stop interfering with the farm economy.

There will be a shakeout and some farmers will go bankrupt—but the more farmers who leave farming, the easier it will be for the survivors to earn a living in the marketplace. We already have the reality of scores of thousands of farmers leaving farming via the set-aside programs. It is only the annual sacrifice of taxpayers that allows the number of farmers who remain to be far higher than it would otherwise be. Is there any reason to support scores of thousands of idle farmers, solely to perpetuate the notion that America has more farmers than it really does? If a farmer isn't farming, is he really a farmer? How much is it worth to the nation to have an individual work as a farmer rather than as a computer repairman or store manager? How many Americans should go hungry in order that farmland can continue to be owned by relatively inefficient farm operators?

An Invigorated Economy. The elimination of farm subsidies would be a massive shot in the arm for the American economy, releasing vast amounts of labor and capital from inefficient uses. The United States is entering a period of labor shortages. It makes no sense to continue paying talented individuals not to work. There is no economic benefit in having a rural leisure class. Thanks to the current low unemployment rates, the ex-farmer's adjustment to city life would be relatively easy. It is a crime to spend tens of billions of dollars to deter adjustment now, when the adjustment could more easily be made now than later. The question is not how many farmers Congress wants, but the best future for the individuals who are currently farming or considering farming as an occupation. Congress may be able artificially to increase the number of farmers for a few years, but at some point in the future the public's willingness to support surplus farmers will evaporate.

Alternatives

Federal price-support programs were created to protect farmers against declines in crop prices while insuring that they could still capture the profits of price increases. Recently the Chicago Mercantile Exchange began trading options contracts on major crops. Option contracts allow a trader to buy or sell a certain amount of a commodity at a future date at a set price. A "put" option provides a farmer with a guarantee that he can sell his crop for a set price, though he is under no obligation to sell at that price if market prices go higher. The cost of put options depends, among other things, on the price of the underlying commodity, the volatility of the market, and the duration of the contract. Put options protect farmers against excessive losses while setting no limits on their profits. Options provide the maximum freedom for the producer while also providing a floor of security.

Options contracts are superior to existing federal programs because they allow farmers to get a guaranteed price without impeding their efficiency or, in rewarding overproduction, engendering huge surpluses that hang over the markets and depress prices. Grain elevators in the Midwest are now providing price guarantees in return for the farmer's pledging to sell his grain to the elevator. If federal programs were abolished, there would probably be a huge increase in the number of grain elevators and grain companies willing to offer farmers guaranteed prices for their crops. Price insurance would effectively be privatized. Privately provided price insurance would not destabilize markets the way government-provided price insurance does.

Many farmers under financial stress have sold their farms to a bank or company and then rented it back and continued farming, often with a profit-sharing arrangement. The farmer still gets to keep much of the fruit of his labor while not being exposed to the risk of skyrocketing interest rates or plummeting land values. Some farmers are selling equity shares in their operation, thereby raising the capital to expand and improve their efficiency. As Kathleen Lawrence, a former USDA deputy assistant secretary, notes,

> As society changes, we must look for new ways to do things. Ownership of all of the aspects that go into production is not necessary to maintain the family farm. We can keep the family farm operating by leasing estate and equipment—until that farmer builds up sufficient cash equity or can get partners into his business—so that he is then able to purchase farmland.[6]

Roadblocks

Most discussions of the phaseouts of farm benefits presume that if the government gave farmers money in the past, it is obliged to continue giving them money in the future. In 1981, farm price supports cost taxpayers only $3 billion. If farm programs had been abolished then, there would have been little loss to farmers and very little disruption of the economy. But the farm lobbies succeeded in railroading through a budget-busting, Christmas-tree package of farm benefits in the 1981 four-year farm bill. In 1985, after mandating the most expensive farm programs in history, congressmen insisted that it would be unfair to give farmers less in the future than they had received in previous years.

Though some farmers will suffer from the abolition of government programs, the losses of individual farmers will be closely proportional to (and probably far less than) their previous windfalls from government subsidies. The only clear exception will be those who have recently purchased farmland. Farmers who have received few handouts will be little affected by the end of federal aid. Most farm subsidies go to a small minority of farms, so most farmers will suffer little from an end to subsidies.

Some farmers will need to make adjustments. Do taxpayers owe people compensation for leaving an overcrowded profession? In cases where government has withdrawn de facto subsidies—the Motor Carrier Act of 1980 that deregulated the trucking industry is an example—established firms have lost heavily. But because the original benefit was unearned, the government held that no compensation was merited. Federal policy-makers encouraged many people to enter the teaching profession in the 1970s, resulting in a huge glut of teachers. The government offered no special compensation to unemployed teachers.

Why should the government give a dairy farmer a million dollars to quit his trade when a typical laid-off worker receives little government aid to help him start a new career? Thousands of private companies are government contractors. Each year, hundreds of them routinely fail to have their government contracts renewed. Sometimes the companies have been contracting with the government for ten, twenty, or thirty years. Does the government then owe special compensation to the company's employees? Such obligations would make as much sense as the offer of severance pay to food stamp recipients who no longer qualify for handouts. Many farmers have essentially spent most of their careers as government contractors producing surplus grain. Like others who change occupations or lose their jobs, farmers abandoning farming could be temporarily eligible for unemployment compensation.

All plans to "compensate" farmers for the reduction of subsidies propose to reward only the producers of surplus, government-subsidized crops. This would mean giving tens of thousands of dollars to cotton growers while providing nothing to sunflower growers. Apparently, only the farmers who received handouts in the past are entitled to receive compensation for the end of federal control over farming. This is a peculiar concept of fairness. What justification is there for taxing one farmer to reward another farmer to stop producing a given crop?

The federal government has spent the equivalent of more than $500,000 on every full-time farmer since 1980. What sense does it make to force the average taxpayer to compensate someone worth almost ten times as much as himself for the abolition of annual subsidies that often exceed that taxpayer's salary? The first premise of any solution to the agricultural crisis should be that taxpayers owe farmers nothing except the opportunity to get a fair price in the marketplace. And the best definition of fairness is a price on which a buyer and seller can voluntarily agree upon.

Some critics worry that the withdrawal of government subsidies will make it less likely that farmers will be able to own the land on which they farm. But a public policy designed to ensure that farmers own their own farms makes no sense when the average farmer is worth nearly a million dollars. Federal policy designed to ensure that farmers own their land—the explicit justification for the FmHA's million-dollar loans to farmers—simply means that it is in the public interest for farmers to be millionaires and semi-millionaires. High land values are the single biggest impediment to young Americans who want to begin a career in farming.

Former USDA chief economist Robert Thompson estimates that the abolition of farm programs would result in a one-time decline of $113 billion in farmland value.[7] This amounts to roughly 20 percent of the value of American cropland, and is far less than the 35 percent, $297 billion decline in cropland values that occurred between 1982 and 1986 despite the highest federal agricultural spending in history. As with the 1982–86 decline, the land that would be hit hardest is land in areas that rely heavily on federal subsidies to preserve their value. Farmers would suffer in close proportion to how much they had received in subsidies in previous years. In 1986, when farmland values hit bottom before re-escalating, young farmers could actually afford to buy farmland with their cash flow—the profits from renting land and raising crops on it. Now farmland values in many prime growing areas are 20 percent higher than they were in 1986—and the possibility of young farmers being able to finance their land purchases with their own sweat appears to be vanishing.

The Problem of Foreign Farm Subsidies

In July 1987 President Reagan proposed a mutual pact of all major agricultural countries to end trade-disrupting farm subsidies and to move to nearly complete free trade in agriculture worldwide. Reagan's idea was excellent, but the United States should do more to reform American agriculture than have interesting discussions with foreign dignitaries in plush hotels in Geneva. The question of whether poor families in Harlem continue to be sacrificed to benefit Wisconsin dairymen should not depend on the Diet in Japan or the actions of the

European Economic Community. America should not abuse its tax-payers simply because foreign governments abuse theirs. If we wait until everyone in the world agrees to end agricultural boondoggles, it will be too late for American farmers to benefit. Regardless of the agricultural policies of foreign governments, free-market agriculture is in the interest of most Americans.

The obsession with foreign export subsidies has been debilitating to U.S. farm policy. Foreign subsidies have provided American policy-makers with an excuse for postponing reform, giving more handouts, and coddling American farmers. The unfairness of foreign agricultural trade practices has been greatly exaggerated in order to justify per-petuating unfair American trade practices. The European Economic Community (EEC), like the United States, provides huge subsidies for its farmers and, like the United States, dumps huge amounts of crops on the world market. Yet wheat is the only major crop for which the United States and the EEC are in head-to-head competition—and EEC wheat exports equal only a small percentage of U.S. exports. The United States and the EEC also compete for dairy exports. U.S. tax-payers could survive quite nicely if their government stopped buying butter for $3,000 a ton and selling it on world markets for $1,000. New Zealand dairy farmers, with vast amounts of pastureland providing low-cost feed, have a huge advantage in their costs of production over both American and European farmers.

There is an accelerating revolution in agricultural efficiency and productivity occurring throughout the world. In the last decade, Saudi Arabia, Sweden, Hungary, and Tanzania have become grain exporters. Farming is in the midst of a genetic revolution, with new seed varieties engineered by biotechnology that allow the expansion of cropland in the desert, in the Sahel, and throughout Latin America. In the 1980s, rice yields rose by 40 percent, wheat yields by 30 percent, and new corn varieties will grow in regions hundreds of miles closer to the North and South poles. Ray Daniel, the vice president of Chase Econometrics, notes that "the population of the world is slowing below 2 percent growth. The productivity of the world [agriculture] is growing faster, about 2.6 percent."[8] While the United States increased its yields faster in the 1970s than its competition did, foreign countries are now boosting yields faster than American farmers are. This revolu-tion in productivity has received little or no recognition from Congress, which is struggling not only against the laws of supply and demand, but also against the advances of modern science. The only way that American farmers will be able to compete in the future is by lowering their cost of production.

The United States lacks the power to set world crop prices, but it can make it very expensive for other countries to continue subsidies after abandoning its own. The United States is waging a Vietnam-type offensive against the EEC, willing to let regions of American taxpayers be slaughtered but unwilling to make the hard policy decisions necessary to win the conflict. The more the U.S. government restrains American farmers, the easier it is for foreign governments to pamper *their* farmers. The abolition of all set-aside programs and restrictions on output would have a powerful effect on foreign politicians. Free-market agriculture in the United States is the greatest threat to the EEC's Common Agricultural Program. If the United States were only to unleash the full efficiency of the American farmer, the Europeans could no longer afford subsidized exports. The EEC has tottered on the edge of bankruptcy almost every year since 1981, and has been saved in large part due to the effects on world markets of massive American set-asides and de facto export taxes.

Federal agricultural policy has long been an albatross around the necks of American trade negotiators. It is difficult for the United States to urge foreign countries to lower their trade barriers against American computers and jet planes when America provides unlimited protection for its own sugar and dairy industries. U.S. industry has often met with retaliation due to American agricultural trade barriers and dumping.

Free trade is the best hope for future world prosperity. Myopic federal agricultural policies in 1929–30 helped derail the world trading system. Government agricultural policy today provides the largest impediment to reform of the General Agreement on Tariffs and Trade and one of the most inflammatory items on the agenda of world trade negotiations. By devastating free trade and endangering the world trading system, federal farm policies cause far more damage to the United States than can be estimated. The sooner we get rid of agricultural programs, the safer the world trading system will be.

The Specter of Mandatory Controls

We have a choice between shifting to a free market and making farmers a permanent welfare class. The faster agricultural comparative advantages shift, the less likely that farmers can survive in a half-free, half-subsidized farm system. The penalties for efficiency and taxes on exports exacted by federal agricultural policy are becoming heavier with each harvest. The higher the subsidies have soared, the more dependent farmers have become, and the more support has arisen for imposing federal controls over all farmers of major crops.

Farm policy debates in coming years could be increasingly dominated by the specter of mandatory controls on all major crops. The Reagan administration already imposed de facto mandatory controls in 1986 and 1987 when it greatly destabilized the cotton, rice, corn, and wheat markets. Over 80 percent of the farmers of those four major crops were effectively forced to comply with USDA-decreed acreage reductions in order to receive federal benefits, or risk being destroyed in USDA-destabilized markets.

The Harkin-Gephardt Save the Family Farmer Act, the most prominent scheme for mandatory controls, is based on the sage insight that if we double or triple food prices, farm income will increase in the short run. This would wreck our export trade, but the same taxpayers who get to pay far more for food would have the privilege of paying additional taxes to dump American crops on world markets at fire-sale prices. Supporters of mandatory controls claim that the United States would earn more from exports after the federal government forced farmers to shut down half their farms, because the crops would be worth more. This is the leading economic fallacy of twentieth-century agricultural policy: Foreign demand is inelastic, and foreigners will buy as much of an American crop at a high price as they would at a low price. Many advocates of mandatory controls argue that the United States can no longer afford to export, because high costs of production make us no longer competitive. But such a view merely continues a sixty-year tradition of looking at mythical averages that are designed to exaggerate costs in order to allow farmers easier access to the Treasury.

Mandatory controls would vastly increase political control of one of America's most important industries. Every proposal for mandatory controls would sacrifice some farmers for the benefit of other farmers. If mandatory controls were in the interests of all farmers, all the farmers would favor them. But they are clearly designed to benefit the least-productive farmers at the expense of the most productive.

Conclusion

Many U.S. farmers could do very well without government aid in world markets. America has the best agricultural infrastructure and the best-educated farmers in the world. America also has many of the world's best research laboratories and by far the world's most efficient marketing system. According to the USDA, American farmers have a comparative advantage in wheat, corn, soybean, and peanut production. A report by the Agricultural Policy Working Group concluded, "The United States enjoys a comparative advantage in the production of many agricultural commodities, especially the grains and oilseeds that make up the bulk of world agricultural commodities."[9] The Former USDA chief economist William Lesher notes, "The U.S. produces over thirteen times as much corn at or below Argentina's cost, as well as six times the quantity of wheat. The U.S. produces two and a half times Brazil's annual soybean output at competitive cost."[10]

Farm lobbies warn that if the USDA does not perpetuate programs that pay farmers not to plant, that pay them to massacre dairy cows and that close the borders to foreign food, there could eventually be a food shortage and terrible disruption in rural America. But even Willard Cochrane, USDA chief economist in the early 1960s and a man who describes himself as "an unreconstructed New Deal Democrat," has pointed out that

> in all likelihood the land acquired by the aggressive neighbor will be incorporated into a more efficient [farm] operation than the one from which it came . . . in the usual case, the demise of a struggling farmer and the reorganization of his assets among his neighbors will increase the total supply of farm products, not diminish them.[11]

Both farmers and politicians will benefit from taking a more realistic perspective on agricultural prices. In policy debates in recent years, politicians have been obsessed with crop prices—as though prices were independent moral entities rather than simply one factor in the overall health of the industry. Congressmen have shown little or no concern about the way in which federal policies have raised the farmers' costs of production. As James Wright Johnson of the National Pork Producers Council put it, "We can care less whether hogs are 36 cents or whether they are 56 cents, as long as there is a profit margin."[12] Wheeler McMillen urged in 1929, "The answer is not higher prices, but lower costs" of production.[13]

As the USDA and Congress surrender their arbitrary power over commodity markets, farming will become more stable, more secure, and less susceptible to the latest political influenza sweeping Capitol Hill. Farmers will not have to wait for a signal from Washington on which crop to plant, or on whether to plow up the crop they just planted. Crop production will shift to those areas with a natural advantage. Some farmers will shift out of corn and wheat production into soybean and sunflower production. More vegetables will likely be grown, and new crops as yet unknown will come into vogue. No one knows precisely what will happen, but the result will surely be more rational, less wasteful, and more efficient than the status quo.

The best aid to farmers during their transition to free markets would be to make a large pyre of wasteful government programs. Many other groups and special interests aside from farmers receive unearned handouts from the government, and these should be abolished. From Community Development Block Grants to the Export-Import Bank and Small Business Administration, from housing subsidies to handouts for the middle class, the federal budget is replete with waste, fraud, and abuse. The best way to stimulate the economy is to reduce taxes, reduce regulation, and allow more scope for individuals and entrepreneurs. As James Wright Johnson told the House Agriculture Committee, "That government is best which governs less—and most of all, spends less."[14]

Chapter 15

Conclusion

How can the government logically appropriate hundreds of millions [of dollars] with the ostensible purpose of increasing production and at the same time hundreds of other millions [of dollars] to decrease production?

—Glenn W. Birkett, March 4, 1931

Almost sixty years ago, Glenn W. Birkett, a "dirt farmer" writing in *The Nation*, complained that federal agricultural policy resembled "Penelope, knitting by day and unraveling by night."[1] Neither thirty sessions of Congress nor ten presidents have been able to construct a rational, consistent, respectable agricultural policy. Farm policy has always been a pointless disruption of markets, a profitless fleecing of taxpayers, and a perennial proof of the limits of government. The sixty-year, federal agricultural policy civil war has disrupted our economy, crippled a major industry, and squandered hundreds of billions of dollars.

Federal agricultural policy has been a hodgepodge of senseless contradictions ever since 1929—with conflicting programs to boost and slash production, programs for driving up prices at home and driving down prices abroad, one program to save the land and another to encourage farmers to plow fencerow-to-fencerow. The con-

tradictions have always been clear, and politicians have never stooped
to correct them. If politicians can't even decide whether to hit the
accelerator or the brake, why should we let them drive?

Politicians took custody of the agricultural economy—and then
wrecked it. In the name of protecting farmers against themselves, the
government has done a hundred things that no intelligent farmer
would ever have done. The problem is not that farm programs are
malfunctioning in the late 1980s, but that the programs have never
worked well and politicians have never fixed them. Congressmen lack
a political incentive to correct their economic mistakes. As long as
politicians can profit from waste, fraud, and abuse—from government
programs that shovel out money for any reason to voters in the
congressmen's districts—the same boondoggles and contradictory
programs will continue. Congress is like a general that loses every
economic battle but can always conscript more tax dollars to fight
again.

For half a century the federal government has been playing King
Canute, trying to sweep back the waves of economic change—yet the
tide keeps rolling in. For more than fifty years, politicians have justified spending billions of dollars on agriculture each year in order to
save the family farm. Almost every year since the 1930s, the exodus
from farm to city has continued, and America's farm population has
decreased from 30 million to less than 5 million. If the government
had succeeded in "freezing" agriculture as it was in 1933, America
would be a far poorer place and farmers really would be as indigent as
the farm lobbies claim they are. The only thing worse than the failures
of agricultural policy would have been its success.

Farm policy is based on a blind faith in giving some men arbitrary
power over other men's livelihood. Farm programs are testament to
the great economic fallacy of modern times: that government can create wealth through waste, that there is a political alchemy that can
increase prosperity by repressing productivity, that government can
enrich society by doing things that would impoverish any individual.
Farm programs are justified with the belief that mindless government
intervention is better than no intervention at all, that political control
is beneficial regardless of how much damage politicians do.

The worse politicians have failed, the more powerful they have
become. Each new farm crisis increases the power and prestige of the

congressional agricultural committees, even though they were the captains that ran the ship aground. The cure for every subsidy is another subsidy, and the answer for every failed control is a tighter control, and there is no problem caused by political manipulation that cannot be cured by more manipulation. No matter how many mistakes congressmen and bureaucrats make, policy marches forward on the tacit assumption that next time they will get it right.

Agriculture is a classic case of brain-dead federal policy—of a zombie government agency that appears destined to repeat the same bumbling steps forever. Agricultural policy today is built on the same foolish premises that it was built on in the 1930s: that farmers will never respond to market price signals by reducing production, that farming is so noble that it is better to pay people not to farm than for them to do something useful, and that politicians and bureaucrats can effectively foresee developments better than markets can. Government began with a mistake sixty years ago and has been unable to stop repeating the mistake ever since.

"We meant well" has been the USDA's motto for sixty years. Almost all the sins of agricultural policy-makers have been excused by their claim of good intentions—as though good intentions were a waiver to do unlimited harm. Whatever boondoggle occurs, regardless of how much money is wasted, politicians and bureaucrats always repeat the refrain, "We were only trying to help farmers." But what excuse is there for seizing power over an industry or an individual and then exercising that power blindly, ignorantly, and irresponsibly?

It is not pro-farmer to bankrupt a cattleman in order to enrich a dairyman. It is not pro-farmer to drive up all farmers' rental payments in a desperate attempt to keep the least-competent farmers on the land. It is not pro-farmer to restrict the amount the most-productive farmer can sell in order to boost the profits of the least-productive farmer. It is not pro-farmer to force peanut and tobacco farmers to pay tribute to dentists, doctors, and lawyers. It is not pro-farmer to repeatedly disrupt markets in hare-brained schemes to boost farm income.

Is it paternalism to destroy a farmer's foreign markets? To boost a farmer's cost of production? To force him to leave a quarter of his cropland idle? To perpetually disrupt markets and leave farmers hiding in the bomb shelters awaiting the next USDA surprise? Is it paternalism to impair a man's ability to stand on his own two feet promising that he will be better off after the government knocks him down?

For every rich farmer who receives another million-dollar check from the government, there are a slew of fertilizer dealers, farm-equipment dealers, and cattle, poultry, or potato producers who are victimized by the government programs, as well as a throng of farm laborers who are thrown out of work. It makes no sense to direct the national economy in order to further enrich a small group of wealthy landowners; yet this has been a prime effect of farm programs for decades.

As Congressman Glenn English proclaimed in 1986, "Let the word go forth from here today to commodity groups, farmers, and members of Congress: Never, never, never trust this Department of Agriculture."[2] The Agriculture Department is not untrustworthy because of the caliber of its employees and managers; they are generally decent human beings who mean well. But the combination of its almost unlimited arbitrary power and its impossible goals guarantees that the USDA will continue to be a threat to the competent farmer. It is absurd to have a system with a czar of agriculture, a huge bureaucracy, and hundreds of haggling congressmen that insures that no one will be held responsible for mistakes. Does America really need a bureaucratic dinosaur telling farmers how many cartons of oranges they can sell each week, the color of nectarines the American public wants, how much milk should cost in each village and town, the interest rate each farmer should pay, and the fair value of each crop?

There are those who will shrug and insist that the moral ideals of farm policy justify its economic damage. But are there good moral reasons for wasting tens of billions of dollars a year? Is America a better society thanks to the government's taxation of janitors, ditch-diggers, and secretaries to pay rich farmers to idle more than 70 million acres of cropland a year? Giving one man power to run another man's life—or a hundred thousand men's lives—does not make society a better place.

Federal agricultural policy has long been a conspiracy against the best farmers—against those who did not need a handout to survive and prosper. Congress is always changing the rules of the game to protect the losers from their own mistakes. Farm policy has been designed for the benefit of the mediocre farmer—the inefficient farmer who can't survive without politicians disrupting the market and constraining his competition. Congress' attention is always on the farmer who can't make it, who needs another Farmers Home Administration bailout to survive, and whose cost of production is above that of efficient, competent farmers. Should government manage a major industry for the benefit of its weakest producers?

Government cannot help individual farmers without worsening the plight of farmers as a class. Government cannot try to help farmers as a class without driving up farmland values, thereby barring young would-be farmers from the occupation and reducing American competitiveness. Every farm rescue package sacrifices some farmers to other farmers and encourages all farmers to rely on the government instead of on themselves. Every farm bailout in the 1980s has made it more difficult for the independent, unsubsidized farmer to survive.

In the future, farm policy should be based on the forgotten farmer, the farmer who asks only to be left alone by the government to sell his crop at a price that he can agree on with his customer, the farmer who asks only that no more political tidal waves sweep away his markets, the farmer who does not feel entitled to other people's paychecks without their consent, the farmer who is proud of his independence, who can stand on his own two feet and compete with any other farmer in the world. This is the farmer who embodies the agrarian ideals that should have influenced public policy. If we respect him, we must respect his markets, and stop driving up his cost of production and restricting his freedom in a series of quixotic efforts to permanently raise farm prices. Poll after poll conducted by farm magazines shows a large percentage of farmers calling for the government to end all intervention in agriculture. These are generally America's best farmers, and if we want a strong agricultural sector in the future, these are the farmers we must respect.

The word *farm* is a red herring in the farm policy debate. A few politically powerful groups managed to get their hands into the Treasury generations ago and have stayed on the dole ever since. Farm policy reform is simply a question of treating all farmers as we currently treat cattlemen, pork and poultry producers, avocado growers, cashew and pecan growers, dry-bean growers, potato growers, grapefruit growers, flower growers, and broccoli and cabbage and onion and spinach and tomato and apple and cranberry growers. It is not a question of helping farmers per se, but of ending handouts to the groups of farmers who, through political clout, have turned themselves into agricultural aristocracies. Why should each sugar grower receive an annual benefit of roughly a quarter of a million dollars from the USDA while maple syrup producers receive not a cent? Why should the government spend $125,000 on each rice grower, but not a cent on a carrot grower? Why should the government maintain a feudal system to enrich peanut growers, but not spend a cent on his neighbor, who grows pecans? Why should congressmen fawn over dairymen while casually wrecking cattlemen's markets? These are distinctions based solely on political clout and campaign contributions.

The clearest effect the USDA is having in the 1980s is to decrease the productivity of American agriculture. The more welfare government has given farmers, the less competitive they have become. Every farm bailout has discouraged farmers from maximizing their productivity and efficiency. The higher the federal government drives up prices, the less efficient American farmers will be. Costs of production will always tend to rise to the guaranteed price, thus ensuring that Americans spend more to produce what they could have produced much more efficiently. How much is it worth to ensure that land is planted by less-competent FmHA farmers instead of more-competent independent farmers? How many city families should we sacrifice in order to keep one unsuccessful businessman on his tractor for one more year?

Farm programs have always cost taxpayers and consumers far more than they have benefited farmers. Agricultural policy has perennially squandered two, three, four, or more dollars to give one dollar in benefits, always wasting money and then spending more to camouflage the waste. For too many years, much of the USDA's budget has been spent concocting plausible excuses for giving the rest of the budget to farmers. This is simply the measure of Congress' incompetence—designing a transfer program that loses most of the loot in the shuffle.

It was a common saying in the 1930s: "We cannot squander ourselves into prosperity."[3] Every year for sixty years, federal agricultural policy has made America a poorer place than it otherwise would have been. American agriculture is dominated by government-caused artificial scarcity of land, government's artificial price incentives, and government's artificial restrictions on farm operation. Farm policy has injected far more capital into agriculture than farmers could productively use, and then lavishly rewarded farmers to leave their assets idle. This capital could have been used to build new factories, new hospitals, new houses, and new cities.

It is difficult to conceive of the full cost of the $200 billion that the USDA has squandered in this decade; it is the equivalent to the combined assets of several of America's largest corporations. If the government had annihilated the capital assets of the country's four largest corporations in a scheme to benefit other corporations, there would be protests in the streets. When it comes to agriculture, as long as there is no smoking gun, as long as the economic devastation is covert, there is no outcry. How much more of our capital—our economic future—can we afford to burn?

For sixty years politicians have driven farmers out of world markets and onto the government dole. While the U.S. government measures American farmers' tobacco fields to the hundredth of an acre, foreign farmers are planting thousands of acres of new tobacco. While the USDA is idling the equivalent of entire states of farmland, Brazil and Argentina are on the verge of plowing up a major part of a continent to increase their harvest. While the United States is forcing farmers to abandon hundreds of millions of fresh lemons and oranges, foreign farmers are expanding at full speed and pouring their crops onto the U.S. market. The United States Congress should admit that it cannot control the world and cease its efforts to control American farmers who must rely on world markets.

As *The Nation* observed in 1930, "Every effort at fundamental control of [world commodity prices] through market manipulation has ultimately resulted in disaster to the controllers."[4] No matter how much politicians and farmers want to control them, markets will still not be controlled. No matter how much money government spends propping up prices this year, prices will shift to a market-clearing level next year, unless the government once again represses market signals. The illusion that politicians control markets lasts only as long as politicians continue to burn tax money.

Sentimentality could be the death of American agriculture. Ten more years of the existing crippling welfare system and American farmers could be totally outclassed in world markets. There is a farm revolution occurring around the world, and neither the decrees of Congress nor the regulations of the USDA can stop it. Wheat, rice, and corn yields are soaring in Europe, Australia, Asia, and Africa. The only way that the United States can maintain its benchmark of parity is by closing its borders, shutting down most American farms, and driving food prices through the ceiling.

Agriculture has been the biggest political intervention in the economy for more than fifty years—the most constant federal effort to manage the economy, to control producers, and to reallocate capital— and the most consistent failure. Agricultural policy is the clearest example of the economic debility of our political system. Government economic interventions are almost always the union of power and ignorance. Congress' contempt for farmers' efficiency is the clearest proof of congressmen's inability to manage the American economy intelligently.

To realize the full costs of federal farm programs, one must consider what might have been. If it were not for federal agricultural programs, farm exports might be $10 billion or $20 billion higher, America would dominate world grain markets, American farms would be far more efficient, low-income Americans would have healthier diets, the government's role in the average American's life would be reduced, our environment would be cleaner, the world trading system would be more open, America would be more respected abroad, and workers would be allowed to keep a greater share of their paychecks. Farmers' debt would be lower because government would not have begged them to borrow, and farmers' earned income would be higher.

On March 7, 1938, Henry Wallace, praising a new farm law that required federal licenses for production and imposed strict controls on output, declared: "Agriculture has a plan which is a challenge to industry. . . . If industry follows the trail blazed by agriculture, both farm and city people will make more rapid gains."[5] What would America be like if other industries had been managed as agriculture has been managed, if America had shut down half the factories in Detroit to drive up car prices, shut down half the textile mills in the Carolinas to drive up clothing prices, and provided half of all the capital for every industry according to a system based on political clout rather than productive ability? What would our economy look like if the government had repressed Apple Computers in order to ensure IBM's continued dominance of the computer industry? What would happen to efficiency if every factory owner had to beg federal permission each week to discover what percentage of his finished products he would be allowed to ship to market? What would happen if government fought change and adjustment as vigorously in other industries as it has fought change in agriculture? What justice would there be if all the court cases were handled according to the practices of the USDA's administrative laws by which political appointees can overturn a judge's decisions with the flick of a pen? America has prospered only because politicians have less control over most industries than they have over agriculture.

British economist J. R. McCullogh observed in 1815:

> The nations of the earth are not condemned to throw the dice to determine which of them shall submit to famine. There is always abundance of food in the world. To enjoy a constant plenty, we have only to lay aside our prohibitions and restrictions, and cease to counteract the benevolent wisdom of Providence.[6]

These thoughts written more than 170 years ago have never been more true than they are now. Most of the hunger in the world today is due largely to the various governments' foolish economic policies. Americans tend to look at farm policy reform solely in the light of American farmers' income. But American agricultural policy has caused misery throughout the world, alternately driving up food prices by reducing American production and withholding American crops and bombing Third World farmers with floods of free food and predatory prices. American policy has given every country in the world a good pretext for closing its own borders to free trade in agriculture and lavishing benefits on its own farmers. At the same time as we follow such disruptive policies, the President and Congress dole out $15 billion in foreign aid each year. This is only one more absurdity of government policy. If we truly wish to help the world's poorest citizens, the best thing we can do is to end our subsidies, end our dumping, and open our markets. Allowing Third World farmers to sell us their sugar and other farm products will do them more good than all the paternalistic schemes dreamed up by the U.S. Agency for International Development. We should not add to the world's misery with mindless schemes to inflate a few hundred thousand American businessmen's income.

Agricultural policy is fundamentally corrupt. It is corrupt because the people who make it almost always lie about the real purpose of a handout, regulation, or intervention. It is corrupt because it sacrifices one group to another group: city taxpayers to rural farmers, fertilizer and seed dealers to grain farmers, and self-reliant farmers to welfare farmers. It is corrupt because it is redistribution on false premises, with politicians always hollering about poor farmers while making millionaires of rich farmers. It is corrupt because it divorces power from responsibility, as with the Dairy Termination Program with which the USDA wrecked the cattle markets. It is corrupt because it creates a hostility of interests where none existed previously, making the livelihood of farmers dependent on how much farm-state politicians can filch from nonfarmers. It is corrupt because it reduces the majority's freedom solely in order to boost a minority's profit. It is corrupt because it forces farmers to rely on the arbitrary power of government and politicians for their survival and prosperity. And it is corrupt because it turns a normal business into more of a crap-shoot and demands that people spend their time begging for handouts instead of boosting their productivity.

Secretary of Agriculture Henry Wallace declared in 1936: "It is essential for this generation to learn to live with more and more social controls."[7] Wallace and other New Dealers felt that the concept of individual freedom had failed and that the only solution was more government control to protect people and markets from themselves. After fifty-six years of assorted "farm dictators," it is clear that Wallace was wrong. Farm policy has sacrificed individual liberty to an endless series of desperate political schemes to drive up farm prices. But political rule has brought only instability, endless coercion, and senseless policies.

In the end, farm policy will always rest on the wisdom of bureaucrats and the honesty of politicians. Farm policy will never be greater than the moral and intellectual sum of farm policy-makers.

Nineteenth-century reformers built their utopias on the expectation of an imminent change in human nature. Twentieth-century reformers have built Leviathans and then awaited a change in politicians' nature. Faith in changing the masses has been replaced by faith in changing their rulers. Almost every expansion of government power is premised on the hope that politicians will not act in the future as they have acted in the past. Each new program is justified only by denying the character of the people who will be controlling the program's levers. Einstein warned in 1945 that with the invention of the atomic bomb, mankind had far more destructive power than people were capable of controlling responsibly. It is the same with government power: Governments have now amassed far more economic power than politicians are capable of responsibly and intelligently wielding.

Reform is the opiate of the welfare state. Farm programs will never be much better run than they are today. It is not a question of finding the right person to play farm czar—of finding a wise man to be secretary of agriculture or chairman of the House Committee on Appropriations. There is no person on earth who can make contradictory farm policies serve the public. The failures of government agricultural programs and interventions are predestined in the nature of government and politics. The problems are inherent in the political process—in managing the economy to harvest the most votes for the most congressmen.

Just because government cannot square the economic circle does not mean government is a useless institution. People have lost respect for government largely because politicians have lost respect for their own limitations. To say that politicians should not manage the economy, set prices, and enrich their friends is not to condemn representative government. There are some things government can do well and many things it cannot do well. But there is no evidence that Congress and the federal bureaucracy can manage the economy better than private citizens. We don't need government "plans" that trample the plans, lives, and businesses of private citizens. The more government attempts, the less it will achieve.

Markets are less imperfect than bureaucrats, voluntary agreements are fairer than bureaucratic decrees, and private citizens move faster than government workers. These should be the guiding principles in judging future government interventions in the economy. The private sector is not perfect—but at least private businesses do not hatch schemes to idle 70 million acres, massacre cows, or mindlessly drive up the cost of production. In the long run, both farmers and their customers will be better off when politicians stop managing American agriculture.

As long as people need food, farmers will be able to produce and sell at a profit. There is no perversity in the economic system itself that prevents farming from being as profitable as other professions. The farm problem is a problem only because politicians need votes. The only solution to the farm problem is to depoliticize agriculture.

Notes

1: Introduction

1. *New York Times*, July 21, 1930.

2. U.S. Congress, House Agriculture Committee, *Policy Alternatives to the Food Security Act of 1985* (Washington, D.C.: Government Printing Office, March 12, 1987), p. 101.

3. Thomas W. Hertel, Robert Thompson, and Marinos E. Tsigas, "Economy Side-Effects of Unilateral Trade and Policy Liberalization on U.S. Agriculture," paper prepared for the Global Agriculture Trade Study organized by the Center for International Economics, Canberra, Australia, May 1988.

4. Rexford Tugwell, *Our Economic System and Its Problems* (New York: Harcourt Brace, 1934).

2: The USDA's Sixty-Year War Against the Market

1. Henry Lee, *An Exposition of Evidence in Support of the Memorial to Congress* (Boston, Mass.: Boston Press, 1832), pp. 3–4.

2. Ibid., p. 6.

3. Ezra Taft Benson, *Freedom To Farm* (Garden City, N.Y.: Doubleday, 1960), p. 112.

4. *New York Times*, June 3, 1934.

5. U.S. Congress House Agriculture Committee, *Wheat Price Guaranteed by Congress*, (Washington, D.C.: Government Printing Office, February 3, 1919), p. 166.

6. Ibid., p. 150.

7. Benson, *Freedom to Farm*, p. 66.

8. Ibid., p. 64.

9. Cited in Bernard Ostrolenk, *The Surplus Farmer* (New York: Harper, 1932), p. 62.

10. Ibid., p. 45.

11. James H. Shideler, *Farm Crisis 1919–1923* (Westport, Conn.: Greenwood Press, 1957), p. 39.

12. Warren Hickman, *The Genesis of the European Recovery Program* (Geneva, 1949), p. 9. Cited in Allan Francis Rau, Jr., "Agricultural Policy and

Trade Liberalization in the United States, 1934–1950," dissertation, Université de Genève, 1957, p. 9.

13. Theodore Saloutus and J.D. Hicks, *Agricultural Discontent in the Midwest*, cited in H. Thomas Johnson, *Agricultural Depression in the 1920s* (1961; reprint ed.; New York: Garland, 1985), p. 135.

14. League of Nations, Economic Committee, *The Agricultural Crisis*, vol. 1, June 15, 1931, p. 21.

15. Cited in Julia E. Johnson, ed., *Agriculture and the Tariff* (New York: H. W. Wilson, 1927), p. 446.

16. H. L. Mencken, *Prejudices: Second Series* (New York: Alfred A. Knopf, 1924), p. 57.

17. *The New Republic*, March 4, 1925.

18. Johnson, *Agricultural Depression in the 1920s*, p. 1.

19. U.S. Department of Agriculture, *Agriculture's Share in the National Income* (Washington: Government Printing Office, 1935), p. 9.

20. G. M. Peterson, "Wealth, Income and Living," *Journal of Farm Economics*, July 1933, p. 442.

21. Joseph S. Davis, *On Agricultural Policy* (Palo Alto, Calif.: Stanford University, 1938), p. 435.

22. Johnson, *Agricultural Depression*, p. 213.

23. Ibid.

24. William D. Rowley, *M. L. Wilson and the Campaign for the Domestic Allotment* (Omaha: University of Nebraska Press, 1970), p. 14.

25. Cited in Johnson, *Agricultural Depression*, p. 125.

26. James H. Shideler, "Herbert Hoover and the Federal Farm Board Project, 1921–1925," *Mississippi Valley Historical Review*, March 1956, p. 721.

27. Wheeler McMillen, *Too Many Farmers* (New York: Morrow, 1929), p. 13.

28. Vernon Carstensen, "The Past Fifty Years," *Journal of Farm Economics*, December 1960, p. 998.

29. Johnson, *Agricultural Depression*, p. 214.

30. Ibid., p. 63.

31. U.S. Department of Agriculture, *Yearbook of Agriculture* (Washington, D.C.: Government Printing Office, 1923), p. 150.

32. Frank C. Platt, *Is the Farmer Going Bankrupt?* (Painted Post, N.Y.: privately published, 1925), p. 96.

33. H. C. Taylor, "The New Farm Economics," *Journal of Farm Economics*, April 1929, p. 357.

34. Millard Peck, "Reclamation Projects and Their Relation to Agricultural Depression," *Annals of the American Academy of Politics & Social Sciences*, March 1929, p. 177.

35. G. S. Wehrwein, "Which Does Agriculture Need—Readjustment or Legislation?" *Journal of Farm Economics*, January 1928, p. 20.

36. Cited in Cassius M. Clay, *Mainstay of American Individualism* (New York: Macmillan), 1934, p. 110.

37. Cited in Ostrolenk, *The Surplus Farmer*, p. 108.

38. Ibid.

39. Ibid., p. 117.

40. Ibid., p. 132.

41. *New York Times*, December 18, 1932.

42. U.S. Congress, Senate Agriculture Committee, *Agricultural Conference and Farm Board Inquiry*, (Washington, D.C.: Government Printing Office, November 24, 1931), p. 141.

43. S. D. Myers, ed., *The Cotton Crisis* (Dallas, Tex.: Southern Methodist University, 1935), p. 27.

44. Lionel Robbins, *The Great Depression* (London: MacMillan, 1934), p. 135.

45. Geta Feketekuty, interview with the author, January 14, 1988.

46. Jude Wanniski, interview with author, June 10, 1988. See also, *The Way the World Works* (New York: Simon & Schuster, 1978).

47. Milton Friedman and Anna Schwartz, *A Monetary History of the United States* (Princeton, N.J.: Princeton University Press, 1963).

48. B. H. Hibbard, "Taxes a Cause of Agricultural Distress," *Journal of Farm Economics*, January 1933, p. 1.

49. Ibid., p. 3.

50. Ibid., p. 5.

51. E. C. Young, "The Farm Mortgage Credit Situation in the U.S.," *Journal of Farm Economics*, February 1935, p. 200.

52. Cited in Arthur Schlesinger, Jr., *The Coming of the New Deal* (Boston: Houghton Mifflin, 1959), p. 368.

53. Ibid.

54. Schlesinger, *Coming of the New Deal*, p. 61.

55. William E. Leuchtenberg, *Franklin D. Roosevelt and the New Deal* (New York: Harper & Row, 1963), p. 77.

56. This was widely reported by commentators and polemicists in the 1930s. A letter from Douglas Bowers, USDA chief historian, to the author November, 1988 confirms that 1935 was the Depression year that food consumption was lowest, though he stops short of drawing a connection between the New Deal policies and food consumption levels.

57. *New York Times*, May 7, 1933.

58. *New York Times*, November 11, 1934.

59. O. B. Jesness, "Validity of the Fundamental Assumptions Underlying Agricultural Adjustment," *Journal of Farm Economics*, February 1936, p. 29.

60. B. H. Hibbard, "The First Year of the Agriculture Adjustment Administration," *The Nation*, July 4, 1934.

61. Theodore W. Schultz, *Vanishing Farm Markets and Our World Trade* (Boston: World Peace Foundation, 1935), p. 5.

62. M. L. Wilson, "Validity of the Fundamental Assumptions Underlying Agricultural Adjustment," *Journal of Farm Economics*, February 1936, p. 19.

63. Chester C. Davis, "The Problem of Agricultural Adjustment," *Journal of Farm Economics*, January 1935, p. 92.

64. Ashner Hobson, "International Aspects of the Agricultural Adjustment Program," *Journal of Farm Economics*, July 1934, p. 379.

65. Franklin D. Roosevelt, *Address on the Accomplishments of and Future Aims for Agriculture*, speech, September 28, 1935, in *Public Papers and Address of Franklin D. Roosevelt*, (New York: Random House, 1938).

66. Cited in William Peterson, *The Great Farm Program* (Chicago: Henry Regnery, 1959), p. 103.

67. Jesse H. Jones, *Fifty Billion Dollars* (New York: MacMillan, 1951), p. 88.

68. Rexford Tugwell, *Our Economic System and Its Problems* (New York: Harcourt, Brace 1934), p. 499.

69. Schlesinger, *Coming of the New Deal*, p. 369.

70. Cited in Schlesinger, *Coming of the New Deal*, p. 369.

71. U.S. Congress, Joint Committee on the Reduction of Nonessential Expenditures, *Reduction of Nonessential Federal Expenditures* (Washington, D.C.: Government Printing Office, February 6, 1942).

72. Otis Durant Duncan, "Some Sociological Implications of the Agricultural Adjustment Program," *Journal of Farm Economics*, July 1934, p. 504.

73. *Milwaukee Journal*, October 8, 1933.

74. Joseph S. Davis, "Agricultural Adjustment Administration as a Force in Recovery," *Journal of Farm Economics*, February 1935, p. 14.

75. Don Paarlberg, "Effects of New Deal Agricultural Programs on the Agricultural Agenda—A Half Century Later, and Prospect for the Future," *Journal of Agricultural Economics*, December 1983, p. 1164.

76. William B. Amberson, "The New Deal For Sharecroppers," *The Nation*, February 13, 1935, p. 186.

77. David E. Conrad, *The Forgotten Farmers: The Story of Sharecroppers in the New Deal* (Urbana: University of Illinois Press, 1965).

78. Benson, *Freedom to Farm*, p. 164.

79. Willford I. King, "Some Results of Government Attempts to Foster Recovery," *Journal of Farm Economics*, May 1935, p. 240.

80. Robert F. Martin, *Income in Agriculture, 1929–35* (New York, National Industrial Conference Board, 1936).

81. Ibid., p. 42.

82. Ibid.

83. Johnson, *Agricultural Depression*, p. 47.

84. Cited in Martin, *Income in Agriculture*, p. 32.

85. Ibid., p. 122.

86. Davis, "The Problem of Agricultural Adjustment," *Farm Economics*, February 1934, p. 88.

87. Cited in Martin, *Income in Agriculture*, p. 123.

88. Ibid., p. 12.

89. Ibid.

90. Charles Hardin, *Food and Fiber in the Nation's Politics*, vol. 3, National Advisory Commission on Food and Fiber (Washington, D.C.: Government Printing Office, 1967), p. 130.

91. Ibid.

92. Benson, *Freedom to Farm*, p. 157.

93. Cited in Paul Findley, *Federal Farm Fable* (New Rochelle, N.Y.: Arlington House, 1968), p. 106.

94. Ibid.

95. D. Gale Johnson, "Agricultural Price Policy and International Trade," *Essays in International Finance*, no. 19 (Princeton, N.J.: Princeton University, June 1954), p. 16.

96. Cited in Findley, *Federal Farm Fable*, p. 71.

97. John Strohm, "The Farmers Vote for Freedom," *Reader's Digest*, September 1963, p. 95.

98. Cited in Findley, *Federal Farm Fable*, p. 114.

99. Charles Schultze, *The Distribution of Farm Subsidies: Who Gets the Benefits* (Washington, D.C.: Brookings Institution, 1971), p. 2.

100. U.S. Department of Agriculture, *Embargoes, Surplus Disposal, and U.S. Agriculture*, Agriculture Economic Report No. 564 (Washington, D.C.: Government Printing Office, December 1986).

101. Julian Simon, interview with the author, August 7, 1988. See also Julian Simon, *The Ultimate Resource* (Princeton, N.J.: Princeton University Press, 1982).

3: Seven Myths of Farm Policy

1. Don Paarlberg, "The Role of Values, Beliefs, and Myths in Establishing Agricultural Policy," unpublished essay, 1987.

2. U.S. Department of Agriculture, *Economic Indicators of the Farm Sector, National Financial Summary, 1986* (Washington, D.C.: Government Printing Office, 1987), p. 46.

3. *Kansas City Times*, "Special Report on the Farm Crisis," February 1985.

4. H. O. Carter, "A New View on Farm Finance," *Choices*, Spring 1987, p. 23.

5. U.S. Department of Agriculture, *Economic Indicators*, p. 50.

6. U.S. Department of Agriculture, *Economic Indicators of the Farm Sector, Farm Sector Review, 1986* (Washington, D.C.: Government Printing Office, January 1988), p. 13.

7. U.S. Congress, Senate Budget Committee, *The Distribution of Benefits from the 1982 Federal Crop Programs*, (Government Printing Office, November 1984), p. viii.

8. U.S. Department of Agriculture, *Economic Indicators, National Financial Summary*; and *Farmline*, January 1, 1987.

9. U.S. Congress, House Congressional Budget Office, *Crop Price-Support Programs: Policy Options for Contemporary Agriculture* (Washington, D.C.: Government Printing Office, February 1984), p. 14.

10. Lloyd D. Teigen, *Agricultural Parity: Historical Review and Alternative Calculations*, report prepared for the U.S. Department of Agriculture (Washington, D.C.: Government Printing Office, 1987), p.59.

11. *Kansas City Times*, "Special Report on the Farm Crisis."

12. *Detroit News*, October 9, 1986.

13. All comparisons derived from *Statistical Abstract of the United States* (Washington, D.C.: Government Printing Office, 1987), p. 388.

14. *Illinois Agri-News*, January 15, 1988.

15. Lloyd D. Teigen, *Agricultural Parity*, p. 32.

16. U.S. General Accounting Office, *Tax Policy: Economic Effects of Selected Current Tax Provisions on Agriculture* (Washington, D.C: Government Printing Office, August 1986), p. 6.

17. *Washington Post*, March 28, 1985.

18. Dale Hathaway, *Government and Agriculture: Public Policy in a Democratic Society*, (New York: MacMillan), 1963.

19. U.S. Bureau of the Census, *Household Wealth and Asset Ownership: 1984* (Washington, D.C.: Government Printing Office, 1986).

20. U.S. Department of Agriculture, *Economic Indicators*, National Financial Summary, p. 78.

21. Ibid. The figures are as follows:

Sales Class	Net Worth
$500,000+	$2,184,243
250,000–499,999	1,158,886
100,000–249,999	664,731
40,000–99,999	392,613
20,000–39,999	251,284
10,000–19,999	178,095
5,000–9,999	136,829
Less than 5,000	104,136

22. Wheeler McMillen, speech delivered at Rutgers University, February 24, 1936; published in *Vital Speeches*, March 9, 1936, p. 352.

23. Don Paarlberg and M. A. Jacobson, "Parity of Net Worth," *American Journal of Agricultural Economics*, no. 1 (1966), p. 127.

24. Don Paarlberg, speech delivered at Missouri Governor's Conference on Agriculture, December 15, 1987.

25. *Washington Post*, April 17, 1984.

26. National Agricultural Forum, *"Report on the 1985 Farm Bill Conference,"* December 1984, Washington, D.C., p. 9.

27. Julius Daschau, *Taxpayer's Hayride* (Boston: Little, Brown, 1964), p. 66.

28. Gregg Easterbrook, "Making Sense of Agricultural Policy," *The Atlantic,* July 1985, p. 70.

29. *Illinois Agri-News*, February 26, 1988.

30. U.S. Department of Agriculture, *Financial Characteristics of U.S. Farms, January 1, 1987* (Washington, D.C.: Government Printing Office, 1988), p. 60.

31. Teigen, *Agricultural Parity*, p. 27.

32. *Congressional Record*, February 19, 1985, H 429.

33. Ralph Robey, *Roosevelt vs. Recovery* (New York: Harper & Brothers, 1934), pp. 117–18.

34. J. Bruce Bullock, *What Is the 1985 Farm Problem?* Cato Institute, Washington, D.C., July 2, 1988, p. 5.

35. Thomas Babington Macaulay, "Southey's Colloquies," *Critical and Miscellaneous Essays*, vol. 2 (Philadelphia: Carey and Hart, 1843).

36. Franklin D. Roosevelt, *Special Message to Congress*, July 24, 1933, in *Public Papers and Addresses of Franklin D. Roosevelt* (New York: Random House, 1938).

37. *Congressional Record*, September 26, 1985, H 7860.

38. Ibid., H 7828.

39. Chester C. Davis, "The Problem of Agricultural Adjustment," *Journal of Farm Economics*, February 1934, p. 89.

40. *Congressional Record*, October 7, 1985, H 8292.

41. *Congressional Record*, June 16, 1988, H 4394.

42. U.S. Congress, House Committee on Banking and Urban Affairs, *Farm Debt* (Washington, D.C.: Government Printing Office, March 20, 1985).

4: A USDA Honor Roll

1. Franklin D. Roosevelt, *Public Papers and Addresses of Franklin D. Roosevelt*, vol. 3 (New York: Random House, 1938), p. 86.

2. Public Voice for Food and Health Policy, *A Consumer's Guide to Sugar Prices* (Washington, D.C.: Public Voice for Food and Health Policy, 1985), p. 6.

3. *Congressional Record*, September 26, 1985, H 7823.

4. *Journal of Commerce*, May 17, 1988.

5. U.S. Congress, Senate Agriculture Committee, *Reauthorization of the Food and Agricultural Act of 1981*, (Washington, D.C.: Government Printing Office, April 2, 1985).

6. *Economic Report of the President, 1986* (Washington D.C.: Government Printing Office, 1986), p. 137.

7. U.S. General Accounting Office, *Sugar Program—Issues Related to Imports of Sugar Containing Products* (Washington, D.C.: Government Printing Office, June 1988), p. 35.

8. *New York Times*, June 3, 1988.

9. Reed Karaim, "What Do Cory Aquino, Cocaine Addicts, and American Consumers Have in Common?" *Washington Monthly*, November 1987, p. 19.

10. *Wall Street Journal*, September 26, 1986.

11. Ibid.

12. Jonathan Rauch, "Sugary Shakedown," *National Journal*, April 30, 1988.

13. Lippert S. Ellis, *The Tariff on Sugar* (Freepoint, Ill.: Fawleigh Foundation, 1933), p. 152.

14. U.S. General Accounting Office, *Congressional Decision Needed on Necessity of Federal Wool Program* (Washington, D.C.: Government Printing Office, 1982), p. 17.

15. *Wall Street Journal*, April 17, 1985.

16. Ibid.

17. Ibid.

18. U.S. General Accounting Office, *Federal Wool Program,* p. 24.

19. National Wool Growers Association, "Analysis of the National Wool Act," 1985, p. 17.

20. Ibid.

21. U.S. Congress, House Agriculture Committe, *General Farm Bill of 1981 (Dairy, Bee Keeper, and Wool Programs),* March 25, 1981, p. 176.

22. *U.S. Congress, Reauthorization of the Food and Agricultural Act of 1985,* March 7, 1985, p. 137.

23. Peter Myers, to Senator Richard Lugar, February 12, 1988.

24. American Peanut Product Manufacturers Institute, "The U.S. Peanut Industry, the World Market, and U.S. Legislation," Washington, D.C., 1985, p. 7.

25. John Block, speech, Washington, D.C., January 9, 1984.

26. *The Flue-Cured Tobacco Farmer,* June 21, 1980.

27. U.S. Department of Agriculture, *Tobacco: Background for 1985 Farm Legislation* (Washington, D.C.: Government Printing Office, 1984), p. 27.

28. Daniel A. Sumner and Julian M. Alston, *Effects of the Tobacco Program: An Analysis of Deregulation* (Washington, D.C.: American Enterprise Institute, November, 1984), p. iii.

29. Cited in *Congressional Record,* October 8, 1985, H 8538

30. U.S. General Accounting Office, *Losses in the Department of Agriculture's Tobacco Program* (Washington, D.C.: Government Printing Office, September 18, 1988), p. i.

31. U.S. Congress, House Agriculture Committee, *Dark Air-Cured and Dark Fire-Cured Tobacco Quotas* (Washington, D.C.: Government Printing Office, April 1, 1987), p. 28.

32. *Washington Post,* March 30, 1985.

33. U.S. General Accounting Office, *Federal Price Support for Honey Should Be Phased Out* (Washington, D.C.: Government Printing Office, 1985), p. 20. See also U.S. Department of Agriculture, *Report on U.S. Honey Imports in Compliance with Section 4503 of the Agricultural Competitiveness and Trade Act of 1988* (Washington, D.C.: Government Printing Office, November 1988).

34. Ibid, p. 5.

35. *Los Angeles Times,* December 27, 1982.

36. U.S. General Accounting Office, *Federal Price Support for Honey,* p. 33.

37. *Wall Street Journal,* October 4, 1984.

38. Material in this section is taken from my article in the *Wall Street Journal,* December 14, 1988.

39. U.S. Congress, Congressional Budget Office, *Diversity in Crop Farming* (Washington, D.C.: Government Printing Office, 1985), p. 46.

40. U.S. Department of Agriculture, *Rice: Background for 1985 Farm Legislation* (Washington, D.C.: Government Printing Office, 1984).

41. U.S. Department of Agriculture, "Economic Indicators of the Farm Sector," *Farm Sector Review* (Washington, D.C.: Government Printing Office, 1988), p. 13.

5: *Paying Farmers Not to Work*

1. U.S. Congress, Senate Agriculture Committee, *Reauthorization of the Food and Agriculture Act of 1981* (Washington, D.C.: Government Printing Office, March 7, 1985), p. 57.

2. *Monthly Bulletin*, Fertilizer Institute, Washington, D.C., April 1987.

3. M. L. Wilson, "Validity of the Fundamental Assumptions Underlying Agricultural Adjustment," *Journal of Farm Economics*, February 1936, p. 17.

4. *New York Times*, June 4, 1934.

5. *New York Times*, November 12, 1933.

6. Julius Daschau, *Taxpayer's Hayride* (Boston: Little, Brown, 1964), p. 192.

7. Ibid.

8. *Washington Post*, May 17, 1977.

9. Bruce Gardner, *The Governing of Agriculture* (Lawrence: Regents Press of Kansas, 1981).

10. U.S. General Accounting Office, *Department of Agriculture Is Using Improved Payment Procedures for its 1984 Farm Programs* (Washington, D.C.: Government Printing Office, August 6, 1984), p.1.

11. *Des Moines Register*, September 15, 1986.

12. *Des Moines Register*, August 17, 1986.

13. Many of the figures and sources cited in this section are taken from Jim Bovard, "Fiasco on the Farm," *Readers Digest*, April 1984.

14. John Block, "The PIK Program—An Assessment," Washington, D.C.: USDA Press Office, 1983.

15. James Bovard, "Fiasco on the Farm."

16. Donald Ratajckack, "Monthly Projections," Georgia State University study, April 18, 1983.

17. John F. Marten, speech delivered at Annual USDA Outlook Conference, (Washington, D.C., November 2, 1983).

18. *Washington Post*, February 21, 1983.

19. *Washington Post*, July 17, 1983.

20. *Chicago Tribune*, January 6, 1984.

21. U.S. Department of Agriculture, Office of Inspector General, "Report on the Payment-in-Kind Program," July 6, 1983.

22. U.S. General Accounting Office, *1983 Payment-In-Kind Program Overview: Its Design, Impact, and Cost* (Washington, D.C.: Government Printing Office September 25, 1985), p. 59.

23. Ibid., p. 13.

24. *Wall Street Journal*, February 22, 1985.

25. Clifford Hardin, "Toward a New Farm Policy" (St. Louis, Missouri: Center for the Study of American Business, 1985).

26. *Memphis Commercial Appeal*, September 20, 1983.

27. G. Edward Schuh, "The Costs of PIK," unpublished essay, University of Minnesota, April 1983.

28. Don Paarlberg, "A Tarnished Golden Anniversary," speech delivered at Hillsboro College, Michigan, August 2, 1983.

29. Washington Post, November 17, 1983.

30. *New York Times*, March 4, 1984.

31. Charles Reimenschneider, "The Costs of PIK" (New York: Chemical Bank), 1983.

32. Cited in William B. Amberson, "The New Deal for Sharecroppers," *The Nation*, February 13, 1935, p. 185.

33. Ibid.

34. David Harrington, Gerard Schluter, and Patrick O'Brien, *Agriculture's Links to the National Economy* (Washington, D.C.: Government Printing Office, 1986) p. 4.

35. U.S. Department of Agriculture, *Final Regulatory Impact Analysis—1987 Farm Commodity Programs* (Washington, D.C.: Government Printing Office, October 6, 1987), p.1.

36. *Wall Street Journal*, November 9, 1984.

37. *Wall Street Journal*, March 6, 1986.

38. U.S. Congress, House Agriculture Committee, *Establishing Farm Program Payment Yields; Dry Edible Beans Ammendment of 1986; and Nonprogram Crop Ammendments of 1986* (Washington, D.C.: Government Printing Office, February 19, 1986).

39. Ibid.

40. Ibid.

41. Ibid.

42. *Washington Post*, February 16, 1986.

43. U.S. Congress, House Agriculture Committee, *Establishing Farm Program.*

44. *Washington Post*, February 16, 1986.

45. Kathleen Davis, "Officials Anticipate Having to Get OK," *Lubbock Avalanche Journal*, February 23, 1988.

46. *Raleigh Times*, February 29, 1988.

47. James Nathan Miller, "Can Congress Kill the Pork Barrel Habit?" *Reader's Digest*, September 1985, p. 126.

48. Dan Dvoskin, *Excess Capacity in U.S. Agriculture: An Economic Approach to Measurement,* U.S. Department of Agriculture, Agricultural Economic Report No. 580 (Washington, D.C.: Government Printing Office, 1988).

49. Ibid, p. 23.

50. Agricultural Policy Working Group, "Economic Impacts of Commodity Supply Controls," Washington, D.C., July 1987, p. 16.

51. U.S. Congress, House, Agriculture Committee, *U.S. Department of Agriculture's Use of General Commodity Certificates* (Washington, D.C.: Government Printing Office, April 7, 1987), p. 21.

52. General Accounting Office, *U.S. Food/Agriculture in a Volatile World Economy* (Washington, D.C.: Government Printing Office, November 1985), p. 21.

53. U.S. Congress, Senate Agriculture Committee, *Trade Policy Perspectives* (Washington, D.C.: Government Printing Office), 1985.

54. Richard Lyng to Gary Myers, February 20, 1987.

6: *Redistribution via Cows*

1. U.S. Congress, House Agriculture Committee, *Review of Status and Potential Impact of the Bovine Growth Hormone* (Washington, D.C.: Government Printing Office, June 11, 1986), p. 209.

2. Ibid., p.6.

3. George Lardner, Jr., "Anatomy of a Scandal: The Milk Fund," *Reader's Digest*, November 1974, p. 123.

4. Emily Yoffe, "Two Milk Duds," *The New Republic*, July 23, 1977.

5. *Barrons*, September 14, 1981.

6. Cited in John Donahue, "The Political Economy of Milk," *The Atlantic Monthly*, October 1983, p. 62.

7. *Congressional Record*, November 9, 1983, H 9535.

8. *Congressional Record*, October 18, 1983, H 8286.

9. *Economic Report of the President, 1986* (Washington, D.C.: Government Printing Office), p. 144.

10. U.S. General Accounting Office, *Effects and Administration of the 1984 Milk Diversion Program* (Washington, D.C.: Government Printing Office, July 29, 1985), pp. i–iii.

11. *Washington Post*, June 18, 1985.

12. U.S. General Accounting Office, *Dairy Termination Program: A Perspective on its Participants and Milk Production* (Washington, D.C.: Government Printing Office, May 1988), p. 2.

13. U.S. Congress, House Agriculture Committee, *Producer Compliance Regulations and Procedures of the U.S. Department of Agriculture's Milk Production Termination Program* (Washington, D.C.: Government Printing Office, June 11, 1987), p. 66.

14. Ibid, p. 65.

15. Ibid.

16. U.S. General Accounting Office, *International Trade, F.A.S. Management of Livestock Cooperator Program* (Washington, D.C.: Government Printing Office, October 1987), p. 6.

17. U.S. General Accounting Office, *Dairy Termination Program*, p. 2.

18. U.S. Department of Agriculture, "Higher Milk per Cow Boosts Surplus," *Agricultural Outlook* (Washington, D.C.: Government Printing Office, May 1988), p. 7.

19. U.S. Congress, House Agriculture Committee, *Implementation of the Orderly Marketing Provision of the Food Security Act of 1985* (Washington, D.C.: Government Printing Office, September 10, 1986), p. 651.

20. *New York Times*, April 10, 1986.

21. Ibid.

22. *New York Times*, December 17, 1987.

23. U.S. Congress, House Agriculture Committee, *Food Security Act*, p. 679.

24. U.S. Congress, House Government Operations Committee, *Implementation of the Dairy Termination Program: USDA's Slaughter of the Cattle Market,*

House Report 99-890 (Washington, D.C.: Government Printing Office, September 25, 1986).

25. U.S. Congress, House Agriculture Committee, *Food Security Act*, p. 687.

26. Chandler Keyes, interview with the author, December 15, 1987.

27. U.S. Congress House Agriculture Committee, *Producer Compliance Regulations*, p. 15.

28. U.S. Congress, Senate Agriculture Committee, *National Dairy Program* (Washington, D.C.: Government Printing Office), May 11, 1988, p. 140.

29. *Louisville Courier-Journal*, April 13, 1981.

30. U.S. General Accounting Office, *Milk Marketing Orders*, March 1988.

31. U.S. Department of Agriculture, Office of Inspector General, "Audit of the New England Milk Market Order No. 1," 01041-4-NY (Washington, D.C.: Government Printing Office, February 27, 1987).

32. John Donahue, "The Political Economy of Milk," *The Atlantic Monthly*, October 1983, p. 60.

33. "Bureaucracy on the Farm," *U.S. News and World Report*, December 1, 1975.

34. *Louisville Courier-Journal*, April 14, 1981.

35. Ibid.

36. U.S. Congress, House Agriculture Committee, *Milk Marketing Orders* (Washington, D.C.: Government Printing Office, July 17, 1979).

37. *Federal Register*, January 10, 1986, p. 1245.

38. *Federal Register*, March 5, 1986, p. 7579.

39. Rod Leonard, interview with the author, June 7, 1988.

40. *Regulation*, May-June 1983, p. 5.

41. *Washington Post*, June 2, 1980.

42. Ibid.

43. Alden Manchester, *The Public Role in the Dairy Economy* (Boulder, Colorado: Westview Press, 1982), p. 278.

44. Ibid.

45. U.S. General Accounting Office, *Milk Marketing Orders: Options for Change* (Washington, D.C.: Government Printing Office, March 1988), p. 91.

46. *New York Times*, February 12, 1985.

47. Ibid.

48. *New York Times*, February 7, 1987.

49. Rod Leonard, interview with the author, June 7, 1988.

50. U.S. Department of Agriculture, *Economic Indicators of the Farm Sector, Farm Sector Review, 1986* (Washington, D.C.: Government Printing Office, 1988), p. 13.

51. Alden Manchester, *The Status of Marketing Cooperatives under Antitrust Laws* (Washington, D.C.: Government Printing Office, 1982).

52. *Regulation*, May-June 1983, p. 5.

53. Cited in James Bovard, "Feeding Everybody," *Policy Review*, Fall 1983.

54. U.S. Congress, Senate Agriculture Committee, *Reauthorization of the Agriculture and Food Act of 1981* (Washington, D.C.: Government Printing Office, April 15, 1985), p. 478.

55. Bruce Gardner, *The Governing of Agriculture* (Lawrence, Kansas: University of Kansas Press, 1981), p. 134.

56. Manchester, op. cit.

57. Keith Schneider, "Biotechnology's Cash Cow," *New York Times Sunday Magazine*, June 12, 1988.

58. Ibid.

59. U.S. Congress, House Agriculture Committee, *U.S. Department of Agriculture's Implementation of the April 1, 1985, Reduction in the National Support Price For Milk* (Washington, D.C.: Government Printing Office, May 21, 1985), p.4.

7: The Conspiracy Against Competence

1. From H. Allan Nation to the editor of an unidentified Mississippi Gannett newspaper in response to Gannett News Service's series on Farmers' Home Administration problems in Mississippi, reprinted in 1984.

2. U.S. General Accounting Office, *Farmers Home Administration's Losses Have Increased Significantly* (Washington, D.C.: Government Printing Office, December 1988), p.1.

3. U.S. Congress, House Agriculture Committee, *Review of Status and Potential Impact of the Bovine Growth Hormone* (Washington, D.C.: Government Printing Office, June 11, 1986, p. 21.

4. Wheeler McMillen, *Too Many Farmers* (New York: William Morrow, 1929), p. 27.

5. Cassius M. Clay, *The Mainstay of American Individualism* (New York: Macmillan, 1934), p. 215.

6. Cited in Ezra Taft Benson, *Freedom to Farm* (Garden City, N.Y.: Doubleday, 1960), p. 119.

7. William Lesher, speech delivered at the Conference on Alternative Agricultural and Food Policies and the 1985 Farm Bill, Berkeley, Calif., June 11, 1984.

8. U.S. Congress, House Committee on Banking, Finance, and Urban Affairs, *Farm Debt* (Washington, D.C.: Government Printing Office, March 20, 1985), p. 80.

9. *New York Times*, March 10, 1985.

10. Michael Boehlje, *Agriculture Policy and Financial Stress* (Washington, D.C.: American Enterprise Institute, December 1984).

11. *Washington Post*, March 1, 1987.

12. Vance Clark, interview with the author, February 24, 1988.

13. *Wall Street Journal*, December 6, 1985.

14. *Pro Farmer*, April 4, 1987.

15. U.S. Department of Agriculture, *Federal Credit Programs for Agriculture* (Washington, D.C.: Government Printing Office, November 1984), p. 13.

16. Mark Rohner and Dennis Camire, "The Golden Yoke: The Farmers Home Administration in Mississippi," Gannett News Service reprint, 1984.

17. Ibid.

18. Ibid.

19. Ibid.

20. Ibid.

21. Ibid.

22. General Accounting Office, *Debt Restructuring Activities During the 1984–85 Farm Credit Crisis* (Washington, D.C.: Government Printing Office, May 16, 1986).

23. Interview of a federal employee who requested anonymity, January 14, 1988.

24. *Bakersfield Californian*, series on Tex-Cal bankruptcy beginning May 5, 1985.

25. Ibid.

26. Ibid.

27. Rohner and Camire, "Fraud and Fortune."

28. Ibid.

29. U.S. General Accounting Office, *Farmers Home Administration Financial and General Characteristics of Farmer Loan Program Borrowers* (Washington, D.C.: Government Printing Office, January 1986), p. 2.

30. U.S. General Accounting Office, *Farmers Home Administration: Federally Acquired Farm Property Presents a Management Challenge* (Washington, D.C.: Government Printing Office, June 1986), p. 23.

31. Ibid., p. 22.

32. U.S. General Accounting Office, *Farmers Home Administration, Problems and Issues Facing the Emergency Loan Program* (Washington, D.C.: Government Printing Office, November 1987), p. 42.

33. U.S. General Accounting Office, *Federally Acquired Farm Property*, p. 23.

34. Ibid.

35. *Wall Street Journal*, April 23, 1988.

36. U.S. Congress, Senate Agriculture Committee, *The Agriculture Credit Act of 1987* (Washington, D.C.: Government Printing Office, November 20, 1987), p. 46.

37. U.S. Congress, Senate Agriculture Committee, *Proposed Changes in Farmers Home Administration Credit Regulations* (Washington, D.C.: Government Printing Office, March 11, 1987), p. 30.

38. Clark, interview.

39. Kathleen Lawrence, interview with the author, July 3, 1988.

40. U.S. Department of Agriculture, Office of the Inspector General, *Designation of Eligible Lending Area,* no. 04659-1-At (Washington, D.C.: U.S. Department of Agriculture, September 24, 1986), p 2.

41. U.S. Department of Agriculture, Office of the Inspector General, *Survey of FmHA Debt Management on Guaranteed Loans*, no. 04099-118-Te, June 11, 1987, p. 2.

42. U.S. Department of Agriculture, Office of the Inspector General, *Farmers Home Non-Program Real Estate Loan Survey*, no. 04099-259-At, October 6, 1987, p. 2.

43. U.S. Department of Agriculture, Office of the Inspector General, *FmHA Policies and Procedures for Managing and Leasing Acquired Farm Properties Need Strengthening*, no. 046654-2-53, June 1987.

44. *Congressional Record*, September 23, 1987, H 7687.

45. Sheldon Rose to the author, March 8, 1988.

46. *Congressional Record*, February 19, 1985, H 429.

47. U.S. Congress, Senate Agriculture Committee, *The Agriculture Act of 1987*.

48. *Des Moines Register*, March 6, 1988.

49. Cited in a letter from Congressman Joseph DioGuardi, May 31, 1988.

50. Ibid.

51. *Richmond News Leader*, March 3, 1988.

52. *New York Times*, March 2, 1988.

53. *Congressional Record*, October 6, 1987, H 8183.

54. Lawrence, interview.

55. Clark, interview, April 2, 1988.

56. Robert A. Bennett, "Has Farm Aid Gone Too Far?" *New York Times*, September 3, 1987.

57. Lawrence, interview.

58. *Atlanta Journal*, May 25, 1987.

59. *Congressional Record*, September 26, 1987, H 768.

60. *Washington Post*, May 13, 1985.

61. *Washington Times*, January 31, 1985.

62. *New York Times*, February 9, 1985.

63. *Washington Post*, March 26, 1987.

64. U.S. Congress, Senate Agriculture Committee, *Proposed Changes*, p. 22.

65. *Fargo Forum*, February 7, 1987.

66. Wheeler McMillen, *Too Many Farmers*, (New York, William Morrow, 1929), p. 66.

8: Export Schizophrenia

1. U.S. Congress, Senate Agriculture Committee, *Agricultural Conference and Farm Board Inquiry* (Washington, D.C.: Government Printing Office, November 24, 1931), p. 71.

2. Ibid.

3. Bernard Ostrolenk, The Surplus Farmer (New York: Harper, 1932), p. 130.

4. Cited in Arthur Cyril Bunce, *Economic Nationalism and the Farmer* (Ames, Iowa: Collegiate Press, Inc., 1938), p. 52.

5. *Congressional Record*, September 26, 1985, H 7423.

6. Ibid., H 7828.

7. U.S. Department of Agriculture, *Options, Futures, and Agricultural Commodity Programs* (Washington, D.C.: Government Printing Office, February 1988), p. 17.

8. U.S. Congress, Congressional Research Service, *What Agricultural Policy Would Best Serve the Economic Interests of the U.S.?* (Washington, D.C.: Government Printing Office, 1986).

9. Thomas Grennes, *Domestic Commodity Programs, the Value of the Dollar, and U.S. Agricultural Exports* (Washington, D.C.: American Enterprise Institute, 1987), p. i.

10. U.S. Congress, House Agriculture Committee, *U.S. Export Competitiveness* (Washington, D.C.: Government Printing Office, April 16, 1985), p. 5.

11. *Wall Street Journal*, March 28, 1985.

12. *Congressional Record*, October 2, 1985, H 8067.

13. *Congressional Record*, October 8, 1985, H 8476.

14. U.S. Congress, Senate Agriculture Committee, *Trade Policy Perspectives* (Washington, D.C.: Government Printing Office, 1985).

15. Agricultural Policy Working Group, "The Competitiveness of U.S. Agriculture," Washington, D.C., 1987.

16. Edward Madigan, speech delivered Washington, D.C., March 29, 1988.

17. *Congressional Record*, October 8, 1985, H 8538.

18. Thomas Hertel, Robert L. Thompson, and Marinos E. Tsigas, "Economy-Wide Effects of Unilateral Trade and Policy Liberalization in U.S. Agriculture," paper prepared for the Global Agricultural Trade Study, op. cit., p. 37.

19. Andrew Feltenstein, "Agricultural Policy and the U.S. Federal Budget and the Trade Deficits," paper prepared for the Global Agricultural Trade Study, op. cit., p. 2.

20. John Ford, interview with the author, January 15, 1988.

21. U.S. Congress, House Agriculture Committee, *Review of Grain Quality Issues and Legislation to Amend the Grain Standards Act* (Washington, D.C.: Government Printing Office, July 21, 1986).

22. *Pro Farmer*, April 30, 1988.

23. U.S. Congress, House Agriculture Committee, *Review of Grain Quality Issues.*

24. *Milling & Baking News*, July 8, 1986.

25. *Wall Street Journal*, May 7, 1986.

26. *Pro Farmer*, November 22, 1986.

27. *Wall Street Journal*, February 4, 1988.

28. Ibid.

29. Ibid.

30. U.S. General Accounting Office, *Implementation of the Agricultural Export Enhancement Program* (Washington, D.C.: Government Printing Office, March 1987), pp. i–iii.

31. U.S. General Accounting Office, *Agricultural Trade: Review of Targeted Export Assistance Program* (Washington, D.C.: Government Printing Office, May 1988), draft copy.

32. Ibid.

33. Ibid.

34. Ibid.

35. Ibid.

36. Ibid.

37. *Wall Street Journal*, July 2, 1984.

38. Ibid.

39. U.S. General Accounting Office, *Disincentives to Agricultural Production in Developing Countries, November 26, 1975* (Washington, D.C.: Government Printing Office, 1975, p. 1; idem, *Agricultural Overview: U.S. Food/Agriculture in a Volatile World Economy* (Washington, D.C.: Government Printing Office, November 1985).

40. *Wall Street Journal*, July 2, 1984.

41. Ibid.

42. Scott D. Tollefson, "Jamaica: Limits of a Showcase Policy," *S.A.I.S. Review*, Summer/Fall 1985.

43. U.S. Agency for International Development, *Audit of the PL-480 Title I Program in Somalia* (Washington, D.C.: Government Printing Office, January 26, 1987), p. 10.

44. Former AID official interview with the author, June 7, 1988.

45. *Wall Street Journal*, July 2, 1984.

46. James Bovard, "How American Food Aid Keeps the Third World Hungry," Heritage Foundation, Washington, D.C.: August 1, 1988.

47. *Wall Street Journal*, July 2, 1984.

48. *Congressional Record*, October 3, 1985, H8196.

49. *Pro Farmer*, October 2, 1986.

50. *Wall Street Journal*, May 7, 1986.

51. *Congressional Record*, February 19, 1985, H 433.

52. *Washington Post*, May 25, 1985.

9: Trampling Individual Rights

1. Rexford Tugwell, *Our Economic System and Its Problems* (New York: Harcourt Brace, 1934).

2. Cited in Lawrence Shepard, "Cartelization of the California Orange Industry, 1934–81," *Journal of Law and Economics*, April 1986, p. 83.

3. M. R. Benedict, "Production Control in Agriculture and Industry," *Journal of Farm Economics*, August 1936, p. 454.

4. Thomas M. Lenard and Michael P. Mazur, "Harvest of Waste," *Regulation*, May/June 1985, p. 25.

5. Perry Walker, interview with the author, April 23, 1988.

6. *New York Times*, August 3, 1986.

7. James Moody, interview with the author, October 3, 1987.

8. U.S. Small Business Administration, "Docket No. AO-144-A14-R01: Proposed Amendments of Marketing Order 910," October 15, 1984.

9. *Federal Register*, July 31, 1987, p. 28,535.

10. Ray Martin, to Charles Brader, January 31, 1988.

11. U.S. Small Business Administration, p. 212.

12. Walker, interview.

13. *California Farmers*, February 16, 1985.

14. Robert Samuelson, *Newsweek*, March 25, 1985.

15. *Bakersfield Californian*, December 16, 1984.

16. *Sequioa v. USDA*, CV-F-88-98, January 29, 1988, p. 163.

17. *Federal Register*, October 16, 1987, p. 38,432.

18. Cited in *Sequoia v. USDA*, p. 58.

19. U.S. Congress, House Committee on Small Business, *The Regulatory Flexibility Act* (Washington, D.C.: Government Printing Office, April 16, 1986), p. 857.

20. Shepard, "Cartelization," p. 97.

21. Lenard and Mazur, "Harvest of Waste," p. 24.

22. U.S. Department of Agriculture, *Economic Effects of Terminating Federal Marketing Orders for California-Arizona Oranges*, Technical Bulletin no. 1664, (Washington, D.C.: Government Printing Office, November 1981).

23. U.S. Department of Agriculture, *Agricultural Statistics, 1987*, (Washington, D.C.: Government Printing Office, 1987), p. 233.

24. *Federal Register*, October 26, 1987, p. 39,901.

25. Ibid., p. 39,903.

26. U.S. General Accounting Office, *The Role of Marketing Orders in Establishing and Maintaining Orderly Marketing Conditions* (Washington, D.C.: Government Printing Office, 1985), p. 13.

27. *Federal Register*, July 1, 1985, p. 26,977.

28. Ibid.

29. Ibid., p. 26,978.

30. U.S. General Accounting Office, *The Role of Marketing Orders*, p. 9.

31. U.S. Department of Agriculture, Post-Hearing Memorandum Correspondence, *Re: Wileman Bros., Elliot, Inc., Kash, Inc., a California Corp.*, Administrative Law Judge Dorothea Baker, Agricultural Marketing Service Docket Numbers, F/V, 916-1, 916-2, 917-2, March 16, 1988, p. 3.

32. Shepard, "Cartelization," p. 87.

33. U.S. Small Business Administration, Docket No. AO-144-A14-R01, p. 217.

34. U.S. Department of Agriculture, Administrative Proceeding *In Re: Sequoia*, April 23, 1987.

35. James Gattuso, *The High Cost and Low Returns of Farm Marketing Orders* (Washington, D.C.: Heritage Foundation, 1985), p. 4.

36. U.S. Department of Agriculture, *Post-Hearing Memorandum Re: Wileman, Elliot, Kash*, p. 7.

37. U.S. Department of Agriculture, Administrative Proceeding, *In Re: Wileman Bros. & Elliott, Inc., & Kash, Inc.—Petitioners' Joint Trial Brief*, AMA Docket Numbers 916-1, 917-3, January 18, 1988.

38. Ibid.

39. Ibid.

40. Ibid.

41. Brian Leighton, interview with the author, February 7, 1988.

42. U.S. Department of Agriculture Administrative Proceeding, *In Re: Saulsbury Orchards and Almond Processing, Compliant for Declaratory Judgment; Preliminary and Permanent Injunction; Mandatory Injunction and Writ of Mandamus; Compensatory and Punitive Damages and Request for Jury Trial Pursuant to Local Rule 201*, March 27, 1987.

43. U.S. Department of Agriculture, press release AMS-263-86, January 23, 1987.

44. Leighton, interview, February 22, 1988.

45. Leighton, interview, April 7, 1988.

46. 781 *Federal Reporter*, 2nd series, p. 78, case no. 85-1324.

47. *Block vs. Community Nutrition Institute*, 467 US 340, 342, 346 (1984).

48. U.S. Department of Agriculture Administrative Proceeding, *In Re: Saulsbury Orchards and Almond Processing, Cal-Almond, Inc., Petitioners' Objections to the Administrative Law Judge's Order Granting Respondent's Motion for an Extension of Time; Motion for a Declaration that the Administrative Proceedings Provide the Petitioners with an Inadequate and Untimely Remedy*, March 21, 1988.

49. U.S. Department of Agriculture, Administrative Proceeding *In Re:* AMA Docket #1 F&V 981-4, 1987.

50. *Sequoia v. USDA*, p. 183.

51. Ibid., p. 117.

52. Ibid., p. 121.

53. Ibid., p. 120.

54. Ibid.

55. Ibid.

56. *Block v. Community Nutrition Institute*, 467 US 340, 342 (1984).

57. 7 USC, § 602, 608c 11, cited in *Sequoia v. USDA*, p. 4.

58. *Sequoia v. USDA*, pp. 141, 146.

59. *Oakland Tribune*, July 27, 1984.

60. U.S. General Accounting Office, *Role of Marketing Orders*, p. 13.

61. Roy Smith, to Carl Pescosolido, February 5, 1986.

62. *Bakersfield Californian*, June 19, 1983.

63. U.S. Small Business Administration, Docket No. AO-144-A14-R01; p. 103.

64. *Wall Street Journal*, January 24, 1985.

65. Moody, interview, July 29, 1988.

66. James Gattuso, *Farm Marketing Orders*, p. 7.

67. U.S. General Accounting Office, *Role of Marketing Orders*, p. 57.

68. U.S. Congress, House Committee on Small Business, *The Regulatory Flexibility Act*, (Washington, D.C.: Government Printing Office, April 16, 1986).

69. U.S. Department of Agriculture, *Criteria for Evaluating Federal Marketing Orders* (Washington, D.C.: Government Printing Office, 1986).

70. *Federal Register*, October 26, 1987, p. 39,901.

71. Moody, interview, July 29, 1988.

10: Uncle Sam: Super Sodbuster

1. Henry A. Wallace, *Democracy Reborn* (New York: Reynal and Hitchcock, 1944), p. 114.
2. H. R. Tolley, speech delivered to American Farm Bureau, December 10, 1936.
3. Charles Hardin, *Food and Fiber in the Nation's Politics*, vol. 3, National Advisory Commission on Food and Fiber (Washington, D.C.: Government Printing Office, 1967), p. 144.
4. Franklin D. Roosevelt, press conference, January 10, 1936, *Public Papers and Addresses of Franklin D. Roosevelt* (New York: Random House, 1938).
5. Hardin, *Food and Fiber*, p. 144.
6. G. Nourse, Joseph S. Davis, and John D. Black, *Three Years of the AAA* (Washington, D.C.: Brookings Institution, 1936), p. 385.
7. Joseph Davis, *On Agricultural Policy* (Palo Alto, Calif.: Stanford University Press, 1939), p. 473.
8. Paul Findley, *Federal Farm Fable* (New Rochelle, N.Y.: Arlington House, 1967), p. 98.
9. Ibid., p. 99.
10. Cited in Hardin, *Food and Fiber*, p. 171.
11. U.S. Department of Agriculture, *An Economic Analysis of USDA Erosion Control Programs: A New Perspective*, ed., Roger Strohbehn, (Washington, D.C.: Government Printing Office, 1986), p. 21.
12. Bruce Gardner, *The Governing of Agriculture*, (Lawrence, Kansas: University of Kansas Press, 1981), p. 32.
13. U.S. General Accounting Office, *Continuation of the Resource Conservation and Development Program Raises Questions* (Washington, D.C.: Government Printing Office, August 1981), p. 7.
14. U.S. General Accounting Office, *Agricultural Overview—U.S. Food/Agriculture in a Volatile World Economy* (Washington, D.C.: Government Printing Office, November 1985).
15. *Wall Street Journal*, September 23, 1984.
16. U.S. Department of Agriculture, *Erosion Control Programs*, p. 23.
17. *Wall Street Journal*, September 23, 1984.
18. Ibid.
19. Ibid.
20. Cited in Hardin, *Food and Fiber*, p. 146.
21. Katherine Reichelderfor, *Do USDA Program Participants Contribute to Soil Erosion?*, study prepared for U.S. Department of Agriculture (Washington, D.C.: Government Printing Office, 1985), p. 3.
22. *Pro Farmer*, October 21, 1986.
23. Ken Cook, interview with the author, April 15, 1988.
24. U.S. Department of Agriculture, *Agricultural Outlook*, April 1987, p. 28.
25. U.S. Department of Agriculture, *Erosion Control Programs*, p. 3.
26. *Wall Street Journal*, September 23, 1984.
27. *Washington Post*, April 29, 1988.

28. Ibid.

29. Ibid.

30. *Wall Street Journal*, April 6, 1987.

31. Ibid.

32. *Fargo Forum*, February 19, 1988.

33. *Wall Street Journal*, September 23, 1984.

34. Cited in Lloyd Jones, "Implementing Swampbuster: A View," *Journal of Soil and Water Conservation*, January/February 1988, p. 30.

35. Jan Goldman Carter, interview with the author, April 4, 1988.

36. *Wall Street Journal*, September 23, 1984.

37. *Lubbock Avalanche Journal*, March 5, 1988.

38. Interview with the author, of a Senate aid who requested anonymity, March 2, 1987.

39. Lloyd Jones, interview with the author, March 28, 1987.

40. *Wall Street Journal*, July 17, 1987.

41. *Kansas City Star*, April 24, 1988.

42. Cited in Michael Dicks, "More Benefits with Fewer Acres Please," *Journal of Soil and Water Conservation*, May/June 1987, p. 171.

43. Pierre Crosson, "Soil Conservation—It's Not the Farmers Who Are Most Affected by Erosion," *Choices*, Spring 1986, p.33.

44. *Cargill Bulletin*, (Minneapolis), November 1987

45. Ibid.

46. U.S. Department of Agriculture, *Agriculture's Links to the National Economy* (Washington, D.C.: Government Printing Office, 1986).

47. *Kansas City Times*, January 19, 1988.

48. Ibid.

49. Charles M. Benbrook, "First Principles: The Definition of Highly Erodible Land and Tolerable Soil Loss," *Journal of Soil and Water Conservation*, January/February 1988, p. 37.

50. Pierre Crosson, "Soil Conservation," p. 37.

51. Mack Gray, "What Constitutes Compliance?" *Journal of Soil and Water Conservation*, January/February 1988, p. 39.

52. *Washington Post*, March 27, 1987.

53. *Journal of Soil and Water Conservation*, January/February 1988, p. 19.

11: The Congressional School of Economics

1. Wheeler McMillen, *Too Many Farmers* (New York: William Morrow, 1929), p. 252.

2. *Congressional Record*, October 3, 1985, H 8188.

3. *Congressional Record*, December 10, 1987, H 11522.

4. *Congressional Record*, June 16, 1988, H 4394.

5. *Congressional Record*, October 3, 1985, H 8188.

6. *Congressional Record*, December 10, 1987, H 11529.

7. *Congressional Record*, September 26, 1985, H 7844.

8. U.S. Congress, House Agriculture Committee, *U.S. Department of Agriculture's Implementation of the Orderly Marketing Provisions of the Food Security Act of 1985* (Washington, D.C.: Government Printing Office, September 10, 1986), p. 93.

9. *Congressional Record*, June 16, 1988, H 4370.

10. Cited in David Stockman, *The Triumph of Politics* (New York: Harper & Row, 1986), p. 167.

11. Cited in Charles Hardin, "The Tobacco Program: Exception or Portent," *Journal of Farm Economics*, November 1946, p. 920.

12. *Congressional Record*, 1983, S13863.

13. Ibid.

14. *Washington Post*, December 13, 1987.

15. *Congressional Record*, September 26, 1985, H 7853.

16. U.S. Department of Agriculture, *Ethanol: Economic and Policy Tradeoffs* (Washington, D.C.: Government Printing Office, August 1986).

17. Michael Fumento, "Some Dare Call Them Robber Barons," *National Review*, March 13, 1987, p. 57.

18. Ibid.

19. *Congressional Record*, June 18, 1985, H 4394.

20. *Congressional Record*, June 18, 1985, H 4398.

21. *Congressional Record*, October 3, 1985, H 8185.

22. *Congressional Record*, October 1, 1985, H 7936.

23. Ibid., H 7948.

24. U.S. Congress, House Agriculture Committee, *Policy Alternatives to the Food Security Act of 1985* (Washington, D.C.: Government Printing Office, March 31, 1987), p. 284.

25. *Congressional Record*, September 26, 1985, H 7846.

26. *Congressional Record*, September 26, 1985, H 7821.

27. Ibid.

28. *Congressional Record*, September 26, 1985, H 7827.

29. *Congressional Record*, October 3, 1985, H 8308.

30. *Congressional Record*, October 3, 1985, H 8185.

31. *Congressional Record*, September 26, 1985, H 7845.

32. Ibid., H 7852.

33. *Congressional Record*, 1986, H 2823.

34. Dan Dvoskin, *Excess Capacity in U.S. Agriculture*, study prepared for the U.S. Department of Agriculture (Washington, D.C.: Government Printing Office, 1988), p. 2.

35. *Congressional Record*, December 10, 1987, H 11529.

36. *Congressional Record*, September 26, 1985, H 7824.

37. *Congressional Record*, October 3, 1985, H 8186.

38. U.S. Congress, House Agriculture Committee, *Food Security Act of 1985* (Washington, D.C.: Government Printing Office, September 13, 1985).

39. U.S. Congress, Senate Agriculture Committee, *Reauthorization of the Agriculture and Food Act of 1981* (Washington, D.C.: Government Printing Office, March 7, 1985), p. 13.

40. *Congressional Record,* March 4, 1986, S 1993.

41. *Congressional Record,* June 16, 1988, H 4391.

42. *Congressional Record,* October 8, 1985, H 8362.

43. *Congressional Record,* September 26, 1985, H 7824.

44. *Congressional Record,* February 19, 1985, H 431.

45. *Congressional Record,* December 10, 1985, H 11528.

46. Ibid., H 11527.

47. *Congressional Record,* November 20, 1985, S 15913.

48. *Congressional Record,* October 8, 1985, H 8398.

49. U.S. Congress, House Agriculture Committee, *Review of the Egg Products Inspection Act* (Washington, D.C.: Government Printing Office, November 21, 1985), p. 55.

50. *Washington Times,* October 21, 1985.

51. Ron Phillips, interview with the author, December 15, 1987.

52. *Washington Post,* June 23, 1985.

53. U.S. Congress, House Agriculture Committee, *Producer Compliance and Procedures of the U.S. Department of Agriculture's Milk Production Termination Program* (Washington, D.C.: Government Printing Office, June 11, 1987), p. 43.

54. *Washington Post,* June 23, 1985.

55. U.S. Congress, Senate Agriculture Committee, *Generic Payment-in-Kind Certificates* (Washington, D.C.: Government Printing Office, 1987).

56. *Pro Farmer,* April 4, 1987.

57. U.S. Congress, House Administration Committee, *Studies Dealing with Budgetary Staffing and Administrative Activities of the U.S. House of Representatives, 1946–1978* (Washington, D.C.: Government Printing Office, 1978), pp. 66–77.

58. Fred Barnes, "The Unbearable Lightness of Being a Congressman," *The New Republic,* February 15, 1988, p. 17.

59. *Congressional Record,* December 10, 1985, H 11527.

60. *Washington Post,* March 9, 1984.

61. Kathleen Lawrence, interview with the author, July 13, 1988.

12: Our Agricultural Industrial Policy

1. *New York Times,* June 19, 1934.

2. *New York Times,* March 12, 1933.

3. Michael Fumento, "Some Dare Call Them Robber Barrons," *National Review,* March 13, 1987, p. 38.

4. G. Edward Schuh, "International Agriculture and Trade Policies: Implications for the United States," in Bruce Gardner, ed., *U.S. Agricultural Policy: The 1985 Farm Legislation* (Washington: American Enterprise Institute, 1985), p. 163.

5. U.S. Congress, House Agriculture Committee, *Review of the Department of Agriculture's Alternative Procedure for Exchanging Generic Commodity Certificates for Wheat and Related Matters* (Washington, D.C.: Government Printing Office, November 17, 1987).

6. Ibid.

7. *Pro Farmer*, May 23, 1987.

8. U.S. Congress, House Agriculture Committee, *Exchanging Generic Commodity Certificates*.

9. Ibid.

10. Ibid.

11. *Wall Street Journal*, March 11, 1988.

12. Ibid.

13. Jackie Patterson, interview with the author, December 17, 1987.

14. Cited in Charles Hardin, *The Politics of Food and Fiber*, vol. 3, National Advisory Commission on Food and Fiber (Washington, D.C.: Government Printing Office, 1967), p. 109.

15. Ibid., p. 73.

16. Ibid., p. 101.

17. John Strohm, "The Farmers Vote for Freedom," *Reader's Digest*, September 1963, p. 71.

18. U.S. General Accounting Office, *Farmer Payments and Loans: Consistency Needed in USDA Crop Yield Estimates* (Washington, D.C.: Government Printing Office, 1986), pp. i–iii.

19. U.S. Congress, House Agriculture Committee, *Policy Alternatives to the Food Security Act of 1985* (Washington, D.C.: Government Printing Office, March 12, 1987), p. 101.

20. Bruce Gardner, *The Governing of Agriculture* (Lawrence: University of Kansas Press, 1981), p. 31.

21. U.S. Congress, House Agriculture Committee, *Exchanging Generic Commodity Certificates*.

22. U.S. Congress, House Agriculture Committee, *Establishing Farm Program Payment Yields; Dry Edible Beans Amendments of 1986; and Nonprogram Crop Amendments of 1986* (Washington, D.C.: Government Printing Office, February 19, 1986), p. 44.

23. U.S. Congress, House Agriculture Committee, *Food Security Act of 1985*.

24. Dean Kleckner, "Implementing the CRP: A Private Perspective," *Journal of Soil and Water Conservation*, January/February 1988, p. 18.

25. U.S. Congress, House Agriculture Committee, *1988 Wheat Program Announcement and County Loan Rates for the 1987 Wheat Crop* (Washington, D.C.: Government Printing Office, July 13, 1987), p. 1.

26. U.S. General Accounting Office, *USDA's Commodity Program: The Accuracy of Budget Forecasts* (Washington, D.C.: Government Printing Office, April 1988), p. 18.

27. Ibid., p. 43.

28. Ibid., p. 48.

29. Ibid., p. 71.

30. Ibid.

31. U.S. General Accounting Office, *Federal Crop Insurance Corporation Needs to Improve Decision-Making* (Washington, D.C.: Government Printing Office, July 1987), p. 25.

32. U.S. Congress, House Agriculture Committee, *Minority Report on HR 12* (Washington, D.C.: Government Printing Office, 84th Congress, January 1956).

33. *Wall Street Journal,* June 27, 1967.

34. U.S. Department of Agriculture, *Economic Indicators of the Farm Sector—Farm Sector Review, 1986* (Washington, D.C.: Government Printing Office, 1988), p. 13. See also, U.S. Department of Agriculture Budget Summaries.

35. *Economic Report of the President* (Washington, D.C.: Government Printing Office, 1986), p. 143.

36. D. Gale Johnson, Kenzo Hemmi, and Pierre Lardinois, *Agricultural Policy and Trade* (New York: New York University Press, 1985), p. 162.

37. *Economic Report of the President,* p. 142.

38. World Bank, *World Development Report, 1986* (New York: Oxford University Press, 1986).

39. Thomas W. Hertel, Robert Thompson, and Marinos E. Tsigas, "Economy Side-Effects of Unilateral Trade and Policy Liberalization in U.S. Agriculture," paper prepared for the Global Agricultural Trade Study organized by the Center for International Economics, Canberra, Australia, May 1988, p. 37.

40. U.S. Department of Agriculture, Office of the Inspector General, "ASCS Administration of 1986 Cotton and Rice Loan Programs," Audit Report no. 03641-1 Te, March 1988, p. 1.

41. U.S. General Accounting Office, *Decision-Making Process for Farm Program Policies Needs to Be Improved* (Washington, D.C.: Government Printing Office, June 4, 1985).

42. U.S. Department of Agriculture, Office of Inspector General, "Review of Disaster Payment Programs," March 30, 1987.

43. *Des Moines Register,* August 17, 1986.

44. Cited in G. Nourse, Joseph S. Davis, and John D. Black, *Three Years of the AAA* (Washington, D.C.: Brookings Institution, 1936), p. 432.

45. Rexford Tugwell, *Our Economic System and Its Problems* (New York: Harcourt Brace, 1934), p. 541.

46. Ibid., p. 542.

47. Robert Conquest, *The Harvest of Sorrow* (New York: Oxford University Press, 1986).

48. U.S. General Accounting Office, *1983 Payment-In-Kind Program Overview: Its Design, Impact, and Cost* (Washington, D.C.: Government Printing Office, September 25, 1985) p. 124.

49. Nourse, Davis, and Black, *Three Years of the AAA.*

50. Chester C. Davis, "The Problem of Agricultural Adjustment," *Journal of Farm Economics,* February 1934, p. 344.

51. U.S. Congress, House Agriculture Committee, *U.S. Department of Agriculture's Implementation of the Orderly Marketing Provisions of the Food Security Act of 1985* (Washington, D.C.: Government Printing Office, September 10, 1986), p. 143.

52. Ezra Taft Benson, *Freedom to Farm* (Garden City, N.Y.: Doubleday, 1960), p. 27.

53. Ibid, 28.

54. B. H. Hibbard, "A Long-Range View of National Agricultural Policy," *Journal of Farm Economics*, February 1934, p. 22.

55. *New York Times*, December 5, 1983.

56. Janos Kornai, *The Economics of Shortages* (Stockholm: University of Stockholm), 1979.

57. Cited in Vernon Carstensen, "The Past Fifty Years," *Journal of Farm Economics*, 1960, p. 998.

58. Ibid., p. 997.

59. Cited in Heritage Foundation, *Agenda 83* (Washington, D.C.: Heritage Foundation, 1983), p. 32.

60. Lloyd Teney, "The Bureau of Agricultural Economics: The Early Years," *Journal of Farm Economics*, November 1947, p. 1023.

13: *The Morality of Agricultural Policy*

1. Henry Wallace, "Farm Economists and Agricultural Planning," *Journal of Farm Economics*, February 1936, p. 3.

2. Cited in Arthur Schlesinger, *The Coming of The New Deal* (Boston: Houghton Mifflin, 1959), p. 72.

3. U.S. Congress, House Agriculture Committee, *Policy Alternatives to the Food Security Act of 1985* (Washington, D.C.: Government Printing Office, March 31, 1987), p. 460.

4. Cited in Carl Pescosolido, *An Analysis of the Legislative History of the Agriculture Adjustment Act* (Exeter, Calif.: privately published, 1984), p. 87.

5. U.S. Congress, House Agriculture Committee, *Food Security Act of 1985*, p. 443.

6. *The Nation*, March 12, 1930.

7. M. R. Benedict, "Production Control in Agriculture and Industry," *Journal of Farm Economics*, August 1936, p. 463.

8. U.S. General Accounting Office, *Examples of USDA's Application of the $50,000 Payment Limitation*, (Washington, D.C.: Government Printing Office, 1985), pp. 1–3.

9. *Des Moines Register*, July 6, 1986.

10. U.S. Congress, House Agriculture Committee, *Review of the Cotton Stabilization Program* (Washington, D.C.: Government Printing Office, March 18, 1987), p. 67.

11. *Wall Street Journal*, October 10, 1980.

12. U.S. Department of Agriculture, *Economic Indicators of the Farm Sector, National Financial Summary, 1986* (Washington, D.C.: Government Printing Office, 1987), p. 50.

13. Cited in Willard Cochrane, "A New Sheet of Music," *Choices*, no. 1, 1986, p. 12.

14. U.S. Congress, House Agriculture Committee, *Review of the State of Agriculture* (Washington, D.C.: Government Printing Office, February 25, 1987), p. 102.

15. *Congressional Record*, April 13, 1933, p. 1642. Cited in Pescosolido, *History of the Agriculture Adjustment Act*, p. 97.

16. *Congressional Record*, November 9, 1983, H 9535.

17. *National Agricultural Forum*, December 1984, p. 9.

18. Don Paarlberg, "Role of Values, Beliefs, and Myths in Establishing Policy: Agriculture and Rural Policy," unpublished manuscript, 1988.

19. U.S. Congress, Senate Agriculture Committee, *Current Status of Farm Programs* (Washington, D.C.: May 21, 1987), p. 77.

20. *United States v. Butler et al., Receivers of Hoosac Mills Corporation*, 297 U.S. 1-88 (1936).

21. U.S. Congress, House Agriculture Committee, *Food Security Act of 1985*, p. 474.

22. Cited in Jon Bartlett, *Familiar Quotations*, Emily Morison Beck, editor (Boston, Mass.: Little & Brown, 1980), p. 631.

23. U.S. Congress, House Agriculture Committee, *Producer Compliance Regulations and Procedures of the U.S. Department of Agriculture's Milk Production Termination Program* (Washington, D.C.: Government Printing Office, June 11, 1987), p. 125.

24. Ibid.

25. U.S. Department of Agriculture, *A History of Price Support Programs, 1933–1984* (Washington, D.C.: Government Printing Office, 1984), p. 6.

14: The Solution

1. Peter Samuel, "New Zealand's Higher Prices for Their Machinery," *Reason*, March 1988, p. 33.

2. *Washington Post*, November 11, 1987.

3. Interview with the author of a senior USDA aide, July 11, 1988.

4. U.S. Congress, Office of Technology Assessment, *Technology, Public Policy, and the Changing Structure of American Agriculture*, Summary (Washington, D.C.: Government Printing Office, 1986).

5. Dennis Avery, interview with the author, September 6, 1988. Much of the author's analysis of the effects of ending subsidies is derived from Avery's work.

6. Kathleen Lawrence, interview with the author, July 3, 1988.

7. Thomas W. Hertel, Robert Thompson, and Marinos E. Tsigas, "Economy Side-Effects of Unilateral Trade and Policy Liberalization in U.S. Agriculture," paper prepared for the Global Agriculture Trade Study organized by the Center for International Economics, Canberra, Australia, May 1988.

8. U.S. Congress, House Agriculture Committee, *U.S. Export Competitiveness* (Washington, D.C.: Government Printing Office, April 16, 1985).

9. Agricultural Policy Working Group, "The Competitiveness of U.S. Agriculture," Washington, D.C., 1987.

10. William Lesher, interview with the author, August 21, 1988.

11. Willard Cochrane, "A New Sheet of Music," *Choices*, No. 1, p. 13.

12. U.S. Congress, Senate Agriculture Committee, *Reauthorization of the Food Act of 1981* (Washington, D.C.: Government Printing Office April 7, 1985), p. 104.

13. Wheeler McMillen, *Too Many Farmers* (New York: William Morrow, 1929).

14. U.S. Congress, Senate Agriculture Committee, *Reauthorization of the Food Act*, April 7, 1985, p. 105.

15: *Conclusion*

1. Glenn W. Birkett, "A Dirt Farmer Wonders," *The Nation*, March 4, 1931, p. 241.

2. U.S. Congress, House Government Operations Committee, *Implementation of the Dairy Termination Program: USDA's Slaughter of the Cattle Market*, House Report 99-890 (Washington, D.C.: Government Printing Office, September 25, 1986), p. 20.

3. Joseph Davis, *On Agricultural Policy* (Palo Alto, Calif.: Stanford University Press, 1939), p. 211.

4. *The Nation*, March 12, 1930.

5. Henry Wallace, radio address, National Radio Forum, March 7, 1938.

6. Cited in David Ricardo's *Principles of Political Economy and Taxation* (New York: Penguin, 1971), p. 316.

7. Henry Wallace, "Farm Economists and Agricultural Planning," *Journal of Farm Economics*, February 1936, p. 11.